Emerging Technologies and Applications for Cloud–Based Gaming

P. Venkata Krishna
VIT University, India

A volume in the Advances in
Multimedia and Interactive
Technologies (AMIT) Book
Series

Information Science
REFERENCE
An Imprint of IGI Global

Published in the United States of America by
    Information Science Reference (an imprint of IGI Global)
    701 E. Chocolate Avenue
    Hershey PA 17033
    Tel: 717-533-8845
    Fax: 717-533-8661
    E-mail: cust@igi-global.com
    Web site: http://www.igi-global.com

                    Library of Congress Cataloging-in-Publication Data

Names: Krishna, P. Venkata, 1977- editor.
Title: Emerging technologies and applications for cloud-based gaming / P.
   Venkata Krishna, editor.
Description: Hershey, PA : Information Science Reference, [2016] | Includes
   bibliographical references and index.
Identifiers: LCCN 2016012764| ISBN 9781522505464 (hardcover) | ISBN
   9781522505471 (ebook)
Subjects: LCSH: Internet games--Technological innovations--Handbooks,
   manuals, etc. | Cloud computing--Handbooks, manuals, etc. | Internet
   programming--Handbooks, manuals, etc. | Internet games
   industry--Handbooks, manuals, etc.
Classification: LCC QA76.76.C672 E44 2016 | DDC 004.67/82--dc23 LC record available at
https://lccn.loc.gov/2016012764

This book is published in the IGI Global book series Advances in Multimedia and Interactive
Technologies (AMIT) (ISSN: 2327-929X; eISSN: 2327-9303)

British Cataloguing in Publication Data
A Cataloguing in Publication record for this book is available from the British Library.

Advances in Multimedia and Interactive Technologies (AMIT) Book Series

ISSN: 2327-929X
EISSN: 2327-9303

MISSION

Traditional forms of media communications are continuously being challenged. The emergence of user-friendly web-based applications such as social media and Web 2.0 has expanded into everyday society, providing an interactive structure to media content such as images, audio, video, and text.

The **Advances in Multimedia and Interactive Technologies (AMIT) Book Series** investigates the relationship between multimedia technology and the usability of web applications. This series aims to highlight evolving research on interactive communication systems, tools, applications, and techniques to provide researchers, practitioners, and students of information technology, communication science, media studies, and many more with a comprehensive examination of these multimedia technology trends.

COVERAGE

- Mobile Learning
- Multimedia technology
- Multimedia Streaming
- Audio Signals
- Social Networking
- Digital Watermarking
- Digital Technology
- Gaming Media
- Digital Games
- Multimedia Services

IGI Global is currently accepting manuscripts for publication within this series. To submit a proposal for a volume in this series, please contact our Acquisition Editors at Acquisitions@igi-global.com or visit: http://www.igi-global.com/publish/.

Titles in this Series

For a list of additional titles in this series, please visit: www.igi-global.com

Contemporary Research on Intertextuality in Video Games
Christophe Duret (Université de Sherbrooke, Canada) and Christian-Marie Pons (Université de Sherbrooke, Canada)
Information Science Reference • copyright 2016 • 363pp • H/C (ISBN: 9781522504771) • US $185.00 (our price)

Trends in Music Information Seeking, Behavior, and Retrieval for Creativity
Petros Kostagiolas (Ionian University, Greece) Konstantina Martzoukou (Robert Gordon University, UK) and Charilaos Lavranos (Ionian University, Greece)
Information Science Reference • copyright 2016 • 388pp • H/C (ISBN: 9781522502708) • US $195.00 (our price)

Emerging Perspectives on the Mobile Content Evolution
Juan Miguel Aguado (University of Murcia, Spain) Claudio Feijóo (Technical University of Madrid, Spain & Tongji University, China) and Inmaculada J. Martínez (University of Murcia, Spain)
Information Science Reference • copyright 2016 • 438pp • H/C (ISBN: 9781466688384) • US $210.00 (our price)

Emerging Research on Networked Multimedia Communication Systems
Dimitris Kanellopoulos (University of Patras, Greece)
Information Science Reference • copyright 2016 • 448pp • H/C (ISBN: 9781466688506) • US $200.00 (our price)

Emerging Research and Trends in Gamification
Harsha Gangadharbatla (University of Colorado Boulder, USA) and Donna Z. Davis (University of Oregon, USA)
Information Science Reference • copyright 2016 • 455pp • H/C (ISBN: 9781466686519) • US $215.00 (our price)

Experimental Multimedia Systems for Interactivity and Strategic Innovation
Ioannis Deliyannis (Ionian University, Greece) Petros Kostagiolas (Ionian University, Greece) and Christina Banou (Ionian University, Greece)
Information Science Reference • copyright 2016 • 378pp • H/C (ISBN: 9781466686595) • US $195.00 (our price)

Design Strategies and Innovations in Multimedia Presentations
Shalin Hai-Jew (Kansas State University, USA)
Information Science Reference • copyright 2015 • 589pp • H/C (ISBN: 9781466686960) • US $225.00 (our price)

www.igi-global.com

701 E. Chocolate Ave., Hershey, PA 17033
Order online at www.igi-global.com or call 717-533-8845 x100
To place a standing order for titles released in this series,
contact: cust@igi-global.com
Mon-Fri 8:00 am - 5:00 pm (est) or fax 24 hours a day 717-533-8661

Table of Contents

Detailed Table of Contents

Chapter 1

Sharon Moses J., VIT University, India
Dhinesh Babu L. D., VIT University, India
Nirmala M., VIT University, India
M. Rajasekhara Babu, VIT University, India
P. Venkata Krishna, Sri Padmavathi Mahila Visvavidyalayam, India

Cloud gaming-as-a-service is emerging as one of the potential revenue generating futuristic fields with a higher growth rate. Cloud gaming service is an entertainment service that depends totally on the cloud computing technology. Cloud gaming delivers games to the gamers, anywhere at any time without any gaming specific hardware and without diminishing the gamer's quality of experience. From getting the user command to rendering the graphics, everything is processed at the gaming service provider end. The only need for the gamer is to use a thin client like web browser to access the cloud game server. In this chapter, we have detailed about the cloud game systems, cloud game services, issues in cloud gaming, economics of cloud gaming, research prospects and the evolution of cloud gaming service.

Chapter 2

Dominik Meiländer, University of Muenster, Germany
Sergei Gorlatch, University of Muenster, Germany

Massively Multiplayer Online Games (MMOG) are a challenging class of applications: they combine high demands on real-time user interactivity and adaptability with the problem of an efficient and economic utilization of resources for the dynamically changing number of users. This chapter studies how MMOG can benefit from Cloud

Computing with its Infrastructure-as-a-Service (IaaS) approach to cost-efficient leasing resources on demand. The chapter makes two major contributions: (1) a new lifecycle model for the development of adaptable MMOG expresses major design and execution aspects of Cloud-based MMOG, and (2) a resource management system RTF-RMS implements efficient load balancing for MMOG on Clouds. The authors illustrate how their lifecycle model and RTF-RMS system support the efficient development and execution of adaptable MMOG on Clouds and demonstrate the advantages of their approach in an experimental evaluation.

Chapter 3

Deverajan Ganesh Gopal, VIT University, India
Sekaran Kaushik, VIT University, India

Cloud computing technology has revolutionized the field of networks and the way of utilizing the resources remotely. In the gaming field this has changed the way of playing traditional games in relation to online on-demand available games which reduces the hassle at the clients' end. In order to play a game online, the game content is processed at the server end and rendered images are transmitted to the client's end. This makes the way of accessing easier and the game can be played even without the hardware or software required for the game. We review the cloud gaming architecture and the different types of streaming used by various cloud gaming platforms. Also, the issues and challenges with the service provider technologies used in the cloud gaming are discussed briefly.

Chapter 4

Prajit Kumar Datta, VIT University, India
Utkarsh Srivastava, VIT University, India

This chapter talks about the architecture required for cloud gaming and various challenges in cloud based gaming. The first part gives a brief introduction about what is actually cloud gaming and the ways in which it is implemented. The subsequent section talks about the cloud gaming system architecture and different server, client components of cloud gaming frameworks involved in the whole process. The next section talks about various cloud based services and their system architecture. In this chapter main aspect is the server client architecture and data flow models via this architecture. A comparative study has been made among various service providers to have a better understanding of the architecture deployed by them in cloud based gaming. The next section discusses about the Challenges of Cloud based Gaming. The future and new improvisations of the Cloud based Gaming System has also been taken up in this chapter.

Chapter 5

Sudha Senthilkumar, VIT University, India
V. Madhu Viswanatham, VIT University, India

Online gaming allows players from different location to play synchronously together for entertainment. Generally multimedia applications which is highly latency sensitive and it requires specific hardware, such as Graphic Processing Units (GPUs) and fast memory. Since recent advances in cloud computing makes it suitable for moving the gaming application to the cloud and streams the video sequence back to the player over the Internet. This is more beneficial for less powerful computational devices that are otherwise incapable of running high-quality games. In addition to this cloud gaming is platform independence means it allow you to play on your android or IOS powered devices. There are several cloud providers like On-Live, G-Cluster and GFACE are provides active game services. However, providing proper access control for games which require license to play various levels is one of the important requirements to play the online games. This paper proposes the suitable access control mechanism to provide the access to cloud gaming applications.

Chapter 6

Ebin Deni Raj, VIT University, India
L. D. Dhinesh Babu, VIT University, India

Cloud computing is the most utilized and evolving technology in the past few years and has taken computing to a whole new level such that even common man is receiving the benefits. The end user in cloud computing always prefers a cloud service provider which is efficient, reliable and best quality of service at the lowest possible price. A cloud based gaming system relieves the player from the burden of possessing high end processing and graphic units. The storage of games hosted in clouds using the latest technologies in cloud has been discussed in detail. The Quality of service of games hosted in cloud is the main focus of this chapter and we have proposed a mathematical model for the same. The various factors in dealing with the quality of service on cloud based games have been analyzed in detail. The quality of experience of cloud based games and its relation with quality of service has been derived. This chapter focuses on the various storage techniques, quality of experience factors and correlates the same with QoS in cloud based games.

Chapter 7

Shivangshu Nag, VIT University, India
Vipul Kumar Srivastava, VIT University, India
Ragam Sai Krishna, VIT University, India

This chapter talks about the latest technology being used for Cloud Gaming. It discusses about various aspects of this technology. The first part gives a brief introduction about what is actually cloud gaming and the ways in which it is implemented. The subsequent section talks about the various servers and units involved in the whole process. The next section talks about the importance of performance and efficiency in the Cloud Gaming system. There are various advantages of implementing such systems over the traditional gaming systems and of course every coin has two sides and thus there are various limitations of this technology which are discussed further in the chapter. What can be the new advancements and the future of the Cloud Gaming System has also been taken up in this chapter. Some case studies have also been included in this chapter to understand the various topics more clearly by analyzing the present scenarios and systems. The companies which offer cloud based gaming services have been discussed about to understand their technologies and implementation mechanisms.

Chapter 8

Raajan N. R., SASTRA University, India
Nandhini Kesavan, SASTRA University, India

Augmented Reality (AR) plays a vital role in the field of visual computing. AR is actually different but often confused to be the same is Virtual Reality (VR). While VR creates a whole new world, AR aims at designing an environment in real time with virtual components that are overlaid on the real components. Due to this reason, AR comes under the category of 'mixed reality'. AR could be viewed on any smart electronic gadgets like mobile, laptop, projector, tablet etc., AR could be broadly classified as Marker-based and Markerless. If it is marker-based, a pattern is used whereas in markerless system there is no need of it. In case of marker, if we show the pattern to a webcam it will get details about it and impose the object on the marker. We are incorporating a new efficient solution for integrating a virtual object on to a real world which can be very much handful for tourism and advertisement for showcasing objects or things. The ultimate goal is to augmenting the 3D video onto a real world on which it will increase the person's conceptual understanding of the subject.

Chapter 9

Nandhini Kesavan, SASTRA University, India
Raajan N. R., SASTRA University, India

The main objective of gesture recognition is to promote the technology behind the automation of registered gesture with a fusion of multidimensional data in a versatile manner. To achieve this goal, computers should be able to visually recognize hand gestures from video input. However, vision-based hand tracking and gesture recognition is an extremely challenging problem due to the complexity of hand gestures, which are rich in diversities due to high degrees of freedom involved by the human hand. This would make the world a better place with for the commons not only to live in, but also to communicate with ease. This research work would serve as a pharos to researchers in the field of smart vision and would immensely help the society in a versatile manner.

Chapter 10

R. Deepthi Crestose Rebekah, Ravindra college of Engineering for
Women, India
Dhanaraj Cheelu, Ravindra college of Engineering for Women, India
M. Rajasekhara Babu, VIT University, India

Cloud computing is one of the most exciting technologies due to its ability to increase flexibility and scalability for computer processes, while reducing cost associated with computing. It is important to share the data securely, efficiently, and flexibly in cloud storage. Existing data protection mechanisms such as symmetric encryption techniques are unsuccessful in preventing data sharing securely. This article suggests Key aggregate cryptosystem which produce constant size ciphertexts in order to delegate decryption rights for any set of ciphertexts. The uniqueness is that one can aggregate any number of secret keys and make them as compact as a single key. This compact aggregate key can be easily sent to others with very limited secure storage.

Chapter 11
Enhancing Quality of Service in Cloud Gaming System: An Active
Implementation Framework for Enhancing Quality of Service in Multi-Player

Balamurugan Balusamy, VIT University, India
P. Venkata Krishna, VIT University, India
Aishwarya T., VIT University, India
Thusitha M., VIT University, India
Tamizh Arasi G. S., VIT University, India
Marimuthu Karuppiah, VIT University, India

In multi-player cloud gaming two or more people from different locations may actively participate in gaming as like they were in a similar geographical location. In such cases handling massive user inputs, performance rendering, bandwidth fluctuations, load balancing, data capturing, data transmission in real time still remains a cumbersome in cloud gaming. In this chapter, we propose a framework that overcomes the major issues associated with quality of service in cloud gaming. The cloud platform consists of two environments namely workbench and runtime environment, where the work bench environment comprises of tools like end user tools, data parsing tools and data integrity tools through which the user input is analyzed and sent to the run time environment for further processing. Each tool present at the cloud platform helps in achieving the quality factors through its functionalities. The user request is processed and the results will be sent to the clients through the runtime environment.

Chapter 12
Impact of Cloud Gaming in Health Care, Education, and Entertainment

Padmalaya Nayak, Jawaharlal Nehru Technological University, India
Shelendra Kumar Sharma, Microsoft, India

With the rapid growth of Cloud Computing, various diverse applications are growing exponentially through large data centers with the use of Internet. Cloud gaming is one of the most novel service applications that helps to store the video games in cloud and client can access the games as audio/video streams. Cloud gaming in practice substantially reduces the computational cost at the client side and enables the use of thin clients. Further, Quality of Service (QoS) may be affected through cloud gaming by introducing access latency. The objective of this chapter is to bring the impact and effectiveness of cloud gaming application on users, Health care, Entertainment, and Education.

Foreword

There are several gaming platforms that gains huge attention with the introduction of cloud gaming such as Gaming Anywhere, Remote play, Cloud Gaming eXtreme, etc. Current gaming systems need to support the new generation applications through on demand services, mobile devices and specialized gaming hardware devices. The Internet plays vital role in connecting the actual game server over cloud platform. This allows access to games without the need of complex hardware resources at user level and provides easy and flexible gaming platforms that gains huge attention among various users. Such an environment requires effective co-ordination of resources like large bandwidth, large server clusters etc. There is considerable growth witnessed with cloud based gaming services as there are many attempts to use open source cloud platforms designed in recent times. It is the most evolving technology at present. To design such challenging environment, many challenges are need to be investigated purposefully. Hence, this domain needs to be explored meticulously to bring out its potential advantages. So, there is a strong requirement for scholarly material regarding cloud based gaming.

Even though few articles have been written on cloud gaming, a comprehensive book such as one edited by Dr. P. Venkata Krishna is not there in the immediate past. So, I congratulate of this book Dr. Krishna for his remarkable efforts in bringing a well-thought out as well as fluently organized book about cloud based gaming with the help of several authors who contributed their valuable work. This book tried to invoke readers thought sphere with fine grained explanations about various components such as overall framework, design methodologies and tools, intelligent interfaces of cloud based gaming. Since the authors have given a wide and detailed vertical coverage of cloud based gaming by addressing the potential challenges and their solutions, this book surely will augment further research in this field. This book will also enlarge the applicability of cloud based gaming in immediate future.

Because of its resourcefulness, this book could also be treated as a reference book for researchers, students and curriculum developers. Hence, this book is a must to read for everyone who works in the field of cloud based gaming.

V. Durga Bhavani
Sri Padmavati Mahila University, India

Preface

Cloud computing created great impact due to its unique characteristics that implements on demand services based on pay and use model. Cloud services include social networking, online business applications, mail communication and related services. The cloud computing model permits to access information and computer resources that are available anywhere in the network connection in short it is a convergence of trends and technologies which makes IT infrastructure and applications more modular and more dynamic. It gives users self-service access to computing resources, while maintaining appropriate control. In this context, cloud based gaming gains huge attention as it requires many resources.

Online gaming is widely popular and gaining more user attention day-to-day. Computer game industry have made considerable growth in terms of design and development, but the scarcity of hardware resources at player or client side is a major pitfall for latest high-end multimedia games. In Cloud Gaming the remote server systems or data center servers provide all necessary gaming actions to the client system like rendering and execution. It has basic advantages like users do not require high-end GPUs and large memory and other gaming necessaries. Thus, it facilitates the user to play the game under any platform and under any hardware requirements and irrespective of the device used by the user.

Although cloud gaming is a promising direction for the game industry, achieving good user experience without excessive hardware investment is a tough problem. This is because gamers are hard to please, as they concurrently demand for high responsiveness and high video quality, but do not want to pay too much. Therefore, service providers have to not only design the systems to meet the gamers' needs but also take error resiliency, scalability, and resource allocation into considerations. This renders the design and implementation of cloud gaming systems extremely challenging. Indeed, while real-time video streaming seems to be a mature technology at first glance, cloud gaming systems have to execute games, handle user inputs, and perform rendering, capturing, encoding, packetizing, transmitting, decoding, and displaying in real-time, and thus are much more difficult to optimize.

The main objective of this book is to throw light on significance of cloud based gaming for the future. And to explain the fundamental architectures with the computing systems to understand the design methodologies of cloud gaming, which addresses the design challenges. It also includes open research issues in cloud gaming. The book consists of the following twelve chapters, each of which contains multiple sections focusing on various aspects in that section. In the following paragraphs, a brief overview for each of the chapters is described.

Chapter 1 provides "A Survey on Strategies, Trends, Economics, and Prospects of Cloud-Based Gaming" authored by Sharon Moses J, Dhinesh Babu L D, Nirmala M, Rajasekhara Babu M and Venkata Krishna P. This chapter presents details about the cloud game systems, cloud game services, issues in cloud gaming, economics of cloud gaming, research prospects and the evolution of cloud gaming service.

Chapter 2 contains "Efficient Development and Execution of Adaptable Online Games on Clouds" authored by Dominik Meiländer and Sergei Gorlatch. This chapter studies how MMOG can benefit from Cloud Computing with its Infrastructure-as-a-Service (IaaS) approach to cost-efficient leasing resources on demand. The chapter makes two major contributions: (i) a new lifecycle model for the development of adaptable MMOG expresses major design and execution aspects of Cloud-based MMOG, and (ii) a resource management system RTF-RMS implements efficient load balancing for MMOG on Clouds. The authors illustrate how their lifecycle model and RTF-RMS system support the efficient development and execution of adaptable MMOG on Clouds and demonstrate the advantages of their approach in an experimental evaluation.

Chapter 3 describes "Emerging Technologies and Applications for Cloud-Based Gaming: Review on Cloud Gaming Architectures" by Deverajan Ganesh Gopal. A comprehensive review on the cloud gaming architecture and different types of streaming used by several cloud gaming platforms is explained in this chapter.

Chapter 4 describes "Cloud Gaming: Design Architecture and Challenges" authored by Prajit Kumar Datta and Utkarsh Srivastava. This chapter talks about the architecture required for cloud gaming and various challenges in cloud based gaming. The future and new improvisations of the Cloud based Gaming System has also been taken up in this chapter. Some case studies have also been included in this chapter to facilitate a clear in-depth understanding of various topics.

Chapter 5 describes "EAC-MPCG Efficient Access Control for Multi-Player Cloud Games" authored by Sudha senthilkumar and V Madhu Viswanatham. This chapter proposes the suitable access control mechanism to provide the access to cloud gaming applications.

Chapter 6 describes "Issues in On-Demand Cloud-Based Gaming Storage: Quality of Service and Quality of Experience" authored by Ebin Deni Raj and Dhinesh Babu L D. In this chapter, the quality of experience of cloud based games and its relation with quality of service has been derived. This chapter focuses on the various storage techniques, quality of experience factors and correlates the same with QoS in cloud based games.

Chapter 7 provides "Cloud-Based Gaming Services" authored by Shivangshu Nag, Vipul Kumar Srivastava and Ragam Sai Krishna. This chapter talks about the latest technology being used for Cloud Gaming.

Chapter 8 provides "Mixed Augmented Reality Systems for Real World Integration" Raajan N.R and Nandhini Kesavan. This chapter details about solution for integrating a virtual object on to a real world which can be very much handful for tourism and advertisement for showcasing objects or things. The ultimate goal is to augmenting the 3D video onto a real world on which it will increase the person's conceptual understanding of the subject.

Chapter 9 illustrates "Gesture Recognition: An Interactive Tool in Multimedia" authored by Nandhini Kesavan and Raajan N.R. This chapter details about gesture recognition with a fusion of multidimensional data in a versatile manner. Vision-based hand tracking and gesture recognition is an extremely challenging problem due to the complexity of hand gestures, which are rich in diversities due to high degrees of freedom involved by the human hand.

Chapter 10 provides "Necessity of Key Aggregate Cryptosystem for Data Sharing in Cloud Computing" authored by Deepthi Crestose Rebekah, Dhanaraj Cheelu, and M. Rajasekhara Babu. This chapter provides importance of cryptosystem which produce constant size cipher texts in order to delegate decryption rights for any set of cipher texts.

Chapter 11 emphasizes "Enhancing Quality of Service in Cloud Gaming System: An Active Implementation Framework for Enhancing Quality of Service in Multi-Player Cloud Gaming" authored by Balamurugan Balusamy, Tamizh Arasi G.S, Ramamohan Reddy, Aishwarya Thangavelu, Thusitha Murali and Marimuthu Karuppiah. In this chapter, a framework that overcomes the major issues associated with quality of service in cloud gaming is described.

Finally, Chapter 12 describes "Impact of Cloud Gaming in Health Care, Education, and Entertainment Services" authored by Padmalaya Nayak and Shelendra Kumar Sharma. With the rapid growth of Cloud Computing, various diverse applications are growing exponentially through large data centers with the use of Internet. The objective of this chapter is to bring the impact and effectiveness of cloud gaming application on users, Health care, Entertainment, and Education.

Cloud based gaming has several issues and challenges due to its robust and complex scenarios. There is significant attempt made by several contributors of this book to present various issues and challenges that address the needs of cloud based gaming. The design of such systems, therefore, requires understanding the joint dynamics of computers, software, networks, and resources. This book would be of considerable interest to researchers, professionals and students with the background of computer science, electrical and electronics communication.

Chapter 1
A Survey on Strategies, Trends, Economics, and Prospects of Cloud-Based Gaming

Sharon Moses J.
VIT University, India

Nirmala M.
VIT University, India

Dhinesh Babu L. D.
VIT University, India

M. Rajasekhara Babu
VIT University, India

P. Venkata Krishna
Sri Padmavathi Mahila Visvavidyalayam, India

ABSTRACT

Cloud gaming-as-a-service is emerging as one of the potential revenue generating futuristic fields with a higher growth rate. Cloud gaming service is an entertainment service that depends totally on the cloud computing technology. Cloud gaming delivers games to the gamers, anywhere at any time without any gaming specific hardware and without diminishing the gamer's quality of experience. From getting the user command to rendering the graphics, everything is processed at the gaming service provider end. The only need for the gamer is to use a thin client like web browser to access the cloud game server. In this chapter, we have detailed about the cloud game systems, cloud game services, issues in cloud gaming, economics of cloud gaming, research prospects and the evolution of cloud gaming service.

DOI: 10.4018/978-1-5225-0546-4.ch001

INTRODUCTION

In the internet era, cloud computing has revolutionised gaming technology to an unimaginable extent. The availability of smart phones and the internet with large bandwidth have provided the possibility for people to access the internet based services frequently. The accessibility of general public to the advanced technology has garnered new entertainment business models. Cloud gaming is one of the fast growing entertainment industry. In the past, in order to play video games, users required high computing power CPUs and expensive graphic cards. The computer will be stationed in one particular place and the user will play the game using that computer. Trying a new game was not that easy because new games required new hardware and software upgradations. This made users to spend more money in updating their expensive graphic cards and processors for each game. Even though users update their computers; each year new upgradation will be released for both software and hardware. If a user likes to play a newly launched game with high definition graphic quality, then he/she has to spend some extra money in buying and updating the game requirements. The upgradation will not last long since the advancements in gaming quality will demand the user to buy new gaming devices in the future.

In today's world, because of cloud computing, the strategy of game playing has changed drastically. Cloud gaming provides high end gaming experience via thin clients no matter what device gamer is using. The only criterion for a gamer is to have an internet connection and a device with a thin client like the browser to play the game. Cloud gaming is one among the popular cloud based services providing game-as-a-service to the end user. Cloud gaming is also known as Game on-demand. In cloud gaming, rendering the video between the user and device, storing the game data and computational tasks like rendering game frame are carried out in the cloud server itself. Cloud gaming attracts a huge number of users since it does not require players to upgrade and change their hardware. Instead, it brings high definition games using the broadband connection and a thin client. A thin client may be a light weight computer with a browser, gaming console, setup box and a Television or a mobile device (Lee, Chen, Su, & Lei, 2012).

CLOUD GAMING OVER TRADITIONAL GAMING

Traditional games that are played by humans are programmed into applications. These programmed applications are called as traditional computer games (Wikipedia, Traditional game, 2015). Video games were not familiar with people until the introduction of computers. Cathode ray tube amusement device is the first known gaming device with a display. This device did not have any storage device or computer program and was totally based on analog signals. After analog games, in the year 1952, interactive visual gaming came into existence. These devices were huge in size and were not available to the public. In 1962 first digital video game called Spacewar was invented by students of Massachusetts Institute of Technology. This game made a revolution among the computer users and got installed on several of the computers. The familiarity of this digital video game made programmers concentrate on the development of the gaming technology. Due to demand and novelty of the gaming among the general public in the year, 1972 commercial video gaming industry came into existence (Wikipedia, Early history of video games, 2014). Personal computer advancements and easy accessibility to the general public nurtured the invention of numerous PC games. Consoles specially designed for playing games were invented and targeted gamers. The invention and advancement in mobile phones paved the way for mobile cloud gaming (Robinson, 2012). The usefulness of World Wide Web made programmers to develop social network games (Wikipedia, Origins of the computer game, 2014). From cathode ray tube amusement device, game development evolved into various forms and attained the cloud gaming in the year 2009 (Kent, 2001). In Figure 1, the evolution of cloud gaming from the traditional gaming is depicted.

Cloud computing redefined the technology with high performance, scalable, reliable and easy to access computing machines. The advantageous nature of the Cloud Computing has made many industries and individuals to adapt Cloud technology. From emails to high end computing, cloud technology is used to provide services based on as-a-service model. Paying for what they use and the access to the cloud irrespective of the user location started gaining more acquaintance among

Figure 1. Evolution of cloud gaming

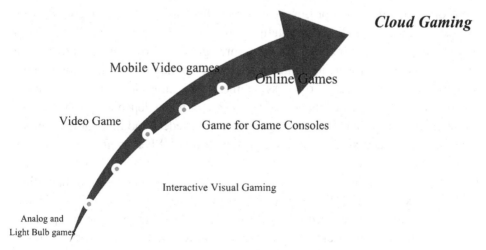

the general public. Gaming in the cloud is offered as one of the services to end users as Gaming-as-a-Service (GaaS). Games based on cloud technology differ from usual desktop games. Normal game development involves building a game for a single client where the game will run on a stationed computer. But in cloud gaming, the game played by the client runs on the server. Cloud gaming enables the developers to develop and manage the game across different territories from a single centralised cloud server. In GaaS, a gamer can enjoy high quality gaming from any device. Earlier, most of the high level games were played using dedicated game consoles. Since most of the computational processes are performed in the cloud servers, users can play the games with simple devices or gadgets like smart phones, personal computers, tablets or laptop computers. GaaS has abolished time constraints and the requirement to have a unique device to play the game. Using GaaS, a gamer can play any game, anywhere and at any time. From saving the game to maintaining the game, every task is taken care by the game developer and service providers. Gamers are free from using disc drives, updating the software and hardware, finding fixes for the bugs and from spending huge money in order to play a single game.

Infrastructure for Cloud Gaming and Desktop Gaming

In the past, game playing infrastructure was totally based on the kind of games the users were playing. For example, if a user likes to play Dangerous Dave game of 1988 then the hardware should be of apple 2 or DOS machine and BASIC language add-on. If a gamer wishes to play AOP2: City of abandoned ships (2009) then the minimum hardware requirement will be Core2Duo Processor, 2GB RAM with an average graphic card and Microsoft windows as the operating system. A game called Assassins Creed: Rogue launched in the year 2015 needs minimum system requirement of Intel Core2Quad processor with the clock speed of more than 2.4 GHz, 2GB Ram, Graphic card of 1Gb and the game can be played only on windows 7 or 8 computer, PS3 and Xbox360. So, these three games, clarifiy the need to have or update to specific software and hardware for every game. In cloud gaming, gaming scenario is totally different. To access a game via the game cloud, users will need a device with thin clients. Cloud server takes care of game dependencies and fixing the bugs. In desktop gaming, gaming devices are needed, and most of the gaming consoles can be accessed only in one particular area. Whereas, in cloud gaming, users can access the server from anywhere in the world with a web browser and can play any game. So, the design of cloud games requires more attention than client centred games. Ensuring the quality aspects of normal games like fixing of bugs, whether the user gets satisfied with the game and other configuration compatibilities are extremely important for game service providers to stay in race. In order to meet cloud gaming quality standards, service providers must test for network connectivity issues, and check how stable the game is when the network has low bandwidth. Similarly, encoding the game in the cloud server and decoding it in the client device, how the game streams in the client device, and bugs in game streaming must be taken care of.

Framework for Cloud Gaming

Cloud gaming framework is totally different from existing game development framework. A framework for cloud gaming is shown in Figure 2. A cloud gamer does require a thin client device to access the cloud gaming servers. Once, the connection is established between the user and the cloud gaming server, the interaction between game logic engine and the gamer starts. Even though, many types of architectures exist for thin clients, instruction based and image based clients are the two major types of architectures. In instruction based client systems, video streams will be transmitted to the client end and after receiving the graphic drawing instructions, the graphics will be rendered at the client side (Nave, et al., 2008). In Image based client systems, the video will be streamed as a real time video at the client end (De Winter, et al., 2006). Instruction based clients consume less bandwidth when compared with image based clients since most of the graphic rendering operations are done at the client end. Gamers send commands to apply or change the game logic. Game commands from gamers reaches the network interface card of a cloud gaming server.

After reaching the cloud gaming server, the game commands are converted into game accomplishments needed by the gamer to apply the game logic. When the commands are successfully applied to the game logic, the game environment gets changed. Change in game environment is rendered by the cloud graphical processing unit (Cloud GPU). Once the game environment is rendered, the video encoding is performed before streaming it to the client.

Figure 2. Cloud gaming framework

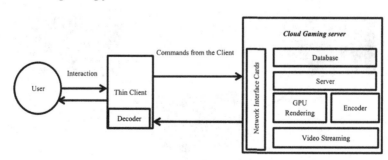

The game video will be streamed to the gamer end. Decoders in the thin clients decode the streaming video for the gamers. The decoded video gets displayed in the thin client and the gamer can find the accomplished change in the gaming environment (Shea, Liu, Ngai, & Cui, 2013). The difference in control flow is depicted in Figures 3 and 4 (Michaud, 2012). The difference in the process takes place after getting the input signal from the user. In traditional gaming, after getting the input signal, the control flows towards processing of input and providing the appropriate output in accordance with the physics of the game.

In cloud gaming, after getting the input command from the user, input to the game logic is transmitted to the game server. In the game server, user input to the game logic is resolved and changes are applied to the game environment. After applying the changes, video frame is encoded and transmitted back to the user. User decodes the video and plays the game. Whereas, in traditional method, after applying the changes to the game scenario, the video frame is returned and changes are displayed on the screen.

Figure 3. Flow of control in traditional gaming

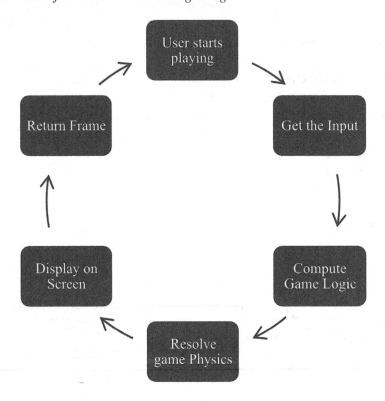

Figure 4. Flow of control in cloud gaming

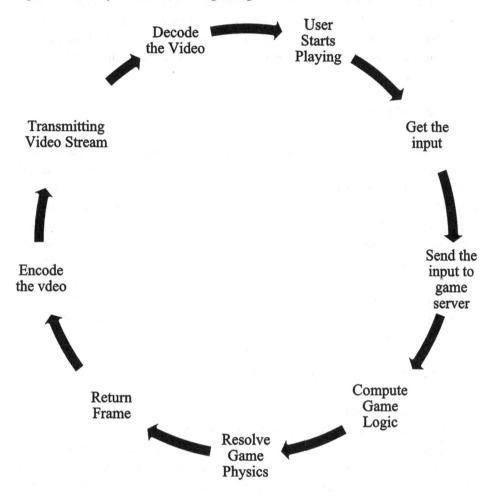

Quality of Experience in Cloud Gaming

Cloud gaming is not just like streaming video between the user and the server. Gaming is about an interaction made between gamer and the game. In Cloud Gaming, it is all about the changes in the experience with respect to the input signal from the user. So the customer view plays a vital role in assuring the service quality of the cloud gaming. Games are designed by considering how gamers will like the game, how novel the game will be to the gamers, how much time gamers will spend on the game and many more aspects that make the gamers get addicted to the game. So, if suddenly something goes out of the box, then it will create frustration among the game players. Denial of service while playing the game will decrease the interest of gamers. A frequent upgrade to the games and server maintenance activities makes the game inaccessible to the gamers for some span of time. Bugs and errors costing the game assets will make a gamer to quit playing the game. Time lagging in opening the game and inconsistent game play are some of the factors where quality assurance is needed.

Latency in Cloud Gaming

In cloud gaming, latency is defined as time response between the game server and thin client. To play a powerful action game, 100ms (milliseconds) of latency is needed where as in role playing games 150ms is required (Jarschel, Schlosser, Scheuring, & HoBfeld, 2013). Different types of delays like playout delay, delay on the network, game delay and processing delay affects the latency of a game (Chen, Chang, Hsu, Chen, Huang, & Hsu, 2014). Network delay is the time taken for transmitting the command from the client to the game server via a network protocol. Game delay is the time taken by the game application in rendering the next frame for the gamer to command. Playout delay is the time needed by the client to decode the video stream after receiving it. Processing delay is the processing time taken by the game server to process, encode and video stream the user command.

Network Traffic in Cloud Gaming

From providing connection to the thin client to getting the rendered video frame from the remote gaming server, everything works on the internet. So, network traffic and reliability of the network proves to be the backbone of cloud gaming. Having an internet connection with the good bandwidth is a necessity to experience a high definition game. In role playing games, if there is a time delay of 10ms, then the impact of the delay will ruin the total game experience of the gamer. Network latency itself is divided into four categories namely time on access, transit, datacentre and isp (Choy, Wong, Simon, & Rosenberg, 2012). Time on accessing is transmission time taken by the client and first connected router. Time on access delay appears to be different for different users, for users with DSL connection, delay is greater than 10ms (Dischinger, Haeberlen, Gummadi, & Saroiu, 2007) and even delay is greater than 40ms in some networks (Sundaresan, De Donato, Feamster, Teixeira, Crawford, & Pescapee, 2011). A home device is connected to a number of active computers on the same network will also end up in time delay. The transmit delay between access router and peer connecting the next hop transit router cause a time delay. Even though, many Internet service providers (ISPs) provide their clients with high and reliable bandwidth, a heavy load of media streaming causes time delay for Internet service providers despite their reliable network (Higginbotham, 2012).

The delay between the front end of the datacentre and the clients hosting server is known as the datacentre time delay (Choy, Wong, Simon, & Rosenberg, 2012). All these network delays are reasons for bad gaming experiences of cloud gamers.

Graphic Quality in Cloud Gaming

Graphics include images or videos on game scenarios to illustrate or entertain the viewers. Graphics quality plays a vital role in the gaming industry. Every year, an improvement in the graphic quality can be experienced by users playing most of the games. The improvements and innovations in graphic quality tempt gamers to explore more games. Hovertank 3D (1991) to FIFA 16 (2015) there is a massive change in the game playing and graphics quality. Cloud gaming service providers have to render high quality graphics to garner more number of active gamers. Stability of network and latency issues remains as a barrier in delivering high definition graphics. Since, cloud gaming involves the process of transmission of signals from the user to server and user receiving the signal from the server it is necessary to maintain good latency and a stable network. Cloud gaming technology aims at rendering 3D games in the server and 2D scenes to the client without any disruptions (Shi, Hsu, Nahrstedt, & Campbell, 2011). The requirements for the game, available bandwidth, network congestion, and latency affect the graphic quality of the Cloud Gaming.

Issues in Cloud Gaming

In spite of its numerous advantageous, cloud gaming has its own share of substantial demerits. In cloud gaming, the video is compressed and transmitted to the client end. Because of the compression, the quality of video gets diminished. Whereas, in high-end gaming consoles, gamers can enjoy high definition gaming. Since, cloud gaming totally depends on the bandwidth, if a gamer plays a game for an hour, he might end up in using more than 1 GB of data. More the amount of data usage, more will be the money spent by the users for data. Latency issues are of great concern in cloud gaming. Latency is defined as the response time taken by the game event over the web. When a gamer plays using the computer, mouse movement will have more latency than that of cloud gaming. To play a high end game in cloud gaming, the user will need strong internet bandwidth. Bandwidth is not same in all the places and in some locations, internet connectivity itself will become an issue. While game publishers will be happy with the DRM (Digital Rights Management) results, many gamers will be at a disadvantage. Cloud gaming also shares all the issues faced by the cloud computing technology (Vouk, 2008). The security risk is high in cloud technology when compared with the traditional way of storage and access (Raj, Dhinesh, Ezendu, Nirmala, & Krishna, 2014). Since Cloud gaming is a service in cloud computing technology, Cloud gaming also experiences the same kind of Cloud security issue (Subashini & Kavitha, 2011). In Cloud, data will not be always in your hand and once uploaded, the data will be in Cloud possession. Servers which are hacked could turn into a rogue and can access the sensitive information of the user (Babu L. D., Krishna, Zayan, & Panda, 2011). Network attacks are always a threat in transmitting data from user end to server (Babu & Krishna, 2013). Cloud gaming platform of Ubisoft called Uplay was hacked by the Russian hackers (Jane, 2013). The hack gave free access to the gamer to access different games and also released forthcoming games prior to its release. This made Ubisoft to shut down the Uplay and fix the issue. EA sports cloud service Origin was hacked in the year 2012 (McCallion, 2012). By this attack, hackers locked many of the gamer accounts by changing the password and user name of gamers. In the year 2011, Sony Online entertainment suffered attack by a hackavist group called anonymous (Schreier, 2011). The network breech compromised information of 24 million users and twenty thousand credit card and bank account details. Security remains as an important concern for the game providers as well as for the gamers.

CLOUD GAMING SYSTEM

Cloud gaming systems involve framing the rules and procedures to manipulate the desired outcome. Framing the rules and procedures for cloud gaming system is totally different from the traditional gaming systems. Cloud gaming systems are known to act in a real time scenario in delivering the remote services to the clients. Cloud gaming systems are classified into video streaming, video streaming with delivering operations, and three dimensional graphic streaming (Huang, Hsu, Chang, & Chen, 2013). Video streaming involves converting the three dimensional commands from the clients into compressed videos and streaming them across the network cards to reach the clients (De Winter, et al., 2006). At the client end, the compressed video will be decoded and displayed on the thin client (Holthe, Mogstad, & Ronningen, 2009). Video streaming does not need any high-cost chips to decode the video. Even the decoder chips coming along with consumer electronics will be sufficient to decode the video. In video streaming with delivering operations, three dimensional graphic rendering operations are done in cloud gaming servers. After encoding the video at the thin client end some more GPU operations are involved in rendering the encoded video (Huang, Hsu, Chang, & Chen, 2013). Three dimensional rendering is like video streaming but involves high cost decoding chips (Jurgelionis, et al., 2009). In three dimensional rendering, the server will not have any graphical unit. The videos are decoded into high definition video using OpenGL and Direct3D at the client's end (Eisert & Fechteler, 2008). Each gaming system has its own unique characteristic feature. Depending on the nature and requirement of the game, game systems are being constructed. There are several gaming systems prevailing with each using one of the game engines in providing their services. GamingAnywhere, Stream In-Home Streaming, Remote Play, Cloud Gaming extreme, Ubitus Game-Cloud, and StreamMyGame are some of the game engines. In the following sections, we intend to explain the deployment of three popular game systems namely GamingAnywhere, Stream In-Home Streaming, and Ubitus GameCloud.

GamingAnywhere

GamingAnywhere is the only available open source cloud gaming system (Chen, gaminganywhere, 2014). It works on a windows server, but it also supports Linux and Mac server. GamingAnywhere client machine is compatible with windows, Linux, mac and android operating system.

Because of the availability of source code, GamingAnywhere is being used by many researchers while researching multimedia supported streaming applications. The standard design of the GamingAnywhere game system is so easy to change or replace the platform independent and platform dependent components. Deployment of Gaminganywhere game system is shown in Figure 5. User logs into the game portal and selects the game. After selecting the game, the portal game server finds for an available game server and schedules the game. There are two types of network interactions in the system namely data flow and control flow. Control flow streams the audio and video signal from the client to server. Data flow streams the video and audio signals from the server to client. Game portal is like an ordinary web service responsible for authenticating the user and an interface to select the game (Huang, Hsu, Chang, & Chen, 2013). All the user requests are sent as http request

Figure 5. Deployment of GamingAnywhere

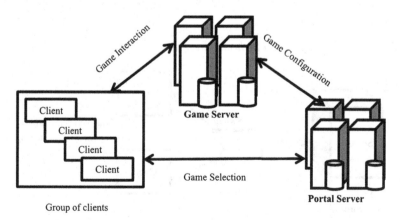

or Representational state transfer. GamingAnywhere supports both the desktop and web based gaming.

Steam In-Home Streaming

An American video game development and digital distribution company called Valve Corporation developed Steam In-Home Streaming Game System. Valve Corporation started working on their steam platform in early 2002. Steam In-Home Streaming server's runs on windows operating system. The main objective of In-Home streaming is to allow users to steam the game for one computer to the other (Figure 6). Any user who has a gaming computer can steam the game from the gaming computer into other low-end devices. The minimum requirement for a computer to act as a server is quad-core CPU with H264 decoding GPU.

Steam In-Home streaming client software should be installed in the computer to act as client and streaming server. Then any one computer can act as an In-Home Streaming server (Slivar, Suznjevic, & Skorin-Kapov, 2015). Currently, In-Home Streaming offers more than 3600 games for different operating systems (Valve, 2014) and there are about 100 million online users registered for Steam In-Home Streaming.

Remote Play

Remote play is the dedicated cloud gaming system for Sony game consoles. Sony released remote play as one of the features of its video game console in the year 2006. Games are streamed from Play Station 3 or 4 gaming consoles to the Play-Station portable or vita. Sony states that all games that are accessed in Play Station 4 can be accessed in remote play. Games which require a camera and PlayStation move cannot be accessed using remote play. Second screen functionality is one of

Figure 6. Deployment of steam in-home streaming

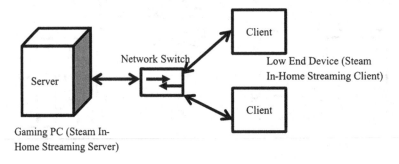

the additional features of Sony remote play. Remote play can be accessed only with Sony consoles (Sony, 2015).

Ubitus GameCloud

Ubitus GameCloud was developed by Ubitus Inc., in the year 2007. Ubitus Inc., provides technical support in deploying cloud based media services and cloud based solutions. Ubitus game cloud offers commercial cloud gaming platform. It supports massively multiplayer online role playing game acts and 4G LTE (Long term Evolution) cloud gaming (Ubitus Inc., 2015).

Ubitus game cloud accepts smart TV, google TV, Set Top boxes, smart phones and web browser as its clients. Ubitus game server runs on windows operating system. Game cloud server is responsible for three processes namely game cloud engine, Integration service and game adaption tools as seen in Figure 7. Game cloud engine is responsible for executing the game, managing and monitoring the game service. Integration service takes the role of managing user account, and also, it acts as a billing gateway. Game adaptation tools provide the game development tool kit. Using the game development tool kit, developers can change the PC platform games into cloud based games without changing the source code. Game commands from the client reach the game server through the network. Real Time Streaming Protocol (RTSP) is used in controlling the streaming servers in entertainment and communication servers. Ubitus cloud uses RTSP protocol for audio and video streaming.

CLOUD GAME SERVICES

User end gaming services offered to the client using cloud gaming technology is known as Cloud game services. Advancement in technology and easy access to the

Figure 7. Deployment of Ubitus Game Cloud

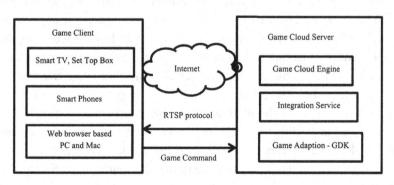

internet has paved way to a lot of users to access cloud gaming services. GameNow, GameFly Streaming, G-Cluster Gface, Kalydo, LoudPlay, Leap Computing, Play Giga, Play Key, PlayStation Now, LiquidSky, Turbo Games are some of the active cloud game services. Most of the game services can be accessed using dedicated gaming consoles. The performance of GeForce Now is 2448 GFlops (Gigabyte Floating point operation per second) and is greater than PlaystationNow and GameFly Streaming. GeForce Now supports maximum resolution of 1080p60 (1920x1080 pixels at 60 Frames per second) whereas PlayStation Now and GameFly Streaming supports 720p30 (Nvidia, 2015). GeForce Now supports google's android platform and nvidia shield devices. PlayStation Now works on Sony PlayStation platform on Sony devices. GameFly Streaming supports amazon fire platform and is compatible with some samsung tvs and some amazon fire tvs. GeForce Now offers 50 plus games, and GameFly Streaming offers around seven to nineteen games for the price of below 10$/month. PlayStation Now charges less than 20$ / month with access to 100 plus games. Sony Entertainment, G-Cluster, Nvidia, Microsoft, and Ubisoft Entertainment are the top vendors of cloud gaming services (ResearchandMarkets, 2015).

Economics of Cloud Gaming

Commercialisation of gaming industry started around the year 1970 and from then onwards, gaming industry instituted itself into huge revenue generating industry. Real world like virtual graphics and animations, power of the gamers to change the virtual environment, and motion capturing sensors have played a vital role in increasing the consumers. Different genres of games make people of all age group and gender to play video based games. A game like modern warfare earned 1 billion dollars in just 16 days (Waugh, 2011). Over the time span of past twenty five years, the growth of gaming industry in a year is stated anywhere between 9% and 15% (Bengtsson, Wilson, & Zackariasson, 2010). Between the year November 23, 2013 to November 22, 2014, Sony had sold 30.2 million units of its PlayStation 4 console worldwide. Microsoft has claimed that it had sold 1.5 million units of its Xbox console in the first quarter of the year 2015. Nintendo, who is the top competitor of Sony and Microsoft, had sold 10.73 million units of Wii U console as of September 30, 2015 (Kharpal, 2015). The technology advancement has made cloud gaming to earn good CAGR (Compound annual growth rate) ratings alongside traditional gaming. Currently, cloud gaming is being dominated by northern America and Western European countries. By 2020, central and eastern Europe, Latin America and Asia will also have a faster growth potential for online cloud based games. Chances of a 33.5% increase in CAGR by 2020 are estimated in the cloud gaming industry (Infoholic, 2015). The current trendsetting change made by cloud gaming in video game scenario will generate more revenue in the upcoming years. Some of the big players started investing billions of money in cloud gaming industry (Marchand & Hennig-Thurau, 2013). IT giant Microsoft invested one billion dollars in their gaming console Xbox one, and it acquired Onlive. Sony purchased Gaikai, a cloud gaming service to increase their hold in Cloud gaming. Amazon and Google are building their own datacentres to support and discover their own cloud ambitions.

Pricing Strategy for Games

Pricing a game varies depending on the nature of game development. Price strategy is one of the most important but undervalued process in game development. Pricing strategy for a game is framed after analysing many aspects of gaming scenarios. Factors like design and concept of the game, production cost, current trends, competitions, market scenario and many other factors must be considered while developing a pricing model. Pricing strategy and factors involved in framing the price are depicted in Figure 8.

One of the most popular pricing strategies is to sell at a high price when the product is new and then to reduce the price when the product is getting old. Most

Figure 8. Pricing strategy for games

of the mobile cloud games are offered as free of cost games but they generate huge profits. These games tempt the game players to buy game currency to level up or to go ahead of their competitors. Strategies of these kinds garner a wide range of audience around the world. Even though the games are marked as freeware, people make in-game purchases to advance faster in the games.

Piracy affects the sales of the video games on a large extent. Piracy started when the game industry started evolving. It was reported that income by pirate game industry equals the revenue generated by the game industry (Zhugeex, 2015). Cloud gaming, tries to bring in the solution to abolish piracy. Playing in the cloud forces the user to get authenticated every time and by this process, the developers can filter the genuine users from the one using pirated versions. By offering basic game as freeware and pro features as in-game purchases, gamers of all economic backgrounds can experience the game with minimum expenditure. If the game is addictive, then it will convince the gamers to buy game currencies and such in-game purchase pricing strategies will be the future of cloud gaming.

Revenue from Advertisements

Freeware games generate revenue even without offering in-game purchases. The proliferation of smart phones and tablets have made public to access many freeware applications and games. Developer monetizes their game by distributing the game without cost and adding interstitial advertisements to monetize the game (Hermet & Combet, 2011). By analysing the experience of gamers in the game, different kinds of advertisements are made to pop up while playing the game. Advertisements in a game can be classified into four categories namely Playable ads, Video ads, rewarded ads, and interstitials ads. Video ads are targeted between level wins, during the waiting time between the players and while starting the game. Playable advertisements are interactive advertisements which enable the audience to play even a demo game. These kinds of advertisements are targeted during the long wait time. Interstitial advertisements are popped during the game play. Rewarded advertisements are non-skippable advertisements which enable the developer to monetise the game form non-paying users (Inmobi, 2014).

Hidden Costs of Cloud Gaming

Since, Game on-demand service evolved over cloud computing technology, the hidden costs of cloud computing services also affect the cloud gaming services. Hidden costs of cloud services affect the game developers in multiple ways than the cloud game users. Inflation in cost over the unused services is a common mistake that cloud developers tend to do like getting more cloud services without estimating the service demand. Unused server instances create loss to developer whereas gains to the cloud provider. The developer will be paying the same amount even though the instance was not used for its purpose. Before hiring storage tiers to store the data, the developer needs to analyse which tier will be suitable for what kind of data. Since for storage tiers, cost varies with the accessibility rate, developers should analyse the need for storage and nature of data instead of paying for storing data which are least accessed by the cloud users. Switching from one cloud provider to the other provider costs the developers more than what they have paid to access the cloud service. In cloud services, trouble shooting is not as easy as fixing the home computer. Cloud troubleshooting is more expensive and time consuming (Froehlich, 2015). The gamer needs to analyse and bare the bandwidth charges while playing the cloud based games. High definition games require nearly gigabytes of data transmission for few hours of game play. Bandwidth charges to play the cloud based game are the hidden cost while adapting cloud services.

Demographical Users

Cloud gaming services are not limited to a particular group of people. It is widely spread across the world and anyone can access the cloud gaming service using the internet and even a thin client. Even, design of the user interface is subjected to the user's cultural heritage (Shneiderman & Ben, 2003). Research to find the relationship between the user's nature of usability and their cultural heritage has proved that beyond cultural heritage, gamers behaviour can get influenced by other factors as well (Zaharias, 2009). So in coming year's demographic variation in cloud gaming will not have any major impact for various localities across the globe. Considering the penetration of World Wide Web and its services, there will only be limited variations between the different cultural and varied demographic users (Badre, 2001). The demand for scalable computation power throughout the world and availability of affordable computational devices will eradicate the demographic variations between users in decades to come.

RESEARCH OPPORTUNITIES IN CLOUD GAMING

Cloud gaming appears to emerge as the future gaming consoles for the gamer. Though it has many advantages, cloud gaming providers have to render cloud gaming services in a lively manner without affecting the cost. This paves way for many types of research in cloud gaming industry. While transmitting command signals and video streams between the gamers and the servers, there is a chance of error during updates or changes made between the game engine and their dependent files in the server (Chen, Huang, & Hsu, Cloud gaming onward: research opportunities and outlook, 2014). These changes will cause an unbalance and wastage of processing time in the server. The integration of game with the service providing cloud gaming platform needs attention. Cloud gaming needs a dedicated video codec-electronic block for video compression. Available H.264 video codec has proved to be the adequate video codec for playing media files, but it is not that efficient for cloud gaming (Shi, Hsu, Nahrstedt, & Campbell, 2011). Chuah and Cheung proposed a layered approach where the graphic frame is divided into two layers namely baseline and enhancement layer (Chuah & Cheung, 2014). Enhancement layer has the graphic rendering commands to the client. The proposed approach used less computational resource in both client as well as server end. Cross layered processing between delivering graphics and video compressing appears to be one of the essential research investigations.

Cloud gaming fully depends on virtualization technology. The cloud gaming quality depends on a number of virtualized game instances on the server. Prevailing gap between the GPU instances and scalable game instances needs a serious investigation to provide gamer the in-home console experience (Chen, Huang, & Hsu, Cloud gaming onward: research opportunities and outlook, 2014). In mobile cloud gaming and in smart phones, most of the control commands are passed by touch buttons instead of joystick and keyboards. The user interface in mobile gaming needs progressions to change the mobile gaming experience of the gamers. The experience of the gamers varies with many factors like the role played in the game, graphics quality, game behavioural pattern, and variation occurs with time and new trends. So, measuring the quality of the cloud gaming experience is not an easy task. Available quality measurement methods like Single Stimulus Continuous Quality Evaluation and Double-Stimulus Continuous Quality Evaluation (Lodge & Wood, 1996) are not sufficient to measure the gaming quality. New inventions are needed in measuring the cloud gaming quality of experience. Since game servers are distributed across the globe, selecting appropriate game server (Babu & Krishna, Applying operations management models for facility location problem in cloud computing environments, 2013) is an issue with the gamers. The game server that has low latency and less traffic can be allocated to the gamer. Scheduling the game server differs from scheduling the normal cloud server (Babu & Krishna, Versatile time-cost algorithm (VTCA) for scheduling non-preemptive tasks of time critical workflows in cloud computing systems, 2013) because each game requires different unique graphical and storage requirements. Analysis of dedicated resource scheduling process (Dhinesh Babu, Gunasekaran, & Krishna, 2014) and server selection for cloud gaming servers can increase the decent gaming experience.

CONCLUSION

Cloud computing services have revolutionized the world to a larger extent. The revolution has eased the task of carrying hardware around us. User's demands to game anywhere and anytime is being fulfilled by cloud gaming services. In this chapter, we have detailed the evolution of cloud gaming, Cloud game systems, its architecture, services, its issues and its future. Economics involved in the gaming industry, revenues generated and detailed analysis to enhance the cloud gaming services were depicted in this chapter. Cloud gaming is going to be the future of gaming industry. Gaming in the cloud will prohibit piracy to a great extent. The user will enjoy the game experience without any hassles in updating or spending more money to buy expensive hardware. Affordable thin clients can make the gamer to feel the game without any heavy gaming consoles. Issues in latency need to be addressed to satisfy user with high definition game playing experience.

REFERENCES

Babu, L. D., & Krishna, P. V. (2013). Applying operations management models for facility location problem in cloud computing environments. *International Journal of Services and Operations Management*, 1-27.

Babu, L. D., & Krishna, P. V. (2013). Honey bee behavior inspired load balancing of tasks in cloud computing environments. *Applied Soft Computing*, 2292–2303.

Babu, L. D., & Krishna, P. V. (2013). Versatile time-cost algorithm (VTCA) for scheduling non-preemptive tasks of time critical workflows in cloud computing systems. *International Journal of Communication Networks and Distributed Systems*, *11*(4), 390–411. doi:10.1504/IJCNDS.2013.057718

Babu, L. D., Krishna, P. V., Zayan, A. M., & Panda, V. (2011). *An analysis of security related issues in cloud computing. In Contemporary Computing* (pp. 180–190). Delhi, India: Springer.

Badre, A. (2001). *The Effects of Cross Cultural Interface Design Orientation on World Wide Web User Performance*. Georgia Institute of Technology.

Bengtsson, M., Wilson, T. L., & Zackariasson, P. (2010). Paradigm shifts in the video game industry. *Competitiveness Review: An International Business Journal*, 139-151.

Chen, K.-T. (2014, July 10). *Gaminganywhere*. Retrieved November 10, 2015, from http://gaminganywhere.org: http://gaminganywhere.org/index.html

Chen, K.-T., Chang, Y.-C., Hsu, H.-J., Chen, D.-Y., Huang, C.-Y., & Hsu, C.-H. (2014). On the quality of service of cloud gaming systems. *Multimedia, IEEE Transactions on*, 480-495.

Chen, K.-T., Huang, C.-Y., & Hsu, C.-H. (2014). Cloud gaming onward: research opportunities and outlook. *Multimedia and Expo Workshops (ICMEW), 2014 IEEE International Conference on* (pp. 1-4). Chengdu, China: IEEE.

Choy, S., Wong, B., Simon, G., & Rosenberg, C. (2012). The brewing storm in cloud gaming: A measurement study on cloud to end-user latency.*Proceedings of the 11th annual workshop on network and systems support for games* (p. 2). Piscataway, NJ: IEEE Press. doi:10.1109/NetGames.2012.6404024

Chuah, S.-P., & Cheung, N.-M. (2014). Layered coding for mobile cloud gaming. *Proceedings of International Workshop on Massively Multiuser Virtual Environments* (pp. 1-6). Singapore: ACM. doi:10.1145/2594448.2577395

De Winter, D., Simoens, P., Deboosere, L., De Turck, F., Moreau, J., & Dhoedt, B. et al.. (2006). A hybrid thin-client protocol for multimedia streaming and interactive gaming applications.*Proceedings of the 2006 international workshop on Network and operating systems support for digital audio and video* (p. 15). Newport, RI: ACM. doi:10.1145/1378191.1378210

Dhinesh Babu, L., Gunasekaran, A., & Krishna, P. V. (2014). A decision-based pre-emptive fair scheduling strategy to process cloud computing work-flows for sustainable enterprise management. *International Journal of Business Information Systems*, 409-430.

Dischinger, M., Haeberlen, A., Gummadi, K. P., & Saroiu, S. (2007). Characterizing residential broadband networks.*Internet Measurement Conference* (pp. 43-56). San Diego, CA: ACM.

Eisert, P., & Fechteler, P. (2008). Low delay streaming of computer graphics. *Image Processing, 2008. ICIP 2008. 15th IEEE International Conference on* (pp. 2704-2707). San Diego, CA: IEEE.

Froehlich, A. (2015, November 05). *Cloud Computing: 8 Hidden Costs*. Retrieved December 01, 2015, from http://www.informationweek.com/cloud/platform-as-a-service/cloud-computing-8-hidden-costs/d/d-id/1321375?image_number=10

Hermet, G., & Combet, J. (2011). Mobile Internet Monetization: A Methodology to Monitor in Real Time the Cellular Subscriber Transactional Itinerary, from Mobile Advertising Exposure to Actual Purchase. *Mobile Business (ICMB), 2011 Tenth International Conference on* (pp. 307-312). Como, Italy: IEEE.

Higginbotham, S. (2012). *Smart TVs cause a net neutrality debate in S. Korea.* San Francisco, CA: Giga OM, Feb.

Holthe, O.-I., Mogstad, O., & Ronningen, L. A. (2009). Geelix LiveGames: Remote playing of video games.*Proceedings of the 6th IEEE Conference on Consumer Communications and Networking Conference* (pp. 758-759). Las Vegas, NV: IEEE Press. doi:10.1109/CCNC.2009.4784713

Huang, C.-Y., Hsu, C.-H., Chang, Y.-C., & Chen, K.-T. (2013). GamingAnywhere: an open cloud gaming system.*Proceedings of the 4th ACM multimedia systems conference* (pp. 36-47). Oslo, Norway: ACM. doi:10.1145/2483977.2483981

Infoholic, R. (2015, June 23). *Global Cloud Gaming Market: Trends & Forecast 2015-2020.* Retrieved November 28, 2015, from http://finance.yahoo.com: http://finance.yahoo.com/news/global-cloud-gaming-market-trends-104100437.html

Inmobi. (2014, December 01). *Monetization Solution for Games.* Retrieved December 03, 2015, from http://www.inmobi.com: http://info.inmobi.com/rs/inmobi/images/InMobi-Monetization-Solution-for-Games.pdf

Jane, M. (2013, April 13). *Publisher's cloud gaming platform hacked, providing access to unreleased games.* Retrieved December 3, 2015, from http://www.cloudpro.co.uk/saas/5470/ubisoft-shuts-down-cloud-gaming-platform-wake-hack

Jarschel, M., Schlosser, D., Scheuring, S., & Hoßfeld, T. (2013). Gaming in the clouds: QoE and the users' perspective. *Mathematical and Computer Modelling, 57*(11-12), 2883–2894. doi:10.1016/j.mcm.2011.12.014

Jurgelionis, A., Fechteler, P., Eisert, P., Bellotti, F., David, H., & Laulajainen, J.-P. et al.. (2009). Platform for distributed 3D gaming. *International Journal of Computer Games Technology, 1.*

Kent, S. (2001). *The Ultimate History of Video Games: from Pong to Pokemon and beyond... the story behind the craze that touched our li ves and changed the world.* New York: Three Rivers Press.

Kharpal, A. (2015, November 25). *Sony PS4 sales top 30 million in battle with Xbox.* Retrieved December 5, 2015, from http://www.cnbc.com: http://www.cnbc.com/2015/11/25/sony-playstation-4-sales-top-30-million-in-battle-with-xbox.html

Lee, Y.-T., Chen, K.-T., Su, H.-I., & Lei, C.-L. (2012). Are all games equally cloud-gaming-friendly? an electromyographic approach. *Network and Systems Support for Games (NetGames), 2012 11th Annual Workshop on* (pp. 1-6). Venice, Italy: IEEE.

Lodge, N., & Wood, D. (1996). New tools for evaluating the quality of digital television-results of the MOSAIC project.*International Broadcasting Convention (IBC)* (pp. 323 – 330). Amsterdam, Netherlands: IET. doi:10.1049/cp:19960828

Marchand, A., & Hennig-Thurau, T. (2013). Value creation in the video game industry: Industry economics, consumer benefits, and research opportunities. *Journal of Interactive Marketing, 27*(3), 141–157. doi:10.1016/j.intmar.2013.05.001

McCallion, J. (2012, November 12). *Gamers find themselves locked out of accounts as hijackers apparently change personal details without permission.* Retrieved November 11, 2015, from http://www.cloudpro.co.uk/cloud-essentials/5022/ea-owned-cloud-gaming-platform-origin-hacked

Michaud, L. (2012). Technical architecture and advantages of cloud gaming. *Communications & Stratégies, 203.*

Nave, I., David, H., Shani, A., Tzruya, Y., Laikari, A., Eisert, P., ... (2008). Games@ Large graphics streaming architecture. *Consumer Electronics, 2008. ISCE 2008. IEEE International Symposium on* (pp. 1-4). Vilamoura, Portugal: IEEE.

Nvidia. (2015, October 03). *Compare streaming platforms.* Retrieved December 10, 2015, from https://shield.nvidia.com/geforce-now-vs-playstation-now-vs-gamefly

Raj, E. D., Dhinesh, B. L., Ezendu, A., Nirmala, M., & Krishna, P. V. (2014). Forecasting the Trends in Cloud Computing and its Impact on Future IT Business. In A. Ezendu (Ed.), Green Technology Applications for Enterprise and Academic Innovation (p. 14). Bedfordshire, UK: IGI Global. doi:doi:10.4018/978-1-4666-5166-1.ch002 doi:10.4018/978-1-4666-5166-1.ch002

ResearchandMarkets. (2015, June 28). *Research and Markets: Global Cloud Gaming Market 2015-2019 - What are the market opportunities and threats faced by the key vendors?* Retrieved December 08, 2015, from http://www.reuters.com: http://www.reuters.com/article/research-and-markets-idUSnBw235751a+100+BSW20150623

Robinson, J. (2012). *The Evolution of the Gaming Industry into the Pockets of the Consumer. Univ. of Southampton.*

Schreier, J. (2011, June 05). *Sony Hack Probe Uncovers 'Anonymous' Calling Card.* Retrieved November 06, 2015, from http://www.wired.com: http://www.wired.com/2011/05/sony-playstation-network-anonymous/

Shea, R., Liu, J., Ngai, E., & Cui, Y. (2013). Cloud gaming: Architecture and performance. *IEEE Network, 27*(4), 16–21. doi:10.1109/MNET.2013.6574660

Shi, S., Hsu, C.-H., Nahrstedt, K., & Campbell, R. (2011). Using graphics rendering contexts to enhance the real-time video coding for mobile cloud gaming.*Proceedings of the 19th ACM international conference on Multimedia* (pp. 103--112). Scottsdale, AZ: ACM. doi:10.1145/2072298.2072313

Shneiderman, B., & Ben, S. (2003). *Designing the user interface*. Pearson Education India.

Slivar, I., Suznjevic, M., & Skorin-Kapov, L. (2015). The impact of video encoding parameters and game type on QoE for cloud gaming: A case study using the steam platform. *Quality of Multimedia Experience (QoMEX), 2015 Seventh International Workshop on* (pp. 1-6). Pilos, Greece: IEEE.

Sony. (2015, November 02). *Remote Play*. Retrieved November 04, 2015, from http://www.sonymobile.com/global-en/apps-services/remote-play/

Subashini, S., & Kavitha, V. (2011). A survey on security issues in service delivery models of cloud computing. *Journal of Network and Computer Applications*, *34*(1), 1–11. doi:10.1016/j.jnca.2010.07.006

Sundaresan, S., De Donato, W., Feamster, N., Teixeira, R., Crawford, S., & Pescapee, A. (2011). *Broadband internet performance: a view from the gateway. In ACM SIGCOMM computer communication review* (pp. 134–145). Toronto, Canada: ACM. doi:10.1145/2018436.2018452

Ubitus Inc. (2015, November 02). *ubitus*. Retrieved November 10, 2015, from http://www.ubitus.net: http://www.ubitus.net/en/aboutubitus.html

Valve. (2014, december 15). *steampowered*. Retrieved December 5, 2015, from http://store.steampowered.com: http://store.steampowered.com/about/

Vouk, M. (2008). Cloud computing--issues, research and implementations. *Journal of Computing and Information Technology*, 235-246.

Waugh, R. (2011, December 13). *Modern Warfare 3 hits $1 billion in 16 days - beating Avatar's record by one day*. Retrieved December 2015, 10, from http://www.dailymail.co.uk: http://www.dailymail.co.uk/sciencetech/article-2073201/Modern-Warfare-3-hits-1-billion-16-days--beating-Avatars-record-day.html

Wikipedia. (2014, December 10). *Early history of video games*. Retrieved december 11, 2015, from https://en.wikipedia.org: https://en.wikipedia.org/wiki/Early_history_of_video_games

Wikipedia. (2014, March). *Origins of the computer game*. Retrieved December 01, 2015, from https://en.wikipedia.org/: https://en.wikipedia.org/wiki/History_of_video_games#Origins_of_the_computer_game

Wikipedia. (2015, January 27). *Traditional game*. Retrieved 12 11, 2015, from https://en.wikipedia.org: https://en.wikipedia.org/wiki/Traditional_game

Zaharias, P. A. (2009). The gamer experience: Investigating relationships between culture and usability in massively multiplayer online games. *Computers in Entertainment*, 26.

Zhugeex. (2015, August 20). *Video Game Piracy On The Rise, Will Cost The Industry As Much As It Makes*. Retrieved November 20, 2015, from http://gearnuke.com/video-game-piracy-rise-will-cost-industry-much-makes/

KEY TERMS AND DEFINITIONS

Cloud Computing: An internet based computational paradigm in which resources comprising hardware as well as software can be hosted as a service to a substantially large number of end users and users pay only for the resources they use per unit time.

Cloud Gaming Services: User end gaming services offered to the client using cloud gaming technology.

Game System: Cloud gaming infrastructure capable of providing gaming service.

Latency: Response time taken between server and client to transmit signal.

Network Bandwidth: Passage of network involved in transferring data from one to the other.

Scheduling: Process of assigning task among CPUs or GPUs.

Video Streaming: Constant receiving and delivering of video media between user end and service provider end.

Video Codec: Electronic/Software components used to compress and decompress videos.

Chapter 2
Efficient Development and Execution of Adaptable Online Games on Clouds

Dominik Meiländer
University of Muenster, Germany

Sergei Gorlatch
University of Muenster, Germany

ABSTRACT

Massively Multiplayer Online Games (MMOG) are a challenging class of applications: they combine high demands on real-time user interactivity and adaptability with the problem of an efficient and economic utilization of resources for the dynamically changing number of users. This chapter studies how MMOG can benefit from Cloud Computing with its Infrastructure-as-a-Service (IaaS) approach to cost-efficient leasing resources on demand. The chapter makes two major contributions: (1) a new lifecycle model for the development of adaptable MMOG expresses major design and execution aspects of Cloud-based MMOG, and (2) a resource management system RTF-RMS implements efficient load balancing for MMOG on Clouds. The authors illustrate how their lifecycle model and RTF-RMS system support the efficient development and execution of adaptable MMOG on Clouds and demonstrate the advantages of their approach in an experimental evaluation.

DOI: 10.4018/978-1-5225-0546-4.ch002

INTRODUCTION

This chapter is motivated by the high performance requirements of Massively Multiplayer Online Games (MMOG): short response times to user inputs (about 0.1–1.5 s), frequent state updates (up to 50 Hz), large and frequently changing number of users in a single application instance (up to 10^4 simultaneously). MMOG combine high demands on the adaptability (i.e., changing the application processing during runtime in order to balance the changing load of application servers caused by fluctuating interactivity between users) and real-time user interactivity with the problem of efficient and economic utilization of resources for the dynamically changing number of users. It is desirable to avoid an up-front investment for building an expensive server pool which would successfully handle peak user numbers in MMOG but would remain underutilized most of the time. Cloud Computing with its Infrastructure-as-a-Service (IaaS) approach to leasing virtual resources on demand is particularly promising for efficient and economic resource provisioning for MMOG: it offers the possibility for small and medium-sized companies to develop and provide large-scale software applications and at the same time avoid risky and expensive up-front investments into hardware resources.

The availability of potentially unlimited Cloud resources leads to large and complex distributed systems and, therefore, increases the demand for adaptable MMOG and efficient load balancing. Common Cloud platforms offer services for monitoring and workload distribution for their Cloud resources, e.g., Amazon Cloud Watch or Amazon Elastic Load Balancing for Amazon Elastic Compute Cloud (EC2) resources (Amazon Web Services, 2015). However, these services currently only provide generic system information about resource utilization (e.g., CPU load, memory consumption, bandwidth, etc.) which are not sufficient for the workload analysis of MMOG according to the previous studies (Ploss, Meiländer, Glinka, & Gorlatch, 2011). Recent studies by Ploss et al. (2011) and Nae, Iosup, Prodan, & Fahringer (2009) show how the performance requirements of MMOG can be fulfilled on commercial Cloud systems like the Amazon Elastic Compute Cloud (Amazon Web Services, 2015).

This chapter addresses the development of adaptable MMOG and their efficient execution in Cloud environments. For this purpose, we utilize our Real-Time Framework (RTF) (Gorlatch, Glinka, Ploss, & Meiländer, 2012) – a high-level framework for developing and efficient execution of highly interactive, distributed applications including MMOG. RTF provides application-specific monitoring values suitable for MMOG workload analysis and efficient parallelization concepts suitable for transparent workload (re-)distribution in MMOG. We use our example application RTFDemo (Gorlatch, Glinka, Ploss, & Meiländer, 2012), which was built using RTF, for illustrating and evaluating the concepts and contributions proposed in this chapter.

The chapter focuses on Infrastructure-as-a-Service (IaaS), rather than other Cloud technologies like Platform-as-a-Service (PaaS) or Software-as-a-Service (SaaS), because we aim at exploiting the processing power of Cloud resources for high-performance MMOG execution. Since MMOG typically have an individual application logic that does not incorporate external services and the application processing is distributed on multiple resources, IaaS is most suitable for MMOG execution on Clouds: IaaS provides services comprising compute and storage resources that are hosted and maintained by an infrastructure provider.

In this chapter, we deal with two main areas:

1. Development of adaptable MMOG suitable for execution in Cloud environments, and
2. Efficient execution and load balancing of Cloud-based MMOG.

For 1, we propose a *novel lifecycle model for MMOG development and execution* in Cloud environments that addresses the following major challenges:

1. Expressing the major design and execution aspects of MMOG executed in Cloud environments.
2. Identifying generic application requirements for Cloud-based MMOG execution.
3. Categorizing scenarios that require load balancing, and proposing suitable load-balancing actions for each such scenario.

For 2, we design and implement a *novel resource management system for MMOG on Clouds* that addresses the following major challenges:

1. Cloud resources have quite long startup times (up to several minutes). Since Cloud resources are typically leased on demand, it is important to find a compensation for these long startup times since MMOG are expected to be highly responsive applications.
2. Cloud resources typically have static leasing periods. In commercial Cloud systems, resources are typically leased and paid per hour or some longer leasing period. Since MMOG often have dynamically changing user numbers, the time after which Cloud resources become dispensable is very variable. However, resources will not be used cost-efficiently if they are shut down before the end of their leasing period. A possible scenario is as follows: a Cloud resource is leased and paid for (at least) one hour, but if this resource is shut down after five minutes (since it has become dispensable), the Cloud provider will not refund any money.

3.   Cloud resources use virtualized hardware. The influence of the virtualization overhead on MMOG performance is analyzed and taken into account for load balancing in our system.

The chapter is organized as follows. Section "Scalable MMOG Development with RTF" briefly describes the class of Massively Multiplayer Online Games (MMOG) and our Real-Time Framework (RTF) used for their development and execution. Section "A Lifecycle Model for Adaptable MMOG on Clouds" presents our lifecycle model and illustrates how it expresses major design and execution aspects of MMOG. Section "Dynamic Resource Management for MMOG on Clouds" presents our dynamic resource management system RTF-RMS, illustrates its strategy for load balancing and Cloud resource allocation and discusses the influence of hardware virtualization on MMOG load balancing. Section "Related Work" compares our approach to related work, and section "Conclusion" concludes this chapter and presents directions for future research.

SCALABLE MMOG DEVELOPMENT WITH RTF

Typically, there are three different actors involved in the development and execution of MMOG:

1.   **Application Developers:** They implement the MMOG application, i.e., server and client programs realizing the application logic, and suitable mechanisms for application state distribution and monitoring,
2.   **Application Providers:** They make MMOG accessible to users by executing application server programs on hardware resources, as well as implement dynamic load balancing for MMOG sessions according to the current user workload, and
3.   **Users:** They connect their personal computers or mobile devices (*clients*) to application servers.

Each user controls his avatar that interacts with application *entities*, i.e., other users' avatars or computer-controlled characters, in the virtual game environment. The application state is shared between all users.

Figure 1 shows the real-time loop model (Valente, Conci, & Feijó, 2005) which describes MMOG execution on hardware resources. Each user is connected to one application server that processes users' inputs (e.g., commands and interactions with other users), computes application state updates and sends them to its users,

Figure 1. One iteration of the real-time loop (left); RTF methods for application state distribution (right)

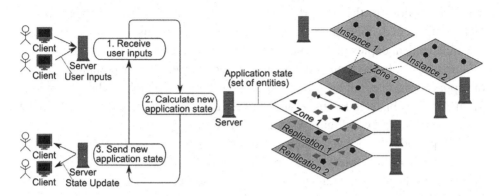

see the left-hand side of Figure 1. One iteration of the real-time loop is called a *tick* and consists of three steps:

1. Each server receives inputs from its connected users;
2. Each server computes a new application state according to the application logic; and
3. Each server sends the newly computed state to its connected users and to the other servers.

Steps 1 and 3 involve communication to transmit the users' inputs and state updates between multiple application servers. The computation of a new application state (step 2) involves quite compute-intensive calculations which apply the application logic to the current state, taking into account the newly received users' inputs. Typically, application servers filter state update information by calculating an *area of interest* for each user, i.e., only changes that are relevant and visible for the user are sent to him, in order to reduce the required network bandwidth. The time required for one iteration of the real-time loop (*tick duration*) is directly related to the application's response time which includes in addition the delay due to the network communication between clients and servers. Hence, the tick duration is used as an important QoS criterion for performance evaluation of MMOG.

The *Real-Time Framework (RTF)* (Gorlatch et al., 2012) is our high-level development platform for scalable MMOG which supports the application developer in three essential tasks as explained in the following:

1. Application state distribution,
2. Communication handling, and
3. Monitoring and distribution handling.

RTF supports three common methods of *application state distribution* among servers (on the right-hand side of Figure 1): zoning, instancing and replication, and combinations of them (Gorlatch et al., 2012). Zoning assigns the processing of the entities in disjoint areas (*zones*) to distinct servers. Instancing creates separate independent copies of a particular zone, such that each copy is processed by a different server. In the replication approach, each server keeps a complete copy of the application state, but each server is responsible for a disjoint subset of entities (*active entities*, black in Figure 1) and receives updates for the remaining, so-called *shadow entities* (grey in Figure 1) from other servers.

RTF provides high-level mechanisms for *communication handling*: automatic (de-)serialization for objects to be transferred over network (user inputs, application state updates, etc.), (un-)marshalling of data types, and optimization of the bandwidth usage. RTF's *monitoring and distribution handling* allows the provider to change the distribution of the application state during runtime, as well as to receive monitoring data from RTF inside an application server. The distribution of the application state can be changed by load-balancing actions which include adding/removing resources to/from the application processing, or migrating users between application servers, i.e., transferring the responsibility for user input processing and state update computation from one server to another.

A LIFECYCLE MODEL FOR ADAPTABLE MMOG ON CLOUDS

Development and execution of Cloud-based MMOG requires *adaptation*, i.e., changing the application behaviour during runtime. While the traditional load balancing techniques primarily adapt to internal influences, i.e., changing load caused by a changing number of users, adaptation also addresses external influences, e.g., unreliable hardware resources used for the execution of application servers, changing user behaviour, etc. While load-balancing actions aim at changing the application state distribution transparently to the users, *adaptation strategies* also consider to adapt the application processing in a non-transparent way (although transparent adaption is preferred), e.g., switching the responsibility for user processing between application servers can be implemented transparently, i.e., unnoticeably for the users, whereas changes to the geography of a virtual environment are usually noticeable by all users (non-transparent). Failures caused by external influences (e.g., failing hardware resources) typically lead to dramatic QoS violations which are difficult to compensate and require non-transparent adaptation strategies in order to prevent a complete system failure. During runtime, the demand for adaptation needs to be identified and the adaptation should be initiated by so-called *adaptation triggers*.

Therefore, suitable monitoring values for indicating QoS violations, and a suitable adaptation strategy need to be chosen.

We propose a novel *lifecycle model* for development and execution of adaptable Cloud-based MMOG by providing suitable adaptation triggers and strategies (Meiländer, Bucchiarone, Cappiello, Di Nitto, & Gorlatch, 2011). Based on RTF as a software framework comprising tools and mechanisms for MMOG communication and distribution, our lifecycle model describes a methodology for MMOG development by identifying major steps during MMOG design and execution. For this purpose, we combine established methodologies from traditional and service-oriented software engineering with the specific QoS requirements of MMOG and the particular characteristics of Cloud environments.

Our lifecycle model supports both:

1.   Development of adaptable Cloud-based MMOG, and
2.   Efficient execution and adaptation of MMOG in Cloud environments.

For 1, we identify the application requirements of adaptable MMOG and propose suitable adaptation triggers and strategies for addressing these requirements. For 2, we illustrate how our lifecycle model provides an abstraction for the main components of an existing service architecture for MMOG execution and, hence, we provide a real-world use case demonstrating the applicability of our proposed lifecycle model for the efficient execution and adaptation of MMOG.

Development of Adaptable Cloud-Based MMOG

A variety of techniques and methodologies for developing adaptable applications have been studied in the domain of *service-oriented software engineering (SOSE)* (Arsanjani, 2008; Papazoglou & van den Heuvel, 2006). In general, *service-based applications (SBAs)* consist of multiple services that interact with each other. Despite different QoS requirements as compared to SBAs, MMOG can still benefit from the established engineering methods for service-oriented architectures. For this purpose, we modify existing SOSE methodologies and make them suitable for MMOG by addressing the specific QoS requirements of MMOG and characteristics of Cloud environments.

A common methodology in software engineering is to use a *lifecycle model* for supporting the design and execution of software systems. A lifecycle model describes an iterative development process which specifies major steps during application design and execution. A number of service lifecycle models have been proposed by both industry and academia. However, most of them address specific application domains (other than MMOG), are not able to express complex system architectures (as required for MMOG) or have not yet reached a sufficient level of maturity. The European Network of Excellence S-Cube (S-Cube European Network of Excellence, 2012) addressed the demand for supporting the design of adaptable applications and developed an abstract lifecycle model which identifies generic tasks and typical software components required for adaptable applications. Our lifecycle model is a specialization of the S-Cube lifecycle model which addresses the specific QoS requirements of MMOG and, thus, enhances its suitability for MMOG development.

Execution and Adaptation of Cloud-Based MMOG

The specific QoS requirements of MMOG pose new challenges for their execution on service-oriented architectures: large number of concurrent users connecting to a single application instance, frequent real-time user interactions, enforcement of precise QoS parameters, adaptivity to changing loads, and competition-oriented interaction between users. Within the European project edutain@grid (Fahringer et al., 2007), a service-oriented architecture for the execution and adaptation of MMOG has been implemented and recommended by a large consortium of multi-disciplinary partners from academia and industry. We analyze this service-oriented architecture in order to decide how our lifecycle model can provide suitable abstractions for the main tasks in MMOG execution and adaptation, and also to demonstrate the applicability of our lifecycle model.

Our lifecycle model is based on the abstract lifecycle model for service-oriented architectures that has been developed by the members of the S-Cube consortium based on a major literature review and input from SOSE experts from different companies (Lane, Bucchiarone, & Richardson, 2012).

While other common models for software development are non-iterative, e.g., the unmodified cascading waterfall model (Benington, 1983), or typically only address the design-time of an application, e.g., the iterative waterfall model (Royce, 1987), our lifecycle model is an iterative model which addresses the design and execution of MMOG. Our lifecycle model shown in Figure 2 includes the so-called *evolution* cycle (right-hand side in the figure) which is complemented by the so-called *adaptation* cycle (left-hand side): (i) the evolution cycle is iterated during the application (re-)design and implementation, and (ii) the adaptation cycle is iterated during runtime and addresses the demand for adaptation in order to balance the application's load (Bucchiarone et al., 2009). The two cycles of our lifecycle model are iterated continuously during the lifetime of an application, including: the initial application development (evolution cycle), execution of the initial application (adaptation), potential redesign of the application (evolution), execution of the redesigned application (adaptation), etc.

Figure 2. The lifecycle model for adaptable Cloud-based MMOG

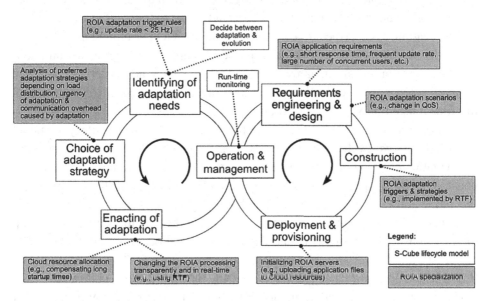

The lifecycle model is specialized for MMOG by identifying specific guidelines and design artefacts (e.g., application requirements, adaptation scenarios, etc.) for each step of the evolution and adaptation cycles (grey in Figure 2). In the following, each step of the lifecycle is described and illustrated using our example application RTFDemo.

The initial development starts with the *requirements engineering & design* phase of the evolution cycle. While this is a common task in software engineering, we identified the specific application requirements and adaptation scenarios for Cloud-based MMOG. Since the development of MMOG is typically focussed on implementing a user-attracting application logic, our lifecycle model supports MMOG developers by highlighting these requirements and scenarios which need to be addressed during the design of adaptable Cloud-based MMOG. In RTFDemo, our empiric observations showed that the users' immersion starts suffering (due to lags) if the update rate falls below 25 Hz or the response time exceeds 100 ms.

During the *construction* phase, the application is implemented according to its previously developed design. While this task commonly follows the application design, our lifecycle highlights the implementation of suitable adaptation triggers (i.e., monitoring mechanisms for identifying QoS violations) and strategies (i.e., mechanisms for changing the application state distribution). Since the implementation of efficient monitoring and adaptation mechanisms is a challenging task, we propose multiple adaptation triggers and strategies (supported by RTF) which are suitable for adaptable Cloud-based MMOG (as described in the next section). In

RTFDemo, we implemented adaptation triggers based on the update rate, CPU load and network bandwidth (amongst others) and adaptation strategies based on zoning and replication, as described in section "Scalable MMOG Development with RTF".

In the *deployment & provisioning* phase, the application provider initializes MMOG server programs on hardware resources (in the Cloud). After initialization, the application is accessed by the users. For RTFDemo, we prepared a custom virtual machine image for execution on Amazon EC2 Cloud resources.

The *operation & management* phase has been included in our lifecycle model to connect its two cycles with each other: on the one hand, this phase concludes the evolution cycle by operating the developed application; on the other hand, this phase starts the adaptation cycle by monitoring the load of MMOG servers. Thus, this phase allows developers to validate the functionality of their application after finishing its development (concluding an iteration of the evolution cycle) or to setup the mechanisms for monitoring and Cloud resource allocation required for adaptation (starting an iteration of the adaptation cycle). In RTFDemo, we utilize the implemented adaptation triggers for monitoring the application's update rate, CPU load and network bandwidth (amongst others). After the operation & management phase, either the evolution cycle is iterated again if the application execution needs to be stopped and redesign is demanded, or an iteration of the adaptation cycle is started if no redesign is demanded. E.g., an iteration of the evolution cycle may become necessary if the application is facing new kinds of attacks by fraudulent users (Gorlatch et al., 2010) or in case of dramatic changes in the behaviour of users which may demand implementing additional adaptation triggers and strategies.

The main task of the adaptation cycle is to adapt the distributed MMOG processing if any of the application servers becomes overloaded. For this purpose, we propose and describe in the following three major steps within the adaptation cycle in order to:

1. Identify the demand for adaptation,
2. Choose a suitable adaptation strategy for the particular adaptation scenario, and
3. Enact adaptation by changing the application processing according to the chosen adaptation strategy.

In the *identifying of adaptation need* phase, the demand for adaptation is identified. For this purpose, the adaptation triggers, implemented during the iteration of the evolution cycle, are used for checking monitoring values against so-called adaptation trigger rules which identify overloaded application servers. In RTFDemo, we implemented a trigger rule that identifies adaptation demand if the update rate falls below 25 Hz. If adaptation triggers identify critical QoS violations and, hence, indicate an adaptation demand that cannot be addressed during execution, the current iteration of the adaptation cycle is stopped and a new iteration of the evolution cycle is started in order to address the adaptation demand by redesigning the application. While the development of adaptation trigger rules is an application-specific task depending on the individual application logic, we present some example trigger rules for a particular example MMOG in the next section.

After the demand for adaptation has been identified, a suitable adaptation strategy is chosen (*choice of adaptation strategy* phase). For this purpose, the particular adaptation scenario is analyzed with respect to the current load of applications servers in order to determine a preferred adaptation strategy. For example, if two RTFDemo servers are replicating the same zone, and one of them becomes overloaded while the other is underutilized, then users are migrated from the overloaded to the underutilized server (as explained in the next section). We present an analysis of preferred adaptation actions for each adaptation scenario in the next section.

In the *enacting of adaptation* phase, the distribution of the application processing is changed according to the chosen adaptation strategy, and Cloud resources (required for redistribution) are allocated. We describe in the sequel the resource management system RTF-RMS that is used for resource management in RTFDemo and addresses hardware virtualization, long startup times and static leasing periods of Cloud resources.

Finally, the "operation & management" phase is iterated again, which is followed by another iteration of the adaptation cycle or an iteration of the evolution cycle if the application requires redesign.

Let us demonstrate how the evolution cycle of the lifecycle model is used for the development of suitable monitoring and adaptation mechanisms for Cloud-based MMOG. We propose three major contributions that support the development of adaptable MMOG according to the evolution cycle: *application requirements*, *adaptation strategies* and *adaptation triggers*, each addressing the specific QoS requirements of MMOG and the characteristics of Cloud environments. Finally, we provide an *analysis of adaptation scenarios* in order to identify preferred adaptation strategies for each scenario.

Application Requirements

The specific application requirements of adaptable MMOG need to be considered during the "requirements engineering & design" phase of our lifecycle in order to support developers in designing suitable mechanisms for adaptation that satisfy the QoS requirements of MMOG. For this purpose, we identified the following generic application requirements of Cloud-based MMOG presented in Table 1.

Table 1. Application requirements for Cloud-based MMOG

Functional Requirements	• Correct execution of the application logic • Practicability to execute the application client program on the users' PCs
Non-Functional Requirements	Client-related requirements: • Short response time (0.1 – 1.5 s) • Frequent interactions between users Server-related requirements: • Suitable adaptation triggers and strategies • High update rate (5 – 100 updates/s) • Compensation for virtualization overhead of Cloud resources • Consistent computation of the application state for a high and variable number of concurrent users • Suitable security mechanisms for preventing fraudulent user behaviour
Adaptation Requirements	• Efficiency of adaptation actions • Transparency of the adaptation • Proactive adaptation • Compensation for long startup times of Cloud resources • Instance-specific adaptation during runtime

Table 1 classifies the application requirements of Cloud-based MMOG into functional, non-functional and adaptation requirements. *Functional requirements* are related to the correct execution of the application logic and the practicability to execute the application client program on users' PCs, which allows users to access the virtual environment and interact with each other. *Non-functional requirements* are related to the application's QoS: we distinguish between client-related requirements (e.g., short response time) and server-related requirements (e.g., suitable adaptation triggers and strategies). It is particularly important to compensate the virtualization overhead of Cloud resources by the efficient implementation of the application logic (e.g., using RTF for communication handling, etc.) and suitable adaptation triggers and strategies during execution. *Adaptation requirements* are related to monitoring and adaptation mechanisms. Our adaptation strategies increase the number of concurrent users in a single application instance by utilizing additional (Cloud) resources efficiently for the distributed application processing, and change the distribution of the application processing transparently to the users in order to not disturb their immersion in the virtual environment. Our adaptation triggers indicate the demand for proactive adaptation in order to avoid QoS violations and compensate for long startup times of Cloud resources.

Adaptation Triggers

One of the main tasks during the "construction" phase of our lifecycle is the implementation of adaptation triggers for monitoring the application processing and identifying or predicting QoS violations. For this purpose, we identify the following four major application scenarios demanding adaptation, and we propose specific adaptation triggers, i.e., suitable monitoring values for identifying the adaptation demand of Cloud-based MMOG for each scenario:

1. **Changes in the Quality of Service:** They denote unexpected QoS violations which are not caused by the application processing or user behavior, but rather related to external influences, e.g., unreliable hardware resources. QoS violations are typically indicated by an inreasing response time to user actions and a decreasing update rate of the application state. Thus, monitoring the response time and update rate provide suitable adaptation triggers for this scenario. However, in order to precisely identify whether the reason for QoS violations is related to computational or network resources, further monitoring values are required (throughput, packet loss, latency, etc.).

2. **Changes in the Computational Context:** They are related to the computational costs for calculating application state updates, e.g., increasing costs can be caused by the virtualization overhead when replacing physical with virtual resources or by increasingly frequent interactions between users. This scenario is identified by monitoring the load of computational resources as well as the incoming and outgoing bandwidth of application servers in order to identify increasingly frequent interactions between users.

3. **Changes in the User Context:** They denote unpredictable changes in the behaviour of users, e.g., many new users connecting to the application due to the increasing popularity of the application or shutting down of competitive applications. This scenario is identified by monitoring the current number of users and the current number of user actions.

4. **Load Prediction:** This is used to gather information about the users' behaviour and to trigger adaptation proactively, e.g., by observing that typically user numbers of online games increase in the evening hours. This scenario is identified by monitoring the user numbers and actions and using these values for predicting load by suitable prediction algorithms or methods based on artificial intelligence as illustrated in the next section.

Adaptation Strategies

Besides implementing adaptation triggers, the implementation of adaptation strategies is the other main task during the "construction" phase of our lifecycle. We provide five major adaptation strategies (supported by RTF) for changing the distributed MMOG processing during runtime:

1.   **User Migration:** Users are migrated from an overloaded server to an under-utilized server which is replicating the same zone, i.e., the responsibility for user input processing and state update computation is moved from one server to another. RTF provides suitable mechanisms for a transparent migration, i.e., the user is not aware of his migration.

2.   **Zone Activation:** A new zone is added to the virtual environment and an additional MMOG server is started that becomes responsible for processing this zone. Zone activation potentially provides the best scalability of all adaptation strategies, i.e., the number of additional users that can be accommodated is increased largely. However, zone activation is not transparent to the users since the geography of the virtual environment is changed and the scalability provided by zone activation depends on the movement of users within the virtual environment: if the users do not enter the new zone, the additional computation power from the server of that zone is not used for application processing. Thus, the application logic should create incentives for the users to enter the new zone. In general, zone activation is used for high numbers of users that cannot participate otherwise.

3.   **Replica Activation:** A highly frequented zone is replicated and an additional MMOG server is started that becomes responsible for processing this replica. When replicating a zone, a number of users are migrated to the new replica in order to distribute the workload equally. While replica activation is transparent for the users, it implies an additional inter-server communication and thus, its scalability is limited. To address the demand for efficient adaptation, the number of active replicas for a particular zone is monitored to decide whether activating additional replicas is feasible or not as compared to the increased communication overhead.

4.   **Instance Activation:** Instancing is used for creating a separate independent copy of a particular zone and an additional MMOG server is started that becomes responsible for processing this instance. Users coming from other zones and entering the corresponding zone are distributed equally on all instances. In contrast to replica activation which allows users on different replicas for the same zone to interact with each other, users in different instances cannot interact with each other. Thus, replica activation is generally preferred to instance activation in order to support high interactivity between users. However, instance activation is useful if the overhead of replica activation would be too high.

5.   **QoS Negotiation:** Hardware resources used for the application processing are changed by negotiating with several distributed hosters (i.e., organisa-

tions providing hardware in Cloud environments) about QoS offered by their resources. A QoS negotiation may include:

a.   Renegotiation of existing contracts, or
b.   Negotiation of contracts with new hosters.

Typical scenarios include the use of more powerful resources of the same hoster or leasing cheaper resources from a new hoster. QoS negotiation provides an alternative to replica activation by allocating more powerful resources that allow to serve more users. In comparison to the other adaptation strategies, QoS negotiation needs a longer time (e.g., due to the startup times of Cloud resources) and, hence, replica and instance activation usually provide faster adaptation. However, QoS negotiation is useful to overcome non-critical peaks in resource shortage or to address a predictable adaptation demand.

Analysis of Adaptation Scenarios

In order to address a particular adaptation demand with an adaptation strategy, we analyse the suitability of each adaption strategy for different scenarios. Table 2 presents suitable adaptation strategies for each scenario identified by our proposed adaptation triggers.

Figure 3 shows how the preferred adaptation action can be determined for each scenario. The first three scenarios have in common that QoS violations occur unpredictably and fast adaptation is demanded for their compensation. Hence, user

Table 2. Relationship between adaptation triggers and adaptation strategies

Scenario	Adaptation Triggers	Example Trigger Rule	Adaptation Strategies
Change in Quality of Service	response time, throughput, resource usage, average packet loss, connection latency, update rate, service availability	update rate < 25 updates/s	user migration, replica or instance activation
Change in comput. context	CPU and memory load, incoming/outgoing bandwidth	CPU load > 90%	user migration, replica or instance activation
Change in user context	number of current users, number of current user actions	number of current users > user capability of application servers	user migration, replica or instance activation
Load prediction	number of users per hour, number of user actions per minute	predicted number of users > user capability of application servers	QoS negotiation or zone activation

migration, replica or instance activation are the preferred adaptation strategies for these scenarios since they allow to overcome performance bottlenecks as fast as possible. We decide between these strategies depending on the amount of free resources and number of active replicas as shown in Figure 3. In order to minimize costs for the application provider and maximize resource utilization, migrating users to underloaded resources is preferred if the additional load can be compensated by running resources; otherwise replica activation is preferred to instance activation in order to support a high level of interactivity between users; if activating additional replicas implies too high communication overhead then instance activation is used.

Load prediction typically leaves more time for adaptation than the above-mentioned scenarios since QoS violations are predicted proactively. Hence, efficient and transparent adaptation strategies are preferred in this scenario: QoS negotiation and zone activation. We decide which of these strategies to use depending on the predicted number of users: QoS negotiation is preferred if it provides enough scalability for accommodating the predicted number of users; otherwise, zone activation is used since it is not transparent but typically provides better scalability as compared to QoS negotiation.

After the "construction" phase, application servers are initialized ("deployment & provisioning" phase) and the application is executed and monitored by the adaptation triggers in order to identify scenarios that demand adaptation ("operation & management" phase). If an adaptation demand is identified, the adaptation cycle is iterated. In the next section, we illustrate how the adaptation cycle supports the efficient execution and adaptation of Cloud-based MMOG.

Figure 3. Preferred adaptation actions for different adaptation scenarios

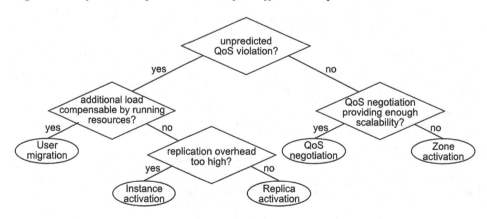

A SERVICE-ORIENTED ARCHITECTURE FOR MMOG EXECUTION AND ADAPTATION

In this section, we demonstrate how the adaptation cycle of our lifecycle model supports application providers in the efficient execution and adaptation of MMOG. For this purpose, we present a case study on the existing architecture for MMOG execution and adaptation that has been developed within the edutain@grid project (Fahringer et al., 2007). We illustrate how our lifecycle model describes the main tasks of the application provider for the efficient execution and adaptation of MMOG. While the edutain@grid architecture comprises a resource management layer for load balancing of MMOG servers in Grid environments, our RTF-RMS resource management system proposed in this chapter is not involved in the implementation of this layer since we target the specific challenges for load balancing in Cloud (rather than Grid) environments. Figure 4 shows a distributed service-oriented architecture that is based on the interaction of four different actors (grey in the figure) (Gorlatch et al., 2008):

1. *End-users* access MMOG sessions via graphical client programs;
2. *Scheduler* identifies appropriate MMOG sessions for a particular end-user based on his QoS requirements (e.g., connection latency, minimum number of users, etc.) and adapts the distributed application processing during runtime if demanded in order to avoid QoS violations;
3. (Potentially Multiple) *Hosters* are organisations that provide computational and network infrastructures (in our case - in the Cloud) for running MMOG servers;
4. The *resource broker* provides a mechanism for the schedulers and hosters (and possibly other actors) to find each other in a large-scale environment and to negotiate QoS relationships.

In the remainder of this chapter, the scheduler is denoted as application provider since we focus on the resource management for application provisioning.

The service-oriented architecture consists of three main layers shown in Figure 4: *user layer*, *resource management layer* and *real-time layer*. In the following, we describe the main services for distributed MMOG execution in each layer (white in Figure 4) and illustrate how the adaptation cycle describes the main tasks of the scheduler responsible for MMOG execution and adaptation:

- **User Layer:** In order to access the virtual game environment and interact with other users, end-users need to execute the application client program on their PCs. For this purpose, the scheduler typically provides the application

Figure 4. The service-oriented architecture for MMOG (edutain@grid)

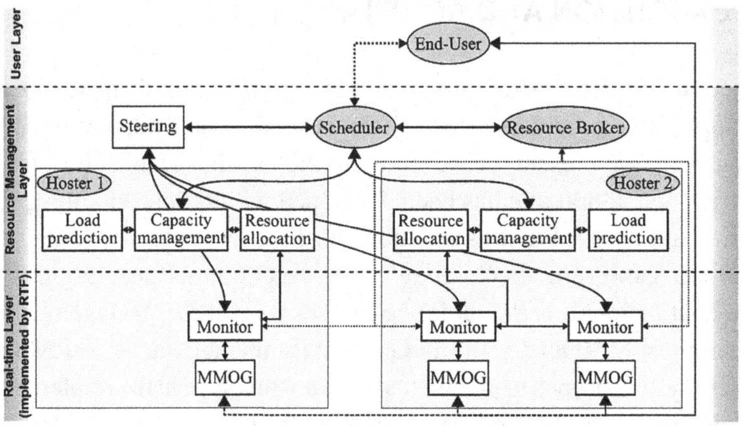

client to the end-users as a DVD or a downloadable file ("deployment & provisioning" phase of our lifecycle model).

- **Resource Management Layer:** The scheduler receives from the end-user his QoS requirements which can be performance-related (e.g., maximum latency) or application-specific (e.g., minimum dimensions of the virtual environment) and identifies application sessions satisfying these QoS requirements for each user. For this purpose, the scheduler negotiates with hosters; the result is a contract, called *service level agreement (SLA)*, between the scheduler and each hoster which describes performance guarantees for resources offered by the hoster (e.g., maximum latency, minimum network throughput, etc.).

The performance of hoster resources may change during application processing, such that the negotiated SLAs cannot be maintained. Typical perturbing factors include external load on shared resources, or overloaded servers due to an unexpected concentration of users in particular parts of the virtual environment. The *steering service* is a software component which interacts at runtime with the monitoring service of each MMOG server and is used by the scheduler for identifying adaptation demand (the "identifying of adaptation need" phase of our lifecycle). For this purpose, we implement in the steering service suitable adaptation triggers for identifying a particular adaptation scenario as illustrated in the previous section. Then, the steering service selects a suitable adaptation strategy for this scenario ("choice of adaptation strategy" phase) and utilizes RTF to change the distributed application processing ("enacting of adaptation" phase).

Typically, each hoster executes a *capacity management service*, a *resource allocation service*, and a *prediction service*. The capacity management service receives from the scheduler a connection request formulated in terms of QoS requirements (e.g., minimum latency or maximum bandwidth) and either accepts or rejects it depending on whether it can be accommodated on available hoster resources. The resource allocation service is responsible for allocating local resources to application servers in a way that satisfies the performance requirements described in the SLA. In order to avoid the violation of performance requirements, the hoster needs to anticipate the future load on its resources. For this purpose, the prediction service may employ neural networks for predicting fluctuations in the number of users (Gorlatch et al., 2008).

- **Real-Time Layer:** The real-time layer of edutain@grid is implemented by the Real-Time Framework (RTF) which is used to distribute the application processing according to the parallelization concepts described earlier. Instead of using web services and SOAP-encoded communication messages which are not suitable for fast real-time communication, RTF internally uses TCP/IP sockets. RTF provides suitable adaptation strategies that are utilized by the steering service as described above and allow to enact adaptation as described in the previous section.

The *monitoring service* provides generic (e.g., latency, bandwidth, etc.) and application-specific monitoring values (e.g., entity positions, messages sent or received, etc.) that are used by the hosters' resource allocation service and by the scheduler's steering service to identify the demand for adaptation

EVALUATION

In this section, we evaluate the scalability and the effect on QoS of three of our proposed adaptation strategies: zone activation, replica activation, and user migration. For this purpose, we conduct two sets of experiments in order to:

1. Evaluate the *scalability* of adaptation actions, i.e., how many additional users can be accommodated by adding a new resource, and
2. Analyze the *QoS improvement* of adaptation actions.

For 1, we analyze how the zone activation and "replica activation" adaptation strategies distribute computational load on multiple resources. For 2, we analyze how the replica activation and user migration strategies improve the QoS transparently during runtime in a particular scenario.

In all experiments, we use RTFDemo (Gorlatch, Glinka, Ploss, & Meiländer, 2012) as our application example. RTFDemo was developed using RTF and is a fast-paced action game from the domain of first-person shooters (FPS), with all typical features of modern online games. In RTFDemo, each user controls his own avatar (robot) in the 3D virtual world, and users can interact by shooting at (and thus damaging) other users' avatars. For adding computational load, we use computer-controlled clients (bots) that continuously send inputs to their servers; bots are allowed to move between zones and thereby generate non-uniform load on application servers.

Scalability

For the evaluation of the scalability, we conducted two experiments using a pool of homogeneous PCs with 2.66 GHz Intel Core Duo CPU, and 4 GB RAM, connected by a LAN. In RTFDemo, a static setup of zones and servers is started for each experiment. We measure the CPU load of each RTFDemo server and calculate the average value of all servers (as presented in Figure 5 and Figure 6).

Figure 5. Scalability of zone activation

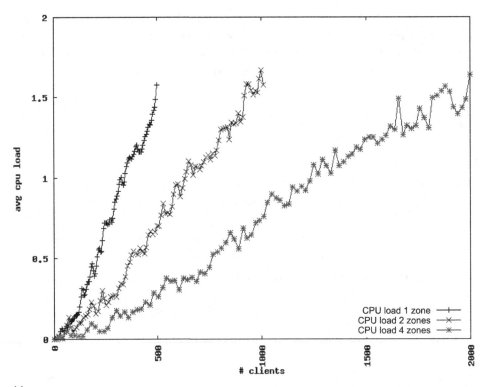

Figure 6. Scalability of replica activation

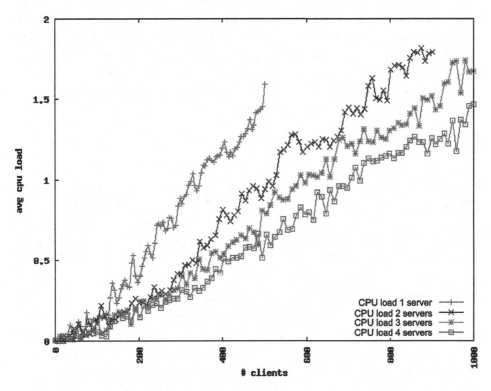

Our first experiment evaluates the adaptation by zone activation: Figure 5 shows how the CPU load increases for an increasing number of clients. CPU load was measured in the IRIX mode in Linux, i.e. the loads of the CPU's cores are summarized. While the implementation of RTFDemo uses multiple threads, we observed that the time required for computing application state updates increases dramatically (leading to lags and QoS violations) if the CPU load exceeds 120%, i.e., one core has a load of 100% and the other core has a load of 20%. This is explained by the fact that the workload is not distributed equally across the threads but rather according to different tasks, e.g., application state calculation, serialization, etc. The "zone activation" adaptation strategy scales almost linearly: 430 clients can be accommodated if one server is used, 820 clients on two servers, and 1600 clients on four servers. This is as expected since zone activation induces only little inter-server communication overhead for interacting users in different zones.

Our second experiment evaluates the adaptation by replica activation: we replicate the computation of a single zone on up to four servers. Figure 6 shows the measured results for the CPU load. One server is able to serve up to 450 clients, which is similar to the results of zone activation (deviations are explained by the random behaviour of bots leading to different numbers of interactions and slight variances in the load). But if more servers are added to the processing of the same zone, the client number can be increased to up to 1000 clients in a four-server setup. This shows that the "replica activation" adaptation strategy allows games to provide a higher level of interactivity in a particular area of the virtual environment. As expected, replica activation provides lower scalability than zone activation due to the inter-server communication overhead.

QoS Improvement

In this experiment, we analyze how the "replica activation" and "user migration" adaptation strategies are able to improve the QoS of a running RTFDemo session. In this scenario, we use a private Cloud with the Eucalyptus framework (version 2.0.2) (Nurmi et al., 2009); servers are Intel Core Duo PCs with 2.66 GHz and 2 GB RAM in a LAN. Moreover, we employ our resource management system RTF-RMS (described in section "Resource Management for MMOG on Clouds") for monitoring the update rate as the QoS criterion and enacting the "replica activation" and "user migration" adaptation strategies. In order to avoid QoS violations, RTF-RMS triggers adaptation if the update rate falls below 25 Hz. Since we use a Cloud environment in this scenario, RTF-RMS starts up an additional resource in advance in order to avoid QoS violations due to the long startup times of Cloud resources. We start a single RTFDemo server on a Cloud resource and connect 260 clients to it.

Figure 7 shows that the measured update rate of server 1 initially drops with the growing number of connected clients. When the update rate of server 1 falls below 25 Hz (horizontal dashed line), adaptation demand is identified by RTF-RMS and a new Cloud resource is added for replicating the overloaded zone. Although the requested resource is started up in advance, we observe that a certain time period is still required to add the new server to the application processing and start user migration. This delay of approximately 15 seconds is caused by the initialization and inter-server communication that are required to integrate the new server from the Cloud in the application processing. After the migration is accomplished, the update rate of server 1 has increased from 20 Hz to about 100 Hz. The update rate of server 1 and server 2 fluctuates between 50 and 200 Hz caused by the continuously changing number of interactions between the 260 clients. Note that if the resource were not in the buffer and had to be started from scratch, the delay would be in the order of 130 seconds, i.e., much longer than 15 sec.

Figure 7. QoS improvement using replica activation

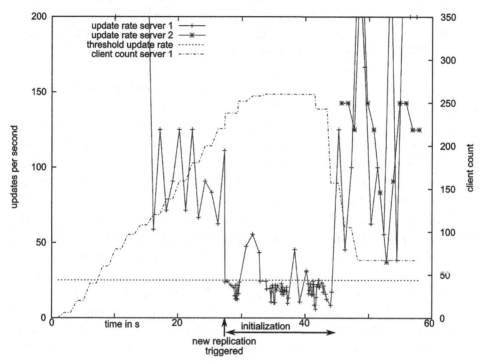

DYNAMIC RESOURCE MANAGEMENT FOR MMOG ON CLOUDS

The high demands on MMOG performance usually cannot be satisfied by a single server. Therefore, distributed, multi-server application processing with suitable load balancing is required. Cloud Computing promises the potential to distribute application processing on an arbitrary number of resources and to add/remove these resources on demand. While several approaches for utilizing Cloud resources for different application domains have already been investigated, none of them targets applications with requirements similar to MMOG (Buyya, Yeo, & Venugopal, 2008; Deelman, Singh, Livny, Berriman, & Good, 2008). On the other hand, load balancing of MMOG on physical resources has been studied in previous work (Bezerra & Geyer, 2009; Lu, Parkin, & Morgan, 2006), but none of these approaches considers the new challenges from utilizing Cloud Computing for MMOG provisioning.

For this purpose, we propose our new resource management system, called *RTF Resource Management System (RTF-RMS)* (Meiländer, Ploss, Glinka, & Gorlatch, 2012), for dynamic up- and down-scaling of MMOG sessions on Cloud resources. The RTF-RMS system implements a novel load-balancing strategy for Cloud-based

MMOG and utilizes RTF for monitoring and distribution of the application processing. The lifecycle model presented in the previous section is directly reflected in RTF-RMS which implements the different phases of the model's adaptation cycle. Thereby, RTF-RMS supports the application provider in the efficient execution and load balancing of Cloud-based MMOG.

RTF-RMS consists of two major software components shown in Figure 8 and described in the following.

The CloudController implements the communication of RTF-RMS with the Cloud using its communication interface (*Cloud API*) which is typically provided by each Cloud and offers functionality for starting and shutting down Cloud resources, monitoring generic system information, etc. The CloudController currently implements Cloud resource allocation for the Amazon Compute Cloud (EC2) (Amazon Web Services, 2015). A particular challenge in the implementation of the CloudController is the compensation for a comparatively long startup time of Cloud resources that can last up to several minutes. Moreover, cost optimization is an important issue since Cloud resources are typically leased for a certain usage period. We address these challenges in section "Cloud Resource Allocation".

The LoadBalancer implements our new load-balancing strategy that dynamically changes the workload distribution between application servers. For this purpose, it receives monitoring values from RTF which are used to determine the load of application servers and utilizes RTF's distribution functionality for re-distributing

Figure 8. Architecture of the RTF-RMS system

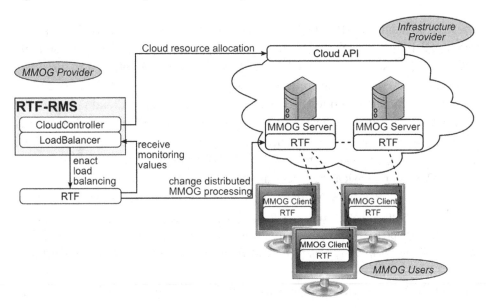

application state processing. Since MMOG typically show lower performance on virtualized Cloud resources than on physical resources with identical hardware configuration, generic system information (CPU, memory, etc.) is not sufficient for load balancing on Cloud resources, For this purpose, RTF-RMS utilizes application-specific monitoring values (tick duration, response time, etc.) for its load balancing. If the LoadBalancer identifies the demand for load balancing, it chooses between four different load-balancing actions, as described below.

Efficient load balancing for MMOG requires suitable mechanisms for *workload analysis* that identify the demand for load balancing, as well as a sophisticated *load-balancing strategy* that chooses suitable load-balancing actions. In this section, we present the mechanism for workload analysis and the load-balancing strategy implemented in RTF-RMS.

Workload Analysis

Our design prescribes that RTF-RMS is configured for workload analysis of a particular application by specifying a so-called *application profile* that defines the (potentially multiple) monitoring values of interest, e.g., tick duration in ms, update rate in Hz, etc., see Table 3 for an example. RTF-RMS allows application providers to specify two thresholds for each monitoring value in the profile: addResourceThreshold and removeResourceThreshold. If a monitoring value leaves the range between its two thresholds, the demand for load balancing is identified. Whether a resource needs to be added or removed is determined by considering the distance of the monitoring value v to the thresholds, i.e., if $|v -$ addResourceThreshold$| < |v -$ removeResourceThreshold$|$, then adding a new resource is demanded, otherwise removing an existing resource is demanded. For example, given a monitoring value v=45 ms and values addResourceThreshold=40 ms and removeResourceThreshold=10 ms, the demand for adding a new resource is identified since the above equation holds: $|45 - 40| < |45 - 10|$

Table 3. Example application profile for a fast-paced action game

```
<appProfile>
  <maxNumReplicas>2</maxNumReplicas>
  <monitoringValue>
    <name>TickDuration</name>
    <monitoringInterval>1</monitoringInterval>
    <addResourceThreshold>40</addResourceThreshold>
    <removeResourceThreshold>10</removeResourceThreshold>
  </monitoringValue>
</appProfile>
```

The application profile also allows application providers to define the maximum number of active replicas for each zone, in order to limit the overhead for inter-server communication caused by the replication. In Meiländer, Köttinger, & Gorlatch (2013), we develop a scalability model that supports the application provider in finding suitable thresholds for all parameters in the application profile of a particular application.

Figure 9 illustrates how workload analysis is implemented in RTF-RMS. The LoadBalancer creates a LoadMonitor object, responsible for collecting the monitoring values specified in the application profile. For this purpose, the LoadMonitor registers an event listener (*monitor*) at each application server in order to receive updates on the monitoring values from RTF. The LoadMonitor aggregates the monitoring values in two different reports: for each server, all monitoring values from this server are aggregated in a *server report*; for each zone, an average value is calculated for each monitoring value and stored in a *zone report*. For example, given servers B and C replicating the same zone and a tick duration of 45 ms on server B and 15 ms on server C, the LoadMonitor creates two server reports and one zone report depicting an average tick duration of 30 ms for this zone (see Figure 10).

The LoadMonitor sends all server and zone reports to the LoadBalancer which analyzes them in order to identify the demand for load balancing and to choose a suitable load-balancing action. In the example in Figure 10, server A processes zone

Figure 9. Workload analysis in RTF-RMS

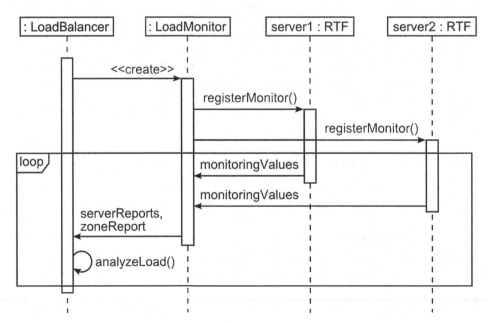

Figure 10. Finding a suitable load-balancing action using zone reports

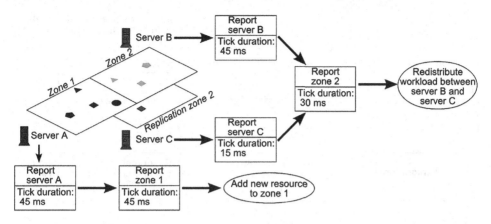

1, and servers B and C are assigned to zone 2. The report of zone 1 identifies a tick duration of 45 ms (on server A). Since addResourceThreshold=40 ms, the Load-Balancer identifies the demand to add a new resource for processing zone 1 (using replication enactment as described in the next paragraph). The report of zone 2 identifies an average tick duration of 30 ms which is below the threshold, but server B has a tick duration of 45 ms. Hence, the LoadBalancer chooses user migration for redistributing the state processing between server B and server C according to our load-balancing strategy described in the next paragraph.

Load-Balancing Strategy

In RTF-RMS, we designed and implemented a load-balancing strategy for Cloud resources that chooses between the following four load-balancing actions (see Figure 11):

1. **User Migration:** Users are migrated from an overloaded server to an under-utilized server which is replicating the same zone. For this purpose, user connections are switched from one server to another. RTF-RMS distributes users by default equally between the application servers for a particular zone. User migration is restricted to the servers replicating the same zone because managing different zones on the same server would considerably increase the inter-server communication for processing user interactions which are typically limited to the nearby users. The user migration action does not activate additional replicas for the zone of the overloaded server; if the zone of the overloaded server is not replicated on other servers, the replication enactment load-balancing action (described next) needs to be chosen. This load-balancing

51

Figure 11. RTF-RMS chooses between four different load-balancing actions

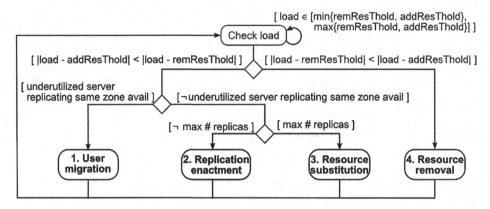

action is an implementation of the "user migration" adaptation strategy presented above in our lifecycle model and is the preferred action if the load of an overloaded server can be compensated by already running resources.

2. **Replication Enactment:** New game servers are added in order to provide more computation power to the highly frequented zone, and a number of users are migrated to the new replica in order to balance the load. Replication implies an additional inter-server communication and thus, its scalability is limited. This load-balancing action is an implementation of the "replica activation" adaptation strategy within our lifecycle model. If the number of active replicas for a particular zone is below the maximum number of replicas specified in the application profile, then replication is used; otherwise the resource substitution action (described next) is preferred.

3. **Resource Substitution:** An existing resource is substituted by a more powerful resource in order to increase the computation power for processing highly frequented zones. For this purpose, RTF-RMS replicates the targeted zone on the new resource and migrates all users to the new server. The substituted server is shut down. This load-balancing action is an implementation of the "QoS negotiation" adaptation strategy presented in the lifecycle model. If no more powerful resources are available for substitution, this means that the application has reached a critical user density, i.e., a large number of users in the same geographical area which cannot be further increased by the generic load-balancing actions offered by RTF-RMS. In this case, the application requires redesign according to our lifecycle model described above.

4. **Resource Removal:** If the demand for removing a server resource is identified, RTF-RMS checks whether the zone that is managed by this server is replicated by other servers. If so, all users managed by the underutilized server are

migrated equally to all other servers replicating the same zone servers, after which the underutilized server is shut down. Otherwise, nothing happens since each zone must be assigned to at least one application server.

There are two main factors that may limit the performance of applications on Clouds: long startup times and static leasing periods of Cloud resources.

Compensating Startup Times

The startup time of Cloud resources may take up to several minutes; since MMOG are highly responsive applications, finding a compensation for long startup times is critical. RTF-RMS implements two mechanisms for addressing this challenge:

1. Parallel startup of multiple Cloud resources, and
2. Starting resources in advance, i.e., before they are demanded by the application.

For 1, the CloudController sends all startup requests consecutively to the Cloud API, i.e., Cloud resources are started in parallel. For each request, the CloudController monitors the startup of Cloud resources in order to identify any potential errors and it sends a new request if required. For 2,, the CloudController introduces a *resource buffer* to which a predefined number of Cloud resources are moved in advance. The CloudController tags the currently running resources as *running* in contrast to *buffered* resources that are currently not used. If any resource changes its state from buffered to running (step 1 on the left-hand side of Figure 12), the CloudController checks whether new Cloud resources must be started in order to keep a certain number of resources in the resource buffer (step 2 in the figure). The number of buffered resources is configured in the application profile.

Figure 12. RTF-RMS starts a new buffered resource (left) and shuts down a dispensable buffered resource (right)

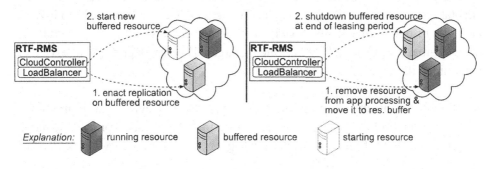

53

By leasing and buffering Cloud resources in advance, additional cost overhead is generated. Therefore, the size s of the resource buffer should be chosen carefully. Given n users and m servers for a particular zone, the time $t_{integr}(r, n, m)$ for integrating a single resource r from the resource buffer is split up into time $t_{intro}(r, m)$ for the introduction of r to m other servers and time $t_{migr}(r, n)$ for migrating users to the new server, i.e.,

$$t_{integr}(r, n, m) = t_{intro}(r, m) + t_{migr}(r, n).$$

The overall time required for integrating all resources $r_1, \ldots, r_s$ from the resource buffer in the application processing should be less than the time $t_{leas}(p)$ required for leasing a new Cloud resource from the infrastructure provider p. Therefore, the following condition describes a reasonable interval of values for the size s of the resource buffer:

$$1 \leq s \leq \max\left\{x \in \mathbb{N} \mid \sum_{i=1}^{x} t_{integr}\left(r_i, n, m\right) < t_{leas}(p)\right\}.$$

Considering Static Leasing Periods

In commercial Cloud systems, resources are typically leased and paid per hour or some longer leasing period. Since MMOG have dynamically changing user numbers, the time after which Cloud resources become dispensable is very variable. However, resources will not be used cost-efficiently if they are shut down before the end of their leasing period. Hence, RTF-RMS removes the resources that have become dispensable from the application processing and moves them to the resource buffer (step 1 on the right-hand side of Figure 12). Cloud resources in the buffer are integrated in the application processing again if required or they are shut down at the end of their leasing period (step 2 in the figure).

Figure 13 illustrates how RTF-RMS implements the different phases of the adaptation cycle of our lifecycle model. While the CloudController of RTF-RMS allocates resources that are used for load-balancing actions, it is not involved in the decision-making process of load balancing targeted by the adaptation cycle. Hence, we omitted the CloudController in the figure.

1.   **Deployment and Provisioning:** The application provider configures RTF-RMS for workload analysis by specifying in the application profile the monitoring values of interest (adaptation triggers) used for identifying the demand

Figure 13. Mechanisms of RTF-RMS for MMOG according to the lifecycle model

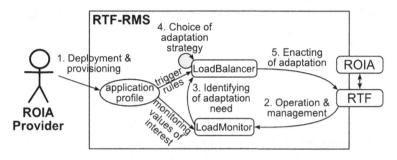

for load balancing. For each specified monitoring value, the LoadMonitor registers a monitor at each application server in order to receive updates on this monitoring value from RTF. Each monitoring value in the application profile has related thresholds, addResourceThreshold and removeResource-Threshold, for identifying the demand for load balancing. Thus, the LoadBalancer generates trigger rules for each monitoring value *v* if:

$$v \notin \begin{bmatrix} \min\{removeResourceThreshold, addResourceThreshold\}, \\ \max\{removeResourceThreshold, addResourceThreshold\} \end{bmatrix}$$

In order to identify QoS violations in each of the application scenarios described above, RTF-RMS supports all of the adaptation triggers mentioned in Table 2, i.e., for each adaptation trigger specified in the application profile, RTF-RMS registers a monitor that receives updates on this monitoring value from each application server.

2. **Operation and Management:** The MMOG is executed and the LoadMonitor receives from RTF updates for all specified monitoring values on each application server. The LoadMonitor aggregates the monitoring values for each server and for all servers of each zone in the server and zone reports, correspondingly.

3. **Identifying of Adaptation Need:** The LoadMonitor sends its server and zone reports to the LoadBalancer which continuously checks the monitoring values against the trigger rules to identify the demand for load balancing.

4. **Choice of Adaptation Strategy:** If the demand for load balancing has been identified, the LoadBalancer chooses between the load-balancing actions: user migration, replication enactment, resource substitution, and resource removal. For this purpose, the LoadBalancer analyzes the number of application servers and their current workload to choose a suitable load-balancing action as shown in Figure 11.

5. **Enacting of Adaptation:** The LoadBalancer enacts the chosen load-balancing action by utilizing RTF's functionality for changing the distributed MMOG processing.

EVALUATION

In this section, we evaluate the suitability of RTF-RMS's load-balancing strategy for overcoming performance bottlenecks in MMOG. For this purpose, we conduct two experiments with our multi-player action game RTFDemo in two particular scenarios:

1. The load on multiple servers becomes imbalanced, and
2. A single server becomes overloaded.

For 1, we analyze how our load-balancing strategy distributes load equally on all application servers. For 2, we verify that our load-balancing strategy efficiently allocates additional Cloud resources for load distribution.

For generating computational load in our experiment, we use computer-controlled clients (bots) that continuously send inputs to their server. We measure the tick duration as the monitoring value for up- and down-scaling of the RTFDemo session. Since we observed that the users' immersion in RTFDemo starts suffering (due to lags) if the tick duration exceeds 40 ms, we configure RTF-RMS by specifying addResourceThreshold=40 ms in the application profile. The value of removeResourceThreshold is set to quite a low value of 10 ms in order to avoid adding and removing resources repeatedly due to fluctuations in the tick duration coming from random interactions between bots.

While the evaluation in Figure 7 already demonstrated how RTF-RMS's replication enactment action improves the QoS of MMOG transparently during execution, here we focus on evaluating RTF-RMS's load-balancing strategy, i.e., whether a suitable load-balancing action is chosen; this complements the previous experiments by evaluating load balancing based on the tick duration, rather than update rate. Thereby, we demonstrate the suitability of another adaptation trigger provided by RTF-RMS and prove the universality of RTF-RMS's mechanisms for workload analysis.

In both experiments, we use a private Cloud environment with the Eucalyptus framework (version 2.0.2) (Nurmi et al., 2009); servers are Intel Core Duo PCs with 2.66 GHz and 2 GB of RAM running CentOS 5.3. Since Eucalyptus and Amazon EC2 use the same API, no modification of the CloudController was required.

Imbalanced Load on Multiple Servers

In this experiment, we start two servers, with all bots initially connected to server 1, which implies an imbalanced load on application servers. As expected, RTF-RMS applies load balancing by user migration without leasing new Cloud resources since server 2 is underutilized. Figure 14 shows that the tick duration of server 1 initially grows with the number of connected bots. When the tick duration reaches the threshold of 40 ms, RTF-RMS migrates half of the users (i.e., 120 users) from server 1 to server 2. This action reduces the tick duration of server 1 from 40 ms to 10-15 ms. Thus, our load-balancing strategy successfully overcomes the performance bottleneck in this scenario.

Single Server Becoming Overloaded

In this experiment, we start a single RTFDemo server and connect an increasing number of bots to it. In order to compensate for the startup time of Cloud resources, we set the size of the resource buffer to 1; the maximum number of replicas is set to 2, so that an additional server can be started in order to compensate the overload

Figure 14. Load balancing: an imbalanced workload on multiple servers

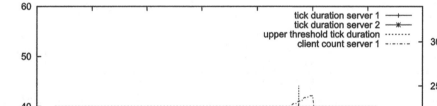

of the initial server. Figure 15 shows that as soon as the tick duration of server 1 exceeds the threshold, RTF-RMS starts a new RTFDemo server for replicating the overloaded zone, since no other servers are available and the maximum number of replicas is set to 2. Although the requested resource is already started up (in the resource buffer), we observe that a delay of 10 sec is still required to add the new server to the application processing and start user migration which is caused by the initialization and inter-server communication required to integrate the new server. After half of the users have been migrated to the new server, the tick duration of server 1 is reduced to 10–20 ms (deviations are explained by the random behaviour of bots). Note that if the resource were not in the resource buffer and had to be started up from scratch, the delay would be much longer (in the order of 130 sec). Thus, our load-balancing strategy successfully overcomes the performance bottleneck in this scenario.

Figure 15. Load balancing: a single overloaded server

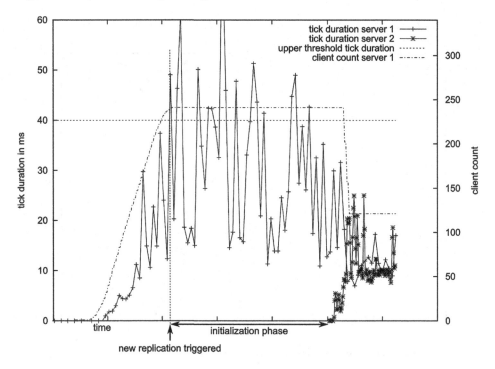

RELATED WORK

The development of adaptable Cloud-based applications has been targeted in multiple research projects. Many of the existing development methodologies are based on the research carried out in the fields of classical software and system engineering and do not address system adaptation (Arsanjani et al., 2008; Papazoglou & van den Heuvel, 2006). Lane and Richardson (2010) carried out a systematic literature review of software development approaches, and they identified 57 such approaches of which there were only eight that addressed adaptation. However, these approaches consider application development and execution as two separated issues (Wirsing et al., 2008; Vale & Hammoudi, 2008; Wautelet, Achbany, Lange, & Kolp, 2009). In contrast, our lifecycle model proposes to consider two cycles for development and execution which are connected to each other and iterate alternating if demanded.

Several approaches (Baresi, Guinea, & Pasquale, 2007; Canfora, Di Penta, Esposito, & Villani, 2005) use so-called built-in adaptation mechanisms, i.e., adaptation trigger rules and actions are static and pre-defined before application execution. However, this is only suitable if all adaptation scenarios are known in advance and do not change during the lifetime of the application. In such kind of applications, specification is performed by extending standard notations or using ECA-like rules (Colombo, Di Nitto, Mauri, 2006) or aspect-oriented approaches (Kongdenfha, Saint-Paul, Benatallah, & Casati, 2006). The main disadvantage of such adaptation approaches is the impossibility to react to unforeseen events. Our approach targets challenging cases in which the adaptation trigger rules and the adaptation actions cannot be completely defined at design time. Some approaches (Verma, Gomadam, Sheth, Miller, & Wu, 2005) address this issue by defining abstract adaptation scenarios during design time while the concrete adaptation mechanism is chosen at run-time. Our lifecycle enables both the built-in and the abstraction-based adaptation, and supports redesigning adaptation mechanisms according to new or changed adaptation demands (Bucchiarone et al., 2009).

The execution of Cloud-based applications has been studied by a number of research projects, each of them limited to a particular application class, e.g., batch execution systems (Freeman & Keahey, 2008), scientific astronomy workflows (Deelman, Singh, Livny, Berriman, & Good, 2008), and market-oriented resource management systems (Buyya, Yeo, & Venugopal, 2008). However, none of these approaches targets applications with requirements similar to MMOG. Our work addresses the particular challenges of cost-effectively leasing Cloud resources and reducing their startup times for MMOG, rather than general challenges for efficient Cloud resource management, e.g., different performance characteristics of identical resource types (Dejun, Pierre, & Chi, 2011) or data inconsistency in Cloud storage solutions (Wei, Pierre, & Chi, 2012).

We showed the impact of virtualized Cloud resources on MMOG (Ploss, Mei-länder, Glinka, & Gorlatch, 2011) and proved that the performance requirements of MMOG can be fulfilled on commercial Cloud systems like the Amazon EC2 (Amazon Web Services, 2015). In (Nae, Iosup, Prodan, & Fahringer, 2009), the influence of Cloud resources allocation on the hosting process of multi-player online games was analyzed, showing that load balancing is a critical challenge for MMOG provisioning on Clouds, as targeted in this chapter.

Cloud platforms offer services that provide monitoring and load balancing for their Cloud resources, e.g., Amazon Cloud Watch or Amazon Elastic Load Balancing (Amazon Web Services, 2015). However, these services only provide generic system information about resource utilization (CPU, memory, bandwidth, etc.). This information is not sufficient for up- and down-scaling of MMOG sessions since MMOG have a specific runtime behaviour: e.g., regardless of the current number of users, an online game may run with a constant CPU load of 100% in order to deliver the highest state update rate possible. In this chapter, we develop a novel lifecycle model and a dynamic load-balancing strategy based on application-specific monitoring information (e.g., update rate) that is better suitable for MMOG running in the Cloud.

CONCLUSION

This chapter targets the development of adaptable Cloud-based MMOG and their efficient execution and load balancing on Cloud resources.

For the development of adaptable MMOG suitable for execution in Cloud environments, we propose a novel lifecycle model which provides two iteration cycles for the development and execution of Cloud-based MMOG:

1. The evolution cycle addresses the initial development and potential redesign of adaptable Cloud-based MMOG. We support the MMOG developer in the major steps during MMOG development by identifying generic application requirements of Cloud-based MMOG and providing adaptation triggers for four major load scenarios, as well as by implementing five efficient adaptation strategies suitable for addressing these scenarios.
2. The adaptation cycle of our lifecycle model addresses the execution of MMOG in Cloud environments. We support application providers in the efficient execution and adaptation of MMOG by providing a case study on the real-world architecture of the edutain@grid project. This case study illustrates how our lifecycle reflects and addresses the main problems of MMOG execution and adaptation and, hence, demonstrates the applicability of our model.

Our lifecycle model has been reviewed positively by software engineering experts from academia and industry and provided a major contribution to the European S-Cube project (Bucchiarone et al., 2011; Di Nitto et al., 2012). Furthermore, our experimental results prove the scalability of our proposed adaptation strategies and demonstrate how they are used for improving the QoS of a particular MMOG.

For the execution and load balancing of MMOG in Cloud environments, we develop our novel RTF-RMS resource management system that leases Cloud resources on demand for MMOG processing and provides transparent mechanisms for load balancing. In order to identify the demand for load balancing, RTF-RMS provides a generic mechanism for workload analysis based on a variety of application-specific monitoring values. RTF-RMS is configured for workload analysis of a particular application by using an application profile for specifying the monitoring values of interest and related thresholds for each value that identify the demand for adding and removing resources.

During MMOG execution, the RTF-RMS system receives monitoring values from each application server and analyzes the load of each server and of each zone of the virtual environment. If the demand for load balancing is identified, RTF-RMS chooses between four possible load-balancing actions: user migration, replication enactment, resource substitution, and resource removal. In comparison to existing monitoring tools, e.g., provided by Amazon EC2, RTF-RMS goes beyond the state-of-the-art solutions which are typically based on generic system information instead of application-specific monitoring values. For Cloud resource allocation, RTF-RMS introduces a resource buffer which efficiently compensates for long startup times of Cloud resources and allows for a cost-effective leasing of Cloud resources on demand by buffering unused resources and compensating static leasing periods. By reflecting and implementing the different phases of the adaptation cycle of our lifecycle model, RTF-RMS supports the application provider in the efficient execution and load balancing of Cloud-based MMOG.

Our experimental results demonstrate the suitability of RTF-RMS's load-balancing strategy for overcoming performance bottlenecks by choosing a suitable load-balancing action for load redistribution on Cloud resources.

Our future work will include further analysis of the impact of hardware virtualization on MMOG performance in order to predict the performance of MMOGs on particular Cloud resources. Moreover, we aim at developing a business model which allows to compare resources from different Cloud platforms and to choose the most cost-efficient resource.

REFERENCES

Amazon Web Services, Inc. (2015). *Amazon Web Services (AWS)*. Retrieved from http://aws.amazon.com

Arsanjani, A., Ghosh, S., Allam, A., Abdollah, T., Gariapathy, S., & Holley, K. (2008). SOMA: A method for developing service-oriented solutions. *IBM Systems Journal*, *47*(3), 377–396. doi:10.1147/sj.473.0377

Baresi, L., Guinea, S., & Pasquale, L. (2007). Self-healing BPEL processes with Dynamo and the JBoss rule engine. In *International Workshop on Engineering of Software Services for Pervasive Environments (ESSPE '07)*. New York, NY: ACM. doi:10.1145/1294904.1294906

Benington, H. D. (1983). Production of large computer programs. *Annals of the History of Computing*, *5*(4), 350–361. doi:10.1109/MAHC.1983.10102

Bezerra, C. E., & Geyer, C. F. (2009). A load balancing scheme for massively multiplayer online games. *Multimedia Tools and Applications*, *45*(1-3), 263–289. doi:10.1007/s11042-009-0302-z

Bucchiarone, A., Cappiello, C., Di Nitto, E., Gorlatch, S., Meiländer, D., & Metzger, A. (2011). Design for self-adaptation in service-oriented systems in the Cloud. In D. Petcu & J. L. Vzques-Poletti (Eds.), *European Research Activities in Cloud Computing* (pp. 214–240). Cambridge Scholars Publishing.

Bucchiarone, A., Cappiello, C., Di Nitto, E., Kazhamiakin, R., Mazza, V., & Pistore, M. (2009). Design for adaptation of service-based applications: main issues and requirements. In A. Dan, F. Gittler, & F. Toumani (Eds.), *Service-Oriented Computing. ICSOC/ServiceWave 2009 Workshops (LNCS)* (Vol. 6275, pp. 467–476). Berlin, Germany: Springer. doi:10.1007/978-3-642-16132-2_44

Buyya, R., Yeo, C. S., & Venugopal, S. (2008). Market-oriented Cloud Computing: vision, hype, and reality for delivering IT services as computing utilities. In *International Conference on High Performance Computing and Communications*. IEEE. doi:10.1109/HPCC.2008.172

Canfora, G., Di Penta, M., Esposito, R., & Villani, M. L. (2005). An approach for QoS-aware service composition based on genetic algorithms. In *Proceedings of the 7th Annual Conference on Genetic and Evolutionary Computation (GECCO '05)*. New York, NY: ACM. doi:10.1145/1068009.1068189

Colombo, M., Di Nitto, E., & Mauri, M. (2006). SCENE: a service composition execution environment supporting dynamic changes disciplined through rules. In *Service-Oriented Computing – ICSOC 2006 (LNCS)* (Vol. 4294, pp. 191–202). Berlin, Germany: Springer. doi:10.1007/11948148_16

Deelman, E., Singh, G., Livny, M., Berriman, B., & Good, J. (2008). The cost of doing science on the Cloud: the Montage example. In *Proceedings of the 2008 ACM/ IEEE Conference on Supercomputing*. Piscataway, NJ: IEEE Press. doi:10.1109/ SC.2008.5217932

Dejun, J., Pierre, G., & Chi, C.-H. (2011). Resource provisioning of web applications in heterogeneous Clouds. In *Proceedings of the 2nd USENIX Conference on Web Application Development*. Berkeley, CA: USENIX Association.

Di Nitto, E., Meiländer, D., Gorlatch, S., Metzger, A., Psaier, H., & Dustdar, S., ... Lago, P. (2012). Research challenges on engineering service-oriented applications. In *1st International Workshop on European Software Services and Systems Research (S-Cube)*. IEEE.

Fahringer, T., Anthes, C., Arragon, A., Lipaj, A., Müller-Iden, J., Rawlings, C. J. ... Surridge, M. (2007). The edutain@grid project. In Grid Economics and Business Models GECON 2007 (LNCS) (Vol. 4685/2007, pp. 182–187). Berlin, Germany: Springer.

Freeman, T., & Keahey, K. (2008). Flying low: simple leases with Workspace Pilot. In *Euro-Par 2008 Parallel Processing (LNCS)* (Vol. 5168, pp. 499–509). Berlin, Germany: Springer. doi:10.1007/978-3-540-85451-7_54

Gorlatch, S., Glinka, F., Ploss, A., & Meiländer, D. (2012). Designing multiplayer online games using the Real-Time Framework. In A. Kumar, J. Etheredge, & A. Boudreaux (Eds.), *Algorithmic and Architectural Gaming Design: Implementation and Development* (pp. 290–321). Hershey, PA: IGI Global. doi:10.4018/978-1-4666-1634-9.ch012

Gorlatch, S., Glinka, F., Ploss, A., Müller-Iden, J., Prodan, R., Nae, V., & Fahringer, T. (2008). Enhancing Grids for massively multiplayer online computer games. In *Euro-Par 2008 - Parallel Processing (LNCS)* (Vol. 5168, pp. 466–477). Berlin, Germany: Springer. doi:10.1007/978-3-540-85451-7_51

Gorlatch, S., Meiländer, D., Bartholomäus, S., Fujita, H., Theurl, T., Hoeren, T., ... Boers, K. (2010). Cheating prevention in virtual worlds: software, economic, and law aspects. In *New Trends in Software Methodologies, Tools and Techniques – Proceedings of the 9th SoMeT_10*. IOS Press.

Kongdenfha, W., Saint-Paul, R., Benatallah, B., & Casati, F. (2006). An aspect-oriented framework for service adaptation. In *Service-Oriented Computing - ICSOC 2006 (LNCS)* (Vol. 4294, pp. 15–26). Berlin, Germany: Springer. doi:10.1007/11948148_2

Lane, S., Bucchiarone, A., & Richardson, I. (2012). SOAdapt: A process reference model for developing adaptable service-based applications. *Information and Software Technology*, *54*(3), 299–316. doi:10.1016/j.infsof.2011.10.003

Lane, S., & Richardson, I. (2010). Process models for service-based applications: A systematic literature review. *Information and Software Technology*, *53*(5), 424–439. doi:10.1016/j.infsof.2010.12.005

Lu, F., Parkin, S., & Morgan, G. (2006). Load balancing for massively multi-player online games. In *Proceedings of 5th ACM SIGCOMM Workshop on Network and System Support for Games (NetGames '06)*. New York, NY: ACM. doi:10.1145/1230040.1230064

Meiländer, D., Bucchiarone, A., Cappiello, C., Di Nitto, E., & Gorlatch, S. (2011). Using a lifecycle model for developing and executing real-time online applications on Clouds. In *Service-Oriented Computing – ICSOC 2011 Workshops (LNCS)* (Vol. 7221, pp. 33–43). Berlin, Germany: Springer. doi:10.1007/978-3-642-31875-7_5

Meiländer, D., Köttinger, S., & Gorlatch, S. (2013). A scalability model for distributed resource management in real-time online applications. In *42nd International Conference on Parallel Processing (ICPP)*. IEEE. doi:10.1109/ICPP.2013.90

Meiländer, D., Ploss, A., Glinka, F., & Gorlatch, S. (2012). A dynamic resource management system for real-time online applications on Clouds. In *Euro-Par 2011: Parallel Processing Workshops (LNCS)* (Vol. 7155, pp. 149–158). Berlin, Germany: Springer. doi:10.1007/978-3-642-29737-3_18

Nae, V., Iosup, A., Prodan, R., & Fahringer, T. (2009). The impact of virtualization on the performance of massively multiplayer online games. In *8th Annual Workshop on Network and Systems Support for Games (NetGames)*. IEEE. doi:10.1109/NETGAMES.2009.5446227

Nurmi, D., Wolski, R., Grzegorczyk, C., Obertelli, G., Soman, S., Youseff, L., & Zagorodnov, D. (2009). The Eucalyptus open-source Cloud-Computing system. In *9th IEEE/ACM International Symposium on Cluster Computing and the Grid*. IEEE.

Papazoglou, M. P., & van den Heuvel, W.-J. (2006). Service-oriented design and development methodology. *International Journal of Web Engineering and Technology*, *2*(4), 412–442. doi:10.1504/IJWET.2006.010423

Ploss, A., Meiländer, D., Glinka, F., & Gorlatch, S. (2011). Towards the scalability of real-time online interactive applications on multiple servers and Clouds. *Advances in Parallel Computing, 20*, 267–287.

Royce, W. W. (1987). Managing the development of large software systems: concepts and techniques. In *Proceedings of the 9th International Conference on Software Engineering (ICSE '87)*. IEEE.

S-Cube European Network of Excellence. (2012). *Software Services and Systems Network*. Retrieved from http://www.s-cube-network.eu

Vale, S., & Hammoudi, S. (2008). Model driven development of context-aware service oriented architecture. In *11th IEEE International Conference on Computational Science and Engineering Workshops*. IEEE. doi:10.1109/CSEW.2008.31

Valente, L., Conci, A., & Feijó, B. (2005). Real time game loop models for single-player computer games. In *SBGames '05 – IV Brazilian Symposium on Computer Games and Digital Entertainment*.

Verma, K., Gomadam, K., Sheth, A. P., Miller, J. A., & Wu, Z. (2005). *The METEOR-S approach for configuring and executing dynamic web processes. Technical report*. Wright State University.

Wautelet, Y., Achbany, Y., Lange, J., & Kolp, M. (2009). A process for developing adaptable and open service systems: application in supply chain management. In *Enterprise Information Systems (Lecture Notes in Business Information Processing)* (Vol. 24, pp. 564–576). Berlin, Germany: Springer. doi:10.1007/978-3-642-01347-8_47

Wei, Z., Pierre, G., & Chi, C.-H. (2012). CloudTPS: Scalable transactions for web applications in the Cloud. *IEEE Transactions on Services Computing, 5*(4), 525–539. doi:10.1109/TSC.2011.18

Wirsing, M., Hölzl, M., Acciai, L., Banti, F., Clark, A., Fantechi, A., … Varró, D. (2008). SENSORIA patterns: augmenting service engineering with formal analysis, transformation and dynamicity. In Leveraging Applications of Formal Methods, Verification and Validation (Communications in Computer and Information Science), (Vol. 17, pp. 170–190). Berlin, Germany: Springer.

KEY TERMS AND DEFINITIONS

Adaptability: The ability to change the load distribution during the runtime of an application in order to balance the load on a distributed set of resources.

Lifecycle Model: A software engineering methodology for describing an iterative development process which specifies major steps during application design and execution.

Load Balancing: Distributing the load of an application on a set of distributed resources according to their computing capabilities.

Massively Multiplayer Online Games (MMOG): A class of distributed applications using multiple servers for the application processing and supporting large numbers of concurrent users interacting in real-time with each other in a virtual game environment.

Quality of Service (QoS) Violation: A failure to meet the deadline for the real-time processing of user inputs leading to users becoming less satisfied with their immersion in the virtual environment.

Real-Time Framework (RTF): A high-level development platform for MMOG which provides mechanisms for application state distribution, communication handling and monitoring.

Resource Management System: A software component for the dynamic load balancing of MMOG and (if demanded) the allocation of Cloud resources.

Chapter 3
Emerging Technologies and Applications for Cloud–Based Gaming:
Review on Cloud Gaming Architectures

Deverajan Ganesh Gopal
VIT University, India

Sekaran Kaushik
VIT University, India

ABSTRACT

Cloud computing technology has revolutionized the field of networks and the way of utilizing the resources remotely. In the gaming field this has changed the way of playing traditional games in relation to online on-demand available games which reduces the hassle at the clients' end. In order to play a game online, the game content is processed at the server end and rendered images are transmitted to the client's end. This makes the way of accessing easier and the game can be played even without the hardware or software required for the game. We review the cloud gaming architecture and the different types of streaming used by various cloud gaming platforms. Also, the issues and challenges with the service provider technologies used in the cloud gaming are discussed briefly.

DOI: 10.4018/978-1-5225-0546-4.ch003

INTRODUCTION

Advancement of technology in cloud computing in the past few decades has shown tremendous results in all the fields, where accessing the resources globally via internet is involved. Cloud Gaming is one of the popular concepts (Shea et al., 2013). Enterprises invest large amount of funds to develop the games that can be played online which is now a popular way of playing games. Cloud gaming systems are providing the services to end clients through internet that makes the gaming job simpler and the client needs to pay some amount to the service provider for the service provided based on some conditions (Hong et al., 2015a). Cloud computing has several opportunities for existing and new applications. Synchronized sharing of files with streaming media files in terms of efficiency of system and usability is an advantage of the cloud computing platform. Based on a research of the market (Huang et al., 2013), gaming platform can be classified into three categories

1. On-solid games,
2. Boxed games, and
3. Cloud games.

One of the major three mainstream architectures, the client server architecture which runs from a centralized server manages the game world peer to peer (P2P) and shares the management load of computational power and resources, and hybrid (Mishra et al., 2014). Mobile online games are the most developing field in the gaming industry while cloud gaming offers several advantages for both the developers and the gamers (Semsarzadeh et al., 2014). Cloud gaming is made possible for a group of clients which is to experience online gaming with groups called cloud federation (Mashayekhy et al., 2015; Chuah et al., 2014). Cost is one of the factors that require to be considered in gaming. The physical hardware for lower graphics game costs US $500 and for higher graphics, game hardware equipment costs US$1200 in order to setup and play the game natively.

Numerous societies, as well as NIST and other government organizations, have suggested different Cloud architectures. For big display place enterprises the architectures scale with traditional large platform IT solutions. However, they might not effectively scale with rapidly evolving computing requirements of corporations and organizations, such as real-time video communication service offerings. Cloud architecture requirements for huge stages intended or varied service types tend to be very diverse from supplies for application specific platforms, such as cloud security platforms. In general, a given cloud architecture model would daze the set of distinctive features.

To run a gaming instance, we need more computational resource. The game instances are dependent on the server capacity for it to run concurrently from a remote location. Even the resource required for the game is dependent on the service provider server. As requests from several gamers are received the number of cloud servers need to be ready with instances of the game to provide sufficient service to the gamers. As the number of online players increases setting up of several servers would ensure maintaining the speed during slow gaming times whereas the absence of maintaining sufficient servers would result in servers becoming overloaded during peak gaming times (Velasco et al., 2015). The on-demand source provisioning service in public clouds provides a promising solution to the above problem. For example, Amazon EC2 delivers g2.2xlarge virtual machine occurrences intended for graphics-intensive GPU computing applications such as cloud gaming. The users can rent the resources (i.e., virtual machines) as and when required in response to workload variation and pay only for the resources that they actually use. This approach frees the users from the complexities of purchasing, engineering, and maintaining hardware infrastructures. The famous cloud gaming company GaiKai has used two public clouds (Huang et al., 2013).

Portability is one of the problems when the game is installed locally. The game cannot be played if the player is in some remote location and hence the gamer needs to carry the laptop or the gaming device. In cloud, the game can be accessed remotely from any location with an internet connection and resume the game from where the player left with the help of any device that has the authentication to cloud server. The cloud service for gaming is termed as 'Gaming as a service (GaaS)'.

Virtualization

Virtual servers are available in cloud and rented by several industries to run their programs that actually serve as cloud servers, minimizing the total renting cost of virtual machines has become one of the major concern to the service providers. The total renting cost of the virtual machines is proportional to the total running hours of all the virtual machines rented by the customers (Hong et al., 2013). Cloud gaming requires several virtual machines in order to render the graphics and provide unstoppable service to the gamer. Workload given to a virtual machine the total running hours of all virtual machines has been dependent on the players request assigned to a virtual machine. During the multi-player gaming heavy traffic occurs in the servers, processing the gaming actions in milliseconds, rendering and returning it to the multiple gamer's devices actually requires lots of processing powers and latency, even a slightest delay it may get the gamer interaction out of the game. Virtual servers are expensive, time consuming and require higher bandwidth connection to perform all the graphics rendering process video content produce in the user device.

Quality of service (QOS) is a major concern for the gaming process need chain network to share the processing in a distributed environment and collect the processed data, since gaming server require lots of hardware and software to make them work together as one and respond to the user. Based on the demand of workload rising can be happen at any time and estimating the future demand add trends towards. Improvements on the commodity hardware better than a specialized hardware for the virtualization, advancement in virtualization technology is also inspiring and a fast growth in the past decades has changed the virtualization in to a new path in computing field. Especially cloud plays major role in virtualization technologies that produces the processing optimal and efficient with the available hardware, renting the cloud servers is still a high cost and for gaming it is an ultimate requirement to process the workload. Developing low cost cloud games will make the gamers interest towards the cloud gaming service providers. The advancement developed in the network function by eliminating specialized processors for networks and multiple heterogeneous environments and making it in to a single architecture which reduces the complexity and cost of owner ship. Cloud provides several features such as low cost, availability, and high level management in expenditures, these welfares are important features for telecom workers, cloud technology appeal is clear from this features. In fact, as discovered in a latest survey, many telecom operators are deploying cloud infrastructures. Notwithstanding, deploying the telecom cloud presents a dissimilar set of trials due to the manufacturing's inherent supplies for availability (5-nines), very low latency, and complex networking (Ethernet, optical, wireless, etc.).

Achieving optimal versions is no easy task because gamers are fussy, and adoration to have both high class of graphics and short interaction delay. However, concurrently optimizing the gamers' both demands is impossible. Therefore, to solve the cloud gaming bitrate adaptation problem, we carefully study the following three main challenges:

1. **Quantifying Gamer Experience via Crowdsourcing:** The metrics of higher level gamer experience and lower level system performance are quite different, and the mapping between them is affected by many factors. Conducting a user study in a laboratory to exercise all the factors requires many participants, and is tedious and expensive. Hence, we leverage crowdsourcing for a user study with many more online participants in Section IV, and derive empirical gamer experience, or mean opinion score (MOS) model. Crowdsourcing also allows us to conduct the user study using gamers' actual client computers for more realistic results, compared with user studies done in a laboratory.

2. **Reconfiguring Video Codecs:** Compared with audio streams, encoding, and transmitting video streams consume much more computation/network resources, and thus video codec is the main control knob for adopting an ongoing cloud gaming session to the available resources. Changing the codec configuration on-the-fly is challenging.

3. **Adapting Videos in Dynamic Networks:** With the gamer experience model and codec reconfiguration mechanism, we develop a suite of techniques to quickly adapt the video codec configurations to dynamic networks. The techniques range from optimal resource allocation algorithms to real-time heuristics to maximize the gamer experience without excessive resource consumption.

Gaming as a Service (GaaS)

Gaming as a service (GaaS) is the new way in gaming industry to develop, deploy and operate the games at the server instead of the same running at the client's end. In cloud, there are several types of services available such as Platform as a service (PaaS), Software as a service (SaaS), and Infrastructure as a service (IaaS). These are the basic services in the cloud terminology. The term 'services' indicates that the connection or communication between the client and the service provider is dependent, here gaming as a service needs specific hardware to run, so the IaaS service will be acquired, to run the game content on any platform PaaS service is required, to deliver the game to the client end device SaaS is required. The basic major services in cloud are together formed as 'Gaming as a service (GaaS)' and are shown in Figure 1. Gaming with a stable (Ameigeiras et al., 2015) 4G or 5G increases the possibility of good experience of cloud gaming and with the success of smart phones it is made possible.

Licensing the architecture increases the development and research in the cloud gaming field. Here, there are two types of licensed systems in cloud gaming and they are (Figure 2):

1. Open source,
2. Proprietary.

Open Source

Open source software for computers enable the source code of the products to be licensed by the copyright owners to modify, change and redistribute publicly (Huang et al., 2013). GamingAnywhere is a gaming platform through cloud, the source code of which is open to access and modify. The openness of the game makes it more portable with high extensibility supported by major operating systems. It is avail-

Figure 1. The gaming as a service view with other available services

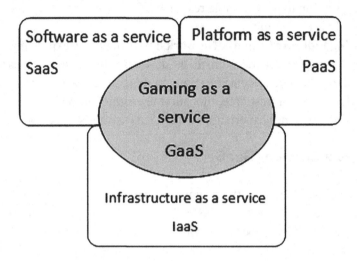

Figure 2. The two license platforms available in clod gaming and service providers available

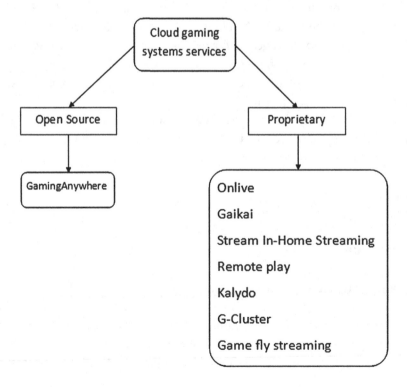

able for windows, Linux, and Mac and source code can be publicly viewed. Games have become more popular since the 80's. With the evolution of cloud it reduces the resources that need to be purchased by the client computer like ram, graphics card and other resources. By making a particular platform open source, the contribution towards the platform will be used and development of the process becomes higher. More ideas will be received from the researchers, students and developers to make the platform acquire high scalability with high quality gaming experience.

Proprietary

Proprietary software is copyrighted by the owner and the source code is closed which cannot be viewed publicly. In gaming, there are several enterprises which offer services on monthly payment based on the game we choose to play. Various enterprises like Nvidia, Onlive, Gaikai, remote play and so on provide cloud gaming services to the end clients to experience the gaming in a different perspective. Expectation of the client will be much higher. Not to compromise with a lag free game with the help of this technology makes the client satisfied with the game. Even the source code is closed in the proprietary systems developing the gaming and experience is still slow process. More researches are being carried out on balancing the load of the game.

ISSUES IN CLOUD GAMING

In a cloud gaming, the system has to collect players' action and transmit them to the cloud game server, process the action, results will be rendered, encode and decode the compression of frames and the resulting changes in the game will be shown to the player's end. All these operations have to happen in milliseconds serially without any delay to ensure the interactivity. This is defined as interaction delay which is to be maintained with much more importance in order to provide rich experience for the cloud game players. For such experiences, critical operations such as rendering and video compression takes more time and high processing unit is needed to do the process which in turn needs more network latency.

Different types of games are available. For games with low graphics, such as Counter Strike, max Payne, GTA Vice City, speed is the most important criterion. For example, for a low graphics game counter strike needs a processor of speed 1.7 GHZ, 512 MB of RAM, graphics card supports DirectiX 8.1 and free disk space of 4.6 GB in secondary memory. Some game needs high end graphics such as Prototype, Call of Duty, Watch Dogs, Far Cry, Saints Row, and so on. For example, for high end graphics game watch dogs needs a processor speed of 2.66 GHZ, minimum 6

GB of RAM, graphics card that supports DirectX 10 and free disk space of 25 GB in secondary memory.

There is a huge difference in the system requirements of low graphics and high graphics games. Here, cloud computing provides us the resources and connectivity and reduces the player's workload of buying this equipment. There is a radical change in the game played traditionally in the local system pc or laptop. Here, the game is uploaded in the server and can be accessed remotely. The action of the player has to be synchronized to the gaming environment thus making the gaming experience as real. Player loses the interaction with the game if the action process reflected in the screen is delayed. For example, in counter strike, the enemy should be shot immediately. Else, the enemy will shoot the player and the player will die on the field creating frustration within the player. Delay tolerance is the major issue in cloud gaming, where action of the player has to reflect in the player's device instantly. Consider in a Real Time Strategy (RTS) games like star craft II legacy of the world delays up to 1000 milliseconds can be tolerable because the player issues many actions and controls several entities in the games that leaves the delay by the player unnoticed. Interaction difference between the traditional gaming and cloud gaming has to be same in order to make the player continue to use the cloud gaming system. When it comes to a multiplayer gaming system streaming the game to more than one client system synchronization is more important to keep the player's interaction. The famous cloud gaming service providers Gaikai and Onlive owned by Sony are encoders to stream the game to client's device. Following are the several issues faced by the users.

- **Resolution:** Game requirements have specified screen resolution like 1200*700 pixels to play the game in traditional method. The client's device needs to be suited to the resolution in order to provide the real experience of gaming. Several gaming has different resolution requirements and the client's device needs to support the control to give actions. High end games has several actions to process in the cloud server and render the actions, thus resulting in the client's device running several frames together at this stage.
- **Network Bandwidth:** Cloud gaming needs a strong internet bandwidth to stream the game from the cloud server to the client's device, with the advancement in technology through 3G, 4G and 5G connections, this is made possible. With high network bandwidth connection can be established easily but the cost for that needs to be considered. Since 2005 several development in communication technologies are evident to solve the network bandwidth.
- **Latency:** Gaming performance is purely based on the game's time latency and based on the delay the gaming interaction of the players will be stable. Client interaction with the game like providing actions has to process in the

game server and replicate to the client's device. Latency has to be less to increase the interaction of the client with the game. For example, counter strike in a shooting game with multiple players has to be processed instantly in the cloud server in order for the enemy to die. Instead of that if rendering is delayed the enemy will shoot the player and the player dies in the gaming process. This will irritate the player and may lead him to discontinue the game.

- **Failure Tolerance:** In the cloud, all the resources of the game will process and renders the result to the client. If any failure occurs like network disconnection, power failure, the system has to tolerate the failure and resume the game status from where the player left. For example, while playing any game, a sudden network failure or power failure at the client's end leading to resuming the game from the first point will make the player to lose the interaction with the game. The game data has to be saved at each of the frames and if failure occurs, server must resume from where the player left proceed further.
- **Security:** Internet has several security flaws and many researches are going on. Cloud gaming entertain the client and if any security problems like frames dislocation and points increase crops up, cheat codes will make the gaming experience bad. Cryptography is necessary to avoid the hackers' attacks on the cloud system and authentication of the client's system may get compromised. Hence, several security measures are needed to make the clients gaming experience more interactive and comfortable.

ADVANTAGES

- **Management of Software:** Software at the client's side is necessary in order to maintain it with regular patches and updates, configuring with different operating systems and platforms needed for different resources and efforts. Software maintenance for a wide-range of stages experiences large working cost for software merchants. Support for older versions is terminated due to the latest release of the new games and update in the software. Cloud gaming provides an advantage of new release available at client's place without any up gradation in client's machine and compatibility issues are also solved, service provider for the game need to maintain the software up to date at the cloud server and manage the software in a cost effective manner with few resources.
- **Management of Hardware:** Technology in gaming platform reached epic heights where new video games release periodically with better graphics. This requires hardware equipment's to be upgraded in the local or client's machine. Hardware may not be utilized well because the requirement of the

game is higher in the latest release. Even if the hardware works fine in the machine, waste electronics are produced unnecessarily. The recent research shows that in United States alone 372.3 million units of waste electronics are sent to disposal (Panke et al., 2015) In this, mobile phones and computers hold 93% of electronic market, cloud gaming reduces the work and cost of upgrading the electronics in our local machine. Storage is also required to store the game files and process them and send back to the consumer to make him interactive with system. Power consumed by the hardware is taken care of by cloud servers where less power is utilized by the client and makes to play the game.

- **Cost for Deployment:** New game release in the market get to sale and distribution of games and delivering the game to several enormous players, pay-per-service model in cloud saves the consumer cost of owning whole software and hardware, where they may lose interest in the game after sometime. For example, Watch dogs is streamed from the cloud and service is provided to user at 720p and 30 fps, this may reduce the overall data volume if the game is played in less than 3.7h, so user can play a trailer to have a quick view on the game and decide to get the game service, thus avoiding high downloading of games data in to local machine. This also provides privacy of game and copyrights issues on the game.

- **Cloud Gaming with Green Data Center:** Cloud gaming requires internet in order to stream the games to client device. Nowadays mobiles clients are connected to internet through high speed wireless connections called as LTE (Long term evolution) and 4G (Fourth generation), the latest technology in communication field via fixed line broadband networks. The cloud gaming consists of graphics rendering, compression of video frames, and network delivery modules in order to work and provide service.

The data center is the delivering center of cloud computing where a group of storage resources and computing resources are gathered and organized to serve clients, divesting these reckonings to the cloud agreements, better deployment of power and hardware in the cloud data center than on separate machines. In the cloud gaming applications, game visuals interpretation and video coding of the extracted images are achieved at such green data centers. To maintain comprehensive calculation of task in a cloud data center, virtual machine (VM) technology has been widely deployed, thanks to its flexibility, reliability, and ease of management. VM technology allows a physical computer to run multiple operating systems (OSs) with strong isolation among the OSs. VMs share the physical hardware that allocates resources among the VMs. Computing resources can therefore be scaled by running more or fewer physical machines according to the client's demands.

- **Platform Independence Gaming:** Many facilities and the test bed need connection to the client browser plugin or software, which are browser dependent or operating system dependent. This requirement results in a lack of portability in cloud gaming deployment, due to development of operating system. Browser plugins for the updated versions of high quality games needs more effort. In addition, maintenance for fewer widespread Operating systems and plugins could be deserted because of cost redeemable by service providers. A platform-independent explanation is wanted for straightforwardness and low cost of conservation for the cloud gaming provider. From the client's lookout, the group of gear can be lengthy by loving cloud service while rejecting the need for frequent software or hardware upgrading. Thanks to the recent advancement in web-based technology, browsers have emerged as an important platform for widely popular web applications. Web applications are getting more popular in providing software services to thin clients independent of OS platform. HTML5, a markup language which provides cross-platform support of multimedia and graphics without the need to install plugins, was recently finalized. The introduction of HTML5 is a promising step in realizing cross-platform design of cloud gaming. With various devices (PCs, TVs, laptops, tablets, and smartphones) equipped with web HTML5-ready browsers, high-end 3D video gaming can be delivered to thin clients via this cross-platform web technology. More importantly, HTML5 was designed considering operating on low-power mobile devices. WebGL is another web technology that provides an application programming interface (API) for 3D graphics over browsers based on HTML5 canvas elements. Access to hardware acceleration for graphics processing in an HTML5 browser allows web games to be rendered at previously unseen graphics quality. HTML5 with WebGL is promising for a truly platform-independent cloud gaming solution.

CLOUD GAMING ARCHITECTURE

Online gaming has become fascinating among all the ages. Recently, cloud gaming has become more attractive because it could be played from anywhere via internet (Chuah et al., 2014). This made it possible to reduce the physical resource in the end client's side (Shea et al., 2015). The games would be streamed in the client computer or handheld devices such as mobiles, tablets that has less physical resources where the game runs on the service provider server through internet (Semsarzadeh et al., 2014). The gaming controls are transmitted to the client's device and button presses of the clients are transmitted directly to the server of service provider and response of the controls are replied to the client's device (Figure 3) (Samba, 2012, pp.19; Hu et al., 2012).

The clients need not download or install the actual game in their physical machine. The content of the game is actually stored in the server side and not in the client's hard disk. Execution of the game code also happens in the service providers' server and the results are transmitted to the client's device (Liu et al., 2013). This enables the client to use less powerful device to play the game even though the game needs more resources to run. Playing game online through wired or wireless connections, streaming the video to the clients are encoded instantly from cloud servers.

Figure 3. The architecture of cloud gaming

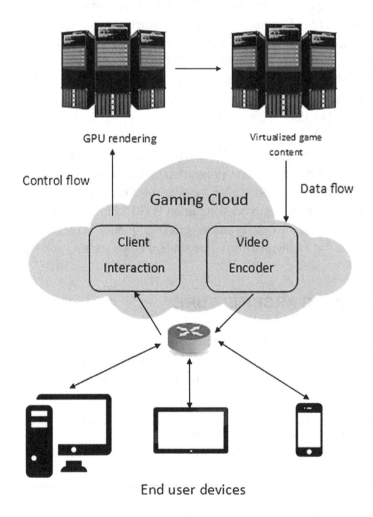

Gaming as a service (GaaS) is named after the cloud gaming service that give tremendous experience in gaming with 3D effect over the traditional gaming system (Panke et al., 2015). There are several cloud gaming systems and services, most of them are proprietary. The first cloud gaming platform in open source, Gaming-Anywhere, was released in April 2013. Several proprietary systems were developed based on the types of streaming and provides Gaming as a service (GaaS) (Velasco et al., 2015).

Reasons for Cloud gaming:

- **Fewer Resources:** No setup, No new hardware, No installation of games, No patches.
- **Game on Any Device:** High quality, gaming in multiple devices, low latency.
- **Click to Play:** Play whenever you want by authentication and start from your saved games.

There are two types of cloud gaming streaming (Hong et al., 2015):

1. Video streaming,
2. File streaming.

Figure 4 presents types of streaming are major types available are in cloud gaming and their services providers in the streaming type.

Video Streaming

Video stream in cloud gaming host and process the entire game content virtually in the service provider's server by making use of the streamed data through internet,

Figure 4. Types of streaming

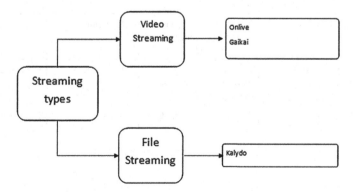

instead of hardware, to run the game. Video streaming demands faster data transfer to process the game content, thus, a stable bandwidth is needed to play the game in cloud which in turn will provide low-latency.

File Streaming

File stream in cloud gaming, which is also known as progressive downloading deploys a client that runs actual game on the clients gaming device such as a tablet, mobile or a personal computer (Cia et al., 2015). The 5% of total size of game is downloaded to start the game instantly. Here, cloud provides scalable way of streaming the content of the game with analysis of big data and virtualization technology (Li et al., 2015; Zhang et al., 2014). This requires a device with hardware abilities to operate the game and the downloaded data is stored at the end client's memory and consumes low bandwidth.

The cloud gaming architecture and type of streaming with its gaming types is indicated in Table 1.

Table 1. Cloud gaming service providers

Architecture	Description	Streaming Type	Game Types
Onlive cloud gaming (Shea et al., 2013)	Online gaming performance with local gaming performance is measured.	Video Streaming	Action, Adventure, Role play.
Gaikai cloud gaming (Shea et al., 2013)	Gaikai is a cloud gaming service provider of cloud gaming with high scalability.	Video Streaming	Adventure, Role play, Arcade games.
GamingAnywhere (Huang et al., 2013)	An open source platform that offers online gaming services	Video Streaming	Open to all types of games
Kalydo	It is a leading enterprise providing gaming service through cloud	File Streaming	Arcade games
Adaptive cloud gaming system (Hong et al., 2015)	To maximize the gaming experience adaptive system is introduced	File streaming	General games
Nvidia grid cloud gaming technology	Revolutionary technology to render 3D games in cloud	File Streaming	High end graphics games

Onlive Cloud Gaming Architecture

Onlive is a provider of cloud virtualization technology that provides gaming service to the consumers through cloud as Gamming as a service (GaaS) and onlive architecture that makes interactions with the consumers. Client sends the game actions to the cloud gaming platform where the interaction and actions are received and passed to game logic the GPU (Graphical processing unit) (Guan et al., 2014). This will render the scene to the action provided and encode the video to video streaming and sends the data to client device. It is implemented in private cloud environment which provides better performance and customization that fully unleashes the potential of cloud gaming.

The version situations used by Onlive are not widely evident. For instance, the situation will be unidentified if Onlive has assisted with antialiasing or with the draw distance. With the specified problems in awareness, we have the subsequent practice to extent Onlive image class. Though we choose the standard game Batman as our examination game we practice the similar test policy defined earlier. To ease the outcome that altered rendering situations over image class, we pick the previously rendered image over the movie into the game. To advance the exactness of our study, we unload the intro video's leading case from the game files of our local copy of Batman. The mined show file has a determination of 1280 x 720 pixels (720p), which effortlessly complete the video spilled by Onlive.

We also organized our local copy of Batman to run at a resolution of 1280 x 720 pixels. Consider our display driver to strengthen a frame rate of 30 FPS to contest the rate of final video. Further, we construct MSI afterburner to record the video uncompressed with a resolution of 1280 x 720 pixels at 30 FPS. The lack of video compression is very significant as we don't apply taint to the glossy compression. We then record the intro sequence of our remoter running game and Onlive running along various bandwidth restrictions. We use Linux software router to tune our bandwidth and hit our target. We examine Onlive running from its optimum bandwidth scenery of 10 Mb/s regularly slowed up to 3.0 Mb/s. It ranges up to broad spectrum of bandwidths usually offered to suburban Internet users. Earlier during runtime, we ensure our bandwidth sceneries are precise by an inquisitive test. Subsequently seizing all the mandatory video systems, we choose 40 second (1200 frame) segment similarly from each video so as to achieve an image quality examination.

We examine the video by means of two traditional measures, specifically Peak Signal-to-Noise Ratio (PSNR) and Structural Similarity Index Method (SSIM). The PSNR technique counts the quantity of fault over the recreated video, which had been added thru compression. The SSIM technique computes the organizational resemblance amongst the two video frames. Thus, our native capture records an extraordinary PSNR and SSIM. Though it will not be an exact solution, it represents certain variance in the verified video and the chief file. Much of this variance is expected, owing to some extent, due to change of brightness and color configurations used by the core video player in the Batman game engine.

When the native capture is associated to Onlive running at any construction rate, we can realize a huge fall in relation to both PSNR and SSIM. Subsequently PSNR and SSIM are not on a direct measure. The dropdown really specifies a substantial filth in image class. Usually a PSNR of 30 dB and beyond is deliberated good class, yet 25 and exceeding is considered suitable for mobile video flowing. Not astonishingly, as we slow down the bandwidth of our test systems, the image class activates to agonize substantial humiliation as well. With the exclusion of the 3.0 Mb/s test, all examples stay beyond a PSNR of 25 dB; so though there is room for enhancement, the image class is quiet suitable.

Gaikai Cloud Gaming Architecture

Gaikai is developed with two public clouds. When the client selects a game, it sends the IP address of the client and the game is ready to run to players. Cloud technology helps to run the high end video games. GamingAnywhere architecture, later acquired by Sony computer entertainment for US $380 million is planning to deploy their own cloud gaming environment to clients. It is implemented in two public clouds namely, Limelight and Amazon EC2 cloud. Ec2 first sends the game client to client device and ping the IP addresses to proxy server to choose the game and when the client selects the game it starts to get actions from the client (Felemban et al., 2013).

GamingAnywhere:

GamingAnywhere is the first platform which is released in open source platform. It works differently than the other available cloud gaming platforms. The architecture consists of Client, Portal clients, and Game servers. Here the client (Huang et al., 2013; Jarschel et al., 2011; Ojala & Tyrväinen, 2011) connects with the portal server and a list of available games will be provided to the client to select. After the game is selected, the portal server sends the configuration of the game to the games server and connects the client to game server. After this, the client can start playing the game. In this model, game server plays an important role in the architecture (Figure 5).

Kalyd

A proprietary technology for cloud gaming service, which is also a file streaming model that allows to play game immediately by selecting the cloud game running

Figure 5. GamingAnywhere architecture

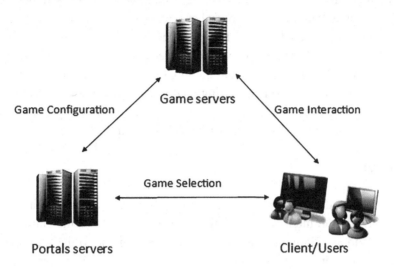

in the file streaming type. This already downloads the game content to the local cache and lets the player to play the game while downloading the next content. It has launched many games even through social media like Facebook. Low bandwidth internet connection is sufficient to acquire the service for gaming. This model initiates low entry pricing and a trial period of one month with access to the tools, customer service and platform to customers, so that they can experience the environment before using the service with full access.

The cloud gaming architecture has been modified from the existing cloud gaming platforms. Here they have added a new feature called bandwidth estimator to monitor sending and receiving of packets with timestamp to the client's end. Codec parameter selector optimizes the bitrate to increase the quality of game and maximizes the experience of the client. This is connected with the MOS model that converts each frame to the gaming dependent rate (Hong et al., 2015). Low internet bandwidth with higher quality outcome of the game shows a promising possibility of cloud gaming.

Nvidia Grid Cloud Gaming Technology

Nvidia, one of the largest graphics card manufacturers and leading game producers based on windows platform has developed a grid technology for cloud gaming and offers its services at $7.99 per month with 3 months' free trial period. Games with high frames ratio is also played with high quality. It can be played in TVs, PCs, and tablets. Performance is most important when it comes to gaming online because even a small lag makes the gamer feel uncomfortable with the gaming experience.

Streaming music and videos to TVs, PCs and tablets using cloud facilities like Netflix, YouTube, Pandora and Spotify has developed the major technique for delight in content for linked devices. The opportuneness of big cloud-managed public library of content with stream-anywhere competence is unbearable to fight. Now with innovative NVIDIA GRID cloud gaming technology, streaming video games from the web just like any other flowing media will soon become a reality. GRID solidifies 3D games in cloud servers, converts each frame promptly and streams the result to any device with a wired or wireless broadband link.

G-Cluster

G-cluster was well-known in the 2000s and had only 25 employees at the initial stage. It provides an interactive gaming platform which stores the gaming service from the cloud as "Gaming as a service". It delivers game to the set-up boxes of televisions or personal computer through a connected stream like internet. Thus, this frees the customer from worrying about the processing of games, processors and operating systems. Configuring the game to the environment with large customer information service, providing unstoppable access to the customer and keeping the network operators in good position has enabled the technology to provide better feasibility in implementing the gaming infrastructure. Initially during start-up G-cluster concentrated on product manufacturing and networking with several companies between 2000 and 2003, but later concentrated on sales and marketing.

CONCLUSION

Billions of dollars are being invested in the field of research and development of cloud gaming. The future of gaming experience is changing with advanced internet connection like 4G and 5G. This technology makes it possible for the enterprise to make an extreme cloud gaming experience. Cloud gaming was developed in the last decade which got an enormous response from the gaming equipment manufacturers and game developers are investing and developing cloud gaming. Major graphics card manufacturing industries like Nvidia, Radeon have already deployed cloud gaming at particular services on monthly subscription basis. A huge burden has gotten reduced by migrating traditional gaming to cloud gaming. This experience takes gamers to a new level of gaming. Cloud gaming has many exciting possibilities and rapidly evolving technology servicing the game experience to mobile and tablet platforms are critical and needs to be concentrated upon.

REFERENCES

Ameigeiras, P., Ramos-Munoz, J. J., Schumacher, L., Prados-Garzon, J., Navarro-Ortiz, J., & Lopez-Soler, J. M. (2015). Link-level access cloud architecture design based on SDN for 5G networks. *IEEE Network*, *29*(2), 24–31. doi:10.1109/MNET.2015.7064899

Cai, W., Hong, Z., Wang, X., Chan, H. C., & Leung, V. (2015). Quality-of-Experience Optimization for a Cloud Gaming System With Ad Hoc Cloudlet Assistance. *IEEE Transactions on Circuits and Systems for Video Technology*, *25*(12), 2092–2104. doi:10.1109/TCSVT.2015.2450153

Chen, K. T., Chang, Y. C., Hsu, H. J., Chen, D. Y., Huang, C. Y., & Hsu, C. H. (2014). On the quality of service of cloud gaming systems. *IEEE Transactions on Multimedia*, *16*(2), 480–495. doi:10.1109/TMM.2013.2291532

Chuah, S. P., Yuen, C., & Cheung, N. M. (2014). Cloud gaming: A green solution to massive multiplayer online games. *Wireless Communications, IEEE*, *21*(4), 78–87. doi:10.1109/MWC.2014.6882299

Claypool, M., & Claypool, K. (2010). Latency can kill: precision and deadline in online games. In *Proceedings of the first annual ACM SIGMM conference on Multimedia systems.* ACM. doi:10.1145/1730836.1730863

Felemban, M., Basalamah, S., & Ghafoor, A. (2013). A distributed cloud architecture for mobile multimedia services. *IEEE Network*, *27*(5), 20–27. doi:10.1109/MNET.2013.6616111

García-Valls, M., Cucinotta, T., & Lu, C. (2014). Challenges in real-time virtualization and predictable cloud computing. *Journal of Systems Architecture*, *60*(9), 726–740. doi:10.1016/j.sysarc.2014.07.004

Guan, H., Yao, J., Qi, Z., & Wang, R. (2015). Energy-Efficient SLA Guarantees for Virtualized GPU in Cloud Gaming. *IEEE Transactions on Parallel and Distributed Systems*, *26*(9), 2434–2443. doi:10.1109/TPDS.2014.2350499

Hong, H. J., Chen, D. Y., Huang, C. Y., Chen, K. T., & Hsu, C. H. (2013). QoE-aware virtual machine placement for cloud games. *2013 12th Annual Workshop on Network and Systems Support for Games (NetGames),* (pp. 1-2). IEEE.

Hong, H. J., Chen, D. Y., Huang, C. Y., Chen, K. T., & Hsu, C. H. (2015). Placing virtual machines to optimize cloud gaming experience. *IEEE Transactions on Cloud Computing*, *3*(1), 42–53. doi:10.1109/TCC.2014.2338295

Hong, H. J., Hsu, C. F., Tsai, T. H., Huang, C. Y., Chen, K. T., & Hsu, C. H. (2015). Enabling adaptive cloud gaming in an open-source cloud gaming platform. *IEEE Transactions on Circuits and Systems for Video Technology, 25*(12), 2078–2091. doi:10.1109/TCSVT.2015.2450173

Hu, G., Tay, W. P., & Wen, Y. (2012). Cloud robotics: Architecture, challenges and applications. *IEEE Network, 26*(3), 21–28. doi:10.1109/MNET.2012.6201212

Huang, C. Y., Chen, K. T., Chen, D. Y., Hsu, H. J., & Hsu, C. H. (2014). GamingAnywhere: The first open source cloud gaming system. *ACM Transactions on Multimedia Computing, Communications, and Applications, 10*(1s), 10. doi:10.1145/2537855

Huang, C. Y., Hsu, C. H., Chang, Y. C., & Chen, K. T. (2013). GamingAnywhere: an open cloud gaming system. In *Proceedings of the 4th ACM multimedia systems conference* (pp. 36-47). ACM. doi:10.1145/2483977.2483981

Jarschel, M., Schlosser, D., Scheuring, S., & Hoßfeld, T. (2011). An evaluation of QoE in cloud gaming based on subjective tests. *Fifth International Conference on In Innovative Mobile and Internet Services in Ubiquitous Computing (IMIS)*, (pp. 330-335). IEEE. doi:10.1109/IMIS.2011.92

Li, Y., Tang, X., & Cai, W. (2015). Play Request Dispatching for Efficient Virtual Machine Usage in Cloud Gaming. *IEEE Transactions on Circuits and Systems for Video Technology, 25*(12), 2052–2063. doi:10.1109/TCSVT.2015.2450152

Liu, F., Shu, P., Jin, H., Ding, L., Yu, J., Niu, D., & Li, B. (2013). Gearing resource-poor mobile devices with powerful clouds: Architectures, challenges, and applications. *Wireless Communications, IEEE, 20*(3), 14–22. doi:10.1109/MWC.2013.6549279

Mashayekhy, L., Nejad, M. M., & Grosu, D. (2015). Cloud federations in the sky: Formation game and mechanism. *IEEE Transactions on Cloud Computing, 3*(1), 14–27. doi:10.1109/TCC.2014.2338323

Mishra, D., El Zarki, M., Erbad, A., Hsu, C. H., & Venkatasubramanian, N. (2014). Clouds+ games: A multifaceted approach. *IEEE Internet Computing, 18*(3), 20–27. doi:10.1109/MIC.2014.20

Ojala, A., & Tyrvainen, P. (2011). Developing cloud business models: A case study on cloud gaming. *IEEE Software, 28*(4), 42–47. doi:10.1109/MS.2011.51

Panke, Q., Xue, C., Lei, W., & Liqian, W. (2015). A novel stateful PCE-cloud based control architecture of optical networks for cloud services. *Communications, China, 12*(10), 117–127. doi:10.1109/CC.2015.7315063

Samba, A. (2012). Logical data models for cloud computing architectures. *IT Professional Magazine*, *14*(1), 19–26. doi:10.1109/MITP.2011.113

Semsarzadeh, M., Hemmati, M., Javadtalab, A., Yassine, A., & Shirmohammadi, S. (2014). A video encoding speed-up architecture for cloud gaming. *IEEE International Conference on Multimedia and Expo Workshops (ICMEW)*, (pp. 1-6). doi:10.1109/ICMEW.2014.6890685

Shea, R., Fu, D., & Liu, J. (2015). Cloud Gaming: Understanding the Support From Advanced Virtualization and Hardware. *IEEE Transactions on Circuits and Systems for Video Technology*, *25*(12), 2026–2037. doi:10.1109/TCSVT.2015.2450172

Shea, R., Liu, J., Ngai, E., & Cui, Y. (2013). Cloud gaming: Architecture and performance. *IEEE Network*, *27*(4), 16–21. doi:10.1109/MNET.2013.6574660

Sommers, J., & Barford, P. (2012). Cell vs. WiFi: on the performance of metro area mobile connections. In *Proceedings of the 2012 ACM conference on Internet measurement conference* (pp. 301-314). ACM. doi:doi:10.1145/2398776.2398808 doi:10.1145/2398776.2398808

Velasco, L., Contreras, L. M., Ferraris, G., Stavdas, A., Cugini, F., Wiegand, M., & Fernandez-Palacios, J. P. (2015). A service-oriented hybrid access network and clouds architecture. *Communications Magazine, IEEE*, *53*(4), 159–165. doi:10.1109/MCOM.2015.7081090

Zhang, C., Yao, J., Qi, Z., Yu, M., & Guan, H. (2014). VGASA: Adaptive scheduling algorithm of virtualized GPU resource in cloud gaming. *IEEE Transactions on Parallel and Distributed Systems*, *25*(11), 3036–3045. doi:10.1109/TPDS.2013.288

Chapter 4

Cloud Gaming:
Design Architecture
and Challenges

Prajit Kumar Datta
VIT University, India

Utkarsh Srivastava
VIT University, India

ABSTRACT

This chapter talks about the architecture required for cloud gaming and various challenges in cloud based gaming. The first part gives a brief introduction about what is actually cloud gaming and the ways in which it is implemented. The subsequent section talks about the cloud gaming system architecture and different server, client components of cloud gaming frameworks involved in the whole process. The next section talks about various cloud based services and their system architecture. In this chapter main aspect is the server client architecture and data flow models via this architecture. A comparative study has been made among various service providers to have a better understanding of the architecture deployed by them in cloud based gaming. The next section discusses about the Challenges of Cloud based Gaming. The future and new improvisations of the Cloud based Gaming System has also been taken up in this chapter.

DOI: 10.4018/978-1-5225-0546-4.ch004

INTRODUCTION

Cloud computing mainly helps in distribution of power among all developing countries. It will provide power to developing nations to access software's once reserved for developed countries. Small scale businesses will save money spent on large expenditures by using services such as Amazon's Elastic Compute Cloud which is mainly used to store and manipulate their data instead of spending huge amounts on buying servers. Sensors will start playing a major role in items such as lights, agriculture tools and handheld devices thus helping in transmitting data across the Web and then into the cloud. Through the utilization of widely deployed data-centers and elastic resources, cloud computing has opened a new field with countless new opportunities for both new and ongoing applications. Existing applications ranging from file sharing, file uploading and data synchronization to media streaming, all have experienced a great leap forward in terms of enhanced efficiency and reusability through cloud computing platforms. Most of the developments in this field have come from exploring the cloud's massive resources with computational offloading and reducing jitter in data transfer along with user access latencies with strategically placed cloud data-centers. Recent developments in field of cloud computing have expanded to allow offloading not only of prevalent computations but also of much more complex tasks such as high definition 3-D rendering, which turns the idea of Cloud Gaming into a reality. Cloud gaming simply accesses an interactive gaming application from a distant place via cloud client servers and streams the scenes as a video sequence back to the player over the Internet with minimal delay. A cloud gaming player interacts with the application through a layered thin client, which is mainly responsible for displaying the video from the cloud rendering server as well as collecting the player's commands and his moves and sending the interactions back to the cloud via server. This will bring a great reform in gaming industry.

SYSTEM ARCHITECTURE

We can see that a player's control moves must be sent over the Internet from its thin client to the cloud gaming platform i.e to the pseudo player on cloud, so once the command or the control reaches the cloud gaming platform they are transformed into appropriate game actions and moves of multi players, which are then understood and executed according to the game logic resulting into changes in the game world. The changes perceived in the game world are then processed by the cloud system's graphical processing unit (GPU) into a combined scene. The interrelated combined scenes must be compressed by the video encoder, and then sent to a video streaming module, which delivers the video stream back to the thin client.

Finally, the thin client decodes the video and displays the video frames in specified sequence to the player. The player on receiving this scene gets a feel of getting one to one correspondence with the gaming environment:

- **The Deployment Scenario of Cloud Gaming:** A user first logs into the system via a portal server, which provides a list of available games to the user. The user then selects a preferred game and requests to play the game. On receiving the request, the portal server finds an available game server in the directory, it launches the selected game on the server, and returns the replica of game server's URL to the user for connecting to the selected game. Finally, the user connects to the game server and starts to play. The portal server is just like most Web-based services and provides only a simple login application (Huang, 2013). Its user interface is also very simple and dynamic. If login and particular game selection requests are sent from a customized client, it does not even need a user interface for its implementation. Actions can be sent via different query messaging protocols.
- **The Architecture of the Game Server and the Game Client of Cloud Gaming:** There are two different types of network flows in cloud based gaming architecture:
  ○ The dynamic data flow, and
  ○ The static control flow.

The data flow is used to send/receive audio and video (A/V) frames from the server to the client whereas the control flow runs in a reverse direction, it is mainly used to send the user's actions from the client to the server. Both the network flows are very arbitrary and independent in functionality but when combined together they make the system complete. This facilitates easy and smooth flow of game control commands and actions. The system architecture of Cloud Gaming allows it to support any types of games, including Desktop-based and Web-based games (Chen & Hsu, 2013). The game selected by a player is executed on a dedicated game server. There is an agent or a pseudo player running along with the selected game on the same selected server. The pseudo player or the agent acts as a bridge between the player's game commands and the cloud server of game. The agent can be a stand-alone process or a cumulative interdependent thread in the selected game. The choice depends on the type of the game and how the game is implemented. The agent has two major responsibilities. The first is to capture the A/V frames of the game, encode the frames using the chosen codecs, and then deliver the encrypted frames to the client via the data flow networks (Chen, 2013). The second responsibility of the agent is to interact with the game (Hsu, 2013). On receiving the user's actions from the client, it must behave as the pseudo user and play with the game by re-playing the received keyboard, mouse, joysticks and gesture inputs from the player. It must be designed so as to behave as a pseudo-user. The client is trivially a self-made game console implemented by combining an RTSP/RTP multimedia player and many other protocols (Chen, 2013). The system architecture of Cloud Gaming allows observers to have a better control on the game by nature because the server delivers encoded Audio/Video frames using the standard RTSP/RTP and many other protocols. In this way, an observer can watch a game play by simply accessing the corresponding replica of game URL with full-featured multimedia players, such as the VLC media player, which are available on most of the OS's (Chang, 2013).

Components of System Architecture

Cloud based gaming architecture is a combination of various independent modules which are dynamic in nature. Cloud Gaming includes a dedicated server and a cli ent, each of which contains a number of modules which are discussed in detail in this section.

Server Module

The relationships among server modules are shown in Figure 4. Some of the modules are implemented in separate threads. When an agent is launched, its four modules, i.e. the RTSP/RTP server, audio inputs, video inputs and input pseudo-player are launched. The RTSP server and the input player modules are immediately started to wait for incoming clients (starting from the path 1n and 1i in the figure). It doesn't wait for any incoming input requests or acknowledgements as compared to audio or video sources. The audio source and the video source modules are kept idle after initialization. When a client is connected to the RTSP server, the encrypted threads are initiated and an encoder must notify the corresponding source input module that it is ready to encrypt the captured frames (Chen & Chang, 2013). The source input modules then start to collect audio and video frames when one or more encoders are ready to work. Encoded audio and video data fragments are generated concurrently in real time dynamically. It accounts for some jitter and latency which will be discussed later in this chapter. However, this can be reduced with proper integration of cloud setup. The data flows of audio and video frame generations are depicted as the paths from 1a to 5a and from 1v to 5v, respectively. The implementation details of each module are explained below.

RTSP, RTP, and RTCP Server

The RTSP server thread is the first thread launched in the agent. It accepts RTSP commands from a client, initiates encoders, and setups up smooth data flows for delivering encrypted frames. The data flows can be implemented via single network connection or multiple network connections depending on the preferred game requirements and transport layer protocol i.e. TCP or UDP (Hsu & Huang, 2013). For more secure and accurate transmissions TCP is preferred while for faster game control transmissions UDP is preferred. If encoded frames are delivered as 0's or 1's i.e. binary data, a raw RTP/RTCP packet can be incorporated by allocating a dynamic packet buffer and then be sent as interconnected binary data. On the other hand, if encoded frames are delivered via RTP over UDP, they are sent directly to the client using libav format.

Video Source

Currently we have two execution model of the video source module to capture the game screens in real time. One implementation is called the PC-capture module, which captures the entire desktop screen at a specified rate, and extracts the desired region when necessary. It picks instances of real-time gameplay and transfers them to pseudo user. Another implementation is called the API intercept module, which intercepts a game's graphics drawing function calls and retrieves the screen directly from the game's back buffer i.e. pseudo user environment immediately whenever the rendering of a new game screen is completed. In this method we have a complete overview of as to where the game has reached and what outcomes have been generated. Given a desired frame rate, the two implementations of the video source module work in a very different manner. The PC-capture module is initiated in a polling manner; i.e. it periodically takes a screenshot of the desktop at a specified frequency (Chen &Hsu, 2013). For example, if the desired frame rate is 50 fps, the capture interval will be 1/50 sec (20 ms). By using a high resolution timer, we can keep the rate of screen captures approximately equal to the required frame rate. On the other hand, the API intercept module works in an event-driven manner. When the game completes the combining process of an updated screen in the back buffer memory, the API intercept module comes into play. The API intercept module captures the screen for further streaming. Because this module captures screens in a periodic manner, we use a token bucket rate controller to decide whether the module should capture a screen in order to achieve the specified streaming frame rate. For example, if we consider that a game updates its screen 500 times per second and the desired frame rate is 250 fps, the API intercept module will only capture one game screen for every two screen updates. In contrast, if the game's current frame rate is lower than the specified frame rate, the module will re-use the last-captured game screenshots to reach up to the level of specified streaming frame rate. All the captured frames of a game have a timestamp associated with it. These captured frames along with their timestamps are stored in a shared buffer by the video source input module and shared with video encoders (Hsu & Chang, 2013). The video source input module basically acts as a buffer writer, while the video encoders act as buffer readers. Main task of encoders is to read the content and store it in the buffer memory for future encryption purposes. In order to implement this, a reader-writer lock must be dynamically acquired every time before accessing the shared buffer and this helps in smooth flow of commands. It also plays an important role in proper resource allocation and usage. Note that although only one video encoder is illustrated in the figure but it is possible to run multiple video encoders simultaneously depending on the usage condition.

Audio Source

Capturing of audio frames is platform-dependent. Here in our discussion, we will focus on the usage of ALSA library for capturing sounds on Linux and Windows audio session API (WASAPI) for capturing sounds on Windows. The audio source module regularly captures audio frames from an audio device (normally the default waveform output device). The captured frames which normally are in default mode are copied by the audio source module to a buffer shared with the encoder. The buffer may either be in lock mode or unlock mode. The encoder will be awakened each time an audio frame is generated to encrypt the new frame. To make the programming interface of Cloud based Gaming simple, we store each sample of audio frames as a 32-bit signed integer. One problem which needs to be handled by audio source module is the problem of frame discontinuity. When no sound is generated in the gaming environment, then audio source has two options. The audio read function may return either 1 (an audio frame with all zeros) or 2 (an error code information indicating that no active frames are currently available). For improved efficiency in the second case, an audio source module must even emit silent audio frames to the encoder because encoders generally expect continuous audio frames irrespective of the case whether the sound is audible or not. Therefore, an audio source input module must emit silent (all 0's) audio frames in the second case to resolve the frame discontinuity problem. This solves the problem of out of order audio packets and also removes jitter (uneven delay in audio packets). It is observed that modern Windows games using WASAPI, suffer from the frame discontinuity problem.

Frame Encoding

Audio and video frames are encoded by two different encoder modules, which are launched when there is a minimum of one client connected to the game server. Cloud based gaming presently supports two encoding modes first is single-encoder-for-all and second is one-encoder-per-client to support different usage conditions. In the single-encoder-for-all mode, the cumulative frames generated by a frame source are only read and encoded by one encoder irrespective of the number of users or game players. Therefore, two encoders, one for video frames and another for audio frames, are responsible for all sorts of encoding tasks. The benefit of single-encoder-mode is enhanced efficiency as the CPU usage doesn't increases when there are multiple users. All the video and audio frames are encoded only once and the encoded frames are delivered cumulatively to the corresponding clients in a unicast fashion (Chen & Huang, 2013). On the other hand, the one-encoder-per-client mode allocates a dedicated encoder for each client, either a player or an observer. The advantage of one-encoder-per-client is that it can use different encoding stimulations and compression techniques, such as bit rate, resolution, and quality parameters, for different clients. However, the consumption of CPU resources will also increase proportionally with the number of encoders. According to a case study an encoder with 1280x720 resolution and 28 fps increases the CPU utilization by nearly 10% on an Intel 2.66 GHz i5 CPU processor. In this way, a game server can only take a load of 10 users or players at most when only one game instance is active. After multilevel comparisons between the single-encoder-for-all mode and one-encoder-per-client mode, decisions are made. It has a huge impact on the performance of a Cloud based Gaming System. Currently, both the video and audio encoder modules are implemented using the libavcodec library.

Input Handling

The input handling module is executed as an independent thread. This module has two major responsibilities. First is to capture input events on the client side and second is to replay the events occurring at the client side of the game server. Unlike audio and video frames, input event fragments are delivered with the help of a unique connection, which can be TCP or UDP. Though it is possible to make use of the RTSP connection for sending input events from the client side to the server side, but it is not used extensively because of following reasons.

1. There might be a delay in delivery of input events due to RTSP packets which are sent via same connection framework.

2. There might be delay in delivery of input events because of RTSP configurations and transfer mechanism. RTSP is text-based and parsing text is very time consuming.
3. There is no mechanism for embedding input events in an RTSP connection. This makes our job tiring and as a result we need to modify the RTSP library and continuously make the system more difficult to maintain and transmit.

The implementation of the input handling module is trivially platform-dependent because the input event structure is more or less OS- and library-dependent. We need different mechanisms for handling input fragments coming from different OS's. They are processed separately according to different configurations. On receiving an input event, the input handling module first converts the received input event into the format compatible with the server and sends the event structure or schema to the server. Cloud based Gaming replays input events using the Send Input function on Windows and the XTEST semantics library on Linux. For most desktop and game applications, the above replay functions work very efficiently but for some games it adopts different approaches for capturing and retrieving user inputs. For example, consider the case of Batman and Limbo, the SendInput function on Windows doesn't works properly which are two popular action adventure games. In such situations, Cloud based Gaming architecture can be configured to use other input replay methods, such as getting access of the GetRawInputData function on Windows to provide input events whenever the function is called by the games.

Figure 1. Client module

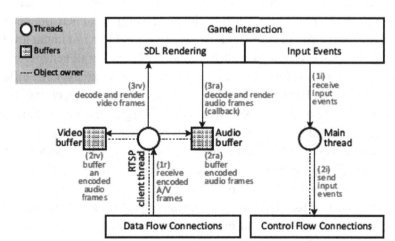

RTSP, RTP, and RTCP Client

In the Cloud based Gaming client, we use the live555 library to incorporate multilevel network communications. The live555 library is completely C++ based with an event-driven architecture. Here the class framework of live555 is exploited to the maximum extent and is incorporated with the RTSP Client and MediaSink classes to register call-back functions that handles multiple network events (Huang & Chang, 2013). Once the RTSP client has successfully initialized the audio and video sessions, then two sink classes are required to manage the encoded audio and video frames that are received from the server. Both sink classes are trivially inherited from the MediaSink class and are implemented with the help of virtual functions called the PLAY command.

Frame Buffering and Decoding

To improve the gaming experience in terms of latency, the video decoder currently doesn't buffer video frames at all. The video buffer is simply used to buffer packets that are associated with the current video frame. It is so because live555 provides enormous amounts of packet payloads without an RTP header and the marker bits labelled on each packet are used to detect whether consecutive packets correspond to the same video frame or not. This means that if a newly received data fragment has a zero marker bit value i.e. the current packet being received is not the last packet associated with the video frame then it will be appended into the buffer otherwise the decoder will decode a video fragment based on all the packets currently present in the buffer slot. It the empties the buffer and places the newly arrived fragment into the buffer. Though this zero-buffering strategy may lead to inconsistency in video playback under prolonged conditions of network delays, but it reduces the input-response delay due to video play out to a minimum level. This design of Cloud based Gaming architecture can yield an overall better cloud gaming experience. In this architecture design the audio frames are handled differently as compared to video frames (Hsu & Chang, 2013). Upon the receiving the audio frames, the RTSP client thread doesn't decodes the fragments, but instead it simply places all the received frames on a shared buffer which generally follows a FIFO implementation. This is because the audio rendering of SDL is performed using recursive demand approach i.e. to play audio in SDL, a callback function needs to be initialized and registered and it is called whenever SDL requires audio frames for playback. The callback function gets the audio packets from the shared buffer setup and then decrypts them and places the decrypted audio fragments into the specified memory address.

Input Handling

The input handling module on the client has two major responsibilities. One is to capture input commands made by game players, and the other is to send captured events to the dedicated server. When an input event is recorded, the complete event structure or schema is sent to the server directly. Even after this the client still has to tell the server the format and the cumulative length of a recorded input event. Presently Cloud based Gaming supports the mechanism for cross-platform SDL event recording. In addition, on certain platforms it also provides more autonomous and dedicated input capture mechanisms to generate information about complete game environment.

SERVICE PROVIDERS OF CLOUD GAMING SERVICES

Cloud Gaming generally called gaming on demand, is a type of online gaming that allows direct and on-demand streaming of games depending on users' choice to his computer via dedicated thin client. In this case the actual game is stored on the company's server and is propagated directly to computers accessing the server through the dedicated client.

The cloud has certainly changed user perceptions. It has created a new plethora of opportunities for various prevalent market products. The idea of storing data and streaming it through off-site servers has drastically changed the way people perceive and act on such situations. All activities ranging from backing up computer info to accessing music, movies and TV shows have changed drastically. The cloud is becoming so common in daily computing that most of the time people don't even realize that their email's and social media accounts are actually an example of cloud-based applications. But that's not the end, cloud gaming is becoming more and more popular day by day. This is clearly visible in many ways, including the fact that Microsoft and Sony's next-gen gaming consoles are heavily based on cloud gaming. It involves the same technique of transferring data via dedicated servers and clients. The main reason behind the success of cloud gaming market is smooth and easy flow of data via dedicated servers and less hardware requirements for game setup. Now day's gamers have lots of options for Cloud Gaming entertainment provided they have a normal computer with a healthy Internet connection. Since then Cloud gaming has generated a lot of interest among entrepreneurs, venture capitalists, and researchers. Startup companies have offered or plan to offer cloud gaming services, such as GaiKai, OnLive, Ubitus, OTOY, and T5-Labs, all of them having varied realizations. For example, some systems are only accessible via clients on PCs through dedicated servers, while others can be accessed via TVs with automated set-top boxes. Let us see the system architecture of some real world service providers of cloud based gaming.

G-Cluster

G-cluster Global Corp. is a company from Finland that offers good cloud gaming service using IPTV set-top boxes provided to operators so that they can make use of white-label cloud gaming platforms which helps users to play across television and various mobile devices. G-cluster is capable of turning the television into a set-top-box-like device with portable multi-platform cloud gaming on TVs, computers and tablets. G-cluster offers pseudo multiple primary screen options as part of a prevalent network-based content offering system. It adds value to wireless high speed data product devices, or OTT as an individual game product. Games are delivered finally with low latency, bandwidth efficient variable bit rate MPEG 2, MPEG 4 or H.294 and streams them client devices using dedicated server technology with fully independent and error-free architecture. It is compatible with Windows Vista, Windows 7, Windows 8, Windows 8.1, Windows 10, iOS, Windows Phone.

OnLive

OnLive was first announced at GDC (Game Developers Conference) 2009. Onlive is one of the most popular cloud-gaming sites. The reason behind this is that it streams some of the most popular games and this service isn't just limited to computers it even streams to mobile devices such as tablets and smartphones as well. Other major reason of its high popularity is due to the fact that it offers no-commitment causes to users and they can easily play after a free signup to the site. The Game system developed by OnLive consists of a Wireless Controller and a console, which is called MicroConsole, which can be connected to a television and directly to the OnLive service, so one can also possibly use the service without the need of a computer. The system comes with several accessories needed to connect all the equipment. MicroConsole supports up to 4 wireless controllers and several Bluetooth headsets. Multiple USB ports are available for controllers, mice, keyboards, and USB hubs. Video and audio output is managed by HDMI, TOSLINK ports and analog stereo minijack. Ethernet port is used for network access, to access the OnLive service. It is compatible with Windows Vista, Windows 7, Windows 8, Windows 8.1 and Windows 10.

Spoon

Spoon is the leading service provider in application virtualization and cloud gaming technologies. Spoon helps users to launch desktop games from the web with no prior installation, so user can test and play games instantly as and when required. Spoon has more than thousand apps which are available from the cloud with a simple browser plugin and no hectic installation. Spoon Cloud Gaming provides huge variety to its users. It allows users to choose from more than 200 games and play them on their will. Spoon provides all services with minimum latency and maximum bandwidth for easy and smooth flow of data via dedicated servers and clients. In order to give users a better gaming experience, Spoon uses both local and remote computer resources and matches up the load to minimize bandwidth requirements and reduces the jitter to an all-time low value. It is compatible with Windows Vista, Windows 7, Windows 8, Windows 8.1 and Windows 10.

StreamMyGame

StreamMyGame is developed as a software streaming solution that enables multiple Microsoft based games and applications to be played remotely on Linux and Windows devices. It was released in October 2007, as a Windows only software. In addition to streaming games over a LAN network, StreamMyGame can also be used over broadband networks, with a prerequisite that these connections should provide a minimum speed of 2 Mb/s. Members have to select any game they want to play on the StreamMyGame website and then the website sends an encrypted signal to the server, and the server responds by starting the game and capturing the video and audio. The video and audio is then sent to the player using a real time streaming protocol and displayed. The player on the user's computer captures keyboard and mouse commands and sends these inputs back to the hosting server, which are fed into the game and are used to control the game. StreamMyGame also enable its members to communicate with a Web 2.0 website, which includes messaging, chat forums and groups. They can use group permissions to enable other members to share and use their games. StreamMyGame's forums are predominantly used to publish the performance details and specs of StreamMyGame, when they are used with new and existing games. It is compatible with Windows 7, XP and Vista, along with Ubuntu, Fedora, Red Hat, Xandros, Yellow Dog Linux and Debian.

Ubitus

Ubitus platform offers cloud gaming services that allows users to play high-end games and console video games processed on remote servers via dedicated thin clients. It allows users to choose from a large variety of games and play them on their will. Ubitus provides all services with minimum latency and maximum bandwidth for easy and smooth flow of data via dedicated servers and clients. In order to give users a better gaming experience, Ubitus uses both local and remote computer resources and matches up the load to minimize bandwidth requirements and reduces the jitter to an all-time low value. It is compatible with Windows Vista, Windows 7, Windows 8, Windows 8.1 and Windows 10. Ubitus was founded in 2007 and now expand office locations in Taipei, Beijing, Guangzhou, Seoul, and Tokyo.

GaiKai

GaiKai was founded in 2008, and since then is at the forefront of cloud gaming revolution. It delivers access to streaming games to millions of users on laptops, PlayStation platforms, PCs, TVs and even more. They claim to have built the world's fastest open cloud gaming platform, thus enabling game streaming on connected smart TVs and mobile devices. In the beginning it started as video game advertising platform, but since then has evolved to streaming games to multiple popular websites available on the internet. Two business models are used by GaiKai for its cloud gaming services namely AD network and Open Platform. In Ad Network model, once the customer has gone through the demo then they are given a choice to purchase the game or product from an online retailer or any reputed source, local retailer or directly download the game. Ad Network, was launched in March, 2011 and has reached over 13 million monthly active users by the end of the year. Several Websites which later joined the network were mainly responsible for multiple high-end PC games as embedded advertising and later received in return a share of the marketing revenue generated from games streamed to users, who got opportunity to play demos free of charge.

CHALLENGES IN CLOUD BASED GAMING

The cloud based gaming has fostered the introduction of multiplayer aspects in majority of games, so that the gaming experiences can be shared with friends and family. Earlier games were sold on CDs and DVDs but now most gamers purchase them on digital platforms like Xbox Live, Steam etc. Though all these advantages seem to be very effective but still cloud based gaming has many challenges ahead before it can truly take off. First and most deadly challenge is that it requires high-speed Internet and huge bandwidth for users to have online gaming experience. Temporary loss of connection, power loss, network congestion etc. could cause great trouble to the gamers. It is not possible for every user to have a high internet speed. The biggest challenge in cloud based gaming is its design considerations, which are currently being addressed by various cloud gaming service providers. A basic Cloud based Gaming system collects player's commands or actions, transmits them to the cloud server, executes the actions, renders the results, encrypts or compresses the resulting changes to the game world environment and finally streams the video (periodically captured game scenes) back to the player/user (Shea, 2013). To make all this hustle free and smooth, all of the above specified serial operations must happen within fraction of seconds. Trivially this amount of time is defined as Interaction delay and efforts must be made to keep this delay as small as possible in order to provide a better gaming experience to the cloud game Player.

Interaction Delay

Though there is much similarity between interaction delay tolerances for trivial gaming and cloud based gaming, we must mark following critical points. Firstly, in traditional gaming the interaction delay was only related to multiplayer online gaming systems and was not considered for single player games but in Cloud based gaming it is not the case. Since here all the games are rendered remotely and cumulatively streamed back to the player irrespective of game being single player or multi player. So now we have to even take care of tolerance delays in case of single player games. In traditional online gaming systems, the effects of interaction delays are not much visible because of the rendering actions on the local system of the user even much before it reaches to the main server (Shea & Liu, 2013). For example, if the user instructs the avatar/hero to move and it spontaneously starts the movement locally on the system whereas the gaming server may not receive the position or command update for several milliseconds. Thus in Cloud based gaming there will be some lag and delay. This lag is accounted because of the player's commands being encoded, transferred, executed on dedicated game servers and then finally the current game environment scene is captured and rendered and sent back to the player via data flow network. The client is not able to hide the interaction delay from the player (Shea & Liu, 2013). Because of this even the mouse cursor movement can be delayed by up to 1000 ms, making it very difficult for the player to tolerate such long interaction delays. Maximum allowed interaction delay for all games hosted in a cloud gaming environment should be at most 200 ms. The situation is even more complicated in case of high action games, where players cannot tolerate even minute interaction delays. So the maximum permitted delay for high action games is 100 ms.

Video Streaming and Encryption

Now we will examine the challenges faced in video streaming and its encryption in cloud based gaming. We observe that the video streaming and encoding needs of a cloud based gaming system is more or less similar to live media streaming. Both these applications i.e. cloud based gaming and live media streaming must quickly encrypt and compress the incoming videos and transmit it to end users. For both cases, we are only concerned with a small set of recent video frames and have no access to future frames. Though we can access previous frames from the buffer but it's also of no use depending on the current gaming environment (Shea & Liu, 2013). This implies that encryption needs to be done only with respect to very few fragments. But on digging deeper we find that live video streaming and cloud based gaming have important differences as well. The most important difference is that Cloud based Gaming has zero buffer capacity on client side as compared to live media streaming which has a very large buffer capacity. This is so because when a player issues a command or a move to the local client, the command must reach to the cloud via internet, must be processed according to the game logic, cumulatively combined by the processing unit, compressed by the video encoder and transmitted back to the player with integrated scenes of current gaming environment. Utmost care should be taken that all these actions and reactions are completed within 100-200 ms. The presence of a video encoder is of paramount importance. It is the efficiency of video encoder which decides the latency incurred (Shea & Liu, 2013). The better the encoding mechanism, the lower will be the latency for the setup. Presently, the major cloud gaming service providers Gaikai and Onlive both implement video encoding via H.264/MPEG-4 AVC encoder. Gaikai totally believes in making tweaks in software setups for improved efficiency whereas OnLive focusses on using specialized hardware to compress its cloud gaming video streams.

Latency

Latency has been one of the major problems in cloud based gaming services. A lot of research by tech giants such as OnLive and Microsoft are still going on to reduce the latency as much as possible, but it is a serious issue which hampers the smooth gaming experience of the user. Latency depends on various factors which when considered together can lead to shocking results (Simon & Rosenberg, 2012). Network delay is the total round trip time which includes the time required to send the game request to the game servers and receiving the response from the servers. It is also usually referred to as the Round-Trip Time (RTT). Processing delay is the difference between the time when the server receives the game request from the client and the generation of the first response signal from the server. In other words, it is the time taken by the server to process the player's command (made from the client). Playout delay is the difference between the time interval when the client receives the encoded form of the response from the server and the time taken by the client to decode the response to present on the screen. The overall response delay (RD) is the sum of network delay, processing delay and the playout delay.

Jitter

Jitter is defined as uneven variation in the delay of received packets. At the sender side, packets are sent in a continuous manner with the packets being spaced evenly but due to network congestion and configuration errors this steady stream comes out of order or the delay between each packet changes unevenly i.e. the packets reach receiver side out of order. Thus it leads to poor game performance and bad user experience. It may lead to a situation where the next effect of the action occurs before the current effect which not only confuses the user but also leads to non-periodic occurrence of events. This creates a situation of dilemma. Most of the companies are currently working on this challenging aspect of cloud gaming.

FUTURE SCOPE OF CLOUD BASED GAMING

Most people have a thought that the future of gaming lies in the cloud. Billions of dollars are currently being invested in cloud gaming from various areas of the video game business. In recent years there has been an influx of activity surrounding cloud gaming. OnLive tried to expand its game catalog to Vizio televisions as well as mobile platforms. Gaikai has partnered with Intel, Bigfoot and EA to provide free game demos directly to the customers. In due course of time, the world's largest retailer—GameStop—jumped into the space with the facilities and support of Spawn Labs and Impulse. Cloud based gaming services obviously has a very bright future. It can provide gaming experiences which has never been felt before. Since cloud gaming has large number of advantages especially that it will greatly reduce the loss which the game industry suffers out of piracy, most of the game developers are focusing on shifting into cloud services. It will also provide gaming experiences to those users who might otherwise have not even picked up video games. Because of easy availability and no much complications, cloud gaming will be made available to most of the audience. The only prerequisite of cloud gaming is a normal computer and good internet speed. In this process, it will indirectly serve to foster further acceptance of the cloud, gradually as more and more users get familiarized with the working of cloud.

Within such a limited span of time, cloud gaming has made great progress in the marketing industry. It has greatly reduced the hardware requirements for playing various high end games. Even as of now, cloud computing has made sufficient amount of progress in gaming industry. We can consider the example of Valve, which offers steam cloud with no independent servers where a user is allowed to upload their profile and save games to an online server which can be accessed by any device connected to the steam cloud thus providing a smooth functioning of file sharing and easy data flow. Considering the amount of progress which has already been made in cloud gaming as is evident, it is obvious that the future of cloud gaming is going to be bright. Different multinational corporations are showing deep interest in the field of cloud gaming. Big firms like Microsoft, Sony, OnLive, Amazon are investing huge amounts of money to promote research works in this particular field. The major field of work in cloud gaming is to reduce the jitter and latency and to maximize the performance with given bandwidth. According to Microsoft, gamers can notice a delay of around 60 milliseconds on a multiplayer game but as the delay gradually increases to above 100 milliseconds and then to 200 milliseconds range the user starts getting annoyed and feels bored. Every game on cloud has some lag/delay but smaller the delay, the better it is from user's point of view. Cloud games with smaller delay's and jitter provide better user experience. Microsoft claims that in near future their product DeLorean can create an awesome gaming experience to the gamers even if the delay is around 200 milliseconds as they are using the trick of keeping the user busy in simultaneous actions. Similarly, Gaikai is Sony's one of the most trusted product after which the company announced a PlayStation.

According to above discussions it is quite evident that cloud gaming has a very bright future. The main obstacle in the advancement of cloud gaming is the delay and jitter during data transfer via dedicated servers. Huge investments are being made in this field to support various research works. If these challenges are overcome in near future then it is very sure that Cloud Gaming is going to be the future of tomorrow's world.

REFERENCES

Alexander, K. (2012, August). *Fat client game streaming or cloud gaming*. Akamai Blog. Retrieved from https://blogs.akamai.com/2012/08/part-2-fat-client-game-streaming-or-cloud-gaming.html

Chen, K.-T., Chang, Y.-C., Hsu, H.-J., Chen, D.-Y., Huang, C.-Y., & Hsu, C.-H. (2014). On the Quality of Service of Cloud Gaming Systems. *IEEE Transactions on Multimedia, 16*(2).

Claypool, M., & Claypool, K. (2006). Latency and Player Actions in Online Games. *Communications of the ACM, 49*(11), 40. doi:10.1145/1167838.1167860

Eisert, P., & Fechteler, P. (2008). Low delay streaming of computer graphics. In *Proc. IEEE ICIP 2008.*

Lai, A., & Nieh, J. (2006). On the performance of wide-area thin-client computing. *ACM Transactions on Computer Systems, 24*(2), 175–209. doi:10.1145/1132026.1132029

Mark Claypool and David Finkel. (2012). *The Effects of Latency on Player Performance in Cloud-based Games.* Burnaby, Canada: ACM Publications.

Pantel, L., & Wolf, L. C. (2002). On the Impact of Delay on Real-Time Multi-player Games. ACM NOSSDAV, Miami, FL. doi:doi:10.1145/507670.507674 doi:10.1145/507670.507674

Shea, R., Liu, J., Ngai, E. C.-H., & Cui, Y. (2011). *Cloud Computing: architecture and performance.* Computer Science and Interactive Media & Game Development Worcester Polytechnic Institute Worcester.

Sony. (2008, November). *Started the company.* Retrieved from https://www.gaikai.com/

Chapter 5
EAC–MPCG:
Efficient Access Control for Multi–Player Cloud Games

Sudha Senthilkumar
VIT University, India

V. Madhu Viswanatham
VIT University, India

ABSTRACT

Online gaming allows players from different location to play synchronously together for entertainment. Generally multimedia applications which is highly latency sensitive and it requires specific hardware, such as Graphic Processing Units (GPUs) and fast memory. Since recent advances in cloud computing makes it suitable for moving the gaming application to the cloud and streams the video sequence back to the player over the Internet. This is more beneficial for less powerful computational devices that are otherwise incapable of running high-quality games. In addition to this cloud gaming is platform independence means it allow you to play on your android or IOS powered devices. There are several cloud providers like On-Live, G-Cluster and GFACE are provides active game services. However, providing proper access control for games which require license to play various levels is one of the important requirements to play the online games. This paper proposes the suitable access control mechanism to provide the access to cloud gaming applications.

DOI: 10.4018/978-1-5225-0546-4.ch005

INTRODCTION

Cloud gaming is one way of online game distribution. The most general way to implement cloud gaming are either by using video streaming or by file streaming. The clients for availing the gaming services are using the computers, consoles or mobile devices or any other thin clients. The games are executed and the results are stored at the cloud server side and finally the graphical results are shown at the users end using any clients. This enables the client system can access and play the game without using large storage devices only by using the internet connection. This will fulfil the user's need who wants to play the games without downloading it and loading it in their system. The user button pressing actions are directly passed to the cloud server, then it will be recorded and finally the response are send back to the cloud users about their gaming score. There are several industries are offering this type of gaming services such as Onlive, PlayKey, G-Cluster and Ubitus. (Shea et al. 2013).

The gaming service utilizes the internet connection, cluster servers and cryptographic technique and compression method to stream the game information to a user's device. At present, MMOGs works as client-server paradigm, where the cloud servers used in game service simulate the game environment and receive the request from users and execute it and distribute the response through the internet. The billing and accounting system are integrated with this game server. Generally, the game servers are introduced by specific companies called as Hosters that rent their computational and network capabilities for executing game servers with assured Quality of Service (QoS). Most cloud online gaming platforms are proprietary.

The file streaming (Cloud Gaming, June 2015) based cloud gaming technique that require the game downloading at the client in which only the small percentage of game is downloaded so that the player can start playing immediately. The rest of the game information is downloaded to the client device while they are playing. This enables the prompt access to games with less bandwidth broadband connections. This type of cloud gaming requires the necessity processor capabilities to play the game. Organization that use this type of cloud gaming comprise Kalydo, Approxy, and SpawnApps.

The multiplayer online game can be played by game server through the internet connection with other game players all over the world. Some known examples of this involve fighting games, sports games and first-person shooters. These games are different from massively multiplayer online game (MMOGs), which do not simulate the persistent world, but create a playing environment for the drive of a single game or round. In other way, they depend on a game listening server which is used for that round, and like that more enormous servers all around the world. Alternatively, MMOGs depend on dedicated servers, since these games must be running constantly. (Hampel et al. 2006; Fiedler et al. 2002).

CLOUD GAMING SYSTEM

Recently, there are several gaming systems available for offering game services. Those are all listed as Steam In-Home Streaming, Remote Play, Cloud Gaming eXtreme, Ubitus GameCloud, and StreamMyGame:

- **Steam:** (Cloud Gaming, 23 January 2016) Offers the installation and automatic updating of games on multiple systems. It delivers a free application programming interface (API) known as Steam works, which is used by the developer to incorporate much of the steam's functions into their products. However originally established for use on Microsoft Windows, later on it is released for Linux operating systems as well. As of September 2015, above 6,400 games are available over Steam, including over 2,300 for Windows OS and 1,500 for Linux.
- **Remote Play:** (Remote Play, 2 January 2016) A feature of Sony Video Console that permits the PlayStation 3 and PlayStation 4 to transmit its video and audio output to a PlayStation Portable or PlayStation Vita.

Remote play is not much implemented on PlayStation 3, it is mandatory feature on all PlayStation 4 games, excluding the games that utilize peripherals for example PlayStation Move.

- **StreamMyGame:** (Cloud Gaming, 23 January 2016) A type of software-oriented game streaming solution that allows Microsoft Windows-based games and applications to be played remotely on Windows and Linux based devices. It was first launched on 26 October 2007 as Windows-only software. Later on it introduces Linux version in January 2008 for its game player. Other than streaming games over a local network, StreamMyGame can also be used through broadband networks though these broadband connections need a minimum bandwidth of 2 Mbit/s.

CLOUD GAMING SERVICES

There are several gaming services offered by cloud environment such as GameNow, GameFly Streaming, G-cluster, GFace, Kalydo, LoudPlay, Leap Computing, Play-Giga, PlayKey, TurboGames. (Huang et al., 2013, pp. 36-47):

- **GameFly:** (Sam et al., 2nd Jun 2015) An online video game subscription service that focuses in providing games for game consoles. The business model of GameFly is more or less similar to the DVD-by- mail subscription service Netflix and Blockbuster online. GameFly rents games to subscribers for a monthly basis.

- **GFACE:** A web-oriented gaming service that is owned and functioned by Crytek. The service is considered to help users come across people and play multiplayer video games with their friends.
- **Kalydo:** a proprietary cloud gaming technology and gaming service based on file streaming method. The Kalydo platform released in market by 2008 and has been in functional yet. The Kalydo file streaming technology permits games to be played directly, without the requirement of downloading and installation in their own system, given that faster and easier access to games. The Kalydo can run on browser or from the PC desktop by installing Kalydo Player plugin.
- **PlayStation Now:** A cloud gaming service that permits users need to pay for access original PlayStation 3 on either a per-game basis or via a subscription. Non-PlayStation devices will require a DualShock 3 or 4 controllers for their service.

All these gaming services require a suitable access control scheme in order to provide an access only to the authorized users who have offered the online gaming services. With the intention of this, we have proposed a scheme that will offer an efficient and fine-grained access control for online gaming which utilizes the cloud servers.

PROPOSED SCHEME

The Figure 1 denotes the cloud gaming architecture which consists of Gaming clients, database server, cloud service provider, Gaming server, Billing and Accounting system:

- **Clients:** The Gaming clients can be a normal desktop, Mobile devices or any other thin client. It requests the cloud service provider to access the online game through the internet
- **Cloud Service Provider:** An entity who will offer the gaming services to the clients. At the same time, it verifies the client credentials and if it is valid it forward the request to the gaming server.
- **Gaming Server:** A dedicated server equipped with high computation power used for installing the online games. (Diao, 2013)

- **Database Server:** An entity used to store the game related contents such as scoring details and the current session details.
- **Billing and Accounting Server:** Used to track usage of the cloud services by the client. According to these values billing details generated and reported to the client.

The client is entities who are accessing the game server through the broadband connection. The client requests the cloud service provider to avail the online game service. The cloud service provider maintains the list of registered users according to the game level they are permitted to play based on their subscription. As per our scheme the user lists are maintained using the cuckoo filter data structure. The cuckoo filter simplifies the item insertion, deletion and lookup operation efficiently than any other data structures such as bloom filter or linked list. Based on the client request, the CSP verifies the user registration details in its database and grants the access if they are the authorized users to play the requested game. The client request redirected to the game server in which the games are installed. Further, the client can directly avail the services from the game server. Whenever their playing time exceeded their subscription time, the notifications send to the CSP from game server. So that the clients are restricted to avail the game service. Simultaneously, the information is transferred to the billing and accounting server (Table 1).

Figure 1. System architecture for cloud gaming

Table 1. Glossary

Notations	Description
C	Client
CSP	Cloud Service Provider
CS	Cloud Server
S_P_H	Subscription_ Period_Hour
Gl	Game Level
client_console_i/p	Client console input
pass_game_result	Pass the game result
Acc_Bill_Ser	Account and Bill Server
DS	Database Server
fetch_store_update_info	Fetches and updates the game information

Procedure for EAC-MPCG Scheme

Algorithm for EAC-MPCG

Step 1: The user requests the cloud service provider for playing online games with its registration details.

$$C \xrightarrow{E_k(id,pwd)} CSP$$

Step 2: The cloud service provider verifies the authentication of the user, their authorization level and their subscription details and, if it is satisfactory, forwards the request to cloud server.

```
if(c (id, pwd) = valid)
{
verify(uAuth(gl))
if(S_P_Hour > 0) then
{
```

$$CSP \xrightarrow{fwd\_req,tk(tkid,s\_p\_hour,gl)} CS$$

```
while(user_complete_play || s_p_hour){
```

$$C \xrightarrow{\substack{client\_console\_i/p}} CS(exec(req\_game))$$

$$CS \xrightarrow{\substack{pass\_game\_result}} C$$

```
}
}
else
msg "your subscription period expired"
}
else
msg "You are not authorized user"
```

Step 3: Subsequently, the cloud server sends the updated information to the database server.

$$CS \xrightarrow{\substack{fetch\_and\_store\_update\_info}} DS$$

Step 4: Further, cloud server passes the usage details to the accounting and billing server.

$$CSP \xrightarrow{\substack{usage\_info}} Acc\_Bill\_Ser$$

Step 5: Subsequently, the CSP updates its user list with the recent user usage information such as subscription period in terms of hours.

```
CSP → user_info_details(s_p_hours)
```

Cuckoo Filter Data Structure

The cuckoo filter (Fan et al., 2013, pp.75-88) is an efficient data structure for set-membership queries in which user information can be inserted and deleted within O (1) computation time. It uses the hash table called as cuckoo hash table which stores the fingerprints (i.e. random hash values) for each user information. We have

112

used the token id as random hash values that could be used to identify the group information. The client subscription details are grouped according to the game license level that they possess. It makes our scheme more efficient in terms of the insertion, deletion and lookup operation.

CONCLUSION

We have proposed the efficient access control scheme for multiplayer cloud games which are currently emerging service offered by the cloud environment. According to our scheme, the cuckoo filters are used for user details insertion, deletion and updation in CSP will drastically reduce the computation complexity of our scheme. In addition all the communications between the various entities are established with secure SSL connection protects the data level threats by the hackers. As a future work, we will implement this scheme in private cloud and evaluate the feasibility of our work in implementing public cloud service providers.

REFERENCES

Claypool, M., & Claypool, K. (2006). Latency and player actions in online games. *Communications of the ACM*, *49*(11), 40–45. doi:10.1145/1167838.1167860

Cloud Gaming. (n.d.). In *Encyclopedia*. Retrieved from 23rd January 2016. https://en.wikipedia.org/wiki/Cloud_gaming

Diao, Z. (2013). *Consistency models for cloud-based online games: the storage system's perspective*. Liebe Teilnehmerinnen und Teilnehmer.

Fan, B., Andersen, D. G., Kaminsky, M., & Mitzenmacher, M. D. (2014, December). Cuckoo Filter: Practically Better Than Bloom. In *Proceedings of the 10th ACM International on Conference on emerging Networking Experiments and Technologies* (pp. 75-88). ACM.

Fiedler, S., Wallner, M., & Weber, M. (2002, April). A communication architecture for massive multiplayer games. In *Proceedings of the 1st workshop on Network and system support for games*. (pp. 14-22). ACM. doi:10.1145/566500.566503

Hampel, T., Bopp, T., & Hinn, R. (2006, October). A peer-to-peer architecture for massive multiplayer online games. In *Proceedings of 5th ACM SIGCOMM workshop on Network and system support for games*.ACM. doi:10.1145/1230040.1230058

Huang, C. Y., Hsu, C. H., Chang, Y. C., & Chen, K. T. (2013, February). Gaming-Anywhere: an open cloud gaming system. In *Proceedings of the 4th ACM multimedia systems conference*. (pp. 36-47). ACM. doi:10.1145/2483977.2483981

Remote Play. (n.d.). In *Encyclopedia*. Retrieved from 2nd January 2016. https://en.wikipedia.org/wiki/Remote_Play

Sam Machkovech. (2015*). GameFly launches cloud-streaming video game service on Amazon Fire TV Ars Technica*. Retrieved from 2nd June, 2015. http://arstechnica.com/gaming/2015/06/gamefly-launches-cloud-streaming-video-game-service-on-amazon-fire-tv/

Shea, R., Liu, J., Ngai, E., & Cui, Y. (2013). Cloud gaming: Architecture and performance. *IEEE Network*, *27*(4), 16–21. doi:10.1109/MNET.2013.6574660

Chapter 6
Issues in On-Demand Cloud-Based Gaming Storage:
Quality of Service and Quality of Experience

Ebin Deni Raj
VIT University, India

L. D. Dhinesh Babu
VIT University, India

ABSTRACT

Cloud computing is the most utilized and evolving technology in the past few years and has taken computing to a whole new level such that even common man is receiving the benefits. The end user in cloud computing always prefers a cloud service provider which is efficient, reliable and best quality of service at the lowest possible price. A cloud based gaming system relieves the player from the burden of possessing high end processing and graphic units. The storage of games hosted in clouds using the latest technologies in cloud has been discussed in detail. The Quality of service of games hosted in cloud is the main focus of this chapter and we have proposed a mathematical model for the same. The various factors in dealing with the quality of service on cloud based games have been analyzed in detail. The quality of experience of cloud based games and its relation with quality of service has been derived. This chapter focuses on the various storage techniques, quality of experience factors and correlates the same with QoS in cloud based games.

DOI: 10.4018/978-1-5225-0546-4.ch006

INTRODUCTION

Online cloud based games have picked up such a great amount of prominence in the most recent years and the credit is shared by distributed computing and the increased utilization of mobile phones. Distributed computing has risen as the most utilized computing system by majority of the clients. The advancement in mobile, cloud and graphics technologies gave rise to a new filed named mobile cloud gaming. A new paradigm named gaming as a service (GaaS) was introduced to stream games across the internet (Cloud Gaming – Gaming as a Service (GaaS) | NVIDIA GRID). GaaS delivers video games to users and reduce the power consumption of the user's mobile device and provide storage for user's game data. Cloud computing enabled better scalability and cost effectiveness and accelerated the growth of online apps (Raj E. D., Babu, Ariwa, Nirmala, & Krishna., 2014). Gaming on-demand has made cloud computing to merge with the online gaming technology (Kamarainen, Siekkinen, Xiao, & Yla-Jaaski., 2014).

The expectation of game players for a better gaming experience and the massively multi player online games (MMOGs) has led to the foundation of cloud gaming. Cloud gaming architecture helps in distribution of workload among multiple cloud servers and clients. The advantages of cloud gaming includes scalability, reduced cost, and elastic nature of cloud computing (L.D. Dhinesh., Gunasekaran, & Krishna, 2014). Games have volatile customer base and there are instances where games become popular overnight. Online gaming performance and experience depends on lot of factors which includes network Quality of service (QoS), and quality of experience (QoE). Cloud based game developers takes into account the network deficiency and game experience from a user perspective. Game engines are the core part of any online gaming system. In traditional online games and cloud based games has a significant difference in the underlying technology. In online games, the user requires the graphic processing units, and powerful processors to play the game effectively. In cloud based games the input from the user is received and sent to the game server and the user requires just a video rendering display. The only constraints in cloud based gaming is how quickly and consistently users can access the game servers deployed over a cloud. The solutions to these constraints are discussed in detail in the sections quality of service and quality of experience in cloud based games.

While the idea of cloud gaming itself is not novel, the exponential levels of popularity for playing games over a scope of different stages has driven up the business sector for facilitating recreations on the cloud (Google App Engine) (Windows Azure). The mobile-friendly market is quickly attesting itself as the bedrock for diversions that most clients appreciate. A mobile game player client joined on a 3G network system would not need to download the whole game to play. The player can play the game without spending energy to install and validate the game in the mobile device. The cloud based gaming platforms interlock two different technologies namely cloud computing and online gaming to provide a better environment for the game lovers.

In the initial years, the players were charged with a nominal subscription fee to play online games. Right pricing for the game is a crucial element in deciding the demand for the game. As already discussed, the game players is a temporary, floating population and instances of games becoming viral overnight is not rare (Li, Liu, & Tang, 2011). The gaming time, preferences, and genre preference varies with different people and geographical location. Cloud based gaming applications has become common with the introduction of smartphones and high speed internet connectivity. The increased popularity of online social networks has also triggered the exponential growth of cloud based games (Raj & Babu, 2015). The revenue of any cloud based game comes from mainly three categories:

1.   Providing Freemium/Lite versions of the game and charging a fee for advanced versions.
2.   In-App purchases from online game stores
3.   Revenue in the form of Advertisements.

This book chapter is arranged in such a way that the initial sections discuss about the storage of games in the cloud, and then about the quality of service and quality of experience in cloud based games. The final sections of the chapter give an overview of the pricing strategies in cloud based games.

CLASSIFICATION OF COMPUTER GAMES

Computer Games were made after a decade from the inception of first computers. As the history of computers and computer games is not within the scope of this chapter, we are not going into the details of that. We focus on the classification of computer games in the present scenario. We have divided the classification as per online/offline games, number of players and the architecture employed in deploying the game (Mishra, Zarki, Erbad, Hsu, & Venkatasubramanian, 2014). Figure 1 shows the detailed classification of computer games. Offline games do not require any internet connectivity to play the game. The game-state will be saved in the respective device where the user is playing the game. The next criterion of classification is the number of players involved in the game. There are single player

Figure 1. Computer game classification

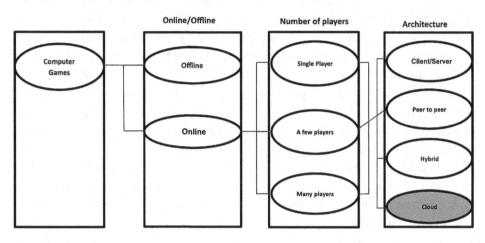

games and multi-player games. The massive multi player online games is a result of the introduction of cloud computing (Shea, Liu, Ngai, & Cui, 2013).

The architectures used in computer games can be broadly classified into four, namely: client/server, peer to peer (P2P), hybrid architectures and cloud architectures. The client/server architecture works with a central server as the hub/ controller of the game (Xu, Nawaz, & Mak, 2014). It is a relatively simple architecture without any complex hardware. The peer to peer architecture was devised to improve the scalability of online gaming. Each of the peers has the capability to work as a client as well as server. In this architecture, the increased load will be distributed evenly among the peers and the bottleneck will be solved. The hybrid architecture will be a combination of one or more architectures including multi server architecture. This architecture treats the global game as different divisions and assigns multiple servers depending on the geographical location. The latest architecture for online games is cloud computing (L.D & Krishna, 2013) (L.D & Krishna, 2013). The cloud based games enables users with basic computing devices with minimal Graphics and processing power to play high end games. The computing power and the graphics are provided by the cloud. The only pre-requisite for cloud based game is high speed network connectivity between the cloud and the game user. Cloud based gaming relieves the user from the burden of possessing high speed processors and graphic cards as the game can even be played in a web browser. Cloud gaming bring together the features of cloud computing and online gaming in a more efficient and user friendly manner.

AN OVERVIEW OF CLOUD BASED GAMING

The interaction between the user and the cloud gaming platform is the key technology in realising the cloud based gaming. The user just requires thin client devices such as browser, mobile devices or smart phones to access the cloud gaming platform. The user commands are sent in to the thin client interaction module of the cloud gaming platform. The user commands are converted to game actions and sent to the Game logic unit in the cloud gaming platform.

The game logic determines how and when to change the game world and render the same to the Graphical processing unit. The graphical processing unit renders the game scene to the video encoder. The encoded video is passed on to the video streaming module. The video stream is sent to the user's video decoder unit which is viewed by the player. Figure 2 shows the architecture of the cloud based game.

STORAGE IN CLOUD BASED GAMES

Storage of data in cloud has become more popular among consumers with the increasing number of free cloud storage providers such as Google drive, Dropbox and Microsoft skydrive (Abu-Libdeh, Princehouse, & Weatherspoon, 2010). Due to the increased usage by customers it is even recognized as storage as a service. Gartner forecasts that by 2016 all internet users will store one third of their data

Figure 2. Cloud based game: an overview of the architecture

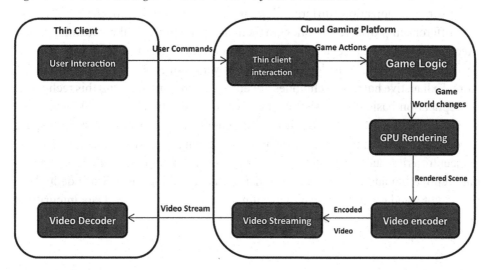

in cloud (Gartner Says That Consumers Will Store More Than a Third of Their Digital Content in the Cloud by 2016, 2012). This data includes game data as well. The exponential growth of data has led to the discovery of new innovative storage techniques for storing data in cloud (Raj & Babu., 2014).

Social Storage Cloud

Social cloud is a term which has become very relevant in the past few years. It is a framework established for process and service sharing by taking advantage of social relationships in accordance with a plan of action adopted by a group of known people, mostly through online social networking. It has become the new face of cloud computing paradigm in resource sharing. Games in social networking sites such as Facebook, Google plus will be stored in the cloud. The various cloud providers include windows azure, amazon web services and other open source cloud providers.

Cloud Storage Service

The digital data growth is so enormous that in house storage systems will be insufficient. This phenomenon is called data deluge, which means data mounts to an overwhelming number or size. Total data size is increasing at a factor of more than two. This means that cloud providers requires more power, more data centres and an increased number of storage resources.

For the sake of more reliability, data is stored in multiple locations (replication) (Dhinesh L.D. & Krishna, 2013). Duplicate files are sometimes used for the ease of working and also play a role in data backup (Hey & Trefethen, 2003).

In some organizations different departments create replicas of the same file so that different employees can work with them independently. To alleviate this process a technology called data deduplication (Meister & Brinkmann, 2009). This technology allows the cloud provider to put almost twenty times the data it can normally store. Exhaustive hashing techniques are employed in implementing this technique. Deduplication basically consist of three types namely block level, file level, and variable block level. As already discussed deduplication reduces the storage space needed, brings down network traffic and scale down the power consumption of the datacentre as it reduces the communication between racks (Geer, 2008). It accelerates data replication and helps in disaster management and recovery. Since deduplication is not standardized it doesn't have higher levels of securities. Data integrity of deduplicted data is still in debate.

Cold Storage in Cloud

The growing digital data amounts to zeta bytes and even to Yotta bytes. It is interesting to note that much of this data is not frequently accessed (Ruiz-Alvarez & Humphrey, 2011). The data that is infrequently accessed is termed as cold. This does not mean that this data has no value or it is irrelevant. This data has great value in analysing business insights and future trends (Mendoza). Big Data analytic techniques are used rigorously to pull out useful perceptions from this data.

The enormous amount of data and budgetary challenges force business organizations to adopt cold storage in cloud. Cold storage data processing has to consider many factors such as cost, governance and the period of time to which a data must be preserved. The longevity requirements have many challenges including storage drive technology becoming obsolete, and data format and media might get out-dated. Cold storage data will obviously have low level performance (Rydning, Reinsel, & Iacono, 2013). Figure 3 depicts the working of cold storage in cloud.

Access speed, access frequency and expected storage life are the prime factors that are considered while moving to cold storage. Cost effectiveness of this change is also taken into account by the business analysts.

Retrieving the cold data in the specified time frame is very critical as failing to do so will result in losing customers. Cold storage in cloud will have separate clause in service level agreements (SLA) which promise the performance, availability and data integrity. The willingness of cloud customers to reduce their cold data access time to few minutes or hours can increase the effectiveness of storage and reduce the cost dramatically.

The storage nodes which store cold data remain in powered off state until the user wants to access or add more data to those nodes. The above figure illustrates the process of differentiating cold storage with normal storage in cloud.

Figure 3. Cold storage working

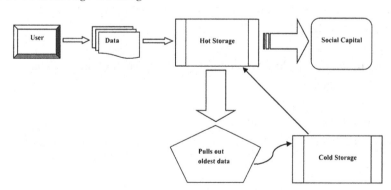

The incoming data is checked against the normal storage location and if vacant space is found it is stored right there. If there is not free space, then the data which is oldest in the location is moved on to the cold storage, and the newly arrived data is moved on to the hot storage.

EMERGING TRENDS IN STORAGE FOR CLOUD BASED GAMES

Emergence of Cloud Drive

Many cloud companies have come up with the idea of cloud drive as storage for the users. The users are provided with a massive storage drive which is nothing but a cloud storage service. Microsoft has launched skydrive, which enables users to store the data online and access it anywhere using internet. DropBox, Google drive, box and amazon drive are some of the cloud drives which store enormous amount of user data. The data consist of personal as well as corporate data. There are still debates on the privacy and security issues of cloud storage (Babu, Krishna, Zayan, & Panda., 2011). The cloud drive providers will have two types of accounts, namely free and enterprise. The free type of account usually offers two Gigabytes to ten Gigabytes of storage space. The goal of cloud based games is to remove pc/gaming console totally in gaming and to provide the same gaming experience in light devices.

Zero Client Computing

Zero client machines will have the CPU and Hard disk and drivers in the network and computation will be done remotely in some other machine (Zero client computing). Thus the end user's terminal has no local storage or processor. Usually zero clients are small boxes with provision of connecting keyboard, mouse, monitor and Ethernet cable. A virtual remote server will be keeping the operating system and drivers of the machine. The numerous advantages of using zero client computing are many and some of them are listed below

1. Power usage is very less when compared to normal computations.
2. It is less expensive.
3. No security vulnerability at client side.
4. Efficient management of resources.
5. High Performance.

Zero clients may run in standard remote device or terminal emulation mode. The device supports protocol which allows communication over wired as well as wireless interfaces. The deployment models for zero client computing vary from point-to-point, multiple point-to-point and point-to-multipoint.

Microserver

This is another emerging technology where performance, energy efficiency, manageability and scalability is better than normal servers. A microserver consists of a set of small servers integrated and composed into a single enclosure. The biggest advantage is that it is possible to choose the processors used in these set of small servers. The idea is to harness more computational power from a group of small servers which are integrated and coordinated to work together. The maintenance cost, performance per watt, performance per square foot and total cost of ownership is more effective when juxtaposed with other server technologies.

This technology is capable to endorse multiple business requirements. It requires less cabling and less flooring thus saving lot of infrastructure space. It drastically rescues energy cost without compromising on performance. The ease of use and maintenance is way ahead of other servers and up gradation from one version to another version is also well-off. It is heavily used along with technologies such as cold storage, content delivery, dedicated hosting and low-end networking.

QUALITY OF EXPERIENCE IN CLOUD BASED GAMES

The Quality of experience in cloud based games depends on responsiveness, fairness and precision from a user's view. QoE is placed as a yard stick in measuring the online gaming experience (Bose & Sarddar, 2015). Cloud based games and online games are significantly different in architecture as well as the quality of experience. Factors determining the quality of experience are delay and loss in communication. There can be downstream delay and upstream delay in gaming. Data loss consists of upstream packet loss and downstream packet loss. There is no universal definition for quality of experience as lot of factors such as user perception, behaviour of the user and relative expectation of the user. QoE metrics has to be identified and measured to discuss more about QoE. QoE in cloud and QoE in cloud based games may have similar or different metrics.

QoE has also a relation with the service level agreement (SLA) with the cloud providers and the game developers. The promised latency and the provided latency decide the quality of experience of the users.

QoE can be based on user feedback using opinion scores. Casa, et al. discuss about a three layer framework for evaluating the QoE in cloud. The layers consist of application, network and user layer. Feedback is collected form the user for the quality of all these layers. Each layer will be given a predefined score which will be used in the calculation of mean opinion score from the users. Cloud games are interactive applications and are more delay sensitive. Network bandwidth and QoE goes hand in hand. A lower bandwidth will result in a low QoE for the user. High Round Trip Time also degrades the QoE of the user.

The work by Chen et.al focuses on QoE and says that QoE is application specific, varies from one domain to another. The factors that depend on QoE in one domain will be different from another. Each of the domains will be different with usage pattern, interactivity and level of complexity. QoE can become a leading standard for quality management in cloud. In cloud based games the factors for QoE can well determine the quality of game and the cloud provider.

The degree of interactivity and the service complexity in cloud games are extremely high and to provide a high QoE is very challenging (Hobfeld, Schatz, Varela, & Timmerer, 2012). Some of the challenges include resource management problems due to colocation and network distance between user and the service. Time varying game conditions require time dependent QoE models.

Some of the factors that affect quality of experience in cloud based games are:

1. Service Reliability,
2. CPU consumptions,
3. Packet Loss,
4. Bandwidth,
5. Jitter,
6. Delay,
7. Response time,
8. Volume of data,
9. Application characteristics,
10. Device usability,
11. User interface,
12. User personality.

Service reliability depends on the up time of the cloud. Most of the CSPs promise 99% up time and some even promise 99.99%. Thus the reliability goes hand in hand with uptime of the cloud. In cloud based games, service reliability contributes to QoE.

CPU consumption should be minimal in cloud based gaming. The computation part of the game is done in the CSP side and thus the CPU consumption from user side should be a minimum. Higher CPU consumption may degrade the QoE and the provider might lose the customer. The CPU consumption will lead to more traffic and congestion in the network.

Packet loss in cloud based games consists of loss of game state update or loss of game play controls which were sent from user to server or vice versa. It is one of the network measures in calculating the network delay, which is directly linked to the quality of experience. Packet loss might result in data delays and result in poor QoE. The available bandwidth and packet loss determine the network condition for good QoE.

Bandwidth is a quality of service determining parameter which also has a role in QoE. Since cloud based games are interactive applications that are more delay sensitive and high RTT will degrade the QoE. Low bandwidth will also degrade the QoE. Latency and bandwidth together determine the QoE in cloud based games (Jarschel, Schlosser, Scheuring, & Hoßfeld, 2011). Resolution of the cloud based games is also a factor in determining the amount of bandwidth, a particular game requires

Jitter in cloud based game is the deviation from the original signal in the communication between player and the cloud game server. Jitter is usually influenced by packet loss in communication. Delay and jitter can be correlated as jitter is mostly caused by RTT delay.

Delay in cloud based games is totally intolerable as the player might lose interest in the game. The delay might be caused by higher cpu consumption, jitter and packet loss. Delay can be caused by the network provider as well. High bandwidth network with infinite resources is desirable for eliminating the delay in cloud based games. Response time and delay are directly proportional. The response time will be more if the delay is large and vice versa.

The volumes of data generated by cloud based games vary from one game to another. The data consist of profile data of players and the game data created by playing. The device usability is also a factor in QoE. Cloud based games mostly uses a light weight browser or will be mobile based app that requires less power.

Some of the challenges in providing the expected quality of experience to the players in cloud based gaming include latency, security and packet loss. These challenges are discussed in detail.

Latency

Latency can be defined as the time required by a cloud based game to process a gamer's input and produce the corresponding response in the player's video console (Lee, Chen, Su, & Lei, 2012). The quality of gamer's experience depends on the degree of latency and the strictness of the game. Latency is a challenge for traditional online gaming as well and delay compensation techniques are employed to counter the same. Cloud based gaming is more susceptible to latency than online gaming as the graphical process and rendering is done by the cloud game server. Latency varies from one game to another in cloud. Response latency consist of network latency, play-out latency and the latency due to the cloud gaming system (due to encoding and decoding of game screens) (Wu, 2014).

The cause of latency can be network delay as well as process delay (Chen, Chang, Tseng, Huang, & Lei, 2011). It has been found that the latency for the same game at different stages will be different. QoE experiments reveal that certain stages in some games could be prioritized to deliver better quality of experience to the user. Bandwidth usage while playing the game depends on the scene complexity and terms of motion. The response latency in cloud based games is mostly dependent on the type of game the user is playing. The design of the game plays a crucial role in determining the latency. The challenge of reducing latency lies with game designers, and developers to create games with efficient architecture. A game which can be played using cloud based game technology without discomfort can be labelled as a cloud gaming friendly.

Although QoE can be affected by number of factors such as network bandwidth restrictions, latency is considered to be the crucial factor in determining QoE of the payer. It is worthy to note that it is almost impossible to eliminate latency in cloud based games because of game screen encoding- decoding time. The cloud gaming friendliness can be determined by measuring how the game's QoE degrades with respect to latency.

Security

Personal data and the geographical location details of the players are stored by the cloud based gaming systems. Data and privacy risks are projected as the main concerns of any cloud computing environment (Jansen & Grance, 2011). The game data of the players will be stored in the game server along with the location details. The users might be concerned about the storage of personal data with/without their consent. Majority of the cloud based game systems will be hosted in public or hybrid cloud models. This increases the chance of privacy breaching and data theft. The security in cloud computing is still a hot debated topic.

Packet Loss

Packet loss greatly affects the experience of user and it can range from user command lost during delivery to the game server to irresponsive video streaming from the game console. Congestion and packet loss gives the worst experience to the game players. The network traffic between the user and the game server plays a great role in checking the packet loss. Packet loss reduces the confidence of the user in that particular game and the player might lose interest in playing that game permanently (Clincy & Wilgor, 2013). The research by Clincy and Wilgor concluded that 1% packet loss will make the game player to lose patience to experience a game. Frequent packet loss will lead to very high player loss and economic loss to the game company.

QUALITY OF SERVICE IN CLOUD BASED GAMES

The cloud based games allow the user to easily play 3D games without buying any extra hardware. The prerequisite for playing cloud based games is to have a high bandwidth networks and less network latency. The reduction of network bandwidth should never compromise on the quality of the rendered game (Shi, Hsu, Nahrstedt, & Campbell, 2011). While QoS properties have gotten steady attention well before the coming of distributed computing, execution heterogeneity and allocation of resources in various cloud stages have fundamentally convoluted QoS research, prediction and validation. The research on cloud gaming QoS is difficult as most of the games are proprietary and as the internal mechanisms of the game is closed. The Quality of service in cloud based games depends on traffic characteristics, latency and graphic quality. Nieh and Lai proposed a way to deal with assess the QoS of a few slender game development frameworks on different undertakings utilizing moderate slow motion of the game (Lai & Nieh, 2006). But this strategy can't be connected to cloud gaming frameworks in light of the fact that the video rendering would need to be changed with the goal that they can keep running in slow motion. The delays in cloud based gaming systems consist of network delay, processing delay, game delay and play out delay. Network delay is the time required to transmit a player's command to the game server and the game screen back to the player. Processing delay is defined as the time required for the cloud based game server to receive and process a player's command and to provide the corresponding response back to the player. Game delay is the time required by the software in the cloud based game server to process a player's command and render the correspond-ing video frame back to player's video console. Playout delay is the time for the player to receive, decode and display a frame form the video encoder present in the cloud based game server.

In addition, the QoS measurements utilized, for example, the measure of infor-mation exchanged, don't precisely evaluate the transient and spatial nature of cloud gaming frameworks. This chapter focuses on five aspects of Quality of service, namely storage QoS, 3D rendering quality, remote gaming architecture, video streaming quality and video streaming with rendering operations quality.

Storage QoS

Storage QoS is similar to network QoS. The goal of storage QoS is to ensure that the game application always get a certain performance level at all time (Crump, 2014). In storage QoS, the performance is expressed in terms of Input/output Operations per Second (IOPS). The storage system calculates and sets a particular number of IOPS as the threshold level and will be allocated to each game present in the cloud. Some cloud providers has the provision of over allocating the IOPS, but has the risk of thin provisioning. The logic behind ensuring storage QoS is that not all games require the same amount of storage at the same time. It is also interesting to note that, for the same game, different players require different storage space.

3D Rendering

The most common 3D rendering technique is the 3D graphics streaming approach (Zhu, Luo, Wang, & Li, 2011). As explained in Figure 2, the cloud server intercepts the commands from the Graphical processing unit and stream the same to the clients after encoding them using the video encoder. The client renders the game scenes with the help of Direct3D or openGL. The 3D rendering approach is less suitable for mobile devices as it is incapable of handling more workload from the server. The compatibility between graphic chip commands of the client and the cloud based game server should be checked to ensure better quality of service. The graphic chips in the clients must be powerful enough to receive the encoded video commands from the cloud based server. The current gaming platforms such as Onlive, Stream-MyGame, and Gaiki are image based systems.

Remote Gaming Architecture

The remote gaming architecture plays a crucial role in interacting with the thin clients. This architecture supports real time graphical applications to enable the user to play the game remotely. Remote gaming architectures fall into two categories namely instruction based architectures and image based architecture (Chen, Chang, Hsu, Chen, Huang, & Hsu, 2014). Instruction based systems consume less bandwidth as the clients render the graphics themselves according to the instructions received from the server. Image based remote gaming architecture renders and streams real video from the server and thus consume more bandwidth.

Video Streaming

Interestingly, with the video streaming methodology the cloud servers render the 3D video into 2D recordings, pack the recordings, and stream them to the game players. The customer devices then decode and show the video streams. The deciphering should be possible utilizing minimal effort video decoder chips mainly produced with the common consumers. This methodology alleviates the customers from computationally- serious 3D design rendering and is perfect for slim customers on asset compelled gadgets. Since the video rendering methodology does not depend on particular 3D chips, the same clients can be promptly ported to distinctive stages, which are possibly GPU-less.

Video Streaming with Rendering Operations

The methodology of video streaming with post-rendering operations lies between the 3D graphic streaming and video streaming. While the 3D graphics rendering is performed at the cloud servers, some post-rendering operations are alternatively done on the player's thin client devices for enlarging movements, lighting, and surfaces. These post-rendering operations have low computational complexity and keep running progressively without GPUs.

Mathematical Model for QoS in Cloud Based Games

The quality of service in cloud can be mathematically perceived for better understanding of cloud based games in OSNs.

Let Ti be the time between the jth and (j-1)th request to the game server, then

$$i = \{1,2,3,.....\}$$

It will be represented by a sequence of independent identically distributed random variables. Let Task L represent the time from beginning of a process till the lth request.

$$TASK_L = T_1 + T_2 + T_3 + ... + T_l \tag{1}$$

If F(L)(t) denote distribution function of TASKK. F(l) is the l-fold convolution of F with itself.

$$F^{(o)}(t) = \begin{cases} 1 & t \geq 0 \\ 0 & t < 0 \end{cases} \tag{2}$$

The goal is to find the number of requests R(t) between an interval of 0 and t. The process $\{N(t) \mid t \geq 0\}$ will be in a discrete state with continuous time renewal counting process.

We can say that R(t)=n if and only if $Task_n \leq t \leq Task_n + 1$, Then

$$
\begin{aligned}
P\big[R(t) = n\big] &= P\big(TASK_n \leq t \leq TASK_{n+1}\big) \\
&= P\big(TASK_n \leq t\big) - P\big(TASK_{n+1} \leq t\big) \\
&= F^{(n)}(t) - F^{(n+1)}(t)
\end{aligned}
\tag{3}
$$

We assume that M (t) will be the average number of requests reaching the game server in an interval (0, t) then

$$
\begin{aligned}
M(t) = E\big[R(t)\big] &= \sum_{n=0}^{\infty} nP\big[R(t) = n\big] \\
&= \sum_{n=0}^{\infty} nF^{(n)}(t) - \sum_{n=1}^{\infty} nF^{(n+1)}(t) \\
&= F(t) + \sum_{n=1}^{\infty} F^{(n+1)}(t)
\end{aligned}
\tag{4}
$$

F(n+1) is the convolution of F(n) and F. Let f be the density function of F so,

$$
F^{(n+1)}(t) = \int_0^t F^{(n)}(t - x) f(x) dx
\tag{5}
$$

Therefore,

$$
\begin{aligned}
M(t) &= F(t) + \sum_{n-1}^{\infty} \int_0^t F^{(n)}(t - x) f(x) dx \\
&= F(t) + \int_0^t M(t - x) f(x) dx
\end{aligned}
\tag{6}
$$

The rate of average requests on the game server can be defined as the derivative of M(t)

$$M(t) = \frac{dM(t)}{dt} \tag{7}$$

For very small values of h, M(t) h shows the probability of a request arrival in the interval (t, t+h). In order to find M(t), we make use of Laplace transform and convolution property of the transform and apply to the Equation (7)

$$L\big(m(t)\big) = L\big(f(t)\big) + L\big(M(t)Lf(t)\big) \tag{8}$$

Thus we can rewrite Equation (8) as

$$L\big(m(t)\big) = \frac{L\big(f(t)\big)}{1 - L\big(f(t)\big)}$$

and

$$L\big(f(t)\big) = \frac{L(m(t)}{1 - L\big(m(t)\big)} \tag{9}$$

When the function F (n) (t) is a gamma or n-stage Erlang distribution, we can write

$$F^{(n)}(t) = 1 - \left[\sum_{k=0}^{n-1} \frac{(\lambda t)^k}{k!} \right] e^{-\lambda t}$$

and also from (3)

$$P\big[N(t) = n\big] = F^{(n)}(t) - F^{(n+1)}(t)$$
$$= \frac{(\lambda t)^n}{n!} e^{-\lambda t} \tag{10}$$

Thus the function N (t) is having a poisson distribution with parameter λt.

We assume that, request holding times are not exponential. If X (t) is the number of requests in the game server at time t and N (t) is the total number of requests in an interval (0, 1). The number of service requests $D(t) = R(t) - X(t)$

We can say that for $n \geq 1$ the request arrival in the interval (0, t), the conditional joint Poisson distribution function of the arrival time T1, T2, T3...Tn is given by

$$f\left(t_1, t_2, t_3, \ldots t_n \mid R(t) = n\right) = \frac{n!}{t^n} \tag{11}$$

When game requests arrive at time, $0 \leq y \leq t$ from Equation (11), the time of request arrival will be independently distributed on (0, t) i.e.

$$f_Y(y) = \frac{1}{t}, 0 < y < t$$

The probability of completion of this request in the stipulated time t, by assuming that it arrived at time y is 1-G (t-y). The unconditional probability of completing the updating at time t is

$$P = \int_0^t \left[1 - G(t - y)\right] f_Y(y) \, dy$$
$$= \int_0^t \frac{1 - G(t - y)}{t} \, dy \tag{12}$$
$$= \int_0^t \frac{t - G(x)}{t} \, dx$$

Simultaneously, if n requests to server arrive, and each has a probability p of independently not completing by time t, then we can obtain a sequence of n Bernoulli trials as shown below.

$$P\left[X(t) = \frac{j}{N(t)} = n\right] = \begin{cases} nC_j p^{j(1-p)^{n-j}} & j = 0,1,\ldots.n \\ 0 & otherwise \end{cases}$$

By theorem of total probability

$$P\left[X\left(t\right)=j\right]=\sum_{n=j}^{\infty}nC_jP^{j\left(1-p\right)^{n-j}}e^{-\lambda t}\frac{\left(\lambda t^n\right)}{n!}$$

$$=e^{-\lambda t}\frac{\left(\lambda tp\right)^j}{j!}\sum_{n=j}^{\infty}\frac{\left[\lambda+\left(1-p\right)\right]^{n-j}}{\left(n-j\right)!} \tag{13}$$

$$=e^{-\lambda tp}\frac{\left(\lambda tp\right)^j}{j!}$$

The number of request for resource in the cloud game system at time t has a Poisson distribution with parameter

$$\lambda=\lambda tp=\lambda\int_0^t\left[1-G\left(x\right)\right]dx \tag{14}$$

When request holding times are exponentially in relation with a parameter μ then,

$$G\left(x\right)=1-e^{-\mu x}$$

$$\int_0^t\left[1-G\left(x\right)\right]dx=\frac{1}{\mu}-\frac{e^{-\mu t}}{\mu} \tag{15}$$

Even though, the CSP doesn't not possess infinite resources it is assumed that cloud possesses unlimited resources.

So when $\rightarrow\infty$, $\lambda'=\dfrac{\lambda}{\mu}$ Let us assume that there are C server racks in the game server in cloud based gaming. The probability of losing a request to the game server from the player is as follows:

$$P\left[X\left(t\right)=C\right]=e^{-\lambda tp}\frac{\left(\lambda tp\right)^C}{C!} \tag{16}$$

Equation (16) can be rewritten for a steady state as

$$P\big[X(t)=C\big]=\frac{\varrho\dfrac{C}{C!}}{\displaystyle\sum_{i=0}^{C}\dfrac{\varrho i}{i!}} \tag{17}$$

where ϱ is the traffic request intensity calculated as $\varrho=\dfrac{\lambda}{\mu}$.

This mathematical model for quality of service in cloud based gaming clearly depict the aspects of quality in games.

CONCLUSION

We have thoroughly surveyed the different strategies used in cloud based gaming in this chapter. The various aspects like QoE, QoS and storage in cloud based games were surveyed and discussed in detail. The chapter mainly focus on the Quality of service in cloud based games. Various methods in QoS and QoE are considered to find the influence among both in cloud based games. The proposed mathematical model for QoS in cloud based games can be used in deciding the benchmarks for QoS in cloud gaming. This mathematical model gives a clear view of the issues that has to be monitored and handled in cloud based games.

Cloud based gaming makes it possible to have any device gaming, click to play simplicity, has less hassle and provides a console free gaming environment. It provides high quality gaming experience to the players and vast business opportunity to the cloud service providers. Cloud based gaming provides extensibility, portability, configurability and openness in gaming. Cloud based gaming is definitely the future of online games and has lot of scope for the game developing companies to generate huge profit.

REFERENCES

Abu-Libdeh, H., Princehouse, L., & Weatherspoon, H. (2010). RACS: a case for cloud storage diversity. *Proceedings of the 1st ACM symposium on Cloud computing*, (pp. 229-240).

Babu, L. D., Krishna, P. V., Zayan, A. M., & Panda, V. (2011). An Analysis of Security Related Issues in Cloud Computing. *Springer Communications in Computer and Information Science*, *168*, 180–190. doi:10.1007/978-3-642-22606-9_21

Babu, L. D. D., & Krishna, P. V. (2013). Versatile time-cost algorithm (VTCA) for scheduling non-preemptive tasks of time critical workflows in cloud computing systems. *International Journal of Communication Networks and Distributed Systems*, *11*(4), 390–411. doi:10.1504/IJCNDS.2013.057718

Bose, R., & Sarddar, D. (2015). A new approach in mobile gaming on cloud-based architecture using Citrix and VMware technologies. *Brazilian Journal of Science and Technology*, *2*(1), 1–13. doi:10.1186/s40552-015-0012-1

Chen, K.-T., Chang, Y.-C., Hsu, H.-J., Chen, D.-Y., Huang, C.-Y., & Hsu, C.-H. (2014). On the quality of service of cloud gaming systems. *Multimedia. IEEE Transactions*, *16*(2), 480–495.

Chen, K.-T., Chang, Y.-C., Tseng, P.-H., Huang, C.-Y., & Lei, C.-L. (2011). Measuring the latency of cloud gaming systems.*Proceedings of the 19th ACM international conference on Multimedia* (pp. 1269-1272). ACM. doi:10.1145/2072298.2071991

Clincy, V., & Wilgor, B. (2013). Subjective evaluation of latency and packet loss in a cloud-based game. Information Technology: New Generations (ITNG) (pp. 473-476). Las Vegas, NV: IEEE.

Cloud Gaming – Gaming as a Service (GaaS) | NVIDIA GRID. (n.d.). Retrieved April 10, 2015, from http://www.nvidia.com/object/cloud-gaming.html

Crump, G. (2014, March 26). *What Is Storage QoS?* Retrieved December 13, 2015, from www.networkcomputing.com: http://www.networkcomputing.com/storage/what-is-storage-qos/a/d-id/1127906

Dhinesh, L. D. (2014). A decision-based pre-emptive fair scheduling strategy to process cloud computing work-flows for sustainable enterprise management. *Int. J. Business Information Systems*, *16*(4), 409–430. doi:10.1504/IJBIS.2014.063929

Dhinesh, L. D. B., & Krishna, P. V. (2013). Applying operations management models for facility location problem in cloud computing environments. *Int. J. Services and Operations Management*, *15*(1), 1–27. doi:10.1504/IJSOM.2013.053252

Gartner Says That Consumers Will Store More Than a Third of Their Digital Content in the Cloud by 2016 . (2012, June 25). Retrieved March 25, 2015, from http://www.gartner.com/newsroom/id/2060215

Geer, D. (2008). Reducing the storage burden via data deduplication. *Computer*, *41*(12), 15–17. doi:10.1109/MC.2008.538

Google App Engine. (n.d.). Retrieved February 25, 2015, from https://appengine.google.com/

Hey, A. J., & Trefethen, A. E. (2003). The data deluge: an e-sicence perspective. In *Gid Computing: Making the Global Infrastructure a Reality*. Wiley. doi:10.1002/0470867167.ch36

Hobfeld, T., Schatz, R., Varela, M., & Timmerer, C. (2012). Challenges of QoE management for cloud applications. *Communications Magazine, 50*(4).

Jansen, W., & Grance, T. (2011). *Guidelines on security and privacy in public cloud computing*. NIST Special Publication, 144.

Jarschel, M., Schlosser, D., Scheuring, S., & Hoßfeld, T. (2011). An evaluation of QoE in cloud gaming based on subjective tests.*Fifth International Conference on Innovative Mobile and Internet Services in Ubiquitous Computing* (pp. 330-335). Seoul, South Korea: IEEE. doi:10.1109/IMIS.2011.92

Kamarainen, T., Siekkinen, M., Xiao, Y., & Yla-Jaaski, A. (2014). Towards pervasive and mobile gaming with distributed cloud infrastructure.*13th Annual Workshop on Network and Systems Support for Games (NetGames)* (pp. 1-6). Nagoya: IEEE. doi:10.1109/NetGames.2014.7008957

Lai, A. M., & Nieh, J. (2006). On the performance of wide-area thin-client computing. *ACM Transactions on Computer Systems, 24*(2), 175–209. doi:10.1145/1132026.1132029

L.D., D. B., & Krishna, P. V. (2013). Honey bee behavior inspired load balancing of tasks in cloud computing environments.*Applied Soft Computing, 13*(5), 2292–2303. doi:10.1016/j.asoc.2013.01.025

Lee, Y.-T., Chen, K.-T., Su, H.-I., & Lei, C.-L. (2012). *Are all games equally cloud-gaming-friendly? an electromyographic approach. In Network and Systems Support for Games (NetGames)* (pp. 1–6). Venice, Italy: IEEE.

Li, H., Liu, J., & Tang, G. (2011). A Pricing Algorithm for Cloud Computing Resources.*Conference on Network Computing and Inform. Security*. doi:10.1109/NCIS.2011.22

Meister, D., & Brinkmann, A. (2009). Multi-level comparison of data deduplication in a backup scenario.*Proceedings of SYSTOR 2009: The Israeli Experimental Systems Conference*. doi:10.1145/1534530.1534541

Mendoza, A. (n.d.). *Cold Storage in the Cloud: Trends, Challenges, and Solutions*. Retrieved February 15, 2015, from https://www.intel.it/content/www/it/it/storage/cold-storage-atom-xeon-paper.html

Mishra, D., Zarki, M. E., Erbad, A., Hsu, C.-H., & Venkatasubramanian, N. (2014). Clouds+ games: A multifaceted approach. *Internet Computing,* (3), 20-27.

Raj, E. D., & Babu, L. D. (2014). Analysis on enhancing storm to efficiently process big data in real time.*5th International Conference on Computing, Communication and Networking Technologies (ICCCNT)* (pp. 1-5). Hefei, China: IEEE. doi:10.1109/ICCCT2.2014.7066747

Raj, E. D., & Babu, L. D. (2015). A firefly swarm approach for establishing new connections in social networks based on big data analytics. *International Journal of Communication Networks and Distributed Systems*, *15*(2/3), 130–148. doi:10.1504/IJCNDS.2015.070968

Raj, E. D., Babu, L. D., Ariwa, E., Nirmala, M., & Krishna, P. V. (2014). Forecasting the Trends in Cloud Computing and its Impact on Future IT Business. In *Green Technology Applications for Enterprise and Academic Innovation* (pp. 14–32). Hershey, PA: IGI Global. doi:10.4018/978-1-4666-5166-1.ch002

Ruiz-Alvarez, A., & Humphrey, M. (2011). An automated approach to cloud storage service selection.*Proceedings of the 2nd international workshop on Scientific cloud computing*. doi:10.1145/1996109.1996117

Rydning, J., Reinsel, D., & Iacono, D. (2013, May). *Cloud storage is hot again.* Retrieved February 11, 2015, from http://www.storiant.com/resources/Cold-Storage-Is-Hot-Again.pdf

Shea, R., Liu, J., Ngai, E.-H., & Cui, Y. (2013). Cloud gaming: Architecture and performance. *IEEE Network*, *27*(4), 16–21. doi:10.1109/MNET.2013.6574660

Shi, S., Hsu, C.-H., Nahrstedt, K., & Campbell, R. (2011). Using graphics rendering contexts to enhance the real-time video coding for mobile cloud gaming. *Proceedings of the 19th ACM international conference on Multimedia* (pp. 103-112). New York: ACM. doi:10.1145/2072298.2072313

Windows Azure. (n.d.). Retrieved February 25, 2015, from http://www.windowsazure.com/en-us/

Wu, Z. (2014). *Gaming in the cloud: one of the future entertainment.* Retrieved 12 12, 2015, from University of Southamtpon: http://mms.ecs.soton.ac.uk/2014/papers/17.pdf

Xu, Y., Nawaz, S., & Mak, R. H. (2014, November 1). *A Comparison of Architectures in Massive Multiplayer Online Games.* Retrieved December 15, 2015, from www.researchgate.net

Zero Client Computing . (n.d.). Retrieved March 10, 2015, from http://www.digi.com/pdf/wp_zeroclientcomputing.pdf

Zhu, W., Luo, C., Wang, J., & Li, S. (2011, March). Multimedia cloud computing. *Signal Processing Magazine*, 59-69.

KEY TERMS AND DEFINITIONS

Cloud Based Games: The type of games in which the game design and logic resides in the game server and the players will be free from overhead expenses such as platform and graphical processing.

Cloud Computing: A computing paradigm in which computational resources including hardware and software can be pooled and provided to a large number of end users and is billed according to the usage.

Cold Storage: The data in cloud which is less frequently accessed by the users.

Hot Storage: The data in cloud which is latest and more frequently accessed by the users.

Latency in Game: The time lapse between a request and response from a game player to the cloud based game server.

Online Gaming: The type of games in which the game design and logic resides with the game players while the servers preserve only the game state of the players.

Chapter 7
Cloud–Based Gaming Services

Shivangshu Nag
VIT University, India

Vipul Kumar Srivastava
VIT University, India

Ragam Sai Krishna
VIT University, India

ABSTRACT

This chapter talks about the latest technology being used for Cloud Gaming. It discusses about various aspects of this technology. The first part gives a brief introduction about what is actually cloud gaming and the ways in which it is implemented. The subsequent section talks about the various servers and units involved in the whole process. The next section talks about the importance of performance and efficiency in the Cloud Gaming system. There are various advantages of implementing such systems over the traditional gaming systems and of course every coin has two sides and thus there are various limitations of this technology which are discussed further in the chapter. What can be the new advancements and the future of the Cloud Gaming System has also been taken up in this chapter. Some case studies have also been included in this chapter to understand the various topics more clearly by analyzing the present scenarios and systems. The companies which offer cloud based gaming services have been discussed about to understand their technologies and implementation mechanisms.

DOI: 10.4018/978-1-5225-0546-4.ch007

INTRODUCTION

Computer games are very popular in today's world. People of all age groups enjoy playing different kinds of games. It has been observed that people in the recent years are spending above 25 billion USD on games and hardware required for playing the high requirement games.

Traditionally games are offered on optical drives or are available on the Internet. The games have to be installed on the physical machine by the user. This process sometimes becomes very tedious because the computer games are too complicated and also big in size whereas the computer software is very fragmented. Also with the popularity of new high requirement games it is often that users find that they need to upgrade their hardware to be able to play the game without lags and glitches.

These limitations of the traditional games have been the motivation of developing cloud based gaming systems. It has been seen as a new opportunity which will be more affordable for the users and also has promising future for the business giants. Ina cloud gaming system the games run on powerful cloud servers and the users can play them on their devices which eliminates the necessity of always having a very powerful console and updating it after short periods of time which makes cloud gaming systems more affordable for the user and thus it becomes beneficial for them and also for the companies implementing this system because of increase in number of users. A market report has come up which says that the cloud gaming market will increase 9 times between 2011 and 2017.

Although the cloud gaming systems have many advantages over the traditional systems but due to users always asking for better audio and graphics, implementing the cloud system is a very challenging task which can meet the user's demands. Fortunately, this technology and its benefits have gained the attention on researchers and thus there is vast research going on to make better ways to implement the system which can both be easy and also efficient and cost effective.

The chapter goes deeper into these topics and tries to explain them.

DESIGN PHILOSOPHY

Before going into the implementation of the cloud gaming systems here we will discuss that with which aims in mind these systems are being developed:

- **Extensibility:** Extensibility means that the components related to the gaming components like codecs can be easily replaced and with the same system used for cloud gaming other things can also be done like any real time multimedia application such as live casting.

- **Portability:** Today apart from computers, mobile phones and small consoles are also getting very popular which are not as powerful as the computers. Portability of the cloud gaming system will enable the users to play good quality games even on their mobiles and will also be able to access and play in many places where playing on computers is not possible.
- **Configurability:** This will enable the cloud based gaming systems to be compatible to various types of audio and video services or codecs. This will enable real time multimedia streaming applications with diverse system parameters.
- **Openness:** The cloud based gaming systems can be much more open to users and even the developers provide academic research facilities for users free of cost. So accessing a cloud based gaming system will be easy.

Types of Implementation

The two basic ways of providing cloud gaming services to a user are by streaming the video on the user's device and the other is by streaming or we can say by making the user download the file consisting of the game.

The video streaming process is more complex of the two types and requires better resources to run without lags and glitches. The whole process involving the delivery of the gaming service by the process of video streaming should be done very quickly and thus there is no margin of buffer in the whole system. The process of receiving the incoming video from and encoding and compressing it for delivery and then delivering it to the end user should be done quickly and also the quality of the video should not be compromised by the cloud server. The encoding process is done with respect to very few frames as the server doesn't have access to the future frames.

The file streaming process is less complex and the game file is downloaded on the user's device and then executed and the game can be played by the user. It has less complication because the whole game file is available with the user so there is no chance of any latency. However, it requires the user to first download the game file in fragments and then play the game. (Wikipedia)

Framework of the Video Streaming Technique

This is similar to the concept of video on demand. The actual copy of the game is on the game company's server, nothing has to be downloaded by the user. The basic framework involves receiving the commands given by user through button presses on his device and sending these commands over the internet to the cloud gaming platform where the commands are converted to appropriate actions happening in the game environment, The actions are then processed by the cloud gaming's graphical processing unit into rendered scenes which are then compressed and encoded and sent to the video streaming module and finally this module sends the video to the user's device. The whole process's speed and efficiency requirements also depends on the type of game, here a good example is that if we are playing a game not requiring time critical actions like the World of Warcraft then a little lag is not largely noticed and does not affect the game where as faster games like Counter Strike a little lag can also lead to a large game change and can even change the final outcome of the game for the user and thus this type of games require large efficiency and speed from the server.

A number of companies use this type of implementation using Gaikai which is now a part of Sony Entertainment.

Framework of the File Streaming Technique

With file streaming technology decent quality games can be played on less resourceful devices, the games on social media sites also this technology. As the game file is downloaded so there is no latency while playing the game which makes the experience more promising and smooth.

The whole game file might be a little big in size and downloading the whole of it in one go might take time which may result in the users getting impatient and deciding against playing the game, to avoid this the file is downloaded in fragments. If the player is downloading or streaming the game, the data necessary for the resumption of the game is streamed first that is priority is given to the data which is immediately necessary for running the game ahead. After the downloading of five to ten percent data the user can start playing the game. The downloading continues in the background which results in the availability of the next parts of the game without any delay. As the data is streamed in fragments thus there is no need for huge disk space.

File streaming gaming services are getting popular as compared to video streaming because of their less requirements and thus affordable nature.

DIFFERENT UNITS IN A CLOUD BASED GAMING PLATFORM

A cloud gaming platform is gateway mainly consist of three basic units the gateway server, the gaming server farm and the management server. The gateway provides users with the initial connecting point. The gaming server farm is responsible for the execution of the game and for the delivering of the scenes to the user's device. The management server provides an administrator platform which interworks with the systems which are responsible for a user's authentication.

- **The Gateway Server:** The initial connection is received by the gateway server, from a user to request the cloud gaming service then the user is authenticated with the internetworking legacy systems and the user is redirected to the gaming server which currently has the minimum load in the gaming server farm.
- **The Gaming Server:** The video and audio scenes of the game being played are captured by the gaming server which then encodes the captured scenes to compressed stream and streams this encoded data to the user's device. The gaming server is also responsible to process the game player's input event and to manage sessions for supporting multiple game players concurrently.
- **The Management Server:** The management server is responsible for monitoring and keeping track of the status of the various factors related to the gaming server like the number of sessions in each gaming server, the load on the CPU, GPU and the NIC of the gaming server with real time. The monitoring is very important to handle the load being put on the machines because if it exceeds a threshold level it might lead to their damage.

All the units grouped together can be called the Game Server. The user's gaming console which has the input buttons, audio and video decoder is called the Game Client. There are two types of network flows between the Game Server and the Game Client, one is the Data flow and the other is the Control flow. The data flow has the responsibility of streaming the audios and videos from the game server to the game client, whereas the control flow runs in the opposite direction and is responsible for the transmission of the user's inputs and commands to the game server (Figure 1).

Figure 1. The whole units and their functions graphically

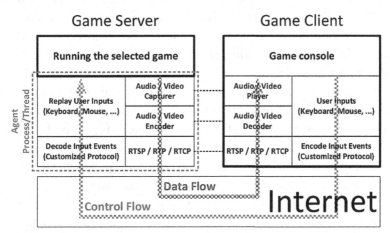

PERFORMANCE OF THE CLOUD GAMING SYSTEM

The performance of a cloud based gaming system can be up to the level of satisfying the players only when there is very little or no latency in the system. Studies have shown that the cloud gaming systems are sensitive to even modest amounts of latency and the user performance degrades by 25 percent with each 100 milliseconds of latency. These studies have shown the developers of cloud gaming systems that they should be extremely careful about how efficient their systems are. The gaming system should deploy the highest and most efficient technology if they want to be successful.

The so high sensitivity of the cloud gaming systems can be easily understood by the following argument. The nature of user interaction with cloud-based games differs from that with the traditional games. Ina traditional game, the local game engine can immediately handle the user action however in cloud based gaming the user actions can only be shown after the whole process of transmitting the input to the cloud, applying its resulting actions to the gaming environment and finally rendering the scenes back to the user is over. Thus due to the already long process the responsiveness of a cloud gaming system is directly impacted by even small amounts of latency.

Real World Implementations of Cloud Gaming Services

The first known venture into the domain of "On demand Video game "services is known to be taken by a company called Infinium Labs, in the year 2002. The company started with making computer keyboards. In January 2003, it released a press release that it is going to release "a revolutionary new gaming platform" which will deliver games through an online subscription. The revolutionary gaming service used a gaming console named "The Phantom" by the company. But this product went through a series of failures in production and hence its release was continuously delayed. The Phantom never made it to the market, but was very popular because of the concept on which it was being developed.

The Phantom was said to have the capability to be able to stream video games. The device would have a large initial game library. This would it easier for developers to produce games for the system. The device used a feature called direct-download content delivery service, instead of the disc and cartridges used by most game consoles. Although the device was never released, the company changed its name to "Phantom Entertainment" in the year 2006. The concept behind the product still grew further and inspired many such ventures in the coming years.

Since then Cloud gaming has generated a lot of interest among entrepreneurs, venture capitalists, and researchers. Startup companies have offered or plan to offer cloud gaming services, such as OnLive, GaiKai, OTOY, Ubitus, and T5-Labs, all of them having varied realizations. For example, some systems are only accessible via clients on PCs, while others can be accessed via TVs with set-top boxes. Because of the large design space of cloud gaming systems, it is not yet known which systems deliver better Quality of Service (QoS) than others and which design elements play a vital role in constituting a good cloud gaming system. (Kuan-Ta Chen, 2014)

Let's have a deeper insight into some of the famous cloud gaming service providers and know how each of them are working towards revolutionizing the entire gaming industry.

OnLive

OnLive was first announced at GDC (Game Developers Conference) 2009. The company provides an on-demand gaming service. The company started with the intention of changing the way games are played. The endeavor has potential which is still being scaled and analyzed by experts and may well be the next big thing in the gaming industry. (OnLive, 2009)

The company believes it is building the future of cloud computing. Steve Perlman founded the company, who is a noted entrepreneur and inventor who has spent years working on the technology before officially releasing it through the OnLive service in 2010 and from then onward progressed at a rapid rate. A total of over 120 games were offered by OnLive by the end of 2011.

It has operated since then serving millions of users in Europe and the United States. The service claims to cater to any device with high-end visual computing experiences. Through the company's proprietary technology, console-quality games can be played instantly on Android tables, PCs, Macs and TVs — either with OnLive's MicroConsole, or on some digital TVs and connected devices that include the required software. OnLive Desktop is a mobile app developed by the company, which provides a remote desktop experience on a mobile device.

After loading up the service and choosing a game to play, the game starts immediately. The game is hosted and played on one of OnLive's several servers, therefore removing the need to download anything on the user's device. Using any input device such as a mouse, keyboard or controller, one can play the game as if it were installed in their own local machine. The inputs are read by the plugin or any standalone device that is being used and then is uploaded to the server. The server then simulates the game just as the user would have played it, sitting at the local machine, except that instead of producing a video on the display, it now gets compressed and streamed to the computer where all the action can be seen and enjoyed.

The Game system developed by OnLive consists of a Wireless Controller and a console, which is called MicroConsole, which can be connected to a television and directly to the OnLive service, so one can also possibly use the service without the need of a computer. The system comes with several accessories needed to connect all the equipment. MicroConsole supports up to 4 wireless controllers and several Bluetooth headsets. Multiple USB ports are available for controllers, mice, keyboards, and USB hubs. Video and audio output is managed by HDMI, TOSLINK ports and analog stereo minijack. Ethernet port is used for network access, to access the OnLive service.

The technology and equipment used is a custom set up by OnLive that consists of video compression chip, along with standard GPU and PC CPU chips. For some older, less graphic intensive games, multiple instances of the game can be played using virtualization. High-end games require one GPU per game. Specifically, 2 video streams are created for each game, where one is optimized for gameplay, and several real-world internet considerations, while the other one is a video stream that is server-side and is used for spectators or for users to record videos of their game. Minimum bandwidth requirement is 3 Mbps, whereas the recommended connection should be 5 Mbps or faster. All games are delivered in 720p format.

Games themselves vary by title and publisher, and there are multiple ways in which one can purchase them. One option is to pay outright and own it indefinitely, or one could rent a title for a pre-specified amount of time. The advantage with the last option is that kind of market is not prevalent today as piracy of games would then run rampant and unchecked. But since now everything is housed online, OnLive services won't be subject to piracy, and game rentals can take place effectively. This possibility is certainly attractive and will interest a lot of game publishers looking for such a market in the gaming industry.

Most games will have a demo which will be available to play, which like all other services, starts instantly with no downloading of files. OnLive hopes that even if gamers intend to buy games as per the current scenario and play content locally on their own high-end rigs, their service will still be an attractive option to try out game demos as the user would not have to download anything.

StreamMyGame

StreamMyGame is developed as a software streaming solution that enables multiple Microsoft based games and applications to be played remotely on Linux and Windows devices. It was released in October 2007, as a Windows only software. In addition to streaming games over a LAN network, StreamMyGame can also be used over broadband networks, with a prerequisite that these connections should provide a minimum speed of 2 Mbit/s. (StreamMyGame, 2010)

StreamMyGames members can install a server and player application from the website. The server has to be installed on the same computer where the game is installed. The server then automatically searches the user's hard drive for these games and then uploads the links to these games onto the StreamMyGame website. The server is compatible with Windows 7, XP, and Vista. The player is also installed on the computer or on the device on which the game will be played and is compatible with Windows 7, XP and Vista, along with Ubuntu, Fedora, Red Hat, Xandros, Yellow Dog Linux and Debian. Server and player software both require continuous access to the internet. Also in addition to streaming games StreamMyGame enables members to record the games being played to a video file. This video file then can be shared anywhere and can be uploaded on site such as YouTube.

Members have to select any game they want to play on the StreamMyGame website and then the website sends an encrypted signal to the server, and the server responds by starting the game and capturing the video and audio. The video and audio is then sent to the player using a real time streaming protocol and displayed. The player on the user's computer captures keyboard and mouse commands and sends these inputs back to the hosting server, which are fed into the game and are used to control the game. StreamMyGame also enable its members to communicate with a Web 2.0 website, which includes messaging, chat forums and groups. They can use group permissions to enable other members to share and use their games. StreamMyGame's forums are predominantly used to publish the performance details and specs of StreamMyGame, when they are used with new and existing games.

GaiKai

GaiKai was founded in 2008, and since then is at the forefront of cloud gaming revolution. It delivers access to streaming games to millions of users on laptops, PlayStation platforms, PCs, TVs and even more. GaiKai is a Japanese word that translates to "vast and open ocean" .(GaiKai,2008) In the beginning it started as video game advertising platform, but since then has evolved to streaming games to multiple popular websites available on the internet. They claim to have built the world's fastest open cloud gaming platform, thus enabling game streaming on connected smart TVs and mobile devices. Two business models are used by GaiKai for its cloud gaming services:

- Ad Network, and
- Open Platform.

In Ad Network model, after the customer has gone through the game demo, they are given a choice to purchase the game or product from a online retailer, local retailer or directly download the game. Ad Network, which included the GaiKai affiliate network, launched in June, 2011, reached over 10 million monthly active users by the end of the year. Several Websites which later joined the network were able to stream multiple high-end PC games as embedded advertising, and later received in return a share of the marketing revenue generated from games streamed to users, who got opportunity to play demos free of charge. GaiKai enabled games are also being integrated into EA's Origin, YouTube and Ubisoft's UBIshop. In April 2012, GaiKai launched a service embedded inside Facebook, allowing several games too be streamed inside of Facebook, allowing games to be streamed directly in the Facebook canvas.

The Open Platform model allowed streaming games to digital TVs, PCs, mobile devices and tablets. The first mobile partnership came in May 2012, where streaming games on the Wikipad tablet was started. In June 2012, Samsung announced a cloud gaming service powered by GaiKai to stream games to its high end Smart TVs.

Gaikai vs. OnLive

The one levelling factor between these two services it that they both have little in the way of network resources to utilize. Current levels of internet bandwidth shed light on the fact that there exists a really tight budget for transmitting HD video encoded at real time. The end result is that OnLive and Gaikai have taken different paths in how the bandwidth is utilized, giving varied results.

OnLive's major target is known to be temporal resolution, where the player enjoys 60 frames per second gaming. This helps in overcoming latency vulnerabilities and this induces a sense that there exists a faster moving image that makes it harder for the human eye to track the compression artifacting. GaiKai's approach is quite the opposite, which is to double the image quality. Also there are more are powerful servers running the games as much high graphical specifications and thus resulting in an improved experience when the games are being played. But there is a noticeable lack on inconsistency in the way the frames are rendered.

Gaikai is marginally ahead when the lag factor is considered. OnLive is known to be vulnerable to poor response rates and inconsistency in latency. The overall experience does not compare to that on the Xbox 360 or PlayStation 3. On the other hand, Gaikai enjoys an advantage as they have more locally based datacenters. On noticeable drawback is that if any game drops frames server-side in Gaikai, the resultant impact to response rates is more noticeable than it is with OnLive.

Cloud gaming technologies are still in their nascent phase. Technologies used by OnLive and Gaikai are still first gen products in which the technology used is far from mature. Cloud gaming has certainly shown genuine promise, and the concepts being developed has a lot of potential. OnLive's main advantage over GaiKai are frame-rate, while GaiKai are ahead in terms of game specifications, video encoding and overall latency. Based on current user feedback, certain games on Gaikai are known to be running with the same latency as on the Xbox 360. This is a clear indication that cloud could be a viable contender in the future. The technology being used has already shown that it is capable of achieving miracles and with further advance in resources used and infrastructure, cloud gaming experiences are only going to get better and better.

Nvidia Grid

Nvidia Grid is built on the concept of cloud gaming, where large cloud managed libraries of content can be streamed to all devices connected to the grid. It took over 20 years of software and hardware innovations in the accelerated graphics field to deliver such a rich graphics experience to various users running grid-connected virtual desktops or applications.

Nvidia calls this system as "revolutionary clod-gaming architecture", where such technology can allow the user to render graphics completely in the cloud. In the near future, this allows for any user to play full graphics games via the internet from anywhere. This system will be able to provide gaming experience on par with the traditional gaming consoles and personal computers connected at home. The system uses a tablet ASIS Transformer Prime packed with Nvidia Tegra-3. The tablet works with an Nvidia Grid app that is connected to the grid of cloud.

This system can be synced with any device, not just a smart TV or a computer, but also be able to play full feature, graphically immersive games in the cloud. This may change the way we play games from top to bottom. The Grid renders 3D games in cloud servers, encode each frame instantly and streams the result to any device with a wired of wireless broadband connection.

Several service providers can use Nvidia grid as the foundation for their on demand gaming as a Service (GaaS) solution, where users can experience tremendous advantages over traditional systems such as:

- **Device Independent Gaming:** High-quality, low-latency, multi device gaming on any connected device.
- **Inherent Simplicity:** Anytime access to a library of games and saved games in the cloud. One can save, play and continue games anytime.
- **Simple Setup:** No changes in hardware. No complications in setting up the game. Game discs and digital downloads are not required. Also no need for installing the game or even installing patches. The games will be updated frequently directly on the server, where the responsibility of delivering such updates solely depends on the game manufacturer.

Nvidia Grid GPU

Nvidia's Kepler based Grid K1 and K2 boards are specifically designed and used to enable rich graphics and experience in cloud based virtual environments. Some of the significant features of the GPU used are:

- **Maximum User Density:** These boards have an optimized multi-GPU design that helps to increase user density in the system. The K1 board features 4 GPUs and 16 GB of memory. Combined with Nvidia Grid vGPU technology, this supports up to 32 users on a single board.
- **Power Efficiency:** These board are designed to enable data center-class power efficiency, including ta streaming multiprocessor, called "SMX". This results in an innovative solution that delivers high performance per-watt for the enterprise data center.
- **Reliability:** The grid boards are designed for high degree of reliability. Using various existent technologies for such kind of servers by vendors such as Cisco, Dell, HP, IBM, and SuperMicro ensures that the cards perform optimally for the life of the system.

Nvidia has developed a low-latency remote display technology which greatly improves the user experience by reducing the lap that users experience when using the virtual machine. This technology encodes the virtual desktop screen and then is pushed directly to the remoting protocol. Every Kepler GPU is a high performance H.264 encoding engine that is capable of encoding multiple continuous streams with superior quality. This increases the cloud server efficiency by offloading the CPU from the encoding functions and allowing the encoding function to scale the all the GPUs in a server. The grid remoting technology is available in industry leading remote display protocols, such as Citrix HDX 3D Pro, VMware Horizon View and NICE DCV.

- **Grid Virtualization:** Grid cards are essential in GPU-capable virtualization solutions from Citrix, Microsoft and VMware, delivering the flexibility to select one among a wide range of solutions. Grid GPUs can be used by a single high-end user of shared among multiple users.

Nvidia GRID vGPU

The grid boards feature Kepler based GPUs that allow hardware virtualization of the GPU. This means that a single GPU can be shared by multiple users, thus improving overall user density while providing true PC performance and high application capability.

Grid solutions improve the overall performance of virtual desktops and applications, thus resulting the enterprise IT to deliver high quality graphics to any user on the network. The technology consists of both hardware and software including Nvidia Grid vGPU technology that enables hardware virtualization of the GPU. (Nvidia, 2010)

Benefits of Nvidia Grid to **IT**:

- Industry leading virtualization solutions,
- Cater to graphic intensive user by providing them with virtual solutions,
- Increase in productivity and mobility for users,
- Efficient IP security for assets.

Benefits of Nvidia Grid for Users:

- 3D-intensive applications are accessible,
- Rich, highly responsive experiences,
- Access independent of location and device.

Advantages of Cloud Based Gaming Services

1. **Development of Games Not Constrained by Individual Configurations:** Normally game developers face many hardships to develop games which can run smoothly in various different platforms, different architecture base or different OS. Apart from these hardships it is observed that the limitation of graphics support by different devices has been a major issue in game development. It has been felt and noticed since the evolution of gaming industry that graphics>gameplay. Hence to overcome these hardships, majority of the gaming industry giants are switching over to cloud.

2. **Running High End Games in Mobile Devices:** In present day scenario, most of the high end games run primarily on PCs which have powerful configurations and architecture support to meet the requirements of those games. But by using cloud, passionate mobile gamers can therefore enjoy the high end games on mobile itself. Mainly the limited hardware support and graphics of mobile devices were a limitation for running the high end games, but with the usage of cloud, the mobile devices will just act like a dummy client with the actual game running on the powerful cloud servers.

3. **Storage Space of the Client Will Be Saved:** Much of the storage area of the host device will be saved and can be utilized for important purpose rather than

just storing the game files since the actual game will be stored on the cloud servers. The size of high end games has always been a concern since they consume large amount of storage capacity of the device, escaping this will certainly be encouraged by the gamers and can really prove a boon to further encouragement in usage of cloud based gaming services.

4. **Integrating Gaming into Televisions and Similar Devices:** The television manufacturers can integrate gaming options into their products using cloud gaming services wherein they need not embed specific gaming hardware's into their television sets yet giving the pleasure of gaming experience to the users thereby enhancing their sales. Recently Playcast Media Systems have become the first gaming on demand technology for IPTV and Cable TV in the world and has partnerships with major video game developers such as Disney, Atari and Activision. The integration of gaming into televisions will give a better gaming experience to the users because of the large and better displays on televisions.

5. **Simplifying the Multiplayer Online Gaming Experience:** Since the game is actually running on a common device being shared by different gamers currently playing therefore the chances of any lagging of the game at the user's end is reduced. If some error occurs to the server it will be a common problem to all users and won't be specific to a particular player, so each and every player will always be at par with others. Similarly, it will be much easy to host international gaming competitions wherein the game will be monitored just at the cloud servers rather than individually monitoring the different participants.

6. **The Host Device's Operating System Won't Affect Gaming Experience:** The presence of a particular Operating System on the client's device won't affect the gameplay since the resources of the client are hardly used to execute the background files for running the game. Normally cloud servers have multiple OS running, and it is the responsibility of the game developers to properly execute the games on different OS as per the client request is made. Therefore, a game which has been designed to run on Android can actually be accessed by a person using Mac and vice versa thereby providing platform independence and even more flexibility.

7. **Prevention of Piracy:** Piracy has been one of the serious issues which are incurring heavy loss to the game developers. If the games are installed on cloud servers instead of local hosts it will be almost impossible to pirate. So, if not to the gamers, but this aspect of cloud gaming will be highly advantageous to the developer's point of view.

Limitations/Disadvantages of Cloud Based Gaming Services

1. **Quality of Gaming Experience Might Be Hampered:** Since cloud gaming is entirely dependent on the available bandwidth to the client, therefore the quality of video game is highly dependent on the bandwidth utilization. Depending on the available bandwidth many of the aspects of the games are compressed thereby definitely affecting the quality. Normally it's the video quality which is affected the most. The fps(frames/second) will reduce thereby giving a poor visual experience. Furthermore, this becomes a critical condition in multiplayer games where the data has to be transmitted thrice, once to the cloud servers making a game request, a return data from the servers to the clients and finally the data are transmitted to the different end users interacting in the multiplayer game. This creates further load on the communication link thereby reducing the available bandwidth.

2. **Security Breaches:** This is undoubtedly the most important issue and must be dealt with details. Before going further into details of security breaches, one should have an overview of the basic cloud model. It is divided into three types of services:-

   a. **Infrastructure as a Service (IaaS):** Under this, basic computer resources such as storage, networking etc are provided to the clients wherein they can deploy/use their applications. Here the extensibility is very high as the user can perform a lot of tasks on the cloud platform.

      i. **Threat in IaaS:** Since IaaS provides a pool of resources such as the basic hardware, storage allocation and many more to the clients, majority of security breaches occur at the IaaS. Let us suppose that a game provider is using the IaaS facility provided in cloud. Now he performs virtualization in order to create or roll back virtual machines so that he may run variety of games on the same infrastructure. Now as a virtual machine is deployed there are high chances of security breaches since there comes two boundaries, a virtual and a physical unlike physical servers which have just a physical boundary. Virtual Machine security is further more important due to sharing of the same CPU or the shared memory in the same game server. A malicious virtual machine can corrupt all the game files stored in the game servers via the shared memory.

   b. **Platform as a Service (PaaS):** In PaaS, the cloud provider supports the users by giving him privileges to use various platforms wherein he can execute his applications without installing them on their systems. This provides a greater extensibility is obviously more than IaaS but certainly less than SaaS.

     i.   **Threat in PaaS:** In PaaS developers don't have access to the un-derlying layers of the game servers. Even if they secure their own platform they are not assured that the underlying layer provided by the PaaS providers are totally secured. Another threat can arise because of non-timely and desynchronized updates of platforms and the applications. Developers must be cautious enough to understand that any updation or changes in the platforms can significantly pose a security threat to their application. Normally, the security breaches in PaaS are not much as compared to IaaS since much of the control is in the hands of the PaaS providers rather than the clients.

    c.   **Software as a Service (SaaS):** Herein, the users are allowed to use the various functionalities or software services deployed in the cloud, such as email applications, file converter softwares etc. Here the extensibility is certainly the least as compared to other two.

     i.   **Threat in SaaS**: With reference to cloud gaming, SaaS services can be such as online market where users can buy or upgrade certain aspects of the game. Now since these applications are typically car-ried using a web browser, any defects or lose ends in the browser can serve as a serious threat to the application. There can always be a man in the middle between the client and the SaaS application who can intercept the data and manipulate them thereby completely affecting the gaming experience of the client.

3.   **Costly Operation:** Cloud gaming is costly to operate from user's point of view. The user has to be constantly connected to the internet during the entire course of play since the game files are actually stored in the cloud servers and are rendered on the clients, secondly if the user plays games that utilize a lot of resources like a first person shooter or MMO, this method can become costlier. Normally there is always a lag in cloud gaming due to dropping of frames. Even the best setups have certain amount of lag. To make the situa-tion similar in experience to that of playing on a console, it would require a very high quality of fibre optic connection to the servers that is as close to the client as possible. This would in a way mean, setting up more data centers to cover the entire population. As per the research from the Fiber to the Home Council, a fiber optic advocacy group, a general project of such a scale can cost something on the order of $89.2 billion.

4.   **Latency:** Latency has been one of the major problems in cloud based gam-ing services. A lot of research by tech giants such as OnLive and Microsoft are still going on to reduce the latency as much as possible, but it is a serious issue which hampers the smooth gaming experience of the user. Basically the latency can be calculated taking into consideration the following criterions:

a. **Network Delay (ND):** The total round trip time which includes the time required to send the game request to the game servers and receiving the response from the servers is known as Network delay. It is also usually referred to as the Round-Trip Time (RTT) (Hong et al, 2015).

b. **Processing Delay (PD):** The difference between the time when the server receives the game request from the client and the generation of the first response signal from the server is known as processing delay. In other words, it is the time taken by the server to process the player's command (made from the client) (Hong et al, 2015).

c. **Playout Delay (OD):** The difference between the time interval when the client receives the encod0ed form of the response from the server and the time taken by the client to decode the response to present on the screen is known as playout delay (see Figure 2, Hong et al, 2015).

As shown in the Figure 3, there is a client device which has pressed the escape button to display the menu screen. The key event is sent as a request to the game server where the processing occurs and the response frame is generated and sent to the client. Now let us assume, the escape key is pressed at time to. This request is received at the server end at time t1, the frame is sent from the server at time t2. Now (t2-t1) is the processing delay when the request gets executed in the servers. At time t3 the frame is received by the client from the server and is displayed at time t4. The time interval t4-t3 is therefore the playout delay. Now summing the entire flowchart, t4-t0 is the actual response delay of the ESC button.

Figure 2. The overall response delay (RD) is the sum of network delay + processing delay + playout delay.

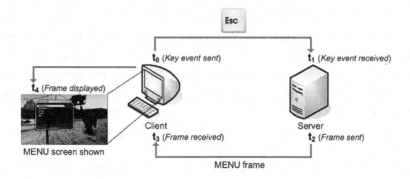

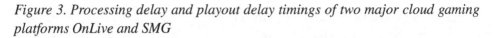

Figure 3. Processing delay and playout delay timings of two major cloud gaming platforms OnLive and SMG

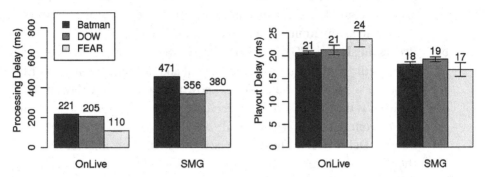

5. **DRM- DRM:** Stands for Digital Rights Management. It refers to the class of technologies, used by the hardware organisations, publishers, or individuals with the intent of controlling the use of the products after sale, thereby controlling piracy. Game developers love DRM which is properly implemented by using cloud, but many gamers would be at a loss if cloud gaming became the primary source of playing video games (Hoffman, 2013). In the third world countries, the slow internet speed acts as a major hindrance in cloud gaming resulting in latency or dropping of frames thereby giving a poor gaming experience. Therefore, the gamers in those areas will be at a disadvantage if cloud gaming becomes the only option for their recreation.

FUTURE OF CLOUD GAMING

Cloud based gaming services obviously has a very bright future. It can provide gaming experiences which has never been felt before. It will provide gaming experiences to those users who might otherwise have not picked up video gaming. Since cloud gaming has large number of advantages especially that it will greatly reduce the loss which the game industry suffers out of piracy, most of the game developers are focusing on shifting into cloud services. This is one major reason for a bright future of cloud gaming. By tapping into the enormous advantages in the field of network technology over the past several years, gaming can reach those who might otherwise would have never picked up gaming. In this process, it will indirectly serve to foster further acceptance of the cloud, gradually as more and more users get familiarized with the working of cloud.

Even as of now, cloud computing has made sufficient amount of progress in gaming industry. Take for example, Valve, which offers steam cloud wherein a user is allowed to upload his/her profile, saved games to an online server which can be accessed by any device connected to the steam cloud thereby providing a smooth functioning of sharing of game files or information. Considering the amount of progress which has already been made in cloud gaming as is evident, it is obvious that the future of cloud gaming is going to be bright.

Different MNC's are showing interest in the field of cloud gaming. Big giants such as Microsoft, Amazon, Sony, OnLive are pouring huge amount of money to research in this particular field. The major field of future research in cloud gaming is to reduce the lag. Microsoft is currently working on it product known as DeLorean which they term as 'speculative execution engine'. In near future if everything goes right the lagging issue can almost come to an end. According to Microsoft, gamers can notice a lag of around 60 milliseconds on a multiplayer game but as the lag gradually increases to over 100 milliseconds and into the 200 milliseconds range the gamers start getting annoyed. Microsoft claims that in near future their DeLorean can create a smooth gaming experience to the gamers even if the lag is around 200 milliseconds on their back end.

Similarly, Sony's $380-million acquisition of Gaikai, after which the company announced PlayStation Now—an extremely ambitious initiative which will certainly revolutionize the distribution of video games. PlayStation Now will let you stream PlayStation 3 games over the internet using the cloud servers to almost any device imaginable, from Sony PS Vita or the Sony TVs or the smartphones and tablets.

Thus, it is quite evident going through the above real world examples that cloud gaming has a very bright future. The main concern as of now is the advancement in the internet technology to support the cloud infrastructure, especially in the developing nations. Once it is achieved, cloud gaming will in a way become the major source of gaming for enthusiast gamers.

REFERENCES

Chen, K. T., Chang, Y. C., Hsu, H. J., Chen, D. Y., Huang, C. Y., & Hsu, C. H. (2014). On the quality of service of cloud gaming systems. *Multimedia. IEEE Transactions on*, *16*(2), 480–495.

Gibbon, D. (2010, April 05). *PS3 to allow PC games to run on it*. Retrieved from www.digitalspy.com

Hong, H. J., Chen, D. Y., Huang, C. Y., Chen, K. T., & Hsu, C. H. (2015). Placing virtual machines to optimize cloud gaming experience. *Cloud Computing. IEEE Transactions on*, *3*(1), 42–53.

Ricker, T. (2009, March 20). *OnLive killed the game console star?*. Retrieved from Engadget.com

Sony Computer Entertainment to Acquire Gaikai Inc., a Leading Interactive Cloud Gaming Company. (2008, November) Retrieved 2015-12-12.

Sun. (2010, March 26). *NVIDIA GeForce GTX480 Video Card Review: Streaming Multiprocessor*. Retrieved from Motherboards.org

Chapter 8

Mixed Augmented Reality Systems for Real World Integration

Raajan N. R.
SASTRA University, India

Nandhini Kesavan
SASTRA University, India

ABSTRACT

Augmented Reality (AR) plays a vital role in the field of visual computing. AR is actually different but often confused to be the same is Virtual Reality (VR). While VR creates a whole new world, AR aims at designing an environment in real time with virtual components that are overlaid on the real components. Due to this reason, AR comes under the category of 'mixed reality'. AR could be viewed on any smart electronic gadgets like mobile, laptop, projector, tablet etc., AR could be broadly classified as Marker-based and Markerless. If it is marker-based, a pattern is used whereas in markerless system there is no need of it. In case of marker, if we show the pattern to a webcam it will get details about it and impose the object on the marker. We are incorporating a new efficient solution for integrating a virtual object on to a real world which can be very much handful for tourism and advertisement for showcasing objects or things. The ultimate goal is to augmenting the 3D video onto a real world on which it will increase the person's conceptual understanding of the subject.

DOI: 10.4018/978-1-5225-0546-4.ch008

INTRODUCTION

Many systems today are too difficult to use because of complex user interfaces. This is partially due to a lack of competence in designing user interfaces many engineers suffer from. A more important reason is that with the growing computational power of modern systems, devices and applications become more complex and integrate more features. Soft- and hardware that was only available to a small amount of specialists a few decades ago, is now a well-integrated part of everyone's daily life. Go o d user interface design is therefore no longer an option but a hard requirement for developing highly usable applications. Augmented Reality (AR) research aims at developing new human computer interfaces. Instead of showing information on isolated displays, it puts data right where it belongs: into the real world. AR thereby blurs the distinction between the real world and the user interface and combines them in a natural way allowing the creation of simple and intuitive user interfaces even for complex applications.

MOTIVATIONAL OVERVIEW

Since the birth of computing technology, humans have used computers as a tool to further their progress. Numerical computation has always been the backbone of computing technology, but as this technology advances, a wider range of high-level tools are realized. AR is ultimately the addition of computer-generated information related to the user's current perception of reality. The more information we have ab out our surroundings, the better equipped we are to function in that environment. This concept of information as a useful tool has been seen in all aspects of life. Equipped with a map and compass, someone can more easily navigate through an unfamiliar environment. The map informs the user of environmental information while the compass provides a sense of direction relative to that environment. These tools are useful aids, but they still leave room for human expertise for their effective use. Imagine the same user equipped with a wearable computer continuously providing directional information to keep this user on course. This technology could guide a user with limited knowledge through completely foreign environments. AR has many known uses and will continue to advance the human toolset as its technology advances. The medical field has been significantly impacted by the introduction of AR. The ability of a surgeon to visualize the inside of a patient can greatly improve the precision of operation. Other fields have also been positively impacted. From the augmentation of live NFL broadcasts, where the "first down line" is added to the assisted maintenance of aircraft through heads-up information, AR is proven to be a useful and powerful tool in our society. These forms of human-computer interaction involve one-way communication. The computer system acquires knowledge pertaining to the user, position and orientation for example and uses this knowledge to communicate to the user in context. The user's view of the environment is then augmented with pertinent information. It is understood that the power of AR would be taken a step further with the introduction of user interaction with the augmented information. This interaction would allow the user to decide if, how, when and where information is augmented. The ability of the user to interact with and control the augmented world is currently missing in AR systems. For AR to become as common as the wristwatch, an acceptable mechanism for such two-way communication must be established.

History

The first arrival of augmented reality dates back to 1901 when L. Frank Baum, proposed a concept of electronic displays / spectacles that overlaps virtual information onto reality. It was named as character marker. Next, in 1962 Morton Heilig built a model called Sensorama that could encompass all the senses (sounds, vibrations, smell, and visuals) in an effective way, thus drawing the viewer into the onscreen motion. Sutherland designed the HMD in 1966. In the year 1968, he was the only person to introduce an optical catch by HMD using AR system. In late 1970s, Myron Krueger generates video place, in a way that permits consumers to correlate with simulated articles. Subsequently, David Mizell and Tom Caudell from Boeing coined the term AR while assisting doers to accumulate cables and wires for aviation industry. Simultaneously, L.B Rosenberg designed the initial working model of AR and revealed its value on mankind operations although Steven Feiner, Doree Seligmann and Blair MacIntyre laid out the presented on an AR system model so-called KARMA. The reality virtuality range was vague till 1994 by Fumio Kishino and Paul Milgram as a continuum that ranges from the actual to practical surroundings (Figure 1). Reality and virtuality are sited in mid-point with AV found closer to virtual surrounding and AR intimate to natural world. By 1997, Ronald Azuma initiated AR enabling a widely recognized resolution of AR by naming it as collating virtual and natural world as both recorded in 3-D and synergistic in real time. The foremost open-air mobe AR game was AR Quake is designed by Bruce Thomas in the 21st century and revealed in International Symposium on Wearable Computers. As the study of Horizon forecasts that AR engineering science will rise completely within the adjacent years and to authorize that forecasting, see through systems that can inspect forcible surroundings in physical time and share points among surroundings and objects are designed in 2005. This system of tools has become the

Figure 1. Milgram's reality-virtuality continuum

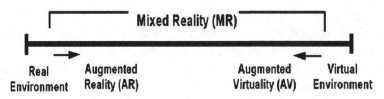

Reality-Virtuality (RV) Continuum

foundation to mix reality with virtuality in AR model. In future years, increasingly AR usage are designed mainly with smart-phone apps for example Wikitude AR Travel Guide established in 2008.

Objective

This report describes a method to generate real-time virtual views in which real objects observed by a camera are replaced with virtual objects. We are aimed augmenting a virtual thing (3D video) over a single marker or real world were the 3D video has to be displayed when the object is recognized. Here when a user looks at some objects or pictures through the smart phones, the system captures the image and search it over the database which consists of pattern files and 3D video. The program links the corresponding pattern files with the 3D video. The main feature of this is 3D video playback, 3D video rotates according to the marker. If user is seeing the interactive 3D video regarding the object, due to some unconditional circumstances part of the object will not be in frame so the video gets disconnected, but our proposed method, users will be able to see the video from where it got disconnected. Our approach to the virtual view generation will be based up on a full 3D structure of the scene is constructed and then reprojected in order to generate a virtual which requires relatively cheap computational cost. To avoid numerical instability of 3D reconstruction, our method finds and tracks only a moderate number of apparent feature points. This is will be very much helpful for tourism, for instance even if we are at forest looking at a tree with the help of AR we can see museum style information and video regarding what tree it is, how it will be useful for curing some disease and many more, this all information will pop ups on the screen. I f we look at another example like if you are looking at some monument or statue, you will be eager to know information regarding what it is instead of giving 30 or 50 bugs to the guide and asking him to tell all the information regarding monument we can use AR by simple pointing out the smart phone over it, we will get interactive 3D video regarding monument history. So there are just very early concepts what kind of things we can do with AR to day this is not a science fiction it will get much more advanced as this decade goes on and AR will be next mass media.

Capturing the 3D content of a live feed with the help of web cam is a sequential process that involves several steps:

1.   The web cam of the system is integrated with the software application using appropriate commands.
2.   The appropriate view of the live feed is generated.
3.   The view is rendered into the scene possibly taking into account the occlusions.

AR makes the working environment more appealing and interesting with its animation and certain other features. AR finds its application in our day to day life. In case of Marker-based AR, the first and foremost step is to create the marker. Here, marker creation could be done using two main methods namely creating marker using toolkit and marker creation using self. In the first method, a pattern is selected in such a way that it should have the combination of binary (Black and white) information alone. It should have a particular size and particular width for outer and inner boundary. The toolkit is specially made for generating marker. In the second method, the dimensionless markers are created and analyzed over AR. It needs to have the same condition with color. In *digitizing the marker*, the marker is first created which is then fed into the webcam which is followed by sampling and quantization. Creating the entity could be done either by using open source or with the help of third party software. While creating using open source, many open source software are available for visualizing 3D animated pictures. Marker as the identity the 3D animated image can be made over the marker. In the second method, it is also possible to execute the after creation of marker to have it as a tool. After digitizing the marker, the digital data that integrates with the software will act as the input entity and the animated data will be available as the output entity for this we need to recognize marker pattern for the same. As soon as the camera is interfaced with the system the tool tries to recognize the marker and play appropriate animation for markers available. It is an integration of real world entity and artificially animated entity.

In case of marker less the marker is recognized. Select any specific color images and create it as marker. For example: a world renowned car company is launching a new model on showroom, usually they give ads to the public and the particular pattern (car or model) can be made as a marker where the procedure remains the same as of marker based AR model and it tries to follow the below steps for recognition namely Pattern matching, Pattern classification and BW/Color. Once the marker is created, it is digitized then the entity is created which is then followed by fixing the entity towards a marker and playing with the marker.

REVIEW OF RELATED LITERATURE

Adhitya et al. (2010) and Hull et al. (2007) describes that all information in the real world could be brought to a white paper such that people need not move about in search of details. The authors have achieved better performance when they tried to load information of a particular region. Clay et al. (2012) expresses their interest in using the tools in AR to cultural platform such as a live dance show whereas Zoellner et al. (2009) and Raajan et al. (2012) explains the visualization of the historic scenes, photos, paintings etc., Kim (2012) deals with the users who wish to pursue research in AR and VR, the basic facts that are to be taken into account in order to continue their research. Nakamura et al. (2012) and Vladimir Geroimenko (2012) discusses how multimedia services with high quality could be delivered to users according to their expectations and Lyu et al. (2005) and Yang (2011) tells how AR could bring a different viewing experience to the viewers, Herold et al. (2008) and Suganya et al. (2012) describes the viewing experience of OLED-on-CMOS technology. Fischer et al. (2005) and Nojima et al. (2002) discusses how improvement in the immersion of AR could be done using stylization techniques where Wang et al. (2010) deals about the usefulness of rendering and relighting in AR. Juan et al. (2004) and Raajan et al. (2012) explains how people who have phobias for cockroach could be treated with AR tools. Bajura and Neumann (1995), and Gammeter et al. (2010) discusses how visual registration problem occurs when the same person views the same image naturally and with the help of webcam. Based on visual recognition, mobile augmented reality system is generated. Arcella et al. (2008) chooses a school student with some knowledge on kinematics, mixes real world data and synthetic data and helps in viewing the physical experiment with the help of a webcam. Hincapié et al. (2011), and Deffeyes and Katz (2010) makes us realize the usefulness of AR. It tells how it is possible to interact with the hardware when they are in the data center. Tokunaga et al. (2003) and Ferreira et al. (2007) discusses the design and development of software infrastructure for the purpose of building AR applications for ubiquitous computing environments.

VISION-BASED TRACKING FOR REGISTRATION

Introduction

The AR interaction system described in this report uses computer vision-based tracking to solve the registration problem. This chapter outlines the details of the tracking system which is based on the work introduced and is used as a platform for extending the system capabilities to allow interaction in the augmented environment. The key to extracting the camera parameters in a given image sequence is to understand the motion characteristics of the captured scene throughout that sequence. The intrinsic and extrinsic parameters of the camera are directly reflected in the captured scene. Inferring scene characteristics through the detection and tracking of natural features can often be fruitless and time-consuming when the computer system has no prior knowledge with which to start. To simplify this process, preconstructed planar patterns are used as reference elements in the scene giving the analysis process a target to detect and track. This simplification results in camera motion being computed relative to the target in the captured scene. Describing the planar tracking system in more detail manner is very essential to have a better understanding of the various AR applications.

Camera Calibration

Camera Calibration is the process of calculating the intrinsic (focal length, image center and aspect ratio) camera parameters. This is accomplished by viewing a predefined 3D pattern from different viewpoints. Along with the intrinsic camera parameters the extrinsic parameters (pose) of the camera are also computed. Figure 2 shows an example of a calibration pattern where the 3D world coordinates of the butterflies are known ahead of time.

Figure 2. A camera calibration setup

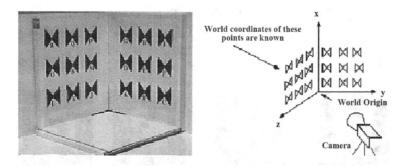

The calibration procedure used in is outlined as follows:

1. The camera is pointed at the calibration grid.
2. A copy of the camera image is read into the computer via a frame grabber.
3. The centers of the butterfly patterns are located within the grabbed image which gives the 2D image coordinates corresponding to the known 3D locations of the actual butterflies. This step can be performed with manual point selection or by an automatic method.
4. This process is repeated for a number of different camera positions. The known 3D coordinates of the pattern points are used to find both the intrinsic and extrinsic camera parameters. The accuracy of such a camera calibration procedure can be affected by the nonlinear lens distortions of the camera. Pinhole camera model that is used assumes that there is no nonlinear distortion, whereas the lenses on real cameras sometimes distort the image in complex ways. Fortunately, in standard video based AR systems this distortion is often insignificant, and hence ignored. Another important point is that for augmented reality the final output is viewed by a person, and people can tolerate a small amount of visual distortion. So the radial distortion can be ignored in many AR applications.

PLANAR PATTERNS

The appearance of the patterns used is tightly coupled with the requirements of the video analysis algorithms. Therefore, a rigid set of constraints is placed on patterns used by the system. The stored visual representation of each pattern is a 64x64 pixel bitmap image. This image is essentially a black square containing white shapes defining a set of interior corners. A text file, storing the corner locations, accompanies the image file to form the internal representation of the pattern. Figure 3 shows some samples of patterns used by the system. The scene representation of a pattern, herein referred to as a target, is printed on white paper in such a way as to leave a white border around the black square.

Figure 3. Sample patterns

This high contrast pattern, and hence target, simplifies delectability and ensures a well-defined set of interior and exterior corners. These corners are used as the fundamental scene features in all the camera parameter calculations. Between any two `frames of video containing the planar target, the position correspondences of the corner points define a 2D to 2D transformation. This transformation, known as a planar homography, represents a 2D perspective projection representation of the camera motion relative to the target. Over time, this definition of the camera path would accumulate errors. In order to avoid such dynamic error, the homography transformation is instead defined from pattern-space to image-space. In other words, a homography is computed for each frame using the point locations in the original pattern and their corresponding locations in the image frame. Figure 4 shows the relationship between the camera, image and target (world) coordinate systems.

PLANAR HOMOGRAPHIES

A planar homography, H, is a 3x3 matrix defining a projective transformation in the plane (up to scale) as follows:

$$\begin{bmatrix} x' \\ y' \\ 1 \end{bmatrix} = H \begin{bmatrix} x \\ y \\ 1 \end{bmatrix} \tag{1}$$

Figure 4. Camera, image, and target coordinate systems

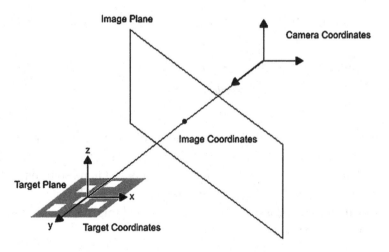

This assumes that the target plane is z = 0 in world coordinates. Each point correspondence generates two linear equations for the elements of H. Dividing by the third component removes the unknown scale factor:

$$
x' = \frac{h_{11}x + h_{12}y + h_{13}}{h_{31}x + h_{32}y + h_{33}}
$$
$$
y' = \frac{h_{21}x + h_{22}y + h_{23}}{h_{31}x + h_{32}y + h_{33}}
$$

(2)

Multiplying out Equation 2 and rearranging them will give:

$$
\begin{bmatrix} x & y & 1 & 0 & 0 & 0 & -x'x & -x'y & -x' \\ 0 & 0 & 0 & x & y & 1 & -y'x & -y'y & -y' \end{bmatrix} h = 0
$$

(3)

where,

$$
h = \left(h_{11}, h_{22}, h_{13}, h_{21}, h_{22}, h_{23}, h_{31}, h_{32}, h_{33} \right)^T
$$

is the matrix H written as a vector. For 4 point correspondences we get:

$$
\begin{bmatrix} x_1 & y_1 & 1 & 0 & 0 & 0 & -x_1'x_1 & -x_1'y_1 & -x_1' \\ 0 & 0 & 0 & x_1 & y_1 & 1 & -y_1'x_1 & -y_1'y_1 & -y_1' \\ x_2 & y_2 & 1 & 0 & 0 & 0 & -x_2'x_2 & -x_2'y_2 & -x_2' \\ 0 & 0 & 0 & x_2 & y_2 & 1 & -y_2'x_2 & -y_2'y_2 & -y_2' \\ x_3 & y_3 & 1 & 0 & 0 & 0 & -x_3'x_3 & -x_3'y_3 & -x_3' \\ 0 & 0 & 0 & x_3 & y_3 & 1 & -y_3'x_3 & -y_3'y_3 & -y_3' \\ x_4 & y_4 & 1 & 0 & 0 & 0 & -x_4'x_4 & -x_4'y_4 & -x_4' \\ 0 & 0 & 0 & x_4 & y_4 & 1 & -y_4'x_4 & -y_4'y_4 & -y_4' \end{bmatrix} h = Ah = 0
$$

(4)

The solution h is the kernel of A. A minimum of 4 point correspondences, generating 2n linear equations, are necessary to solve for h. For n = 4 correspondences, A is a 2n x 9 matrix. In this situation there will not be a unique solution to $Ah = 0$. It is necessary to subject h to the extra constraint that $h = 1$. Then h is the eigenvector corresponding to the least eigenvalue of ATA, and this can be computed using standard numerical methods.

AUGMENTATION WITH PLANAR PATTERNS

Dimensional Augmentation

Using the homography directly provides a mechanism for augmenting 2D information on the plane defined by the target in the image sequence. This is done by projecting the 2D points defining the virtual object into image-space and rendering the virtual objects with respect to their image-space definition. This augmentation method is performed without camera calibration, since the camera parameters are not needed in order to compute the required homography.

In order to augment virtual content that is defined by a set of 3D coordinates, a new projection transformation must be defined. This transformation describes the relationship between the 3D world coordinates and their image-space representations. This projection can be computed by extracting the intrinsic and extrinsic parameters of the camera using a separate camera calibration process. As shown, the camera parameters can also be estimated using the computed homography to construct a perspective transformation matrix. This removes the need for a separate camera calibration step. This auto-calibration feature allows planar-centric augmentation to occur using any camera hardware. The perspective matrix is constructed as follows. The homography, H, can be expressed as the simplification of the perspective transformation in terms of the intrinsic and extrinsic parameters of the camera which gives:

$$
H = \begin{bmatrix} f_u r_{11} & f_u r_{12} & f_u r_{13} & f_u t_1 \\ f_v r_{21} & f_v r_{22} & f_v r_{23} & f_v t_2 \\ r_{31} & r_{32} & r_{33} & t_3 \end{bmatrix} \tag{5}
$$

where f_u and f_v are the respective horizontal and vertical components of the focal length in pixels in each of the u and v axes of the image, r_{ij} and t_i are the respective rotational and translational components of the camera motion. The orthogonality properties associated with the rotational component of the camera motion give the following equations:

$$
r_{11}^2 + r_{21}^2 + r_{31}^2 = 1 \tag{6}
$$

$$
r_{12}^2 + r_{22}^2 + r_{32}^2 = 1 \tag{7}
$$

$$
r_{11} r_{12} + r_{21} r_{22} + r_{31} r_{32} = 0 \tag{8}
$$

Combining Equation 8 with 5 gives:

$$\frac{h_{11}h_{12}}{f_u^2} + \frac{h_{21}h_{23}}{f_v^2} + h_{31}h_{32} = 0 \tag{9}$$

Similarly, combining Equation 8 with 6 and 7 gives:

$$\lambda^2\left(\left(\frac{h_{11}^2}{f_u^2}\right) + \left(\frac{h_{21}^2}{f_v^2}\right) + h_{31}^2\right) = 1 \tag{10}$$

$$\lambda^2\left(\left(\frac{h_{12}^2}{f_u^2}\right) + \left(\frac{h_{22}^2}{f_v^2}\right) + h_{32}^2\right) = 1 \tag{11}$$

for some scalar λ. By eliminating λ^2 in Equations 10 and 11 we get

$$\frac{h_{11}^2 - h_{12}^2}{f_u^2} + \frac{h_{21}^2 - h_{22}^2}{f_v^2} + h_{31}^2 - h_{32}^2 = 0 \tag{12}$$

We can then solve for f_u and f_v as follows:

$$f_u = \sqrt{\frac{h_{11}h_{12}(h_{21}^2 - h_{22}^2) - h_{21}h_{22}(h_{11}^2 - h_{12}^2)}{-h_{31}h_{32}(h_{21}^2 - h_{22}^2) - h_{21}h_{22}(h_{31}^2 - h_{32}^2)}} \tag{13}$$

$$f_v = \sqrt{\frac{h_{11}h_{12}(h_{21}^2 - h_{22}^2) - h_{21}h_{22}(h_{11}^2 - h_{12}^2)}{-h_{31}h_{32}(h_{11}^2 - h_{12}^2) - h_{21}h_{22}(h_{31}^2 - h_{32}^2)}} \tag{14}$$

Once these intrinsic focal lengths have been computed, a value for λ can be found using Equation 10 as follows:

$$\lambda = \frac{1}{\sqrt{\dfrac{h_{11}^2}{f_u^2} + \dfrac{h_{21}^2}{f_v^2} + h_{31}^2}} \tag{15}$$

The extrinsic parameters can be computed as follows:

$$r_{11} = \lambda \frac{h_{11}}{f_u} \quad r_{12} = \lambda \frac{h_{12}}{f_u} \quad r_{13} = r_{21}r_{32} - r_{31}r_{22}t_1 = \lambda \frac{h_{13}}{f_v} \tag{16}$$

$$r_{21} = \lambda \frac{h_{21}}{f_u} \quad r_{22} = \lambda \frac{h_{22}}{f_u} \quad r_{23} = r_{31}r_{12} - r_{11}r_{32}t_1 = \lambda \frac{h_{23}}{f_v} \tag{17}$$

$$r_{31} = \lambda h_{31} \quad r_{32} = \lambda h_{32} \quad r_{33} = r_{11}r_{22} - r_{21}r_{12}t_1 = \lambda h_{33} \tag{18}$$

PLANAR TRACKING SYSTEM OVERVIEW

In this section we will describe how the planar pattern tracking system is implemented. The system, outlined in Figure 5, uses computer vision techniques to detect, identify and track patterns throughout the real-time captured video sequence. The system begins by scaling the captured frame of video to 320 x 240 pixels and enters the detection mode if it is not already tracking a target. In this mode, an intensity threshold is used to create a binary representation of the image, converting each pixel intensity to black or white. This operation exploits the high-contrast of the target to isolate the target from the background. The binary image is then scanned for black regions of connected pixels, also known as blobs. A simple boundary test is performed on the blob pixels to choose four outer corners. These corner locations are used to define an initial homography, computed as described in the previous section. This homography is used to un-warp the target region in order to compare it with all patterns known to the system. If a pattern match is found, the system moves into tracking mode. In this mode, the previous corner locations and displacement are used to predict the corner locations in the current frame. A search window is positioned and scanned for each predicted corner to find its location with high accuracy. These refined corner locations are then used to update the current homography. The tracking facility continues until the number of detected corners is less than four. At this point the system returns to search mode.

Image Binarization

In order to detect a target in the image frame, it must stand out from its surroundings. The black and white pattern printed with a white b order supports this target isolation. To simplify the localization of potential targets in the image, a common

Figure 5. Tracking system overview

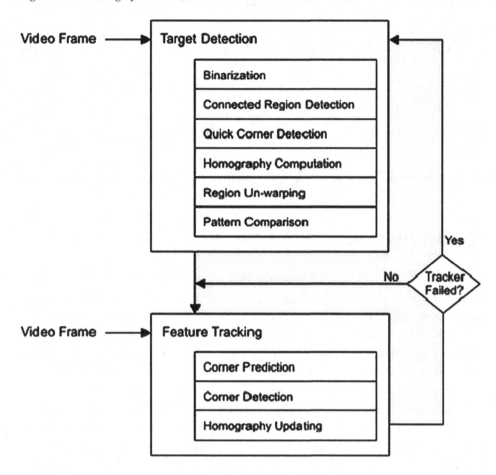

computer vision technique known as image binarization is employed. The image binarization process used by this system converts a grayscale image to a binary representation based on a threshold value, shown in Figure 6. The resulting binary image has the form:

$$P_B(X,Y) = \begin{cases} 0 & P_G(x,y) < T \\ 255 & P_G(x,y) > T \end{cases} \tag{19}$$

where $P_B(x, y)$ is the binary image pixel value at position (x,y), $P_G(x, y)$ is the grayscale image pixel value at position (x,y) and T is the threshold value. In this system the threshold value is constant over the entire image.

Figure 6. Image frame binarization

Connected Region Detection

In the binary representation of the captured frame, a planar target is represented by a connected region of black pixels. For this reason, a full-image scan is performed to locate all such regions.

A connected region of pixels is defined to be a collection of pixels where every pixel in the set has at least one neighbour of similar intensity. Figure 7 shows the 8-pixel neighbourhood of the central black pixel. To find a connected region, the system adds visited black pixels to a stack in order to minimize the overhead created by using a recursive algorithm.

Each pixel popped off the stack has its neighbourhood scanned, and each neighbouring black pixel is pushed onto the stack. This process continues until the stack

Figure 7. A sample pixel neighbourhood

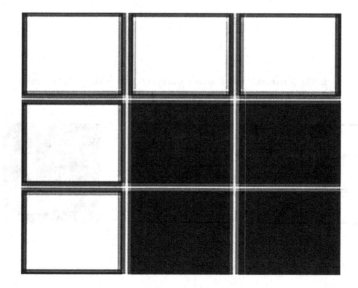

is empty. This connected region detection continues for all blobs in the image. The largest blob is chosen as the target candidate.

Quick Corner Detection

In order to verify and identify the detected target, a comparison must be made between the detected region and each pattern in the system. A proper verification is done by performing a pixel-by-pixel comparison of all 4096 pixels in each original pattern with those in the pattern-space representation of the target. This is done by computing a homography between pattern and image space and using it to un-warp the detected planar target into pattern space. To quickly find the four corners of the target, a simple foreground (black) to background (white) ratio is calculated for each pixel in the blob. As shown in Figure 8, it is assumed that the outer corners of the blob are the four pixels that have the lowest ratios.

Region Un-Warping

The homography H is then used to transform each of the pixel locations in the stored pattern to their corresponding location in the largest binary blob. These two values are compared and their difference is recorded. Where Figure 9 shows (Region un-warping (a) The original image frame (b) the un-warped target (c) the original pattern). The point location in the binary blob, P_B, is found by transforming the corresponding point location in the pattern image, P_p, using the following equation:

$$P_B = H(P_P) \tag{20}$$

Figure 8. Pixel classifications: (a) corner pixel, (b) boundary pixel, and (c) interior pixel

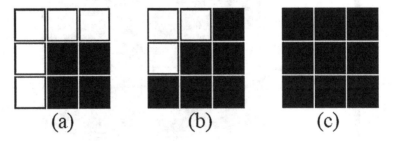

Figure 9. Region un-warping: (a) the original image frame (b) the un-warped target (c) the original pattern

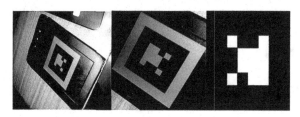

Pattern Comparison

An absolute difference value between each pixel in the stored pattern and warped binary image, $d_{P,B}(x, y)$, is then computed using the following formula:

$$d_{P,B} = I(P_P) - I(P_B) \tag{21}$$

Here I is the intensity value at a given pixel location in the binary blob and the pattern. This information is used to compute an overall score, $S_{P,B}$ for each pattern comparison given by:

$$S_{P,B} = \sum_{X=1}^{64} \sum_{Y=1}^{64} d_{P,B}(X,Y) \tag{22}$$

This process is repeated for each stored pattern in the system. To account for the orientation ambiguity, all four possible pattern orientations are scored. For n system patterns, 4n scores are computed and the pattern and orientation that produces the best score is chosen as the candidate pattern match. If this minimum computed score is less than a given threshold set by the system, the system decides that the chosen pattern corresponds to the target. It is important to note that with this identification process, target occlusion can greatly increase the computed scores due the potentially significant intensity changes introduced by such occlusion. When portions of the pattern are outside the video frame, the scoring mechanism will consider the hidden pixels values to be zero. This will also increase the score when white regions are outside the frame. For this reason, it is necessary for the intended target to be un-occluded and completely visible when the tracking system is in search mode. When a pattern match occurs, the system uses the known corner positions in the pattern to place initial search boxes in the image frame. These search boxes will be used as local search regions for the corner detection algorithm. By predicting the corner positions in each subsequent frame, corner detection can be performed directly within the updated search regions without the need for target detection. This behaviour occurs when the system is in the feature tracking mode.

Feature Tracking

Tracking features through a video sequence can be a complex task when the camera and scene features are in motion. To simplify the process, it is assumed that the change in feature positions will be minimal between subsequent frames. This is a reasonable assumption, given the 20-30Hz capture rate of the real-time system. Under this constraint, it is possible to apply a first order prediction scheme which uses the current frame information to predict the next frame.

Corner Prediction

For any captured frame, the system has knowledge of the homography computed for the previous frame along with the previous corner locations. The prediction scheme begins by applying this homography to the previous corners to compute a set of predicted corner locations in this frame. The previous corner displacements, in other words how much the corners moved from the previous frame, are then reapplied to act as the simple first-order prediction. Search windows are positioned around the newly predicted corner locations to prepare the system for corner detection. Figure 10 shows the set of search windows that produced by the corner detection system. An interesting capability of the system is the ability to relocate corners that were once lost.

Figure 10. Corner localization search boxes

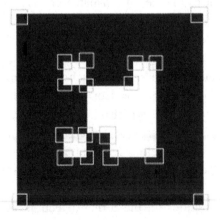

When a feature is occluded or it moves outside the cameras field of view, the corner detection process will fail for that corner. As long as the system continues to track a minimum number of corners it is able to produce a reasonable homography, and this homography can be used to indicate the image-space location of all target corners. This includes a prediction of locations for corners that are occluded. These predicted positions will have an error that is proportional to the error in the homography. As the invisible features become visible, this prediction scheme will place a search window with enough accuracy around the now visible corner to allow the corner detection algorithm to succeed.

Corner Detection

With the search windows in place, a Harris corner finder with sub-pixel accuracy is run on the local search window. The second step in the detection process is to extract the strongest corner within the search window, and to threshold the corner based on the corner strength. Corners that fail to be detected by this process are marked and excluded from further calculations for this frame. Successful corner detections are used to compute a new homography describing the current position of the target relative the camera.

Homography Updating

The detected corners in the current frame are used to form a set S of feature correspondences that contribute to the computation of a new homography. Using the entire correspondence set can result in significant homography error due to potential feature perturbation. The Harris operator can detect false corner locations when the corners are subjected to occlusion, frame boundary fluctuation and lighting changes. The error observed by the homography is in proportion to the sum of the feature position errors. Result of slight feature detection drift is slight homography error, which directly translates into slight augmentation drift. To minimize this homography error, a random sampling algorithm is performed. It has the goal of removing the features that generate significant homography error. The random sampling process generates a random set S, where $S \subseteq C$. A homography is then computed using the correspondences in S. This homography is then tested by transforming all features in c to compute an overall variance with respect to the actual detected corner locations. This process continues by choosing a new random set S, until a set producing a variance below a given maximum is found. If no such set S is found, the system exits tracking mode and attempts to perform target detection. Using random sampling allows for greater robustness in the presence of occlusion or detection of the wrong feature.

Camera Parameter Extraction

Using the described mathematics of planar homographies, the homography computed by the feature tracking system provides enough information to augment two dimensional virtual information onto the plane defined by the target in the world coordinate system. Using this homography, any 2D point relative to the center of the pattern in pattern-space can be transformed to a similarly positioned 2D point relative to the center of the target in image-space. For this reason, it is not necessary to compute the intrinsic and extrinsic camera parameters for this form of augmentation. Hence, two-dimensional augmentation can be performed by the system without requiring camera calibration. This avoids any complication of introducing any variety of camera and lens technology. Table 1 explains different tools based on ARToolKit.

AUGMENTED REALITY DEVICES

Presentation, stimulus devices, tagging, and estimators these are the major devices used for Augmented Reality.

Displays

Handheld displays, head bestrode displays (H MOUNTED D) and spatial displays are the three major types of display devices used in AR. H MOUNTED D is worn on the head which is a display device or as part of a spectacles and that combines both images of the virtual and real environment. H MOUNTED D can either be optical catch by or video-catch by and binocular display optic or monocular dis-

Table 1. Different tools based on ARToolKit

Name	Platform	Language
ARToolKitplus	*	C++
NyARToolKit	*	C++,java,AS3
osgART	*	C++
ARToolKit	*	C++
ArUco	*	C++
AndAR	Andriod	Java
SLARToolKit	WP7	Silverlight

play optic. Optical-catch by systems are less commanding than the video -catch by systems as the user has to hold cameras on his head which needs the processing of the two images coming from the cameras to deliver the enhanced part of scene by adding the computer generated virtual information. As the optical-catch by works on magic mirror technology to authorize the vision of real world to go over the lens and diagrammatically superimpose info to be replicated in the users senses (eyes). Then again, Video catch by systems enhanced vision is previously compiled by the PC and allow a check over the solution. Hence, checking all around the timing of the actual sight will be attained through coordinating the computer generated figure with the scene. In optical catch by apps, the picturing of actual data should not be late (delayed), so the delay of processing of images is apparent from user to user. Such properties in figure may not be attached to the actual object but they are made to be equate, due to this there will be unbalanced, floating when the user look on to it. Hand-held display devices consist of small processing devices that user can clamp in their reach Figure 11. Hand-held device usage moving picture-catch by methods to superimpose visuals on the physical world and uses sensing elements for example GPS and compasses for their 6th DOF tagging sensing elements, indicator systems, for instance machine vision methods (SLAM) or ARToolKit. There are presently trio different modules of commercially obtainable portable devices: PDAs, Tablet PCs and smart-phones. Mobile-phones are particularly handy and on the latest development present is a mixture of sinewy PC, GPS, measuring device etc. compass, creating them an identical promising stand for AR.

Figure 11. Handheld display

PDAs exist plentiful of the same pros and cons of the smart-phones, but because of recent advances in smart-phone technology for example AOS (AOS operating system) established device, IPhone, Tab PCs remain commanding when compared to interactive mob device, but then again they are expensive, heavy even too lengthy dual-handed usage. Withal, IPad recently released, researchers trust that Tab PCs might turn out to be a hopeful stage for hand-held displays. Spatial Augmented Reality (SAR) is a kind of optical components, RF tags, video projectors, holograms, dogging technology to show computer generated graphics data straight on physical stuffs and there is no need to carry the display Figure 12. Spatial displays differentiate the technology from the user then combine this with the real time. This allows spatial domain reality to logically rescale to clusters and then permitting quislingism in-between consumers. By doing this we can increase the curiosity of AR models in institutions, lab oratory, art and museums. There occur trio diverse methods to SAR which mostly vary in the method they enhance the surroundings: In SAR, apparatuses and normal PC is compulsory. Spatial optical catch by shows figure that are overlay on the real world. Spatial optic mixtures such as planar, optical holograms, curved mirror beam splitters or transparent screens are crucial elements of this display. Still, cover established video catch by, spatial opticcatch by, none of these support smart-phone apps because of spatial adjusted oculi and video exhibit technology. Lastly, optical device-based spatial presenters project figures straight on the real time surfaces.

Tagging

Tagging systems comprises of GPS, accelerometers, digital cameras, wireless sensors, compasses etc. All of these engineering science has diverse degree of precision

Figure 12. Spatial augmented reality

and hinge on system actuality established. Few researchers recognized the over-all tagging technology for AR to be: magneto sensors, mechanical, GPS, inertia, optics and ultrasonic. Researchers use a connect of DiVerdi established on orbit, which has fixed surroundings and resolution.

Processing Unit

AR systems need dominant CPU and momentous increase of RAM to process cam pictures. Up to now mobe processing devices utilize a movable system within a knapsack shape, as there is increase in mobile- phones technology and iPhone, users can have a confidence assure that laptop substituted by a smart-phone and more stylish viewing system. Static systems can use old-fashioned workstation with an authoritative video card.

APPLICATIONS

Augmented Reality has many applications and many possibilities of using it in a pioneering way. In this we have restricted to three types of applications that are mostly used in the field of AR for research: medical, advertising and commercial, education and entertainment. At the commencement, AR had industrial, medical and military attention but later commercial and entertainment usage got into it gained more focus.

Commercial and Advertisement

At present AR frequently used by the traffickers for the promotion of their new pro ducts online. The technique, the marketers are using is users should show the marker given by the marketers to web cam present in front, they use a special software to analyze these markers (software will be running from Ad troupe website). For instance, in the year 2008, MINI the well-known automobile industry promoted their pro duct using the augmented reality in automotive magazines. The user who is reading the magazine has to go the company website and has to present the advertisement ahead of a camera to get 3-D MINI which will app ear in the screen as shown in Figure 13. Beyond reality has issued an advert which doesn't use any markers, the software could recognize and animated, that user has to download from the publisher website.

Figure 13. MINI advertisement

Education and Entertainment

Educations and Entertainment apps comprise of gaming apps, museum guidance and lightseeing with AR usage on mobile applications for education and entertaining role. In some applications which uses AR for virtually constructing the ancient shells or by telling ab out the site history through virtual teaching. Old-style game by augmented reality and AR usage on mobile applications for education and entertainment role. In some applications which uses AR for virtually constructing the ancient shells or by telling ab out the site history through vital teaching. There exists limited systems which uses AR for museum guidance.

There are systems that uses mobe device, however certain systems use smart-phone as an interface while certain other systems use a fairy-tale (magic) lens pattern. Few writers recognized the welfare by means of AR as an interface for social applications as: intuitive and natural technique, well-organized communication through multimedia demonstrations to the user, acquisition costs and low maintenance for the museum in the case of mobile phone being used. Augmented Reality gaming apps gives numerous advantages with the physical board for instance, the capability to present multimedia presentations and animations. The capability is to present animations to add enthusiasm to a game. For instance, signs to assist players study the game or indications to the user after they made an illegal change. Cooper N in 2004, created a game called Chinese checkers using AR (ARCC) that uses tierce markers and cam attached to the roof to trace the markers as so on in Figure 14.

One marker is used for manipulating the game pieces and remaining two indicators are used for positioning the checkerboard. Taking single instrument for controlling the parts permits the writers to adjust their format to dissimilar kinds of game only thing they have to alter is the Graphic User Interface of the game's logic and the board games. Once more, this is typically due to technological improvements for instance tagging model. For instance, we have seen that the little museum guidance models designed were only appropriate to that museum or exhibition they were established for and might not be employed for other museums, due to the fact that together these systems trusted on the exhibition to distinguish the artifacts. Paintings do not existing such a vast trouble for model for instance Google Goggles (Google) due to their even form objects, for example objects of recent art have very uneven shape that makes it tough to track a sharp article.

Medical Applications

Major medical applications deals on robot-assisted surgery and image guided surgery. Because of this, substantial research is going on to implement AR in instruments which incorporate the surgeons' intuitive capabilities. Substantial discovery is made in medical imaging for example endoscopic camera which records video

Figure 14. ARCC

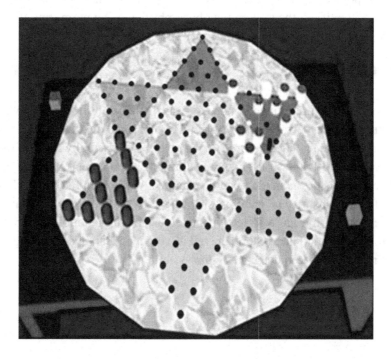

images inside the patient and present it on the monitor. Yet these discoveries will have limitation on physician's direct 3-D vision, natural view of the human anatomy as the physician has to deal with virtual data that is additionally added which will be shown in monitor. AR can be used to like procedural task while surgery is progressing. Bichlmeier C in 2006 designed an AR system that can view real skin through virtual anatomy by polygonal surface model which can be used for real time visualization as so on in Figure 15. Even Bichlmeier designed a system which can use the directed medical tools to enhance the surgeon vision with in the human body. Remote controlled robot assisted surgery will give physician some extra pros with dexterity, visualization and precision. Still enforcing feedback is limited by feelings and it is subjected to physician skills. If there is a lack of feedback, then the performance of operations will be affected. The strength applied by the physician is graphically characterized and superimposed on a streaming live video by means of a system of circles that separately change colours through three programmed ranges (green, yellow, red) permitting to the quantity of winding forces noticed by strain devices. It necessary to decrease surgical processes is not the only one to hinge on seeing medical imaging data on the patient in real time, the need to develop medical analysis also depend on it. In this research field, the ICAR-CNR group of Naples (Giuseppe De Pietro) is functioning on an AR cooperative system for examining patients hand for swelling by superimposing in real time 3-D. Magnetic Resonance visualization data straight on upper part of the patient's hand. Since swelling disabilities are powerfully related with pain, so need a straight operation of the hand region to be identified, the system may back physicians by permitting them to do morphological analyses at the similar time.

RESULTS

When a marker of a predefined dimension was displayed in front of the web cam, it was detected and a corresponding object was displayed on the respective marker (on screen). The object that app eared on the screen is not actually a part of the input fed to the web cam; rather it is an augmentation (virtual object) in a real environment. The patterns of the marker can be changed, and so can the overlaid objects. These virtual objects may be pictures, shapes, solids or others whose location path is specified earlier. In Figure 16 left image tell us ab out the input marker which is showed the camera and the right image tell us ab out appearance of 3D video when the input marker has been detected by the system.

Figure 15. Bichlmeier system

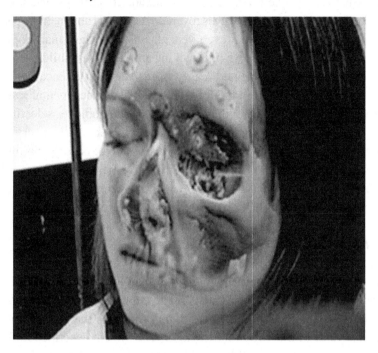

Figure 16. Input image and appearance of a 3D object

CONCLUSION AND FUTURE ENHANCEMENTS

Augmented Reality is at initial phase and forthcoming likely apps are endless. What we want now to embrace is reality will allow you to do amazing things, this will remove barriers that currently exist. AR will allow 3D elements of virtual universe that can take advantage of any were we are, any time What we want now to embrace is computer vision, the ability to see the world as scene and the elements within it like tables, walls and objects once you know that you can relate information very smartly. Augmented reality is the perfect medium for technological magic. In the last five years it really changed the way we live in world and the way we see the world and what great is we think this is next paradigm shift because now we can literally take the content we share we discovered we enjoyed and making a part world

around us. In the future you may even wear glasses which has small display which shows virtual objects that you see, while walking around stores, building, people and pro ducts in that screen. Augmented reality is just very early concept of what AR can do, it gets more advanced in the following yea The experimental results show the efficient use of markers for augmented various virtual objects, selecting options in a game, web, maps over a single marker. This application will be very useful for showcasing of various virtual objects. Occurrence of error is very minimum as the video tracking techniques are highly efficient and camera is precisely calibrated. By this AR will break the barrier we have with conventional desktops, laptops and we want the convenience of having the information were ever you are.

The Power of Augmented Interaction

Interaction in Augmented Reality can take on many forms. One such form is the direct manipulation of the virtual objects in the augmented environment. Another useful form is the manipulation of the system properties that govern the appearance and behaviour of the virtual information. The system described in this report illustrates a mechanism for providing the immersed user with the ability to control the properties of the AR system. The fact that the interface itself is a virtual object in the augmented environment allows it to be used and manipulated in ways that differ from those of physical interfaces while at the same time providing complex functionality. For example, the augmented interface can be altered or positioned arbitrarily by the user or by the system. This means that the interface can change based on environmental conditions or context. As a user moves through rooms in a museum, for example, the options presented through the interface can be contextually altered to reflect the content of each of the rooms. It is important to allow the user the ability to alter the AR interface as he or she may have superior knowledge of the current environment than that of the computer system. As compared to Virtual Reality, where the computer system has knowledge of every aspect of the virtual environment, Augmented Reality should not only merge real and virtual objects, but should also merge the user's intellectual perception of the environment with that of the computer.

Mainstream Potential of Augmented Reality

For Augmented Reality to become a mainstream tool, it must robustly provide useful information at rate that is synonymous with that of human sensory perception. The experimental results of this simple augmented interaction system provide evidence that real-time Augmented Reality is more than a theoretical vision. Using modern computer technology, it is clear that the first step towards the real-time computer perception of human behaviour can be taken. This can be as simple as the classification of basic human actions based on a pre-defined model or as complex as a continuous learning system able to mimic the communication performed by another human being. Many avenues are being explored in this field, all of which await the arrival of the required technology to process the observed information in real-time.

FUTURE WORK

An interesting application of Augmented Reality is AR based training. This application provides a trainer with the ability to provide virtual feedback to a remote and immersed trainee with respect to a given coordinate system. In order for the trainer to visualize the user's perspective, the captured video frames are sent to the trainer. The feedback consists of graphical annotation of the captured video frames by the trainer, followed by the retransmission of these frames to the trainee. In, the transmitted image sequence is paused when the trainer wants to communicate, in order to eliminate the difficult problem of following the user's mobile viewpoint. This form of remote collaboration can be improved by using the real-time stabilization technique introduced in this thesis. By giving visual feedback in the stabilized image sequence, the trainer can more robustly provide augmented information to the trainee in real-time, without the need to pause the input sequence. This feedback information can then be augmented in the users view relative to the initial coordinate system. This mechanism provides an improvement to the accuracy and real-time nature of the AR based training application.

REFERENCES

Adithya, C., Kowsik, K., Namrata, D., Nageli, V. S., Shrivastava, S., & Rakshit, S. (2010). Augmented Reality Approach for Paper Map Visualization. *Proceedings of the International Conference on Communication and Computational Intelligence.*

Arcella, A., Balzano, E., Cavaliere, S., & Iura, R. (2008). A Teaching kinematics: augmented reality and virtualization in the observation. *International Conference on Computer Science and Software Engineering.* doi:10.1109/CSSE.2008.1625

Bajura, M., & Neumann, U. (1995). Dynamic Registration Correction in Augmented-Reality Systems. *Virtual Reality Annual International Symposium, Proceedings.* doi:10.1109/VRAIS.1995.512495

Clay, A., Couture, N., Nigay, L., Rivière, J. B., Martin, J. C., Courgeon, M., & Domenger, G. et al. (2012). Interactions and systems for augmenting a live dance performance. *International Symposium on Mixes and Augmented Reality*, Atlanta, GA. doi:10.1109/ISMAR-AMH.2012.6483986

Deffeyes, S., & Katz, N. (2010). Augmented reality in the data center. IBM Academy of Technology.

Ferreira, P., Orvalho, J., & Boavida, F. (2007). A Middleware Architecture for Mobile and Pervasive Large-Scale Augmented Reality Games. *Fifth Annual Conference on Communication Networks and Services Research, CNSR '07*. doi:10.1109/CNSR.2007.2

Fischer, J., Bartz, D., & Straber, W. (2005). Stylized Augmented Reality for Improved Immersion. *Proceedings of the IEEE Virtual Reality*.

Gammeter, S., Gassmann, A., Bossard, L., Quack, T., & Gool, L. V. (2010). Server-side object recognition and client-side object tracking for mobile augmented reality. *IEEE Computer Society Conference on Computer Vision and Pattern Recognition Workshops (CVPRW)*. doi:10.1109/CVPRW.2010.5543248

Geroimenko, V. (2012). Augmented Reality Technology and Art: The Analysis and Visualization of Evolving Conceptual Models. *16th International Conference on Information Visualisation*. doi:10.1109/IV.2012.77

Herold, R., Vogel, U., Richter, B., Kreye, D., Reckziegel, S., Scholles, M., & Lakner, H. (2008). *OLED-on-CMOS Integration for Augmented-Reality Systems*. International Students and Young Scientists Workshop "Photonics and Microsystems". doi:doi:10.1109/STYSW.2008.5164134 doi:10.1109/STYSW.2008.5164134

Hincapié, M., Caponio, A., Rios, H., & Mendívil, E. G. (2011). An Introduction to Augmented Reality with Applications in Aeronautical Maintenance. *13th International Conference on Transparent Optical Networks (ICTON)*. doi:10.1109/ICTON.2011.5970856

Hull, J. J., Erol, B., Graham, J., Ke, Q., Kishi, H., Moraleda, J., & Olst, D. G. V. (2007). Paper-Based Augmented Reality. *17th International Conference on Artificial Reality and Telexistence*. doi:10.1109/ICAT.2007.49

Juan, M. C., Botella, C., Alcañiz, M., Baños, R., Carrion, C., Melero, M., & Lozano, J. A. (2004). An Augmented Reality System for treating psychological disorders: Application to phobia to cockroaches. *Third IEEE and ACM International Symposium on*. doi:doi:10.1109/ISMAR.2004.14 doi:10.1109/ISMAR.2004.14

Kim, S. J. J. (2012). A User Study Trends in Augmented Reality and Virtual Reality Research: A qualitative study with the past three years of the ISMAR and IEEE VR conference papers. *International Symposium on Ubiquitous Virtual Reality*. doi:10.1109/ISUVR.2012.17

Lyu, M. R., King, I., Wong, T. T., Yau, E., & Chan, P. W. (2005). ARCADE: Augmented Reality Computing Arena for Digital Entertainment. *Aerospace Conference*. doi:10.1109/AERO.2005.1559626

Nakamura, T., Sorbier, F., Martedi, S., & Saito, H. (2012). *Calibration-Free Projector-Camera System for Spatial Augmented Reality on Planar Surfaces*. 21st International Conference on Pattern Recognition (ICPR 2012) Tsukuba, Japan.

Nojima, T., Sekiguchi, D., Inami, M., & Tachi, S (2002). The SmartTool: A system for augmented reality of haptics. *Virtual Reality, Proceedings*. IEEE.

Raajan, N. R., Suganya, S., Hemanand, R., Janani, S. & Ramanan, S.V. (2012). Augmented Reality for 3D Construction. *Procedia Engineering, 38*, 66–72.

Raajan, N. R., Suganya, S., Priya, M.V., Ramanan, S.V., Janani, S., Nandini, N.S., Hemanand, R., & Gayathri, S (2012). Augmented Reality Based Virtual Reality. *Procedia Engineering, 38*, 1559–1565.

Suganya, S., Raajan, N. R., Priya, MV, Philomina, A.J., Parthiban, D., & Monisha, B (2012). Real-Time Camera Tracking of Augmented Reality in Landmarks Environments. *Procedia Engineering, 38*, 456–461.

Tokunaga, E., Zee, A. V. D., Kurahashi, M., Nemoto, M., & Nakajima, T. (2003). Object-Oriented Middleware Infrastructure for Distributed Augmented Reality. *Sixth IEEE International Symposium on Object-Oriented Real-Time Distributed Computing*. doi:10.1109/ISORC.2003.1199250

Wang, Z., Yang, X., Xiao, S., & Li, B. (2010). Relighting in Spatial Augmented Reality. *International Conference on Audio Language and Image Processing (ICALIP)*.

Yang, R. (2011). The Study and Improvement of Augmented Reality based on Feature Matching. *2nd International Conference on Software Engineering and Service Science (ICSESS)*.

Zoellner, M., Keil, J., Drevensek, T., & Wuest, H. (2009). Cultural Heritage Layers: Integrating Historic Media in Augmented Reality. *15th International Conference on Virtual Systems and Multimedia*. doi:10.1109/VSMM.2009.35

KEY TERMS AND DEFINITIONS

Binarization: A preprocessing step where an image is converted from gray scale to binary image.

Camera Calibration: It calculates the intrinsic parameters of the camera.

Homography: In predictive geometry, a homography is an isomorphism of predicitive spaces induced by an isomorphism of the vector spaces from which they are derived.

Marker Based: Marker based AR uses a specific dimensions for analysis and process of the data in AR.

Markerless: Markerless AR typically uses the GPS feature of a SmartPhone to locate and interact with AR resources, service limits, bandwidth requirements and power pulls on the devices.

Tagging: Function used to perform classification.

Tracking: The calculation of the pose of camera in the real world.

Chapter 9
Gesture Recognition:
An Interactive Tool in Multimedia

Nandhini Kesavan
SASTRA University, India

Raajan N. R.
SASTRA University, India

ABSTRACT

The main objective of gesture recognition is to promote the technology behind the automation of registered gesture with a fusion of multidimensional data in a versatile manner. To achieve this goal, computers should be able to visually recognize hand gestures from video input. However, vision-based hand tracking and gesture recognition is an extremely challenging problem due to the complexity of hand gestures, which are rich in diversities due to high degrees of freedom involved by the human hand. This would make the world a better place with for the commons not only to live in, but also to communicate with ease. This research work would serve as a pharos to researchers in the field of smart vision and would immensely help the society in a versatile manner.

INTRODUCTION

Gesture recognition aids human beings to commune with the machine (HMI) and interact in a natural manner without the use of any mechanical devices. Gesture recognition has replaced all input devices like joysticks, mouse and keyboards which

DOI: 10.4018/978-1-5225-0546-4.ch009

have been acting as input devices to the system. For example, if you want to point at a particular diagram in a web page it is enough if we point it with our finger in place of mouse being used to do the same work, so this could be very useful for interactive purpose. Hand gestures can be used for natural and intuitive human-computer interaction. On the other hand, computer vision algorithms are notoriously brittle and computation intensive, which make most current gesture recognition systems fragile and inefficient. Its applications are diverse, spanning a variety of markets. To achieve this goal, computers should be able to visually recognize hand gestures from video input. However, vision-based hand tracking and gesture recognition is an extremely challenging problem due to the complexity of hand gestures, which are rich in diversities due to high degrees of freedom involved by the human hand. Now, gesture recognition is becoming a commonplace technology, enabling humans and computer to interface (HCI) more easily in homes, automobiles, work etc.

Over the past few years, gesture recognition has made its debut in entertainment and gaming markets. Gesture recognition (GR) has been presented by the RGB-D gaming controller which used a stereoscopic 2D image sensor which brought this GR technology to all the electronic devices in one's life. This has altered the way with which users interact with the system. Gestures are useful in identifying hand and body movement. In addition, they could be used as input command which helps in reading the face and speech recognition. This provision of enabling gestures to be given as input commands to the computer makes it very easy and comfortable for the physically-impaired. Hand, body gesture can have modified amplification factor introduced by a controller which integrated with multiple sensors like accelerometer, gyroscope, etc., were connected to a camera to enable the software in the controller can recognize various gestures. Each and every gesture is (needed to) trained (always) for a particular function. For instance, still pose of the palm might indicate stop. In addition to the technical challenges of implementing gesture recognition, there are also social challenges. Gestures must be simple, intuitive and universally acceptable.

The study of gestures and other nonverbal types of communication is known as kinesics. 3D tracking and control software powers gesture control TVs, 3D depth sensing digital signs, digital signage and interactive hand-tracking displays. It caused a revolution in interactive technologies. Natural interaction seems to be the maximum in case of gesture recognition where there is possibility of gaming and 3-D virtual world environment. The whole world is revolving around the gesture recognition which is reaching the pinnacle in terms of the various applications that could be done with the help of it. It interacts tremendously with the real world. Process involved in gesture recognition: Gesture recognition which is an interactive technology and considered a very important tool in multimedia involves sequential process in its identification and recognition. Initially the acquisition of image is done with the help of standard camera or depth camera. This is followed by background subtraction where the foreground is separated from the background as the essential part of an image is only the foreground and noise if any present in the background need not be processed for its elimination. The foreground is then subject to filters depending on the kind of noise of present in the image. The output that is obtained after the filtering process (image free from noise) is then fed to hardware if any used for the purpose. Next in sequence is the use of classifier. There are a number of classifiers that could be used for identification and recognition of gestures they are Support Vector Machine, Neural Network, K - nearest neighbor etc.

The kind of classifier is then chosen which plays a vital role as far as interactive technology is considered. It requires two sets namely training data and test data. Initially the training data is created with few subjects whose feature are extracted and framed into feature vectors. This is then stored in the database. Then when a new subject performs the same set of gestures it first checks in the database for the availability of the same pattern. If a match is found it displays the name of the person or any feature that has been selected for display. Figure 1 explains the different gestures of hand namely victory, good luck and number two. If there seems to be no match as in case of this tool used at workplace it displays the message that he/she is not an authorized person. This could be used to identify the person or the kind of gesture that is being performed. Technique with which interactive technology be handled: The movement of a person can be identified and tracked with the help of various devices. Though there are various devices each has its own pros and cons in terms of the environment, clothing etc., Interface with computers using gestures of the human body, typically hand movements. In gesture recognition technology, a camera reads the movements of the human body and communicates the data to a computer that uses the gestures as input to control devices or applications. For example, a person clapping his hands together in front of a camera can produce the

Figure 1. Different gestures of hand

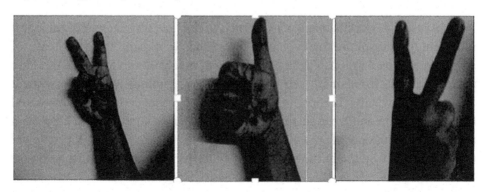

sound of cymbals being crashed together when the gesture is fed through a computer. One way gesture recognition is being used is to help the physically impaired to interact with computers, such as interpreting sign language. The technology also has the potential to change the way users interact with computers by eliminating input devices such as joysticks, mice and keyboards and allowing the unencumbered body to give signals to the computer through gestures such as finger pointing.

Following are the various devices with which interactive technologies be handled:

- **Wired Gloves:** With the use of wired gloves, it is possible to give input to the computer about the position and rotation of the hands. Certain other gloves are available which are used to detect finger bending with a high degree of accuracy.
- **Depth Cameras:** This camera generates a depth map of the object when the camera and object are at shorter range, use this data to approximate a 3d representation of what is being seen. These can be effective for detection of hand gestures due to their short range capabilities.
- **Stereo Cameras:** Here two cameras are used whose relation to one another is known beforehand. This stereo camera generates a 3d representation.
- **Controller Based Gestures:** With the help of this controller the gestures that are performed by human could be actively captured with the software. Mouse gesture is an example of controller based gesture, where the motion of the mouse is correlated to a symbol being drawn by a person's hand which is used to represent the acceleration.
- **Single Camera:** A normal 2D camera will help in the process of gesture recognition. The main problem with such camera is the lighting and environment which it could not control. For simple gesture recognition applications single camera could be used.

SCIENTIFIC IMPORTANCE OF THE WORK

A lot of research work is being concentrated in the area of gesture recognition. It is evident from literature survey that gesture recognition seems to be the center of attraction in smart vision. The applications and practical implications of gesture recognition vary from simply recognizing a wave to gaming applications. One of the main areas where it is concentrated is in sign language recognition. This would help the deaf and dumb people to interact with the environment and to keep them updated. This not only plays a vital role in the lives of deaf and dumb people but also to persons who are in the midst of language problem. Gesture recognition is also being widely used for domestic purposes like increasing and decreasing the volume, switching over channels etc. with no special training being given to the user. Even a layman can make use of gestures to control various appliances and perform certain operations. Though a lot of focus is shown on gesture recognition, it still suffers from various pitfalls. The most common problems encountered is the accuracy and recognition rate.

After a detailed literature survey it has been noticed that gesture recognition is being upgraded in certain areas only even though it could be used in various walks of life. This research work is to make technological developments in a versatile manner. It makes everything touch free and could be easily used by a layman to a technical autocrat. This involves processing the data, fusion of sensor, classification of gestures and providing methodologies for real time implementation. Here the mobile network is cut down such that the information provided does not need any device for transfer of information. The right kind of classifier and appropriate fusion technique is performed to enhance the accuracy and the recognition rate of various gestures. This research addresses the problems not fully explored by smart vision experts.

A gesture control system usually uses one depth sensor to detect persons. This sensor is placed in front of the user and as close to the virtual interaction surface as possible. However, for such a system some gestures might be occluded or undetectable due to the human operator's posture. As it interferes with each other it is placed at least three meters apart, at an angle of approximately 90°. In such a setup the interference is almost negligible. Furthermore, the setup is chosen such that a hand can be detected by at least one depth sensor. Multiple sensors are integrated and calibrated which minimizes the probability of occlusions and enlarges the operating space. The main objective of gesture recognition is to promote the technology behind the automation of registered gesture with a fusion of multidimensional data in a versatile manner. The usefulness are: it is an interactive technology has attained a prominent place in real world the time required for each and every task has reduced considerably.

Gesture is defined as the movement of hands and legs of a person that could be accompanied by expression and feeling. It tells a person about an idea, gives direction, describes about an object. For example, if a person nods his head it means that he is giving consent to a decision. Gesture recognition involves keeping in constant track the position of a human, his head orientation, movement of fingers and identifying the person is trying to communicate by means of signs. There are three vital roles a gesture. They are Semiotic which means the communication has meaningful information, Ergotic which conveys that the gesture gives useful details about the environment and Epistemic which is used to identify the environment by means of touch. There are various gestures that could be identified for instance if a person is sad it could be identified if his head is lowered, his shoulders drooped and very sluggish in his movement. There is a belief that gesture is associated with the physically challenged people but the face is that it is very much prevalent among all. Gesture recognition seems to be a cake walk but the procedure involved and the effort needed to train the various gestures that too in finer level of precision is a herculean task. This would make the world a better place with for the commons not only to live in, but also to communicate with ease.

If gesture recognition is accompanied with voice recognition, eye tracking and lip movement it is known as perceptual user interface (PUI). Its goal is to improve the efficiency and make it user friendly. The most application of gesture is that it is given as input command to the system. Figure 2 tells about the generation of skeleton of a person using depth camera. The problem of keeping the remote elsewhere and searching will soon decrease not because they are going to keep it in the right place but because everything is going to operate without the object in the near future just by means of gestures. If a person wants to delete some files from his computer with the help of a gesture such as putting waste into the dustbin. In a similar manner operating an oven could also be done by means of gesture. In the present scenario, a situation has arrived where one's hand is sufficient to perform any task such that it communicates directly with the computer or any device. Revolution in computer has started hence human computer interaction has been concentrated such that it could be further improved. The limitations in the use of computer should be eliminated as it has become integral part of our day to day life. Previously, a person interacted with the computer with the use of a keyboard or a mouse but now with the advent of gesture technology this has been replaced. An example of this is the touch screen that we are using without which day would be incomplete. This technology will soon be replaced by gesture recognition technology. Similar to handwriting, the way a particular gesture is being done varies from person to person.

This work deals about two of the various applications in the field of computer vision. These two applications cover and benefit people of various strata and under very different circumstances. First application is to locate places for the deaf and vocally disabled people. In general, the deaf and dumb people would be reluctant incoming out and moving along with people as they will not be able to communicate with others. Though the number of such challenged people are relatively less when compared to the total population, their needs are also to be satisfied. This would help such people to face the world with increased confidence. Second main application discussed here is the effective disaster management. Disasters though not common in day to day life, once it occurs it leaves a commotion and that is very difficult to get over. So here, concentration is been focused on rescuing persons who are alive. In order to arrive at a result, unsupervised algorithm is used.

Figure 2. Skeleton generated using depth camera

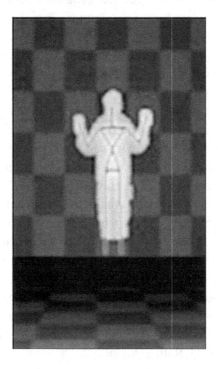

LITERATURE REVIEW

(Bhaskar Purkayastha, 2009; Field. M, S. Gordon, E. Peterson, R. Robinson, T. Stahovich & C. Alvarado, 2010) explains how to integrate speech and gesture and the percentage of accuracy that is obtained using various classifiers. (Cheng-Chang Lien & Chung-Lin Huang, 1998; Dong-IkKo & Gaurav Agarwal, 2012) explains how gesture recognition could be done which enables natural interactions with that of electronics. (Christian Vogler & Dimitris Metaxas, 2001) explains how sign language could be recognized simultaneously and with ease. (Cristina Manresa, Javier Varona, Ramon Mas & Francisco J. Perales, 2000; Daniel Persson & Björn Samvik, 2009) explains how gesture recognition would be used for human computer interaction and the various advantages of it. (Jagdish L. Raheja, Ankit Chaudhary, Nandhini K. & S. Maiti, 2014) describes how help could be offered to patients using gait as a biometric and also discusses the classifier that is best for such an application. (Jia, Pei, Hu, Huosheng H, Lu, Tao & Yuan, Kui, 2007) clearly explains an application that would be very useful for the physically challenged. This work deals about how wheel chair could be operated just by means of head movements and without the use of hands. (Min C. Shina, Leonid V. Tsapb & Dmitry B. Goldof, 2004; James

H. Neilan II, 2012) describes how gesture recognition could be done using bezier curves and ensemble of classifiers. (Nandhini K. & N.R. Raajan, 2013) describes how gesture recognition could be used to save the life of a person when he/she is in danger especially in case of a tot. (Nandhini K., Rakesh Kumar Karn & N.R. Raajan, 2013) briefs that it is possible to recognize gestures in liquid medium using sense of touch in substrates coated with compounds.

(Ahmad Akl, 2005) explains how gestures are being recognized with the help of accelerometers for the purpose of acquiring data, training and testing the obtained data. (Nandhini. K & B. Santhi, 2012; Yu Yuan, 2008) describes the survey conducted on various classifiers and how SVM classifier works good and explains how gesture recognition could be done based on gestures using SVM classifier. (Nandhini.K & B. Santhi, 2012) elaborates the study conducted on various emotions, what is the root cause of various emotions and for what kind of health condition what kind of emotion is expressed by a human. (TiehanLü, 2004; Zannatul Ferdousi, 2008; Siddharth S. Rautaray & Anupam Agrawal, 2012; Byong K. Ko and Hyun S. Yang, 1997) explains how to design a human gesture recognition system with the aid of real time video and finger mouse. (Feng-Sheng Chen, Chih-Ming Fu & Chung-Lin Huang, 2003) describes the process of hand gesture recognition and classification using Hidden Markov models. (Prateem Chakraborty, Prashant Sarawgi, Ankit Mehrotra, Gaurav Agarwal, Ratika Pradhan, 2008; Sanjay Meena, 2011) have done a study on hand gesture recognition. (Parneet Kaur & Prateek Prasanna, 2011; Qing Chen, 2008) explains how gestures are being tracked and recognized with the help of hand movement and by means of blink. (Siddharth S. Rautaray & Anupam Agrawal, 2012; Thomas A. Coogan, 2007) describes how gesture recognition system is used for dynamic applications using transformation invariant method. (Takashi Morie, Hiroyuki Miyamoto & Akitoshi Hanazawa, 2007; Ashvini A. Bamanikar, Sarika Ursal & S. S. Jadhav, 2013) briefs the process of gesture recognition using vision. The dataset used consisted of videos for five gestures. Gesture recognition system has to recognize the start and end of gesture followed by assigning the obtained frames to any of the two classes. Here, the author briefs about a flexible video analysis system that could be widely used for video surveillance applications.

IMPACT OF GESRTURE RECOGNITION IN DAY TO DAY LIFE

A prototype Smart Camera system is developed, which is able to detect and track interested objects, including the detection of people and recognizing their activities in an application environment. It proposes two new background elimination algorithms to increase the performance of Smart Camera systems in the midst of changing background and varying lighting condition. Designers need to balance certain factors such as processing speed, accuracy, system cost and robustness, to provide a practical system. Gesture could be physical behavior or expression that is because of any emotions. This could either be static or dynamic. If it is static it is known as sign, on the other hand if it is dynamic it is known to communicate messages. By using gestures, it is possible to have an efficient and expressive human computer interaction. This system acts as a motivation tool for analyzing, designing, simulation and recognition of gestures. Hand gesture recognition system (HGRS) focuses on various applications. One such application where concentration is high is the medical field. HGRS is developed such that surgeons could remain in a particular place in the operation theater without the need to move about to operate the computer.

This system has replaced touchscreens. The major drawback with the touch screen is that it has to be cleaned every time an operation has been done. This involves initial calibration which recognizes the gestures of the surgeons which is followed by learning the gestures and training them. Here, it is trained in such a way that each gesture indicates a particular action. It is possible for the surgeons to zoom in and zoom out the images during the operation such that they could get a clear idea of the depth of injury and many other minute details. It is possible to avoid casual gestures from being detected by putting the system to sleep mode. The system could be initiated by a wave of the surgeon in front of the camera.

This system is being upgraded for the visually impaired such that they could feel the environment. This tremendous revolution of replacing smart phones by gesture oriented actions would save a lot of power and revenue. Another advantage is that by the use of gestures it is possible to operate the device without seeing and having no physical contact with it. Gesture technology is available in smart phones but the drawback is that if this technology is left in on mode it will drain the entire battery of the mobile. But with the new evolution of gesture recognition technology system it is possible to leave it enabled for the entire day and it consumes very less power that of tens of micro watts. With this technology a person can mute his phone, attend call and change volume of the music player without seeing and touching the mobile. This could be made effective by attaching sensors which costs less than one dollar to household objects and this would help us in interacting with day to day objects. Input devices such as keyboard, joystick and mouse were replaced by touch screens.

This is now being replaced by gesture recognition technology which would be very efficient and cost effective. It is mentioned above that it is possible to operate mobile phones and tablets without touching or seeing it. it is also to be noted that it is possible to operate house hold devices to operate with ease when you are not near it. This is obtained with the help of WIFI which detects minute changes in the amplitude of the signal. New technologies are emerging in which a chip when integrated with the camera gives depth information of the world around the user. This motivates the user in having a 3D experience of the environment around them user. Gesture recognition is a technology which makes life a lot easier than it was expected. It is common to follow a recipe from a tablet. When you are in the midst of cooking procedure and when your hands are wet or covered with flour then you need to flip to the next page in the tablet such that you can continue the cooking procedure. In such an instance this technology comes to the users rescue.

Every time you need not wash or wipe your hands to turn the next page in you tablet, instead a simple wave gesture would turn pages for you without touching the devices. The gestures that are taken into consideration for remote handling of house hold appliances are very simple. They are push, swipe from left to right, swipe from right to left, blink eye, clockwise movement and anti-clockwise movement. This generally uses both kinds of camera such as web cam and stereoscopic cam for these kinds of applications. This is capable of detecting and recognizing gestures in the midst of low light and also it is attire independent. It could work perfectly well when the distance is in the range of five meters. By gesture we not only mean the movement of hands but also that of fingers, face and eyes. As the future unfolds, more and more sophisticated devices are to evolved which makes life much more easy and comfortable. Safety must remain paramount when the application of automotive infotainment is taken into consideration.

Audio and video has entered into automotive and this has become a reason for distraction of drivers which leads to accidents. With the emergence of gesture recognition technology, the drivers could attend phone calls, increase or decrease volume, change songs etc., with ease just by means of simple gestures like wave or swipe. Currently simple gestures are taken into consideration, but research is going on for complex gestures to be trained and used for various other applications with improvement in the robustness of the application. The hand is first detected from the background which is followed by background subtraction using any of the various algorithms. This is followed by segmenting the region of interest and this leads to detection and recognition of palm and fingers.

PITFALL IN THE CURRENT SYSTEM

In the present scenario, gesture recognition is being used mainly in the field of gaming and in identifying simple gestures. Every research work has a modification but only in terms of the classifier being used and the language used for recognizing alphabets. Concentration is mainly given in improving the recognition rate and accuracy but the importance of developing new applications that could serve the society is not stressed upon.

Sensors Used

There are various sensors that could be used for gesture recognition. Of which few of them are mentioned below in detail. Ultrasonic sensor, Infrared sensor and Swept Frequency Capacitive Sensing (SFCS) are sensors that could be used for gesture recognition. Infrared sensor is opted when the sensor is bound to be used in a closed place. The proximity and range when an object is moving towards the sensor capacitive sensing only allows for electrical signals at one frequency whether an action is performed or not, for instance touch or no touch.

Measures Used in Confusion Matrix

Data mining tool is a tool which is useful for the purpose of exploring and analyzing data in large volumes. There are various classifiers available for the purpose of classification of which a few of them are SVM, Naïve Bayes, Random forest and K Nearest Neighbor. Various measures are available to test the input data. They are accuracy (AC), sensitivity (Sn), specificity (Sp), F1 score, Precision (Prec/PPV), Brier score and Matthews correlation coefficient (MCC). TP_t denotes true positive, FP_f denotes false positive, TN_t denotes true negative and FN_f denotes false negative. The systematic errors is termed as accuracy and is defined as the ratio of the sum of TP_t and TN_t values to the sum of positive and negative values. The random errors is associated with precision and is defined as the ratio of TP_t to the sum of TP_t and FP_f.

$$AC = \frac{TP_t + TN_t}{P + N}$$

$$PPV = \frac{TP_t}{TP_t + FP_f}$$

Sensitivity which also be termed as true positive rate is measure of performance in the field of statistics which helps in the calculation of positives which are correctly classified. Specificity which is also termed as true negative rate which is also a measure of performance in the field of statistics which helps in the calculation of the negatives which are correctly classified.

$$\frac{Sensitivity}{TPR} = \frac{TP_t}{TP_t + FN_f}$$

$$\frac{Specificity}{TNR} = \frac{TN_t}{FP_f + TN_t}$$

F1 score which could also be termed as F score is a measure of accuracy in a particular test. The value of the score is calculated based on both precision and recall value. It is a ratio of twice TP_t to the sum of FN_f, FP_f and twice the value of TP_t.

$$F1 = \frac{2TP_t}{2TP_t + FN_f + FP_f}$$

Matthews correlation coefficient could be represented as the ratio of the difference between the product of TP_t and TN_t and FP_f and FN_f to the square root of the product of the sum of TP_t and FP_f, TP_t and FN_f, TN_t and FP_f and TN_t and FN_f. Even if the classes seem to be varying in size this measure could be taken into consideration which is a measure of quality.

$$MCC = \frac{\left(TP_t \, X \, TN_t\right) - \left(FP_f \, X \, FN_f\right)}{\sqrt{\left(\left(TP_t + FP_f\right)\left(TP_t + FN_f\right)\left(TN_t + FP_f\right)\left(TN_t + FN_f\right)\right)}}$$

This is a score function which can measure the probabilistic predictions and accuracy where the set of outcomes could either be binary or categorical.

$$BS = \frac{1}{N}\sum_{t=1}^{N}\left(f_t - o_t\right)^2$$

Classifiers Used in Gesture Recognition

SVM is a very practicable supervised learning algorithm in the arena of machine learning that is capable of analyzing data, pattern recognition and mainly used for the purpose of classification and regression. It could be distinguished as points in space in such a way that there is a wide gap between the various classifiers. If any other example is to be classified, then it checks to which category it may suit and it allocates that data to that category whichever closest. It is not only a binary classifier but it is also capable of performing classification among multiple classes. It is a known fact that SVM is capable of performing linear classification efficiently and effectively. It should also be noted that SVM is capable of performing nonlinear classification effectively with the help of kernel trick and maps the input to high dimensional data. The hyperplane in SVM can be denoted by the following function where β represents the weight vector and the bias is represented by β_0.

$$f\left(x\right) = \beta_0 + \beta^T x$$

Different representations of the optimal hyper plane could be arrived at after scaling β and β_0. There may be various possible combinations but the one that is preferably used is the following function:

$$\left|\beta_0 + \beta^T x\right| = 1$$

SVM is a classifier which is used for the sake of regression and classification. There are various surveys being conducted to bring out the importance of SVM classifier when compared with other algorithms in the arena of pattern recognition. It has its application in diverse fields like categorization of text and classification of images. The recognition rate, accuracy and precision obtained by SVM is high when compared with other algorithms like K Nearest Neighbor, PCA etc., The classification of SVM is linear SVM and non-linear SVM. Its main objective is to separate the target variables from the other category in the hyper plane. There are two types of classification which are possible namely one to one and multi class classifier. It has two kinds of margin as well. They are hard and soft margin. Former is the one which separates two classes without error and the latter is the one which does the classification process by allowing the errors to occur. The main goal of SVM is to analyze the inputs and to classify them based on various parameters. All the test data are classified based on the certain parameters and grouped into a particular class. When a new data enters into the picture it is checked or could be termed as compared with the already existing values or data in the database and if any such match is found it gives a positive reply else informs that no such item found. Any class that is tested is found to be topsy–turvy the classification is performed with a gap which is far as possible. The term attribute is given to predictor variable and the transformed attribute which gives information about the hyper plane is known as a feature. The procedure of picking out the exact representation is termed as feature selection. This set of features which gives accurate information regarding a case is known as a vector. A well-known principle namely SRM (Structural Risk Minimization) is used which reduces the upper bound on the expected risk. The optimal hyper plane is chosen which separates the clusters of vector with one category of the target variable on one side of the plane and with the other category on the other side of the plane.

Naïve Bayes classifier functions on the basis of Bayes theorem and it is a cluster of a variety of simple probabilistic classifiers. It has its application in diverse field namely text and medical diagnosis. It is a highly scalable classifier which involves very large number of features for the purpose of learning. This classifier is a conditional probability model. N features are required for the purpose of classifying a particular problem and it also requires a set of vectors that are given by $X=(x_1,x_2,\ldots,x_n)$. For each of the k possible outcomes, the probability could be given by the following function:

$$p\left(C_k \mid x_1,\ldots x_n\right)$$

In the above mentioned equation, when the value of n is large or when it keeps increasing there arise a lot of problems because the formation of probability would not be feasible. In order to make the calculation simple, understandable and for the easier formulation of table it is essential to reformulate the above formula. The formula mentioned below explains about the conditional probability:

$$p\left(C_k \mid X\right) = \frac{p\left(C_k\right)p\left(X \mid C_k\right)}{p\left(X\right)}$$

The above mentioned equation could also be written in simpler terms as

$$posterior = \frac{prior * likelihood}{evidence}$$

Though it is very simple, it suits well for certain real world situations which are very complex. The main characteristic of Naïve Bayes classifier is that it requires or rather demands each and every feature to contribute independently for identification of a particular object in spite of identifying it based on correlations of features. Both Naïve Bayes learner and classifiers are very fast when compared with various other algorithms. This is a space efficient algorithm and the main advantage is that it is not sensitive to irrelevant features. The training is very fast in this algorithm as it is done in a single scan and also fast enough to classify. It is efficient enough in handling data that are both real and discrete. It also handles the streaming of data very well.

Random forests are also used for classification, regression and various other tasks also and this is an ensemble learning method. This algorithm constructs many decision trees during the training phase and it performs the function of classification and regression for each and every tree. In order to produce large number of decision trees with controlled variance this is constructed with a combination of bagging and random selection of features. In terms of accuracy, no current algorithm could unsurpass random forest. Even though, the data set is large, it is capable of learning efficiently. Though there are thousands of data which are given as input, it effectively handles all data without deletion of any variable. It distinguishes the important variables among the many available variables in the classification process. If a data set is at hand which has lot of missing data then the best algorithm to choose is the random forest so that better accuracy could be obtained. If a forest is generated then it is possible to save them for future use. With the information obtained from the relation between variables and classification, prototypes are computed. The error rate of the forest depends on the following two factors:

1. It depends on the correlation between any two trees in a forest. If the value of correlation keeps increasing, the forest error rate keeps increasing.
2. The individual strength of a tree in a forest.

If there is a tree whose error rate is very low, then it is termed as strong classifier. If, the strength of individual tree keeps increasing then the overall error rate of forest keeps decreasing.

K-Nearest Neighbors algorithm (KNN) is a very easy machine learning algorithm and its main purpose is to do classification and regression. Here the input is a set of k closest training examples and the object is classified by the maximum number of votes it gets by its neighbors and is assigned to the one which is very common among the k nearest neighbors. This is also known as learning method. Here the function is locally approximated and all computations are put off until classification. It has its drawback of being sensitive to the local structure of data. The results obtained using KNN is strongly consistent. By applying proximity graphs, it is possible to obtain improvements in the results of KNN. Its performance could be highly improved by using supervised metric learning. In order to validate the accuracy and precision of KNN an effective tool namely confusion matrix or matching matrix could be used. It is also possible to use statistical methods which are highly robust namely likelihood ratio test. This research work would serve as a pharos to researchers in the field of smart vision and would immensely help the society in a versatile manner.

Pitfalls of Few Classifiers

There are varieties of classifiers all of which perform the same operation of classification. Each algorithm has its cons. Here are few of the drawbacks: PCA is not capable of performing linear separation of classes, it is possible to store only partial information of the input vector and the remaining are discarded. In case of HMM, it is possible to train only positive data and also its difficult to reduce the observation probability of instances from various other sets. The main drawback with KNN is that the time complexity is high and that of neural network it is with respect to computational burden. It has another main con which is the empirical nature of model development. Exhibition of undershoot is the main problem in DWT. This means that the values tend to be negative even though the original series is non-negative. There are so many reasons that tend to have an impact on the recognition rate of various actions performed. Few of the external parameters that affect the recognition rate are the attire of a person, the lighting effects of the surrounding and the ornaments worn by the subject. A comparative study was conducted on how persons were capable of identifying their colleagues using Moving Light Display (MLD) and in random. The former gave a recognition rate of 38% whereas the latter gave recognition rate of 17%. There is another branch in gait recognition as quasi gait recognition. In this technique there is drawback which is certain parameters need to be known beforehand such as the distance between the subject and camera, camera calibration details. For instance, when an example of detection of lane. SVM classifier is opted when compared to other algorithms because it could be applied for any kind of situation and could give accurate results. There will be problems when the snow is covered with fog, snow and heavy rain. This is not the flaw of the algorithm but the weakness in the sensor used.

Applications

Gesture recognition finds its application in various walks of life. They are as follows: traditional applications such as authentication in work place, sign language, for enhanced safety where the nation's security is at stake. Recent applications such as coffee is produced at the instant the machine identifies a person yawn, switching channel without a TV remote, automated homes, possibility of safe driving when the driver is feeling sleepy, gestures for doing a particular task, gaming and video surveillance.

REFERENCES

Akl, A. (2010). *A Novel Accelerometer-based Gesture Recognition System.* (Master of Applied Science thesis). University of Toronto.

Bamanikar, Ursal, & Jadhav. (n.d.). Hand Gestures Recognition Based On Vision. *ASM's International E-Journal of Ongoing Research in Management and IT*.

Byong, K. (1998). Finger Mouse And Gesture Recognition System As A New Human Computer Interface. *Computer Graphics, 21*(5), 555–561.

Chakraborty, P., Sarawgi, P., Mehrotra, A., Agarwal, G., & Pradhan, R. (2008). Hand Gesture Recognition: A Comparative Study. *Proceedings of the International Multi Conference of Engineers and Computer Scientists 2008*.

Chen, F.-S., Fu, C.-M., & Huang, C.-L. (2003, March20). Hand gesture recognition using a real-time tracking method and hidden Markov models. *Image and Vision Computing, 21*, 745–758.

Coogan, T. A. (2007). *Dynamic Gesture Recognition using Transformation Invariant Hand Shape Recognition*. M.Sc. Thesis.

Ferdousi, Z. (2008). *Design and Development of A Real-Time Gesture Recognition System*. (Master of Science in Computer and Information Systems Engineering Thesis). Graduate School of Tennessee State University.

Field, M., Gordon, S., Peterson, E., Robinson, R., Stahovich, T., & Alvarado, C. (2010). The effect of task on classification accuracy: Using gesture recognition techniques in free-sketch recognition. *Computers & Graphics, 34*(5), 499–512. doi:10.1016/j.cag.2010.07.001

Ikko & Agarwal. (2012). *Gesture recognition: Enabling natural interactions with electronics*. Gesture Recognition and Depth-Sensing Texas Instruments, White Paper.

Jia, P., Hu, H. H., Lu, T., & Yuan, K. (2007). Head gesture recognition for hands-free control of an intelligent wheelchair. *The Industrial Robot, 34*(1), 60–68. doi:10.1108/01439910710718469

Kaur & Prasanna. (2011). *Real Time Hand Gesture Recognition and Blink Detection*. Project report.

Lien & Huan. (n.d.). Model-based articulated hand motion tracking for gesture recognition. Image and Vision Computing, 16, 121–134.

Lü, T. (2004). *Design and Analysis of A Real-Time Video Human Gesture Recognition System*. (Ph.D. Thesis). Princeton University.

Manresa, C., Varona, J., Mas, R., & Perales, F. J. (2000). Real –Time Hand Tracking and Gesture Recognition for Human-Computer Interaction. *ELCVIA. Electronic Letters on Computer Vision and Image Analysis, 0*(0), 1–7.

Meena, S. (2011). *A Study on Hand Gesture Recognition Technique*. Thesis of Master of Technology in Telematics and Signal Processing.

Morie, T., Miyamoto, H., & Hanazawa, A. (2007). Brain-inspired visual processing for robust gesture recognition. *International Congress Series, 1301*, 31–34. doi:10.1016/j.ics.2006.12.010

Nandhini, K. (2013). Touchte'l: Nanomaterial Based Touch Sensing. *International Journal of Applied Engineering Research, 8*(17).

Nandhini, K., & Raajan, N. R. (2013). Gesture Based Life Saving Approach. *International Journal of Applied Engineering Research, 8*(17).

Nandhini, K., & Santhi. (2012a). Retrospection of SVM Classifier. *Journal of Theoretical and Applied Information Technology, 38*.

Nandhini, K., & Santhi. (2012b). An in Depth Study of Emotion Analysis. *Research Journal of Applied Sciences, Engineering and Technology, 4*(24).

Neilan, J. H., II. (2012). *Gesture Recognition Using Ensembles of Classifiers*. (Master of Science Thesis). Northern Kentucky University.

Persson & Samvik. (2009). *A System for Real Time Gesture Recognition*. (Master's thesis). Lund University.

Purkayastha. (2009). *Integrating Gesture Recognition and Speech Recognition In A Touch-Less Human Computer Interaction System*. (Master of Science thesis). University at Buffalo.

Raheja, J. L., & Chaudhary, A. (2014). *PreConsultation Help Necessity Detection Based on Gait Recognition. In Signal Image and Video Processing* (Vol. 8). Springer.

Rautaray & Agrawal. (2012). Real Time Hand Gesture Recognition System for Dynamic Applications. *International Journal of Ubi Comp, 3*(1).

Rautaray, S. S., & Agrawal, A. (2012). Real Time Multiple Hand Gesture Recognition System for Human Computer Interaction. *I.J. Intelligent Systems and Applications, 5*(5), 56–64. doi:10.5815/ijisa.2012.05.08

Shina, M. C., Tsapb, L. V., & Goldgof, D. B. (2004). Gesture recognition using Bezier curves for visualization navigation from registered 3-D data. *Pattern Recognition, 37*.

Vogler, C., & Metaxas, D. (2001). A Framework for Recognizing the Simultaneous Aspects of American Sign Language. *Computer Vision and Image Understanding*, *81*(3), 358–384. doi:10.1006/cviu.2000.0895

Yuan, Y. (2008). *Image-Based Gesture Recognition with Support Vector Machines*. (Ph.D. dissertation). University of Delaware.

Chapter 10

Necessity of Key Aggregation Cryptosystem for Data Sharing in Cloud Computing

R. Deepthi Crestose Rebekah
Ravindra college of Engineering for Women, India

Dhanaraj Cheelu
Ravindra college of Engineering for Women, India

M. Rajasekhara Babu
VIT University, India

ABSTRACT

Cloud computing is one of the most exciting technologies due to its ability to increase flexibility and scalability for computer processes, while reducing cost associated with computing. It is important to share the data securely, efficiently, and flexibly in cloud storage. Existing data protection mechanisms such as symmetric encryption techniques are unsuccessful in preventing data sharing securely. This article suggests Key aggregate cryptosystem which produce constant size ciphertexts in order to delegate decryption rights for any set of ciphertexts. The uniqueness is that one can aggregate any number of secret keys and make them as compact as a single key. This compact aggregate key can be easily sent to others with very limited secure storage.

DOI: 10.4018/978-1-5225-0546-4.ch010

CLOUD COMPUTING ARCHITECTURE:

Cloud computing is a model for delivering information technology services in which resources are retrieved from the internet through web-based tools and applications, rather than a direct connection to a servers (Kanchana & Dhandapani, 2013) (Rajasekhara et al., 2014). However, cloud computing structure allows access to information as long as an electronic device has access to web.

Characteristics of Cloud Computing

The five essential characteristics of cloud computing are On-demand self-service, broad network access, resource pooling, rapid elasticity and measured service:

1. **On-Demand Self-Service:** A service provided by the cloud vendors that enable the provision of cloud resources on demand whenever they are required (Zhang et al., 2010).
2. **Broad Network Access:** The resources hosted on a cloud network that are available for access from a wide range of devices such as smart phones, tablets, personal computers etc., and these resources are accessible from different locations that offer online access. (Prakash, 2013).
3. **Resource Pooling:** The computing resources are pooled by cloud vendors to serve multiple consumers using a multi-tenant model, with different physical and virtual resources dynamically assigned and reassigned according to consumer demand [3]. The examples of resources include storage, processing, memory, network bandwidth and virtual machines.
4. **Rapid Elasticity:** It allows the users automatically control and optimize resource by using a metering capability at some level of abstraction appropriate to the type of services (Mell & Grance, 2014). Resource usage can be monitored, controlled and reported providing transparency for both the provider and consumer of the service.

Service Models of Cloud Computing

Cloud service models describe cloud services are made available to users. Figure 1 explains three service models – SaaS, PaaS and IaaS which provide resources to the users:

1. **SaaS:** It provides the customers with ready to use application running on the infrastructure service provider. The applications are easily accessible from several client devices as on demand services. Salesforce, DocLanding, Zoho,

Figure 1. Service models of cloud

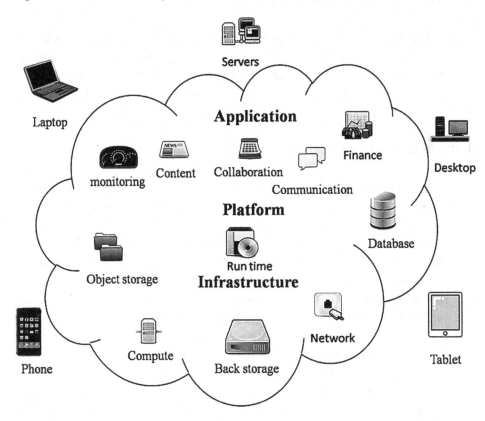

Workday are instances of SaaS are used for different purposes such as email, billing, human resource management etc. (Figure 1),

2. **PaaS**: It provides platform oriented service controlling the installed applications and available hosting environment configuration. Google AppEngine, LoadStorm are the instances of PaaS for running web applications and testing their performance.

3. **IaaS**: It provides infrastructure services such as memory, CPU and storage. The consumer can deploy and run software. It reduces hardware costs. Amazon S3 and FlexiScale, Dropbox are the best examples of IaaS for storing and maintaining virtual servers.

Deployment Models of Cloud Computing

While service models describe the specific capabilities of cloud solutions, deployment models describe where, how, and by whom the cloud's physical servers are

Figure 2. Deployment models of cloud

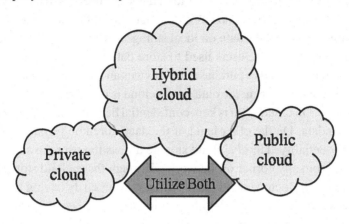

managed (Armbrust et al., 2010). Cloud computing may be deployed as private, public and hybrid, which are shown in Figure 2:

1. **Private Cloud:** A private cloud is a particular model of cloud computing that involves a distinct and secure cloud based environment in which on the specific client/ organization can operate.

    As private cloud is only accessible by a single organization, that organization will have the ability to manage and configure it in line with their needs to achieve a network solution.
    Benefits of private cloud are higher security and privacy, cost and energy efficiency and improved reliability.

2. **Public Cloud:** Public cloud is a deployment model under which resources are made generally available to everyone. However, the cloud provider still owns and manages the actual services. Users can self- provision resources from a web interface, in effect renting them from the provider as pay – as – you – use basis (Shelke et al., 2012).

    The benefits of public cloud are its on- demand setup and vast scalability.

3. **Hybrid Cloud:** A hybrid cloud is an integrated cloud service utilizing both private and public clouds to perform various functions within the same organization [7]. An organization can maximize their efficiencies by employing public cloud services for non- sensitive operations and private cloud services for sensitive operations and also ensure their platforms seamlessly integrated.

The various services offered by the cloud made the users increasingly opting for cloud storage for saving their data. With the data saved on the cloud, users are no longer required to store their data on local storage devices.

Firstly, in the early days, users used to store data on physical devices. If these devices get lost, users need to purchase new devices and also have to pay for backing up services. Secondly, storing the data on the cloud is more secure than storing it on physical devices. On cloud, data is kept confidential because only authorized people can access the data. On the other hand, if the data stored on physical devices may risk the confidentiality. Thirdly, cloud storage allows the users to share their files or documents from any corner of the world. Through these cloud storage services, users can send their documents to others without necessarily having to meet physically, whereas this cannot happen with traditional storage because users must meet physically with the people they want to share the data with.

Finally, the file backup software provides quick online data backup of any lost data. If the users make any changes on their data, automatic data backup software updates it and therefore it keeps their files secure and updated at all times. However, they can lose their data when they use physical devices.

Considering data privacy, a traditional way to ensure it is to rely on the server to enforce the access control after authentication which means any unexpected privilege escalation will expose all data. In a shared- tenancy cloud computing environment, things become even worse.

Data from different clients can be hosted on separate virtual machines (VM) but reside on a single physical machine. Data in a target VM could be stolen by instantiating another VM co-resident with target one (Mathew et al., 2014). Regarding the availability of files, there are a series of cryptographic schemes which go as far as allowing a third- party auditor to check the availability of files on behalf of the data owner without leakage anything about the data (Wang et al., 2013), or without compromising the data owner's anonymity (Wang et al., 2013).

SECURITY ISSUES OF DATA SHARING IN CLOUD

In this section we explain security issues and challenges in cloud computing.

Cloud computing encompasses many technologies including networks, databases, operating systems, virtualization, resource scheduling, transaction management, load balancing, concurrency control and memory management. Security issues for many these systems and technologies are applicable to cloud computing. For example, the network that interconnects the systems in a cloud has to be secure. Furthermore, virtualization paradigm in cloud computing leads to several security concerns, and mapping the virtual machines to physical machines has to be carried out securely.

Data security involves encrypting the data as well as ensuring that appropriate policies are enforced for data sharing (Narkhede et al., 2013). In addition, resource allocation and memory management algorithms have to be secure. Finally, data mining techniques may be applicable for malware detection in the clouds.

There are several types of security threats like are confidentiality, integrity, availability and data sharing to which cloud computing is vulnerable:

- **Confidentiality:** Confidentiality is roughly equivalent to privacy. Measures undertaken to ensure confidentiality are designed to prevent sensitive data from reaching the wrong people, while making sure that the right people can in fact get it, i.e. access must be restricted to those authorized to view the data. Confidentiality of data in cloud may lose due to internal user threats, external attacker threats and data leakage.

Internal user threats are malicious cloud providers, malicious cloud customer users and malicious third party users. External attacker threats are remote software attack of cloud infrastructure, remote software attack of cloud applications, and remote hardware attack against the cloud. Data leakage may happen due to failure of security access rights across multiple domains, failure of electronic and physical transport systems for cloud data and backups.

- **Integrity:** Integrity involves maintaining the consistency, accuracy, and trustworthiness of data. Data must not be changed in transit, and steps must be taken to ensure the data cannot be altered by unauthorized people. Integrity of data may be affected by data segregation, user access and data quality (Cheelu et al., 2013).

Data segregation involves incorrectly defined security perimeters, incorrect configuration of virtual machines and hypervisors. Implementation of poor user access control procedures creates many threat opportunities. The threat of impact of data quality is increased as cloud providers host many customers' data. The introduction of a faulty or misconfigured component required by another cloud user could potentially impact the integrity of data for other cloud users sharing infrastructure.

- **Availability:** Availability is the ability of the user to access data or resources in a specified location and in the correct format. Availability of data may lose due to change management, denial of service threat and physical disruption.

Likewise, cloud users may feel that cloud server is not doing a good job in terms of confidentiality (MohamedInfan, 2014).

CRYPTOGRAPHIC SOLUTIONS FOR DATA SHARING IN CLOUD

To overcome this problem, users can use cryptographic techniques whenever the users don't trust the security of the VM or the honesty of the technical staff. Then users can encrypt their data with their own keys before uploading them to the server.

One of the important functionality of cloud storage is Data sharing. For example, social network users can let their friends view a few of their private pictures; an organization may grant employees access to a portion of sensitive data. The challenging problem is how to share the encrypted data effectively. Obviously, users can download the encrypted data from the cloud storage, decrypt them, and then send them to others for sharing. But it loses the importance of cloud storage.

Imagine that Alice stores all her private photos on Dropbox, and she does not want others to view her photos. Due to various data leakage possibility Alice cannot feel relieved by just relying on the privacy protection mechanisms provided by Dropbox, so she encrypts all the photos using her own keys before uploading. Suppose on one day, Alice's friend, Bob, asks her to share the photos taken over all these years which Bob is appeared in. Alice can then use the share function of Dropbox, but the problem now is how to delegate the decryption rights for these photos to Bob. Certainly, there are two extreme ways for her under the traditional encryption paradigm:

1. Alice can encrypt all the photos with a single encryption key and gives encrypted key to Bob.
2. Alice encrypts photos with different secret keys and sends Bob the corresponding secret keys.

Obviously the first technique is not sufficient since all unchosen data may be also revealed to Bob. For the second method there are practical errors on efficiencies because the number of such keys is as many as number of shared photos.

Encryption techniques come with two techniques, symmetric key encryption and asymmetric key encryption.

1. **Symmetric Key Encryption:** An encryption system in which a single common key is used by the sender and receiver to encrypt and decrypt the message. The symmetric encryption scheme has five ingredients which are present in Figure 3:
   a. **Plaintext:** This is the actual message or data that is fed to the algorithm as input.
   b. **Encryption Algorithm:** The encryption algorithm performs various substitutions and permutations on the plaintext.

c. **Secret Key:** The secret key is also given as input to the encryption algorithm. The exact substitutions and permutations performed depend on the key used, and the algorithm will produce a different output depending on the specific key being used at the time.

d. **Cipher Text:** This the scrambled message produced as output. It depends on the plaintext and the key. The cipher text is an apparently random stream of data, as it stands, is unintelligible.

e. **Decryption Algorithm:** This is essentially the encryption algorithm run in reverse. It takes the cipher text and the secret key as input and produces the original plaintext as output.

The problem with the symmetric key encryption is sender and the receiver must have obtained copies of the secret key in a secure fashion and must keep the key secure. If someone can discover the key and knows the algorithm, all communications using this key is readable.

2. **Asymmetric (Public) Key Encryption:** An encryption system in which a sender uses a public key to encrypt messages and receiver uses a private key to

Figure 3. Symmetric encryption

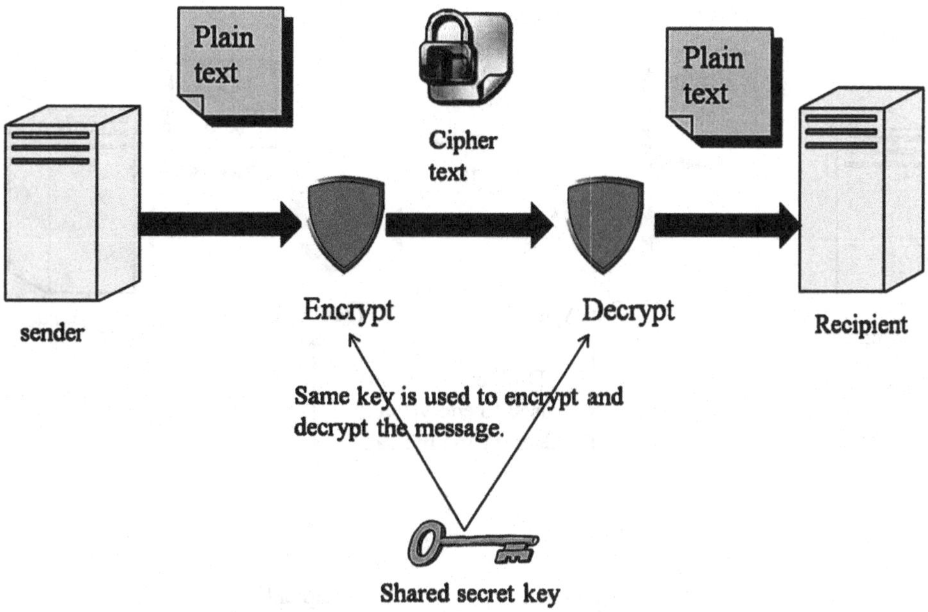

decrypt the messages. The asymmetric encryption scheme has five ingredients which are present in Figure 4:

a. **Plaintext:** This is the readable message or data that is fed into the algorithm as input.

b. **Encryption Algorithm:** The encryption algorithm performs various transformations on the plaintext.

c. **Public and Private Key:** This is a pair of keys that have been selected so that if one is used for encryption, the other is used for decryption. The exact transformation performed by the encryption algorithm depends on the public or private keys that are provided as input.

d. **Cipher Text:** This is the scrambled message produced as output after encryption.

e. **Decryption Algorithm:** This algorithm accepts the cipher text and the matching key as input and produces the original plaintext.

The use of public key encryption gives more flexibility for our applications. For example, in enterprise settings, every employ can upload encrypted data on the cloud storage server without the knowledge of the company's master-secret key

Figure 4. Asymmetric encryption

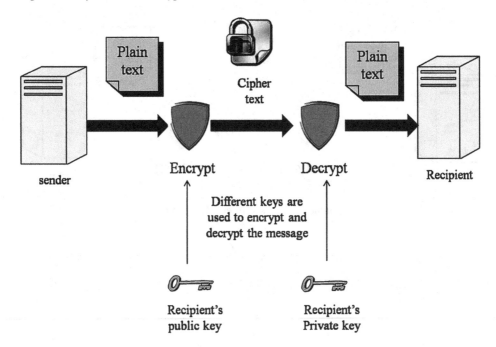

(private key). Therefore, the best solution for the above problem is key aggregate cryptosystem (KAC).

In KAC, users encrypt a message not only under a public key, but also under an identifier of cipher text called class. That means the cipher texts are further categorized into different classes. The key owner holds a master secret called master secret key, which can be used to extract secret keys for different classes. More importantly, the extracted key have can be an aggregate key which is as compact as a secret key for a single class, but aggregates the power of many such keys, i.e., the decryption power for any subset of cipher text classes (Chu et al., 2014).

With our solution, Alice can simply send Bob a single aggregate key via a secure e-mail. Bob can download the encrypted photos from Alice's Dropbox space and then use this aggregate key to decrypt these encrypted photos. The scenario is depicted in Figure 5.

That Alice encrypts photos with different public keys but only sends Bob a single (constant size) decryption key. Since the decryption key should be sent via a secure channel and kept secret, small key size is always desirable.

Figure 5. Alice shares files with identifiers 2, 3, 6, and 8 with Bob by sending him a single aggregate key.

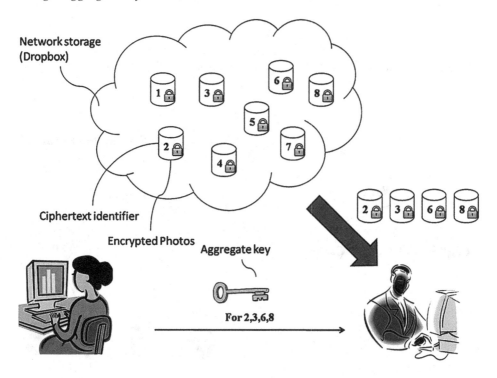

RELATED WORK

This section we compare our basic KAC scheme with other possible solutions on sharing in secure cloud storage.

Cryptographic Keys for a Predefined Hierarchy

The main aim of Cryptographic assignment schemes is to minimize the expense in storing and managing secret keys for general cryptographic use (Akl et al., 1983; Chick & Tavares, 1990; Tzeng, 2002; Ram, 2015). By using a tree structure, a key for a given branch can be used to derive the keys of its descendant nodes. Because granting the parent key implicitly grants all the keys of its descendant nodes.

We take the tree structure as an example. Alice can first classify the cipher text classes according to their subjects like Figure 6(a). Each node in the tree represents a secret key, while the leaf nodes represent the keys for individual cipher text classes. Filled circles represent the keys for the classes to be delegated and circles circumvented by dotted lines represent the keys to be granted. Note that every key of the non-leaf node can derive the keys of its descendant nodes.

In Figure 6, if Alice wants to share all the files in the "personal" category, she only needs to grant the key for the node "personal", which automatically grants the delegatee the keys of all the descendant nodes ("photo", "music"). This is the ideal

Figure 6. Compact key is not always possible for a fixed hierarchy.

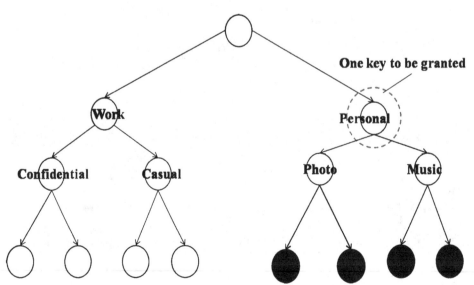

case, where most classes to be shared belong to the same branch and thus a parent key of them is sufficient.

However, it is still difficult for general cases. As shown in Figure 7, if Alice shares her demo music at work ("work"→"casual"→"demo" and "work"→"Confidential"→"demo") with a colleague who also has the rights to see some of her personal data, what she can do is to give more keys, which leads to an increase in the total key size. One can see that this approach is not flexible when the classifications are more complex and she wants to share different sets of files to different people. For this delegate in our example, the number of granted secret keys becomes the same as the number of classes.

Compact Key in Identity-Based Encryption

Identity-based encryption (IBE) is a type of public-key encryption in which the public-key of a user can be set as an identity-string of the user (e.g., an email address). There is a trusted party called private key generator (PKG) in IBE which holds a master-secret key and issues a secret key to each user with respect to the user

Figure 7. Compact key is not always possible for a fixed hierarchy.

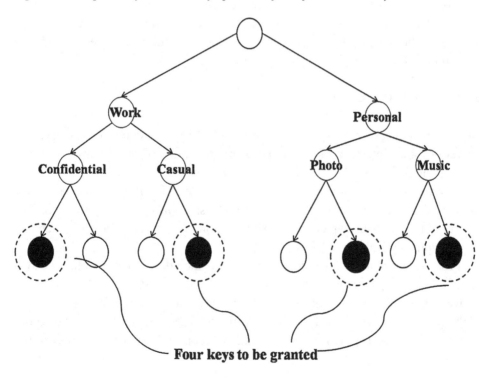

identity. The encryptor can take the public parameter and a user identity to encrypt a message. The recipient can decrypt this cipher text by his secret key.

Guo et al (2007) and Kate & Potdukhe (2014) tried to build IBE with key aggregation. One of their schemes assumes random oracles but another does not. In their schemes, key aggregation is constrained in the sense that all keys to be aggregated must come from different "identity divisions". While there are an exponential number of identities and thus secret keys, only a polynomial number of them can be aggregated. Most importantly, their key-aggregation comes at the expense of O(n) sizes for both cipher texts and the public parameter, where n is the number of secret keys which can be aggregated into a constant siz(N Bhatt et al., 2013) one. This greatly increases the costs of storing and transmitting cipher texts, which is impractical in many situations such as shared cloud storage.

Key-Policy Attribute-Based Encryption

Attribute-based encryption (ABE) is a paradigm, where messages are encrypted and decryption keys are computed in accordance with a given set attributes and access structure on the set of attributes (Tiplea, 2014). Attribute based encryption allows each cipher text to be associated with an attribute, and the master-secret key holder can extract for a policy of these attributes so that a cipher text can be decrypted by this key if its associated attribute confirms to the policy. The major concern in attribute based encryption is collusion resistance but not the compactness of secret keys. Also the size of the key often increases linearly with the number of attributes it encompasses, or the cipher text-size is not constant.

Proxy Re-Encryption

Instead of sending secret key to the delegate (say Bob) one can delegate the decryption power of some cipher texts by using proxy re-encryption (Canetti & Hohenberger, 2007) (Chu & Tzeng, 2007) (Chu et al., 2009) (Chow et al., 2010).

In proxy re-encryption scheme a delegator (say Alice) and a delegatee (say Bob) generate a proxy key that allows a semi trusted third party (say the Proxy) to convert cipher text encrypted under Alice's public key into cipher text which can be decrypted by Bob.

Proxy re-encryption has various applications including cryptographic file system [25]. However Alice has to trust that according to her instruction the proxy only converts the cipher texts, which is what we want to avoid at the first place. Even, if the proxy conspires with Bob, some forms of Alice's secret key can be recovered which can decrypt Alice's cipher texts without the help of Bob. It means that transformation key of proxy should be safeguarded. Proxy re-encryption makes the secure key storage from delegatee to the proxy. Proxy re-encryption makes the storage requirement from the delegatee to the proxy. Thus it is unacceptable to let proxy reside in the storage server. It is also inconvenient because every decryption requires separate interaction with the proxy.

KEY AGGREGATE ENCRYPTION

We first give the framework and definition for key-aggregate encryption. Then we describe how to use KAC in a scenario of its application in cloud storage.

Framework

A key aggregate encryption scheme consists of five polynomial-time algorithms. Initially the data owner establishes the public system parameter via Setup and generates a public/master-secret key pair via KeyGen. Messages can be encrypted via Encrypt by anyone who also decides which cipher text class is associated with the plaintext message to be encrypted. To generate an aggregate decryption key, the data owner can use the master- secret for a set of cipher text classes via Extract. Now the generated keys can be passed to delegatees securely through secure e-mails or secure devices. Finally, any user with an aggregate key can decrypt any cipher text provided that the ciphertext's class is contained in the aggregate key via Decrypt:

1. **Setup ($1^\lambda,n$):** This is executed by the data owner to setup an account on an untrusted server. A security level parameter 1^λ and the number of 'n' cipher text classes (i.e., class index should be an integer bounded by 1^λ and n); it outputs the public system parameter '*param*'.
2. **Keygen:** It is executed by the data owner to randomly generate a public/master-secret key pair (pk, msk).
3. **Encrypt (pk, i, m):** This is executed by anyone who wants to encrypt data. It takes a public key pk, an index i denoting the ciphertext class and a message m as input. It outputs a cipher text C.
4. **Extract (msk, S):** It is executed by the data owner for delegating the decrypting power for a certain set of cipher text classes to a delegatee. It takes the master secret key msk and a set S of indices corresponding to different classes, it output the master-secret key msk and a set S of indices corresponding to different classes as input; and it outputs the aggregate key for set S denoted by K_s.

5. **Decrypt (Ks, S, i, C):** This is executed by a delegatee who receives an aggregate key K_s generated by Extract. It takes Ks, the set S, an index i denoting the cipher text class the cipher text C belongs to and C as input, it outputs the decrypted result m if i∈S.

    a.   There are two functional requirements:

        i.   Correctness for any integers λ and n, any $S \subseteq \{1,...,n\}$, any index i ∈ S and any message m. Pr[Decrypt(Ks,S,i,C)=m:param←Setup(1^λ,n), (pk,msk)←KeyGen(), C←Encrypt(pk,i,m), Ks←Extract(msk,S)]=1.

        ii.   Compactness For any integers λ, n, any set S, any index i ∈ S and any message m; $param$ ←Setup(1^λ, n),

(pk, msk)←KeyGen(),

Ks← Extract(msk, S) and C←Encrypt(pk, i, m);

$|Ks|$ and $|C|$ only depend on the security parameter λ but independent of the number of classes n.

Sharing Encrypted Data

An authorized application of KAC is data sharing. The key aggregation property is especially useful when we expect the delegation to be efficient and flexible. The schemes enable a content provider to share her data in a confidential and selective way, with a fixed and small cipher text expansion, by distributing to each authorized user a single and small aggregate key.

Here we describe the main idea of data sharing in cloud storage using KAC, illustrated in Figure 2. Suppose Alice wants to share her data m_1, m_2, ...,m_i on the server. She first performs Setup (1^λ,n) to get $param$ and execute KeyGen to get the public/master secret key pair (pk, msk). The system parameter $param$ and public key pk can be made public and master secret key msk should be kept secret by Alice. Anyone (including Alice herself) can then encrypt each m_i by C_i=Encrypt (pk, i, m_i). The encrypted data are uploaded to the server.

With $param$ and pk, people who cooperate with Alice can update Alice's data on the server. Once Alice is willing to share a set S of her data with a friend Bob, she can compute the aggregate key Ks for Bob by performing Extract (msk, S). Since Ks are just a constant size key, it is easy to be sent to Bob via a secure email.

After obtaining the aggregate key, Bob can download the data he is authorized to access. That is, for each i ∈ S, Bob downloads C_i (and some needed values in $param$) from the server. With the aggregate key Ks, Bob can decrypt each C_i by Decrpty(Ks, S, i, C_i) for each i ∈S.

CONCLUSION

Cloud computing is a promising paradigm with growing acceptance, but there is still much work to be done if we want to achieve security in the cloud. The important issue of cloud storage is how to protect user's data privacy. Hence we described a new public key cryptosystem which produce a constant size ciphertext such that efficient delegation of decryption rights for any set of ciphertexts are possible. The uniqueness is that one can aggregate any set of secret keys and make them as compact as single key but encompassing the power of all the keys being aggregated.

The limitation in this work is predefined bound of number of maximum ciphertext classes. In cloud storage the number of ciphertexts usually grows rapidly. So we have reserve enough ciphertext classes for the future extension.

REFERENCES

Akl, S. G., & Taylor, P. D. (1983). Cryptographic solution to a problem of access control in a hierarchy. *ACM Transactions on Computer Systems*, *1*(3), 239–248. doi:10.1145/357369.357372

Akl & Taylor. (1983). Cryptographic Solution to a Problem of Access Control in a Hierarchy. *ACM Transactions on Computer Systems*, *1*(3), 239–248.

Armbrust, M., Fox, A., Griffith, R., Joseph, A. D., Katz, R., Konwinski, A., & Zaharia, M. et al. (2010). A view of cloud computing. *Communications of the ACM*, *53*(4), 50–58. doi:10.1145/1721654.1721672

Ateniese, G., Fu, K., Green, M., & Hohenberger, S. (2006). Improved proxy re-encryption schemes with applications to secure distributed storage. *ACM Transactions on Information and System Security*, *9*(1), 1–30. doi:10.1145/1127345.1127346

Bhatt, N., Babu, M., & Bhatt, A. (2013). Automation Testing Software that Aid in Efficiency Increase of Regression Process. *Recent Patents on Computer Science*, *6*(2), 107–114. doi:10.2174/22132759113069990008

Canetti, R., & Hohenberger, S. (2007, October). Chosen-ciphertext secure proxy re-encryption. In *Proceedings of the 14th ACM conference on Computer and communications security* (pp. 185-194). ACM.

Cheelu, D., Babu, M. R., & Venkatakrishna, P. (2013). A fuzzy-based intelligent vertical handoff decision strategy with maximised user satisfaction for next generation communication networks. *International Journal of Process Management and Benchmarking*, *3*(4), 420–440. doi:10.1504/IJPMB.2013.058268

Chick, G. C., & Tavares, S. E. (1990, January). Flexible access control with master keys. In Advances in Cryptology—CRYPTO'89 Proceedings (pp. 316-322). Springer New York. doi:doi:10.1007/0-387-34805-0_29 doi:10.1007/0-387-34805-0_29

Chow, S. S., Weng, J., Yang, Y., & Deng, R. H. (2010). Efficient unidirectional proxy re-encryption. In *Progress in Cryptology–AFRICACRYPT 2010* (pp. 316-332). Springer Berlin Heidelberg.

Chu, C. K., Chow, S. S., Tzeng, W. G., Zhou, J., & Deng, R. H. (2014). Key-aggregate cryptosystem for scalable data sharing in cloud storage. *Parallel and Distributed Systems. IEEE Transactions on, 25*(2), 468–477.

Chu, C. K., & Tzeng, W. G. (2007). Identity-based proxy re-encryption without random oracles. In *Information Security* (pp. 189–202). Springer Berlin Heidelberg. doi:10.1007/978-3-540-75496-1_13

Chu, C. K., Weng, J., Chow, S. S., Zhou, J., & Deng, R. H. (2009, January). Conditional proxy broadcast re-encryption. In *Information security and privacy* (pp. 327–342). Springer Berlin Heidelberg. doi:10.1007/978-3-642-02620-1_23

Guo, F., Mu, Y., & Chen, Z. (2007). Identity-based encryption: how to decrypt multiple ciphertexts using a single decryption key. In *Pairing-Based Cryptography–Pairing 2007* (pp. 392–406). Springer Berlin Heidelberg. doi:10.1007/978-3-540-73489-5_22

Jain, S. (2014). *An analysis of security and privacy issues, Challenges with possible solution in cloud computing.* National Conference on Computational and Mathematical Sciences (COMPUTATIA-IV), Jaipur, India.

Kanchana, D., & Dhandapani, D. S. (2013). A Novel Method for Storage Security in Cloud Computing. *International Journal of Engineering Science and Innovative Technology, 2*(2), 243–249.

Kate, M. K., & Potdukhe, S. D. (2014). *Data sharing in cloud storage with key-aggregate cryptosystem.* Academic Press.

Mathew, M., Sumathi, D., Ranjima, P., & Sivaprakash, P. (2014). *Secure Cloud Data Sharing Using Key-Aggr egate Cryptosystem.* Academic Press.

Mell, P., & Grance, T. (2014). The nist definition of cloud computing, 2011. National Institute of Standards and Technology Special Publication, 800-145.

Narkhede, A., Dashore, P., & Verma, D (2013). *Graphics Based Cloud Security.* Academic Press.

Infan, Muthurangasamy, & Yogananth. (2014). Resilient Identify Based Encryption for Cloud Storage by Using Aggregated Keys. *International Journal of Advanced Research in Computer Engineering & Technology, 3*(3).

Prakash, K. (2013, February). A Survey On Security And Privacy In Cloud Computing. International Journal of Engineering Research and Technology, 2(2).

Rajasekhara Babu, M., Venkata Krishna, P., & Khalid, M. (2013). A framework for power estimation and reduction in multi-core architectures using basic block approach. *International Journal of Communication Networks and Distributed Systems, 10*(1), 40–51. doi:10.1504/IJCNDS.2013.050506

Ram, N. A., Reddy, N. C. S., & Poshal, G. (n.d.). *An Effective Scalable Data Sharing in Cloud Storage using Key-Aggregate Crypto-system.* Academic Press.

Shelke, M. P. K., Sontakke, M. S., & Gawande, A. (2012). Intrusion detection system for cloud computing. *International Journal of Scientific & Technology Research, 1*(4), 67–71.

Tiplea, F. L., & Dragan, C. C. (n.d.). *Key-policy Attribute-based Encryption for Boolean Circuits from Bilinear Maps.* Academic Press.

Tzeng, W. G. (2002). A time-bound cryptographic key assignment scheme for access control in a hierarchy. *Knowledge and Data Engineering. IEEE Transactions on, 14*(1), 182–188.

Wang, B., Chow, S. S., Li, M., & Li, H. (2013, July). Storing shared data on the cloud via security-mediator. In *Distributed Computing Systems (ICDCS), 2013 IEEE 33rd International Conference on* (pp. 124-133). IEEE. doi:doi:10.1109/ICDCS.2013.60 doi:10.1109/ICDCS.2013.60

Wang, C., Chow, S. S., Wang, Q., Ren, K., & Lou, W. (2013). Privacy-preserving public auditing for secure cloud storage. *Computers. IEEE Transactions on, 62*(2), 362–375.

Chapter 11

Enhancing Quality of Service in Cloud Gaming System:
An Active Implementation Framework for Enhancing Quality of Service in Multi-Player Cloud Gaming

Balamurugan Balusamy
VIT University, India

P. Venkata Krishna
VIT University, India

Aishwarya T.
VIT University, India

Thusitha M.
VIT University, India

Tamizh Arasi G. S.
VIT University, India

Marimuthu Karuppiah
VIT University, India

ABSTRACT

In multi-player cloud gaming two or more people from different locations may actively participate in gaming as like they were in a similar geographical location. In such cases handling massive user inputs, performance rendering, bandwidth fluctuations, load balancing, data capturing, data transmission in real time still remains a cumbersome in cloud gaming. In this chapter, we propose a framework that overcomes the major issues associated with quality of service in cloud gaming. The cloud platform consists of two environments namely workbench and runtime environment, where the work bench environment comprises of tools like end user

DOI: 10.4018/978-1-5225-0546-4.ch011

tools, data parsing tools and data integrity tools through which the user input is analyzed and sent to the run time environment for further processing. Each tool present at the cloud platform helps in achieving the quality factors through its functionalities. The user request is processed and the results will be sent to the clients through the runtime environment.

INTRODUCTION

Computer gaming plays a major role in internet, since all type of users (adults, children, teenagers, etc.) play games online for relaxation, fun and entertainment. In recent years, computer program i.e. a adaption of non-computer game is called traditional game. But traditional games do not contain any modern technologies, hence people does not get attracted more. To overcome this cloud gaming was introduced. Cloud gaming as the name indicates, it allows many users to play game online without any problem. It sometimes called as "gaming on demand". Cloud gaming differs from traditional online gaming as it (cloud gaming) provides better network load and less traffic problems when compared with traditional gaming. Cloud gaming is classified into two types they are,

- Cloud gaming on VIDEO streaming, and
- Cloud gaming on FILE streaming.

Cloud gaming on video streaming provides less friction and it also allows direct play ability to users on various devices. As discussed earlier, cloud gaming provides video streaming on users' computers based on demand. The original game is actually stored, executed and implemented on remote server or on that company server, the operations that is performed on cloud is not displayed or known to users only the output of that requested video is displayed on the user's computer with the help of internet. This cloud gaming can be accessed on consoles, computer and also on mobile devices. The controls or the actions performed by user are directed to the server from where the input controls are sent.

Cloud gaming on file streaming will reduce the internet bandwidth level by downloading the small part of the game initially, which will be less than 5% of the total game size. Later the remaining game will be downloaded in the user's device. This will require very less internet bandwidth. Hence it is also called as progressive downloading. This usually deploys a thin client in end user's device. Since it is deployed in cloud it reduces a scalability problem. This type of streaming will have a cache copy of the downloaded game. To operate the file streaming game, the device should have the hardware capabilities.

Design Objectives

The design objectives of cloud gaming include:

- **Extensibility:** Cloud gaming is a modularized design. Platform independent components such as audio and video capturing and platform independent components such as codes and protocols can be easily modified. To develop the capabilities, the developers should follow the programming interfaces of modules. It is not only limited to audio and video capturing, but a live casting is also done using this cloud gaming architecture.
- **Portability:** Since many users uses cloud gaming in wireless network, the gaming should design in such a way that it is easily adaptable in any platform. Platform dependent components can be easily replaced by new platforms. Gaming is played in windows, Linux operating systems, with the help of this portability the gaming can also be played in mobile devices.
- **Configurability:** To make a system into a customized usage scenario it is possible to try some combination of parameters that simply edit a text based file that makes the file customized. The configuration of the system should be easy to use by the users. A wide range of audio and video codecs should be supported.
- **Openness:** It is a free website. So any user can use the gaming service from anywhere. One criterion the user (researcher and developers) should follow is that the license terms provided for that game in their source packages (Figure 1).

Players will send the commands to the users in the form of thin client through internet. The commands will then be converted into game actions where the world of game changes. The changes are then processed by graphical processing unit in the cloud's system. The scene that is rendered is sent to the video encoder module which encodes the video. The encoded video is sent back to the video streaming module, that module will send the encoded rendered video back to the thin client. The decoding of the sent video is done by thin client and it will display the decoded video in the player's system (Table 1).

CLOUD GAMING ARCHITECTURE

The cloud gaming system composes of the gaming servers, portal servers and the clients or the gamers. The portal server is used by the user to log in the cloud gam-

Figure 1. Framework for a cloud gaming platform

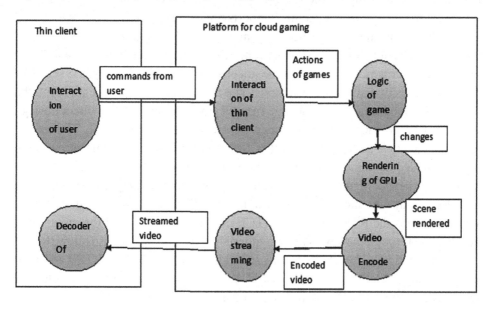

Table 1. System requirements with its descriptions

System Requirements	Descriptions
Operating systems	Linux, MAC, Android, Chrome OS etc
Hardware and upgradation	Existing hardware can be used. So its not expensive
Spectation	Spectating will be easy
Playing	Cloud gaming allows you to play instantly.
Piracy rate	The piracy rate for cloud gaming will be low

ing system for gaming where a list of games that are available are provided and the users could select the preferred game from the list. The request to play the game is provided by the user to the portal server. The user then could be connected to the game server to play the game by the link of the game provided by the portal server. A simple login is provided for the user to log in and also provides a simple gaming user interface. The protocols used for the actions and requests are the REST-like and HTTP or HTTPS.

The cloud gaming architecture work done by Huang et al (2013) provides two types of network flows: the data flow and the control flow. The data flow is used in streaming the audio and video frames from the server to the client where it encodes and decodes the audio, video signals through various protocols. The control flow sends the user inputs encode it and decode it form the client to the server in reversible manner. This architecture supports both the PC-based and the web-based games. An agent runs on the selected gaming server by the user. Depending upon the type and the implementation of the game, the gaming agent runs as a stand-alone process in other words it could also be injected as a thread into the game selected. The agent does two important functions: The first function of the agent is send the audio and video frames in an encoded manner from the server to the client through the data flow and these captured frames are decoded in the client side. The second foremost function done by the agent is to interaction with the game through the input provided by the user from the client side. The inputs actions are provided through the keyboard, mouse, and joystick or even through the gesture recognition in order to play and interact with the game. The client side runs the game console which contains the RTSP, RTP and RTCP multimedia player and the input could be accepted through the keyboard or a mouse logger. This would also allow the client to automatically decode the audio and video frames using the RTSP and RTP protocols and also allows the input events to be sent to the server in encoded format which is customizable. Due to this reason the

URL for accessing the preferred game by the user could be done easily using the multimedia players such as VLC media player which are supported in almost all types of OS. The server side of the gaming architecture deals with the decoding of the input events given by the client and also to encode the audio and video frames captured using the RTSP and RTP standard protocols (Figure 2).

Implementation

The implementation of the gaming system deals with the game server and the thin gaming client as described in the framework. These system works mainly on three important data flows. They are audio data flow, image or video data flow and input data flow. The data for the game audio is carried by the audio data flow. The data for the game frames are carried by the image data flow and the data regarding the input given by the user is carried by the input data flow. These flows represent the communication between the gaming server and the gaming client.

- **Audio Data Flow:** The task of the audio data flow stated by Huang et al (2013) is to collect the audio source and capture it. Then these captured audio frames are taken for the audio encoding and transmission of these encoded frames from the server to the client are done. The received encoded audio frames are later decoded by the client and are made to play through the media players in the game console. The detailed description of each task done in the audio data flow is described below:

Figure 2. Cloud gaming architecture

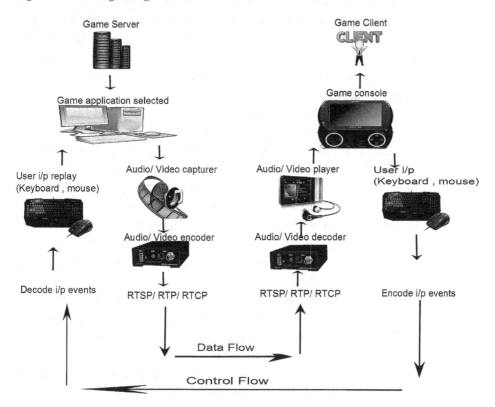

○ **Audio Source:** The audio source is received from the audio listener stated by Huang et al (2013) where all the audio of the game is received and these are played through the speakers of the computers.

○ **Audio Capture:** The audio is captured from the audio source through the audio capture component. This work stated by Huang et al (2013) component approximately gets chunks of audio for every 20 milliseconds which is said to be an array of 2048 bytes. Each and every time the audio data is captured a passed it is converted into an array of 8192 bytes. Then the array of bytes is sent through the TCP socket using a local host to the next process of encoding and transmission of audio.

○ **Audio Encoding and Transmission:** The FFMPEG is stated by Huang et al (2013) is used for the encoding and transmission component of the audio which is said to be the solution for the cross-platform for streaming and conversion of the audio and video frames. This FFMPEG is not shown on the terminal as it runs as a background process. The FFMPEG composes options for the input and output audio streaming with the IP address of the local host which is sent over a TCP socket, encoding bit rate audio codec used and the sample rate of the audio with the number of the channels. The audio compression is done with the MP3 encoder provided and the streaming is done through the UDP to the audio reception and the decoding component in the client side which denotes the IP address of the destination for the output stream

- ○ **Audio Reception and Decoding:** The implementation of the audio reception and decoding component is done using the FFPLAY is stated by Huang et al (2013) which is built using the libraries of the FFMPEG and SDL library. This is used to fetch the stream of the audio sent from the encoding and transmission component from the server. Thus this FFPLAY decodes the audio frame provided for playing.

- ○ **Audio Play:** This component is also implemented using the FFPLAY is stated by Huang et al (2013) similar to that of the previous component. This would receive the decoded audio frames which could be played through the SDL window.

- **Image/Video Data Flow:** The image data flow collects the image or the video from the gaming window from the server side and is captured. Then the encoding process is stated by Huang et al (2013) of the image or the video captured is done followed by the transmission of the encoded image frames from the server to the client. Then these encoded images are received in the client side and is decoded. The decoded video or image frames are displayed in the game console on the client side. The detailed description of each task done in the image data flow is described below:

  - ○ **Screen Capture:** The game screen is stated by Huang et al (2013) from the game window is captured using the screen capture component. Capturing the game screen with and without GUI are the two modes for capturing. The texture 2D format with 24-bit is used in the capture with GUI mode. In this mode the capture rate is synchronized with that of the image compression of the processing rate. In capturing without the GUI mode the capture rate is not synchronized with that of the image compression of the processing rate and the capture rate is set manually according to the rate of the image procession.

  - ○ **Image Encoding:** The JPEG encoder is used to perform the image encoding task. The quality factor and the texture 2D is stated by Huang et al (2013) objects are taken as the input by the JPEG encoder. The value of the quality factor lies between 1 and 100. The lower compression ratio is the indication of the higher quality factor. The compression of the image is done to the byte arrays by getting from the Screen

Capture component the pixel data in Texture2D format running at JPEG Encoder.

○ **Image Transmission:** The RPC method is used to do the image transmission is stated by Huang et al (2013) but it also uses a third party package called uLink to send the big chunk of image data properly which could help in decreasing amount of delay when receiving the data on the client which could make the connection well between the server and the client. The RPC script on the client and the server side is said to be the same in order to interact with one another.

○ **Image Reception and Decoding:** The RPC method on the client side is used to do the image reception. According to the work stated by Huang et al (2013) collects the bytes sent by the Image Transmission component where the rate of reception is same as the invoking rate on the server. The image decoding component decodes the entire image received on the frame basis. These byte arrays are decoded and again are converted to a 24-bit Texture2D format.

○ **Image Display:** The GUI is used for the implementation of the image display component is stated by Huang et al (2013). The image decoding component passes the texture it got and sketches it on the game window on the client's console. The users could customize the position of the window screen and the size of the texture. The image receiving rate is comparatively less to the rate of the image display rate as the method is several times called automatically on each frame.

• **Input Data Flow:** Similarly, the input data flow deals with the capturing of the events from the client side given by the user through the keyboard, mouse or joysticks is stated by Huang et al (2013). Then these are encoded through the customizable protocols and are transmitted from the client to the server. Then the server receives the encoded input events and decodes it to replay the events given by the user while playing a game. The detailed description of each task done in the input data flow is described below:

○ **Input Transmission:** The RPC is stated by Huang et al (2013) which is said to be unreliable is implemented for the input transmission component. The input data that are sent for the transmission are of three types they are positions and clicks of the mouse and the keyboard strokes which could be read from the input devices such as the keyboard and the mouse. The cursor movements of the mouse from the client side console are translated into the vector 3 type coordinates. The clicks of the mouse are translated into the integer value of either 1 or 0. Similarly the arrow keys on the keyboard are translated of values from -1 to 1 with respect to the horizontal and vertical axes and the other strokes of the keyboard pressed are translated into the related values of the keys.

○ **Input Reception:** The input reception is also implemented using the RPC method is stated by Huang et al (2013) which is responsible for the reception of the input data from the client side to the server side. As the interactions are event based and based on the mouse movements and clicks and the keyboard strokes these cannot be transferred to the interactions of the in-built GUI system to the server. This helps the gaming server to respond to the stimuli from the client side action for the game played. Thus after the reception of the input event is got from the client side it responds with the output for the corresponding input event performed.

GAMING AS A SERVICE (GAAS)

Cloud gaming is provided as a service in the name of "GAAS", that stands for gaming as a service. The gaming service is hosted or played by using cloud computing technologies (Figure 3). The gaming service also provides additional features like anti-piracy. Players sometimes download games on their pc's and other devices but they never play in such cases the memory and storage space will be wasted. This can be avoided in this service since it provides instant gaming opportunity. It also provides an enhanced experience of game to the users by allowing them to play games

Figure 3. The model of Onlive service

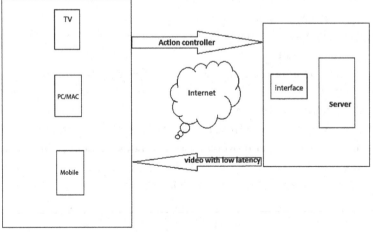

from anywhere, anytime and unexpected gaming service. Cloud gaming also helps commercially. The present commercial cloud gaming is onlive, gaikai, G-cluster.

The above graph represents the research issues and challenges faced by the OnLive in terms of network delay, streaming and encoding. The series 1 and series 2 in the graph describes about interaction delay and RTT in network (Figure 4).

G-cluster has a business model it consists of licensors, end users and network operators. The network operators will send a source code to G-cluster service, which will convert the source code to binary code. The converted code will be sent to network operators by G-cluster and based on demand the service will be provided to end users. The assurance of quality will be given by G-cluster. The server manufacturer will act as an intermediary between the G-cluster and network operators. To provide a flexible performance of cloud gaming in mobile the network environment should adopt some parameters. The parameters are full details, reduced path, and reduced details. The quality experienced by users is mapped to the quality of service in network. The mapping consists of subjective factors, objective factors, perceived quality (Figure 5).

Cloud gaming also supports multiple players to play a requested game. The players involved in the same game will receive a same video quality as other players. The received videos of gaming can be shared by other users with the help of cloudlet of ad-hoc that is developed by secondary level of ad-hoc network. This sharing is possible in clients those who plays in mobile. This sharing will help in reducing the transmission rate of the server. The multiplayer gaming includes cor-

Figure 4. Research issues and challenges faced by the OnLive

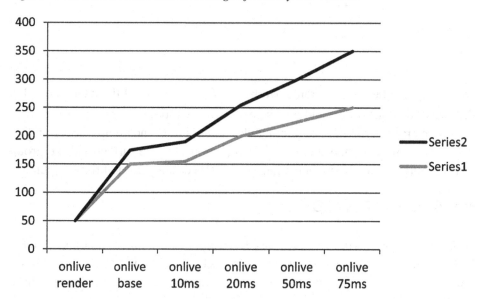

Figure 5. The visual of the mapping

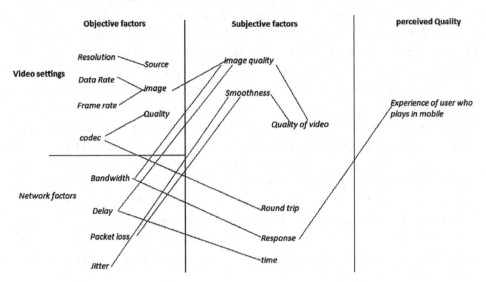

relation of inter-video and video frames. The inter video frame will help in calculating overlapping of frame ratio and size of inter frame. It consists of intra frame size and ratio of compression.

The formula to calculate is given below

$$R_{OP} = \frac{\left[W - \left(\left|X_2 - X_1\right|\right)\right]\left[H - \left(\left|Y_2 - Y_1\right|\right)\right]}{WH}$$

$$P_{in} = \left(1 - R_{OP}\right)I\rho$$

where R_{OP} the ratio of the frame overlap is, P_{in} is the size of the inter-frame, I is the size of the intra-frame and ρ is the compression ratio.

The interaction model of player includes random walk and group chase. Random walk is nothing but choosing a random direction to move further and the group chase is nothing but chasing a random peer for a certain period of time (Figure 6).

Mobile Based Cloud Gaming

A new technology has been aroused based on cloud based mobile computing as stated by Cai et al (2013) as a number of smart phones have been arrived, the smartphones are preferred to that of the computer. But there are also some restrictions on these

Figure 6. System model

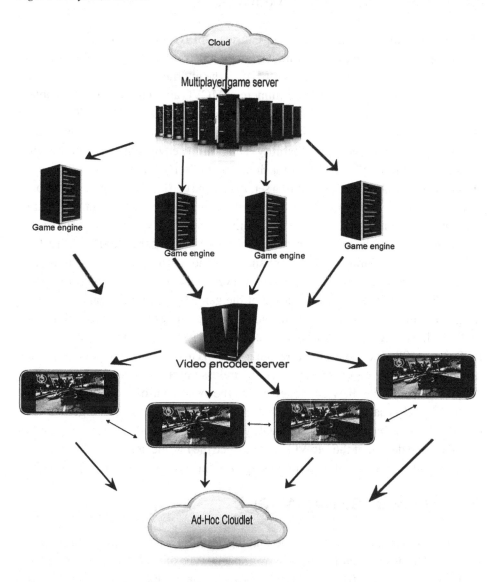

smartphones such as the minimal level of the battery usage time, computational capacity, internal storage memory and RAM of the phone needed to run the game. These mobile phones use the wireless broad band network for internet access. Hence cloud provides gaming also as a service similar to the SaaS, IaaS and PaaS. The mobile gaming provided by the cloud is classified into three types. They are Mobile Cloud Video Gaming (MCVG), Mobile Cloud Gaming (MCG) and Mobile Browser Gaming (MBG).

Mobile Cloud Video Gaming (MCVG)

Many cloud gaming services such as G-Cluster, OnLive, Gaikai and Big fish games provide gaming service by executing it from their private cloud as stated by Cai et al (2013)servers which could be transmitted over the internet to the smartphones, PC's or interactive televisions. The first commercial MCVG application that is available is the OnLive5 a mobile version in the Google Play Android App market. The mobile cloud video gaming (MCVG) is a combination of the Gaming-on-Demand model with wireless communication capability. The runtime environments of the mobiles are stimulated through the virtual machines by the server of the cloud. The game engine servers and the game streaming servers are the two key components composed by the virtual machines to support the mobile gaming on the thin clients. The game content server confirms the connection from the mobile device when a user tries to access the server of the respective game. The factors such as the QoSE which affects the Mobile Cloud Gaming (MCG) are analyzed and it also simultaneous initializes the game engine server. This game engine server later loads the account information of the client and then process the logic of the game by getting the game data from the game content server and the game video is rendered by the user data as described by Wilhelmsen, & Martin Alexander (2014). The game streaming video as stated by Cai et al (2013) encodes the raw game video. This encoded video is sent to the mobile devices i.e. the client through the wireless internet connection. The mobile devices are said to be the video receiver and the event controller whereas the cloud of the MCVG is said to be the video streaming server and the video generator as described by Wu et al (2014). The quality of Service (QoS) is said to be quite important in the design of the MCVG system since the mobile networks have put forth the constraints on rendering, compressing and transmitting the video (Figure 7).

Mobile Browser Gaming (MBG)

Mobile browser gaming is an online gaming services which is provided by social network. This type of gaming is used by a special type of users called massive users as stated by Cai et al (2013). This type of browser gaming has several characteristics they are:

1. **Support of Multiplayer:** As the name indicates it allows multiple user to play. The game will allow 'n' numbers of users to get interact with each other.
2. **Client Acts as Web Browsers:** This game is played online no need to download the game. Users can play directly with the help of internet. Users don't need to install any games on their pc.

Figure 7. Mobile cloud video gaming system

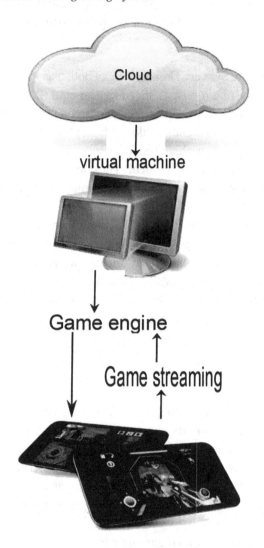

3. **Always On:** Users will get notifications messages regarding attacks even if users are not online.
4. **Varied Timescales:** This type of browser game will be played in a real-time. This happens in a different time scales. This gaming request will be queried in a timescale commands.
5. **Single Account Is Accessed by Separate User:** Each player is allowed to control the game with his/her single account, they can access it in a group or nation of one character. They have different styles /games, they are role-playing games, strategy games, manager games, shooting games, and social

networking games. Browser games are emerging in mobile devices also. The web browsers are the most emerging technique with the game container. This can also be referred as MBG.

a. MBG includes:

i. **Gaming Server:** The scripting of both user side and interface scripting must be robust as stated by Cai et al (2013) and fast-scripting. The server side scripting provides main functionalities and contents that include languages like python, php, jsp, java etc. user interface scripting allows handling of players input, controls etc.

ii. **Communication Protocol:** The communication between the server and the mobile browser is given a major importance in this section. In MBG's JSON, XML are well adopted

iii. **Application Run Time:** The run time in the mobile devices should be installed as plug-ins in a web browser. Some most successful commercial application run-times are Adobe flash player, Adobe shockwave player, Microsoft silver light, java applet. FarmVille on Facebook is one of the social network MBG's that greatly depend on the eco-system (Figure 8).

Mobile Cloud Gaming

The best definition of mobile cloud gaming was not given. The MCVG and MBG as stated by Cai et al (2013) are the two types of mobile cloud gaming. It is a type of interactive gaming that makes use of cloud as an external source to process gaming in a cross-platform as stated by Kamarainen et al (2014). Those who use cloud gaming in mobile will find easy to play when compared to systems because the operations are not visible to the users only they can host and play games without any compatibility.

The advantages of mobile cloud gaming are:

• That it(MCG) does not need its clients to install the game before playing is stated by Cai et al (2013). It only needs its users to install "OnLive" which acts as a thin client in one's device. The OnLive is used to transmit the video and also command. It also allows its user to install some add-ons like gaikai for browsers.

• Major advantage in using mobile cloud gaming is that it can store a vast data and resources to compute is unlimited.

Figure 8. Mobile browser gaming

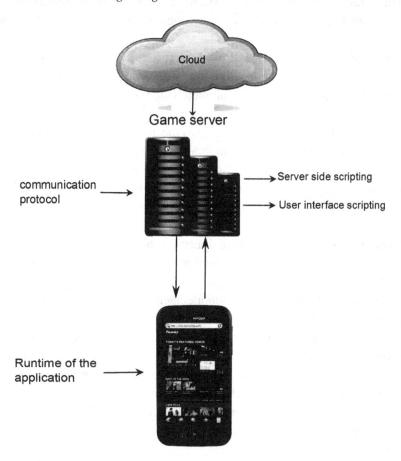

- When a user lost his/her mobile device, they may lose the game data that resides in the cloud-end. But in MCG whenever the players connect to the game the data and status of the game remains the same irrespective of the place. So it automatically provides a better gaming experience to the users.
- If the gaming process is complex it conserves battery on each device, it conserves battery only if the process is complex.

Some of the problems faced by MCG are:

- **Network Dependency Will Be Strong:** Network dependency problem occurs in mobile cloud gaming since cloud gaming will work only with the help of internet id=f the network is disconnected the dependency problem will occur.

- **The Bandwidth Used Will Be High:** It consumes high bandwidth since it must transmit real time video which requires high network load that results in network traffic.
- **Mobile Browsers Will Be Allowed to Access Limited Resources:** The resources available on mobile will not be sufficient for an effective gaming this results in transmitting of an incomplete video frames.

In Shea et al (2013) paper (gaming paper) the authors proposed some novel features which could be act as a future mobile cloud gaming services. The proposed features are Dynamic cloud integration, Augment reality gaming, context-aware gaming, multi-player online interaction and seamless cross platform gaming. The brief description about these features is given below,

- **Dynamic Cloud Integration:** In dynamic cloud integration, the game engine which is present in cloud is divided into video streamer and other components. The transmissions on mobile devices are done by components and the execution on client is done by mobile agents. This type of process is called as onloading where in normal cloud the opposite of this process is called as offloading. Based on the information gained the proportion of the game is onloaded in the user's device. i.e. it first displays the requested game on the user's device and then the cloud will wait for the status(statistics) of that particular device. Based on the statistics the game will be provided to the users. The problem faced by users is the network problem. The network will not remain constant, so to overcome this problem dynamic cloud integration is used.
- **Augmented- Reality Gaming:** The augmented reality gaming is proposed to overcome traditional gaming problem. The traditional gaming is otherwise called as pervasive gaming. This type of gaming is played by users in their mobiles only when the game is downloaded and installed. It is not suited to all types of games. Games like iPhone games or PlayStation is not downloaded and installed. So augmented reality gaming is a type of active, real, direct view or indirect view of gaming that helps the users to play cloud games in mobile devices easily.
- **Context Aware Gaming:** The context aware gaming will generate innovative and adaptive gaming contents in terms of time, place and movement of each player. This is possible since all mobile devices are connected with GPS. It offers a better playing or gaming experience that satisfy users' needs.
- **Multi Player Online Gaming:** Onlive was the first GAAS provider to offer cloud gaming in an android market. As in pc, users can also able to play games in their mobiles. It also provides better video streaming transmissions

to maintain the same quality of service in cloud gaming. Game is available in cloud-end it allows multiple users to play game.

- **Seamless Cross Platform Gaming:** Users will rely only on the contents of gaming. But the platform in which they are playing plays a major role. One game running in different platform contains different faming contents that game cannot be played in different platform so the cross platform for gaming is important. So the seamless cross platform gaming in mobile cloud gaming solves these cross platform problems thereby providing a better gaming experience to all types of users.

Quality of Service

Maintaining Quality of service in cloud gaming as stated by Jebalia (2014) is difficult because of the network dependency, i. e. the network connection may not be constant all the time. When it comes to mobile cloud gaming, it is very hard to maintain the QOS because of the diversity of subjects in each device of end user and also due to the network quality which changes frequently. To overcome these problems stated by Chuah et al (2014) (good) a new type of platform called component based cloud gaming platform is proposed specially for mobile's cloud gaming issues. In this the gaming which is decomposed is offloaded partially into the cloud. By doing this we can balance load in network between terminals and cloud. A prototypes containing three gaming is proposed in a test-bed in order to achieve effective and feasible demonstrations.

In component based cloud gaming test-bed is used to increase the quality of service. In test-bed the first thing is to divide the application into several pieces. This divided piece of gaming application is later executed in either cloud or terminals. The execution of the gaming content will be based on either the status of the network quality or diversity as stated by Zhang The test-bed should be capable of marinating the application in a real-time or run-time environment. This will help in finalizing how much load to allocate and also maintaining the dynamic inter relativity between the cloud terminals.

Cognitive engine will be present in the test-bed which receives all the status (statistical information) once the session of the game starts. This engine will not receive the status directly from session, a terminal will be responsible for sending the status to the cognitive engine, this engine will analyse the performance of each system and send those acknowledgments to the partitioning coordinator to decide its partitioning. The coordinator will then resend all types of messages like control messages and inter component messages based on the decision to maintain the dynamic partitioning. When cognitive engine sends decision to the partitioning coordinator, anon loading process will take place. This process is an optional process that is available in a test-bed.

Platform Independence Gaming

Cloud gaming is preferred by many users because it is platform independent. The gaming does not require any particular OS or platform. Hence there will be no issues like portability. Cloud gaming provider will be demanded low cost because the gaming will not have any compatibility problems like plug-ins etc. so it consumes very low cost which can be easily affordable by all types of users and also by gaming provider. The maintenance cost of the gaming is very low. So users will experience a better gaming environment. Cloud gaming does not need its client to upgrade hardware or software i.e. the client can neglect the frequent up gradation of their system's or device hardware and software and also they can enjoy their gaming by extending the systems lifetime with the help of cloud service. Cloud gaming has some 3 major modules which is named ad rendering of graphics, compressing video, and network communication. The three modules are designed in a cross layer form in order to increase the energy efficiency of the cloud gaming. Based on network statistics a video encoder bit stream can be adapted to achieve quality of experience in gaming by users. The graceful degradation will help in reducing the bit rate by smoothing the video gaming even when the network is congested. The graceful degradation is important for cloud gaming since this gaming is interactive and also it does not allow the user to wait for buffering which irritates many users while playing as stated by Süselbeck et al (2009). Content-Aware network algorithms are proposed; this algorithm will classify all the video packets based on the demand. So the requested packet will be delivered to the users in a requested time which reduces the waiting time of the users. Other two modules will eliminate the unwanted time of computational and energy used for communication. This problem arises due to poor co-ordination. The combination of video encoding and rendering of graphics in cross layer design in a cloud gaming environment helps the provider to achieve an efficient gaming to the user. Different games in a cloud serve different threshold. The threshold helps in finding the delay difference of one game to another game. Usually the delay difference of shooter game will serve 100s delay threshold value whereas other games like real-time gaming will provide only 1s difference. Video coding and network delay plays a major role in cloud gaming. The main task of these two service is that it allocates the needed resources in time thereby it satisfies its client by providing the video within or before they reach the threshold delay's. joint rendering cloud optimization helps in improving the energy efficiency of the gaming with the help of cross layer design in cloud gaming. The games are delivered with low-latency, graceful degradation and also user experiences smooth play

Figure 9. Framework of the joint rendering coding optimization

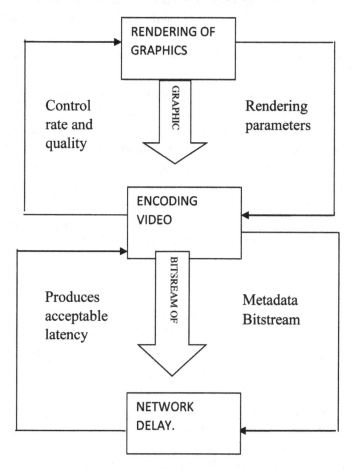

because the network resources with the help of video packets in metadata and game rendering allocate the needed resources. Figure 9 represents the framework of the joint rendering coding optimization with the help of cross layer design.

Rendering of Games Based on User's Device

As 'n' number of users uses cloud gaming we cannot expect that all users will use same type of device. The display screen, performance, power consumption of device will vary for each user. Some users may use PC's and some other users may be mobiles i.e. smart phones. So the video should be rendered in such a way that the user should experience a better gaming experience in their respected devices without any problem. They should achieve better quality of service. The bit rate, video quality, rendering should be achieved without any disturbance. To overcome this issues video resolution is adapted in each device. Adapting this resolution in user's device for large optimization it consumes more energy in the network and cloud servers.

Clients those who play games in a HDTV, set-up boxes and broadband connection will experience a high effective gaming experience since the display screen, performance of those connections will be high so probably the gaming video will also be high. The video resolution in these devices will be high whereas the video resolution in mobiles like smart phone users will be low. The video quality, channel quality will be less because the videos are rendered in such a way that it should be adapted by each user's. The videos are rendered based on the user's device.

Frame rate and frame type is used to avoid worst flaws or worst short comes faced by users in cloud gaming. This frame rate and frame type is adapted in every device of each user. The energy efficiency of devices that adapted this frame rate and frame type will be more when compared to other devices.

Social Gaming

The gaming services are now made available in social networks also in order to grab the user attraction of different age group. One can send request to other user in social networks, e.g. Facebook, where the game played by one user can be played by n number of different users based on the request. This social gaming also allows multiple players to be involved in one game. The user's device will be heterogeneous in nature. For this situation multiple encoding, transcoding is required which is not possible to adapt this service in each device, so Scalable video coding(SVC) will overcome this issues in social gaming easily. This SVC will first divide the video into different layer and encode it, later the user those who request that video will extract the video and decode it. The layered bit stream video can also be partially extracted by the user based on their need for different resolutions and video quality. The main advantage of using this scalable video coding is that it eliminates the duplicated multiple bit stream. This improves the efficiency of the network and cloud resources. Among many gamers and viewers, the gaming video display can be synchronized using SVC, this synchronization will automatically provide an efficient bandwidth. But this synchronization will possess critical issues in a gaming environment where it involves multiple players.

3D Vision Gaming

Action games like FPS and adventure games are played in 3D visioning, 3D visioning games gain popularity among end-users. This significantly improves the efficiency of gaming experience in home TV's. This 3D vision will include two different views, they are multi view or free view and intermediate view. Look around service is adaptable in multi view 3D vision gaming for users to experience realistic gaming service. The drawback in this view is that it needs users device with some computation display capability to view synthesis. Multi view coding(MVC) is used for rendering and coding of gaming video in multiplayer games. This MVC is linearly corresponding to the number of views.

To control the system and gaming mengleo et al proposed a thesis called ubiquitous. It is a cloud based 3d unity and it is an open source as described by Zhang et al (2015). The thesis will help the developers to check and control the game genre, game image quality and game resolution. They also conducted some validations that will show the efficiency of the cloud game.

Features of cloud gaming comes in different aspects they are software, hardware, deployment aspect and computation resources. Each feature is described below:

- **Software Aspect:** In the cloud gaming the software can be maintained easily without any complexity. The software in cloud gaming is designed in such a way that it does not expose any rapport problems on user's or player's device. It provides more security to the game binary.
- **Hardware Aspect:** Hardware performance will be more in cloud gaming environment. The computing resources in gaming will provide high efficient.
- **Deployment Aspect:**
  ◦ Client has no direct cost for playing.
  ◦ The categorizing and sale cost will be less.
  ◦ It does not allow copy rights of game developers.
- **Computing Resources:** The cost used for computing will be low. The up gradation cost of hardware and electronic waste will be low.

Efficient 3D Vision Gaming

High end action intensive video games such as the FPS and action-adventure gain popularity with respect to the 3D vision as described by Shi (2011). With the help of the 3D enabled displays like home televisions the user enhances the gaming experience significantly with the depth perception of the games played. Two views are said to be needed for the conventional stereo 3D vision. For the synthesizing intermediate views depth maps are required for the free view point or the multi view point. For a significant realistic gaming experience multiview 3D vision allows for a "look around" effect as described by Chang et al (2014).] which requires some computation capability at the client devices for viewing. Accurate depth information is readily available in the case of graphics rendering from the rendering similarly the depth information might not be accurately captured in the case of the natural videos which might result in displacement of the pixels with respect to the reconstructions. The multiview video coding as described by Wilhelmsen, & Martin Alexander (2014), coding of the color and the renderings are linearly proportional to the number of views which makes the cloud gaming to be a more efficient one in the case of the multiplayer games also some pipelines are rendered such as geometry processing are performed once and are later made avail for rendering and multiple view coding for multiple players.

Cognitive Mobile Cloud Gaming

Problems faced by existing cloud gaming environment is, that the cloud gaming should provide a good transmission of video gaming. To establish a good transmission, the environment requires a high bandwidth so that it can provide a feasible and rational video transmission as described by Orerdope et al (2013). Another major problem faced by cloud gaming is battery. The gaming environment needs to extend the battery life because the gaming consumes more battery because of screen display. And also decoding consumes more battery.

Main problem faced by cloud gaming is that it provides unstable quality of experience for the players. So, to overcome this as described by Cai et al (2015). in their paper proposed a component based gaming platform. They designed that platform in such a way that it provides cognitive capabilities. The capabilities such as click and play, creative resource allocation, and offline execution partially. And they also performed an experiments based on this to achieve overall latency as described by Leung (2015) to achieve these cognitive capabilities we need to overcome the dissimilarity in devices of end-users and network changes in QOS which changes frequently, responses from cloud. The developed platform will utilize all the cognitive capabilities resources dynamically (Figure 10).

The developed platform will allow users to play game instantly. They no need to install the game in their device in advance. If the user is connected their device to the gaming platform, then they can play game without the need of download and installation. The intelligent resource allocation i.e. the proposed system has the capability to measure the performance, CPU load, bandwidth, transparency, player capacity, spatial distribution etc. So cloud gaming should be able to adapt to the user's system performance and provide a better quality of service (QOS) as described by Shii et al (2015). A better quality of service will automatically provide a better quality of experience to users (QOE).

Figure 10. Architecture of cognitive mobile cloud gaming

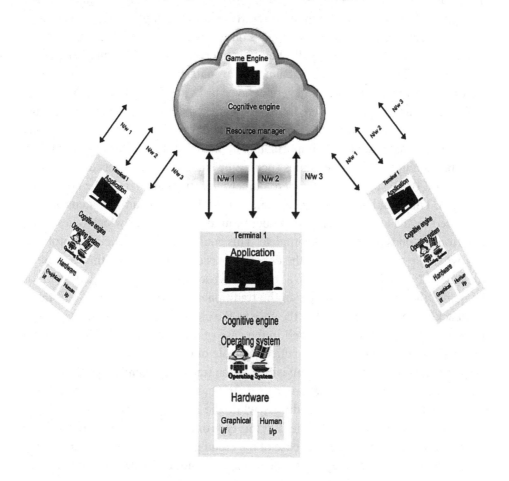

Issues and Challenges

Delay Tolerance

The delay tolerance for different type of games are said to be different and also said to have different thresholds for these delays. Before the degradation of the Quality of Experience (QoE) the maximum delay that could be tolerated by as described by Shea et al (2013) an average player is tabulated in Table 1. A low delay tolerance of 100ms could be seen in the perspective of the first person is said to be action based which could be seen in the games like shooter game, counter strike etc. This also leads to a higher negative rate for the players with higher delay. Also the delay becomes extensively sensitive in games such as the first person shooter (FPS) and a higher tolerance of 500ms could be seen in games such as role playing games (RPG), Multiplayer games such as World of Warcraft. This type of higher delay tolerance is seen as the gaming controls given depends on the avatar of the player. Eg: some of the commands like casting the spells, heal character, use any of the item for opposing the opponent. These actions hence cannot be instantaneous and are said to be done as a timely mannered tasks. If timely or delayed tasks are done, then it would result in disappointing the gamer where for ex: the gamer should be healed before the attack is done but still died due to the late command was given. Here timely actions that are registered is said to be important. A high delay tolerance of nearly 1000ms could be seen in the real time games such as the simulation games as described by Park et al (2013), star craft etc. where numerous entities that are to be controlled are listed. This could be a quite acceptable type of delay as a number of entities are controlled by the user by giving a number of unique commands which takes some time from seconds to minute to complete. This could become a noticeable problem only when the response time for the commands is delayed by more than a minute. This interaction delay is said to be a major drawback for multiplayer games not for the games that need single player in the traditional systems of gaming. But these drawbacks are totally removed in the case of the cloud way of gaming where even a single player game is noticed well in the case of the interaction delay which are rendered and streamed back to the client console of the player. These rendering of the game delays are made to be invisible by the traditional gaming system before the command is received to the gaming server. i.e. if the player instructs to move a warrior to a place it does it immediately while the gaming command is not sent to the server to certain amount of time. But this type of hiding the commands from the server given is not possible in the case of the cloud gaming as the cloud renders the game offloads thus the delay in interaction also cannot be hidden from the player. The cloud gaming would tolerate or manage to an extent the interaction delay occurring i.eupto a delay of 1000ms for some of the gaming actions such as the mouse cursor movements as described by Madani et al (2015) A maximum delay that could be seen is said to be at most 200ms for all the games and action based FPS games are much in need of nearly to 100ms which would not affect the players much in the Quality of Experience (QoE) context (Table 2).

Table 2. Delay tolerance in gaming

Game Type	Person Perspective	Delay Threshold
Real time strategy (RTS)	Omnipresent	1000 ms
First person shooter (FPS)	First person	100 ms
Role playing game (RPG)	Third person	500 ms

Video Streaming and Encoding

Another aspect that is under the examination for proper gaming is to render a quality video streaming and encoding. These Clouds gaming's video streaming are actually influencing the characteristics of the media streaming in live as described by Shea et al (2015)The similarities that could be seen in the cloud gaming and in the live media streaming is that the compression and encoding of the video and transmitting it to the end users as soon as possible. These streaming and encoding of the video focuses on the latest or the recent frames set of the video and do not see after the frames which are said to be produced in the future. The choice of encoding the cloud game of the video encoder is said to be an important task which is a real time sensitive task for the cloud game provider as described by Sun et al (2015). The top leading cloud game providers Onlive and the Gaikai use theMPEG-4 AVC and H264 encoder for encoding purposes. The Onlive compress the video streams of its cloud gaming using a specialized hardware and the Gaikai uses a software based approach for encoding its cloud gaming video streams as described by Wu et al (2015). In order to provide a high compression ratio and a well configuration facility provided for the stringent real-time demands the H.264 encoder is kept as a foremost choice for both these top gaming providers.

Measuring Interaction Delay

Among all the issues a major challenging issue is said to be the interaction delay minimization which is also said to be a critical metric to measure. The following technique used by the Onlive as described by Shea et al (2015) for the measurement of the interaction delay. The first step in testing the system is to install and configure it using a video card tuning software which is used mostly to control the GPU of the system. Also the next configuration set up is to configure the screen capture to start its recording at 100 frames/sec. Then using the zoom vision action the game is started. The interaction delay can be determined with respect to the first frame on looking the video file in which the action becomes evident from the resulting file. As the frames are recorded at 100 frames/sec 10-ms granularity could be seen in measuring the interaction delay by multiplying the frame number with 10ms to calculate in milliseconds. Two optimization techniques are followed to minimize the CPU and hard dish overhead as the recording is done at 100 frames/sec, influencing the performance of the game. The frame is resized to 1/4 of the original image resolution and the next step done is a Motion JPEG compression is applied before writing to the disk. These steps would result in recording at 100 frames/sec also 5 percent of the CPU is used with only 1 Mbyte/sec is written on the disk. The amount of the interaction delay defined by the processing time is due to the logic of the game, GPU rendering and video encoding which of these are not explained by the network delay latency. The overhead of the cloud is also said to be calculated which are not caused due to the network latency or the logic of the core game. The calculation includes the amount of the delay due to the video encoder and streaming system. More designs in terms of the video encoding and the streaming software is needed to attain the optimal interaction delay threshold which indicate the cloud processing overhead is above 100ms.

Green Design of Cloud Gaming

The cloud gaming is done through the connection of the internet via high-speed wireless networks i.e. Fourth generation (4G), WiFi and Long Term Evolution (LTE) by the mobile clients whereas the cloud servers and the home clients are connected through the broadband networks of the fixed line. Some of the energy deficient modules are described below with respect to the cloud gaming platform.

Green Cloud Data Center

A pool of manipulating and storage resources are managed to serve the clients or the users through the processing hub of the cloud computing which is known as the data center. Due to the economy of scale the production scaled up and the cost of the service provided is also reduced. These computations to the cloud when offloaded provide a better hardware utilization and power than on the individual host machine in the data center of the cloud as described by Wu et al (2015). Green data centers help to perform the game graphics rendering and the video coding rendering of the images in the cloud gaming applications. Virtual machine technology has been deployed to complete the computation task in a cloud data center due to its flexibility, ease of management and reliability. It also allows a physical computer to isolate the other OS's strongly from multiple operating systems. The virtual machines allocate the resources through the physical hardware among them thus scaling the number of the needed physical resources accordingly to the demands of the client as described by Huang et al (2014). Liu et al proposed green cloud architecture for the live migration virtual machines, online monitoring and for the placement optimization of the virtual machine aiming to minimize the consumption of power of the cloud ensuring the performance from the client side. Similarly, in order to meet the quality requirements and power consumption scheduling policies and resource allocation were formulated.

Energy-Aware Graphics Rendering

For a good gaming experience, a realistic and smooth game graphics are a needed one henceforth these type of rendering is said to be computationally intensive. Large blocks of parallel data processing are involved in the graphics rendering. Conventional CPU's are replaced by the GPU's (Graphical processing unit) and the power consumption of GPU could be controlled through the dynamic voltage frequency scaling (DVFS) with respect to the cloud gaming hardware rendering as described by Shi et al (2011) and Sheikhi et al (2014). The reduction of the power consumption could be done by the substantial slowdown of the operating frequency. The energy efficiency of the GPU could be improved by voltage frequency adaptation via the incorporation of the DVFS with rendering load accurate prediction. The geometry processing, fragments and logic of the game in the energy models of the rendering pipeline consumes the high power as described by Shi et al (2011) in the pipeline which concludes that at each stage of game rendering algorithms the rendering pipeline attains some complexity in computation. The graphics rendering trade off in various aspects such as the complexity and the quality of the rendering.

- **Resolution:** The frame size and the rate of the frame is composed in the resolution. A rendering algorithm is used to compute the color value of each pixel in the rendering pipeline. Henceforth the game display resolution increases with respect to the increase in the rendering complexity. With accordance to the device screen of the user and the capability the resolution could be adapted with respect to the factors discussed below:
- **Level of Detail:** The detailed level of a 3D game object is defined through the number of polygon i.e. the vertex data. Better details on a 3D object could be provided when there are more number of the polygons are provided in the geometry processing at the cost of more energy.
- **Lighting and Shading:** The depth and the illumination of the color of a 3D scene could be described by the shading and lighting. In order to stimulate light paths complicated algorithms are required for the effects of the photo-realistic rendering. Full simulations of lights rays are not required for the video games as they are often action-intensive which leads to the exploration of a reasonable balance could be done.
- **Texture Map:** The surface details and the 3D model pattern could be added by the texture maps whereas the rough surfaces are simulated by the normal and bump maps. More computations are required for providing realistic effects on the 3D surface through the mappings. The game animations are largely dependent to the pipeline rendering in the context of the power consumption and the computation bottleneck. Computationally efficient render-

ing algorithms could help in achieve energy efficiency in the computer graphics by the rendering pipeline optimization.

Energy-Efficient Video Compression

A sequence of images which are compressed into a video bit stream is done by a graphic rendering pipeline rendered by the game animation. The rate and distortion optimization is said to be a trade–off in the video compression. An image sequence could be compressed by the removal of the redundancies through the coding mode and motion vector searches. This could be said as a layout for a better rate distortion performance when it is unconstrained and the decisions are obtained through the searches. These searching of the coding decisions are said to be computationally demanding in the case of the video coding. The video coding power consumption and the distortion rate could be scaled by the motion vectors search spaces and the mode decisions by limiting the search spaces. The algorithmic complexity with respect to the voltage frequency of CPU's through DVFS integration could help in achieving the video coding energy efficiency. The lower bit rates are said to be the resultant of the high compression efficiency which could ease on the latency and throughput in the case of the network delivery.

Green Communications and Networking

These compressed video bit streams from the video encoder are received by the clients through the internet. For a smooth playout high network throughput and low latency is required for game videos. As the energy-delay trade-off in the communication networks these demands are often said to be power consuming hence energy efficiency is said to be a major focus in the case of the communicational research done. The digital subscriber line (DSL) would consume power at a defined rate which is said to be the wireless access networks. Increasing the power efficiency of the power amplifiers, power converters provide a direct solution to the energy efficiency. Intelligent management of the nodes are done by the critical methods through the Software-defined networking (SDN) and dynamic topology optimization where the Software-defined networking allows the lower layer functionality to be done by the network administrator for the network services management. It helps to adapt the game providers accordingly to the dynamic changes of the demands provided by the gamers without replacing the hardware components of the network or also to reconfigure it. The overall energy consumption is reduced when the traffic demands and the dynamic topology optimization could be adopted by some of the operating nodes through the reorganization being done during off-peak hours. The less network capacity, queue delay and longer routing path could be overcome by multipath transmissions in the heterogeneous networks. The energy efficiency of the wireless networks could be further improved through the transmission power in the accessing networks of wireless such as the LTE which actually depends on the data rate and the coverage distance as defined in the Shannon's channel capacity. For better energy efficiency and for the higher channel capacity in wireless networks transmissions wireless spectrum could be dynamically exploited in the cognitive radio networks. For an efficient cloud gaming the stringent requirements like cloud data center, graphics rendering, wireless networks, video compression and communications overhead and the cloud data center joint optimization which ensures the energy efficiency. A green reconfigurable router is explored by as described by Care et al (2014) which monitors and controls the power aware routing with the power dissipation and rate adaptive processing through the DVFS and a power efficient architecture. By the reconfigurable router each base station or the terminal could be framed in the wired and the wireless networks.

REFERENCES

Shea, R., Liu, J., Ngai, E., & Cui, Y. (2013). Cloud gaming: Architecture and performance. *IEEE Network*, *27*(4), 16–21. doi:10.1109/MNET.2013.6574660

Chuah, S.-P., Yuen, C., & Cheung, N.-M. (2014). Cloud gaming: A green solution to massive multiplayer online games. *Wireless Communications, IEEE*, *21*(4), 78–87. doi:10.1109/MWC.2014.6882299

Jarschel, M., Schlosser, D., Scheuring, S., & Hoßfeld, T. (2011). An evaluation of QoE in cloud gaming based on subjective tests. In *Innovative Mobile and Internet Services in Ubiquitous Computing (IMIS), 2011 Fifth International Conference on*, (pp. 330-335). IEEE. doi:10.1109/IMIS.2011.92

Cai, W., Leung, V., & Chen, M. (2013). Next generation mobile cloud gaming. In *Service Oriented System Engineering (SOSE), 2013 IEEE 7th International Symposium on*, (pp. 551-560). IEEE.

Cai, W., Zhou, C., Leung, V., & Chen, M. (2013). A cognitive platform for mobile cloud gaming. In *Cloud Computing Technology and Science (CloudCom), 2013 IEEE 5th International Conference on*, (vol. 1, pp. 72-79). IEEE. doi:10.1109/CloudCom.2013.17

Luo, M., & Claypool. (2013). *Uniquitous: Implementation and Evaluation of a Cloud-based Game System in Unity*. Academic Press.

Huang, C.-Y., Hsu, C.-H., Chang, Y.-C., & Chen, K.-T. (2013). GamingAnywhere: an open cloud gaming system. In *Proceedings of the 4th ACM multimedia systems conference*, (pp. 36-47). ACM. doi:10.1145/2483977.2483981

Wen, Z.-Y., & Hsiao, H.-F. (2014). QoE-driven performance analysis of cloud gaming services. In *Multimedia Signal Processing (MMSP), 2014 IEEE 16th International Workshop on*, (pp. 1-6). IEEE.

Cai, W., & Leung. (2012). Multiplayer cloud gaming system with cooperative video sharing. In *Cloud Computing Technology and Science (CloudCom), 2012 IEEE 4th International Conference on*, (pp. 640-645). IEEE.

Chen, Huang, & Hsu. (2014). Cloud gaming onward: research opportunities and outlook. In *Multimedia and Expo Workshops (ICMEW), 2014 IEEE International Conference on*, (pp. 1-4). IEEE. doi:10.1109/MMSP.2014.6958835

Lu, & Dey. (2015). Cloud Mobile 3D Display Gaming User Experience Modeling and Optimization by Asymmetric Graphics Rendering. *Selected Topics in Signal Processing, IEEE Journal of, 9*(3), 517-532.

Care, R., Hussein, A. H. H., Suarez, L., & Nuaymi, L. (2014). Energy-efficient scheduling for cloud mobile gaming. In Globecom Workshops (GC Wkshps), 2014, (pp. 1198-1204). IEEE. doi:10.1109/GLOCOMW.2014.7063596

Oredope, A., Moessner, Peoples, & Parr. (2013). Deploying cloud services in mobile networks. In *Science and Information Conference (SAI)*. IEEE.

Xu, L., Li, C., Li, L., Liu, Y., Yang, Z., & Liu, Y. (2014). A virtual data center deployment model based on the green cloud computing. In *Computer and Information Science (ICIS), 2014 IEEE/ACIS 13th International Conference on*, (pp. 235-240). IEEE. doi:10.1109/ICIS.2014.6912140

Huang, J., Wu, K., & Moh, M. (2014). Dynamic Virtual Machine migration algorithms using enhanced energy consumption model for green cloud data centers. In *High Performance Computing & Simulation (HPCS), 2014 International Conference on*, (pp. 902-910). IEEE. doi:10.1109/HPCSim.2014.6903785

Leung, V. (2014). Keynote talk II-Video game as a service: Cloud computing enabled video gaming anywhere on any device. In *Advanced Information Networking and Applications (AINA), 2014 IEEE 28th International Conference on*, (pp. xxxv-xxxv). IEEE.

Cai, & Chan. (2014). *Cognitive Resource Optimization for Decomposed Cloud Gaming Platform*. Academic Press.

Jebalia, M., Ben Letaifa, A., Hamdi, M., & Tabbane, S. (2014). A Coalitional Game-Theoretic Approach for QoS-Based and Secure Data Storage in Cloud Environment. In *High Performance Computing and Communications, 2014 IEEE 6th Intl Symp on Cyberspace Safety and Security, 2014 IEEE 11th Intl Conf on Embedded Software and Syst (HPCC, CSS, ICESS), 2014 IEEE Intl Conf on*, (pp. 1048-1054). IEEE. doi:10.1109/HPCC.2014.176

Zhang, Ranjan, Menzel, Nepal, Strazdins, Jie, & Wang. (2014). *An Infrastructure Service Recommendation System for Cloud Applications with Real-time QoS Requirement Constraints*. Academic Press.

Kamarainen, T., Siekkinen, M., Xiao, Y., & Yla-Jaaski, A. (2014). Towards pervasive and mobile gaming with distributed cloud infrastructure. In *Network and Systems Support for Games (NetGames), 2014 13th Annual Workshop on*, (pp. 1-6). IEEE. doi:10.1109/NetGames.2014.7008957

Sun, K., & Wu, D. (2015). Video rate control strategies for cloud gaming. *Journal of Visual Communication and Image Representation*, *30*, 234–241. doi:10.1016/j.jvcir.2015.03.012

Jarschel, M., Schlosser, D., Scheuring, S., & Hoßfeld, T. (2013). Gaming in the clouds: QoE and the users' perspective. *Mathematical and Computer Modelling*, *57*(11), 2883–2894. doi:10.1016/j.mcm.2011.12.014

Shi, T., Yang, M., Li, X., Lei, Q., & Jiang, Y. (2015). An energy-efficient scheduling scheme for time-constrained tasks in local mobile clouds. *Pervasive and Mobile Computing*.

Sheikhi, A., Rayati, M., Bahrami, S., Ranjbar, A. M., & Sattari, S. (2015). A cloud computing framework on demand side management game in smart energy hubs. *International Journal of Electrical Power & Energy Systems*, *64*, 1007–1016. doi:10.1016/j.ijepes.2014.08.020

Wu, Yuen, Cheung, Chen, & Chen. (2015). *Enabling Adaptive High-Frame-Rate Video Streaming in Mobile Cloud Gaming Applications*. Academic Press.

Süselbeck, R., Schiele, G., & Becker, C. (2009). Peer-to-peer support for low-latency Massively Multiplayer Online Games in the cloud. In *Network and Systems Support for Games (NetGames), 2009 8th Annual Workshop on*, (pp. 1-2). IEEE. doi:10.1109/NETGAMES.2009.5446229

Madani, F. M., & Mokhtari, S. (2015). Virtual optical network embedding over elastic optical networks with set-up delay tolerance. In *Electrical Engineering (ICEE), 2015 23rd Iranian Conference on*, (pp. 450-455). IEEE.

Wu, Xue, & He. (2014). iCloudAccess: Cost-effective streaming of video games from the cloud with low latency. *Circuits and Systems for Video Technology, IEEE Transactions on, 24*(8), 1405-1416.

Chang, W.-C., & Chang, W. C. (2014). Real-Time 3D Rendering Based on Multiple Cameras and Point Cloud. In *Ubi-Media Computing and Workshops (UMEDIA), 2014 7th International Conference on*, (pp. 121-126). IEEE. doi:10.1109/U-ME-DIA.2014.52

Zhang, H., Reardon, C., Zhang, C., & Parker, L. E. (2015). Adaptive human-centered representation for activity recognition of multiple individuals from 3D point cloud sequences. In *Robotics and Automation (ICRA), 2015 IEEE International Conference on*, (pp. 1991-1998). IEEE. doi:10.1109/ICRA.2015.7139459

Park, Yu, Chung, & Lee. (2011). Markov chain based monitoring service for fault tolerance in mobile cloud computing. In *Advanced Information Networking and Applications (WAINA), 2011 IEEE Workshops of International Conference on*, (pp. 520-525). IEEE.

Shi, S. (2011). Building low-latency remote rendering systems for interactive 3d graphics rendering on mobile devices. In *Proceedings of the 19th ACM international conference on Multimedia*, (pp. 859-860). ACM. doi:10.1145/2072298.2072493

Wilhelmsen, & Alexander. (2014). Using a Commodity Hardware Video Encoder for Interactive Video Streaming. *Multimedia (ISM), 2014 IEEE International Symposium on*. IEEE.

Shi, S., Hsu, C.-H., Nahrstedt, K., & Campbell, R. (2011). Using graphics rendering contexts to enhance the real-time video coding for mobile cloud gaming. In *Proceedings of the 19th ACM international conference on Multimedia*, (pp. 103-112). ACM. doi:10.1145/2072298.2072313

Chapter 12
Impact of Cloud Gaming in Health Care, Education, and Entertainment Services

Padmalaya Nayak
Jawaharlal Nehru Technological University, India

Shelendra Kumar Sharma
Microsoft, India

ABSTRACT

With the rapid growth of Cloud Computing, various diverse applications are growing exponentially through large data centers with the use of Internet. Cloud gaming is one of the most novel service applications that helps to store the video games in cloud and client can access the games as audio/video streams. Cloud gaming in practice substantially reduces the computational cost at the client side and enables the use of thin clients. Further, Quality of Service (QoS) may be affected through cloud gaming by introducing access latency. The objective of this chapter is to bring the impact and effectiveness of cloud gaming application on users, Health care, Entertainment, and Education.

DOI: 10.4018/978-1-5225-0546-4.ch012

INTRODUCTION

Cloud Computing: A Quick Review

The term cloud computing defines itself a type of computing that relies on sharing computing resources rather than a personal server or devices to handle the applications. The word "cloud" is used as a metaphor for Internet and the phrase "cloud computing" defines Internet based commuting that integrates different services such as servers, storage and applications etc. It can be defined as a centralized storage of huge no. of remote servers having network connectivity allow on-line access for computer services and resources. Cloud computing services can be represented in four ways. These are Software as a service (SaaS), Platform as a service (PaaS), Infrastructure as a service (IaaS), and business process as a service (BPaaS). SaaS uses the web to develop applications owned by a third party vendor, whose interface is accessed by client side. A complete software application is delivered to the end-users including the associated data and hosted centrally in the cloud. The data can be accessed anywhere through the web browser. PaaS includes software platform including infrastructure elements such as database, middleware, security, and presentation layer to develop custom applications. It allows the users for development and testing of applications in a simple cost effective way whereas the resources are managed and controlled by a third party vendor. IaaS is known as the basic service model of cloud. The company provides resources in terms of servers, network bandwidth, and storage space on pay per use basis. BPaaS provides an external web enabled service for external business process. The general architecture of cloud computing is shown in Figure 1.

The deployment models of cloud computing can be classified as Public, Private, Hybrid, and Community cloud. The deployment model of cloud computing is shown in Figure 2. Private clouds are meant for private usage and owned by a single company located either inside the campus or outside the campus. It can be owned by an external third party that provides a virtual infrastructure for applications and communications for internal business users. Private cloud offers the benefit of on-demand infrastructure with dedicated resources to an organization. But the computing resources are shared across the applications and business units of those applications. This model is highly suitable for enterprisers with strong concern about data security and data privacy. Public cloud is meant for the public users to access over a network and owned by a third party vendor. Unlike private cloud, the public cloud customers never need provision, manage, upgrade or replace any hardware. Of course, pricing depends on the company's utility-style. They pay only for resources they reserve or consume during a defined time span. Hybrid cloud enjoys the benefits of both the private and public cloud. It maintains data confidentiality in private

Figure 1. Architecture of cloud computing

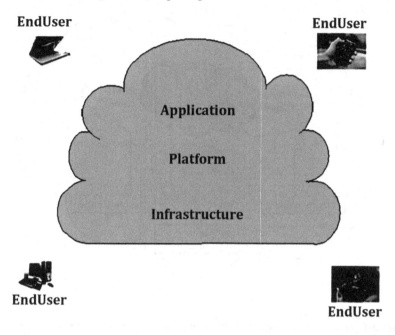

cloud and extends the flexible access for public cloud by offering services provided by public clouds. Community Clouds are collaborative resources shared by different organizations with common interest-most probably in the same industry or based on geographical region. But all of these four forms of cloud computing provide the services at one or four levels. These four levels are defined as application level, platform level, infrastructure level, or business process level.

Over the time, the concept of cloud computing has been changed and new term has evolved "Everything as a Service" (XaaS) such as the applications, infrastructure, processes can be obtained from the cloud. National Institute of standard technology (NIST) defines cloud computing as follows: "Cloud Computing is a model for enabling convenient, on-demand network access to a share pool of configurable computing resources (i.e. Networks, Servers, Storage, Applications and Services) that can be rapidly provisioned and released with minimal management effort or service provider interaction". NIST has derived five essential characteristics or benefits of cloud computing that neither can be provided by simple web server nor virtualized data centres. These are:

- **On-Demand Self-Service:** Users can make use of cloud at any time anywhere.
- **Resource Pooling:** Customers share pool of computing resources and data storage. Cloud customers might know where to store data at a macro level but they do not know the exact location of the application and data storage

Figure 2. Service model of cloud computing

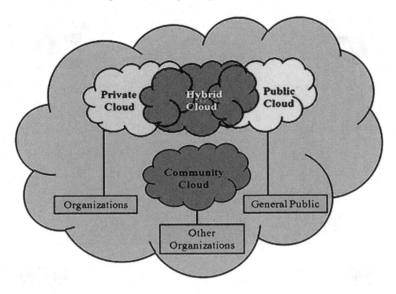

- **Broad Network Access:** All the smart devices having internet connectivity such as Laptops, Mobile phones, iPads and other devices may access the service using clients as the web browsers.
- **Rapid Elasticity:** The storage capacity, network bandwidth, computing capacity is so flexible that it can be increased or reduced at instance and provides an optimal solution for the resource usage.
- **Measured Device:** Cloud system allows the resources to be used and at the same time it can monitor, control, and report usage in a transparent way.

CLOUD COMPUTING IN HEALTH CARE: A GAME CHANGER

In past some years, some health care companies are taking surge of interest for moving health care related applications from traditional infrastructure based systems to cloud based platforms to improve the patient care service. Till today, organizations are relying on paper to maintain medical records, for decision making, and handwritten notes to inform the patient. Sharing of patient's data among clinicians, departments, and even patients is rare and complex. The traditional systems have been highly saturated across the health care Industry. Now, healthcare industries are influenced by other industries such as telecomm industries and finance industries how to minimize the cost by maintaining the data security. Over the years, the health care market is becoming more automatic, more patient centric and more data driven and it cannot be stopped. Beyond the driving shift there is a key question is that whether cloud gaming can be a permanent game changer for every other aspect of health industry such as service offering, collaborative capabilities, end user services etc. Many medical experts view it in variety of ways. But Medical Imaging is the most appropriate example use of cloud in health care. Accenture has a multi-year collaboration with AT &T offering advanced image capabilities in the cloud to the hospitals in the US. The AT &T Medical and Information Management Solution (MIIS) enables the health care professionals such as radiologist, cardiologist to expedite patient care by web enabled virtual collaboration and mutual interpretation of patient images such as X-rays, Computed Tomography (CT) and Magnetic Resonance Imaging (MRI) scans. The users can view the patient images instantly from anywhere attending the physicians.

Role of Cloud Computing in Health Care Services

With the recent advances in multimedia computing (MMC), the use of various multimedia tools, techniques, and services facilitates doctors as well as other health care professionals to access the e-health information for better treatment and decision making. The introduction of multimedia services in e-health brings many new challenges where there is a trade-off between Quality of Services (QoS) and cost in designing the health care. Moreover, e-health media contents such as real time images, videos are required to cache in content delivery networks (CDNs). However, due to the lack of dynamic resource support at the CDN nodes, there is a limitation on computing power, memory, and bandwidth to support e-health information. One of the potential solutions to resolve all these issues is the introduction of cloud based multimedia e-health service. Healthcare organizations with cloud gaming technologies are expected to provide new and improved patient care technologies with reduced cost and time.

The technological advancement along with the increased number of diseases, health care cost is going on increasing since last decade. Especially, in rural areas, the health care infrastructure and services normally very poor. People have little access to quality health care with high quality devices and treatment. However, in emerging market, people do have more and more mobile phones. These mobile phones are now replaced with smart phones with internet connectivity. By linking these smart phones with other smart devices to the cloud platform, health care industry can replace the physical Infrastructure. The smart devices with internet facility can be installed in the rural villages to provide the services like blood tests, scans, prenatal monitoring of pregnant mothers when the people require it. This will provide benefits to both the doctor and patient in number of ways. If we consider from the patient side, they will be provided with scarce healthcare resources with accuracy.

At the same time doctors can save their time from travelling and can spend more time advising patients and analyzing the documents from the cloud. Doctors can keep the e-health reports in their mobile phones and during the doctor's periodical check-up the patient can be monitored and advised if required from the last check-up. So the resources can be utilized effectively and efficiently instead of spending a huge amount in an infrastructure based health centres. A general model of e-health care is shown in Figure 3.

What Does the Cloud Offer to Health Care?

In general, cloud computing defines anything that involves delivery of technology via Internet. The overall goal of cloud is to reduce complexity and manage the particular application in an effective way so that it can accommodate innovation. For instance, health care is shifting towards cloud computing that support coopera-tion, collaborations and information sharing. According to health care informatics (Healthcare informatics, 2012), the services provided by the cloud in health care applications can be derived in number of ways which are given below:

- Computing Resources available on-demand,
- Faster deployment of Electronic Health Records (EHR),
- Data Sharing,

Figure 3. A general model of e-health care through cloud computing

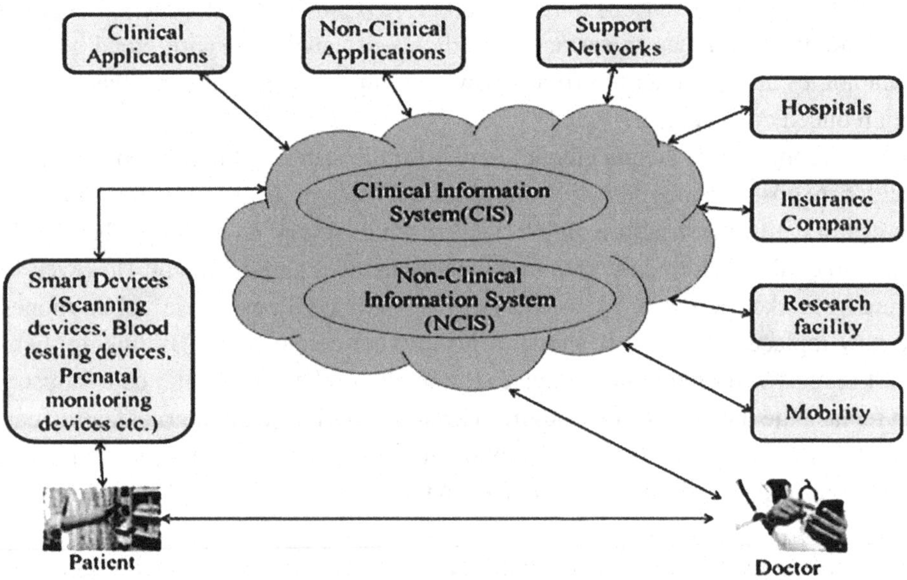

- Enhanced Collaborations,
- Patient Medical Record,
- Revenue Cycle Management,
- Claims Processing,
- Enrolment.

Benefits of Cloud Gaming in Health Care Services

In shifting to the cloud, the health care industry will find new opportunities for data consolidation or aggregation of patient data to help doctors or health care professionals to make decisions for better treatment. While doing so, the organizations can save money through reduced redundancy and cheaper operational costs. According to KLAS (2013) the benefits of cloud based health care model has been discussed here.

- **Clinical Benefit:** The biggest benefit is the clinical benefit that provides to access applications that was not previously possible through traditional health care system. For example, the implementation of digital pathology, managed through the cloud services has huge clinical impact on organization. Earlier access to the pathologist was possible at only through near excellence centres, whereas new services can be provided to access the experts remotely to render their diagnoses. Patient care can be improved through cloud by providing service faster and more efficiently. Since patients need not to be travelled and waiting list can be managed more easily as same tests are conducted at different places with larger number experts. The same experts can access the patient's data remotely on-demand basis through many internet connected devices. Physicians can diagnosis the patient from home and give the advice from any point of location without any delay.
- **Clinical Research:** Cloud based computing provides an enhanced scope for R&D as currently Pharma companies don't have space to store large amount of databases especially DNA sequencing. The size of the data in Pharma firms is overwhelming their computers. Commercial cloud vendors have developed Phama-specific clinical research cloud offing in order to develop new drugs with lower cost.
- **Business Benefit:** Obviously, there is a business benefit with any new technology to be adopted. The healthcare providers are in business to provide better treatment and care for the patient. Cloud offers their providers the ability to access storage experts, network security experts, who can manage different components.
- **Electronic Medical Records:** Hospitals and Physicians are finding that cloud based medical records and medical images archiving services com-

ing on line. The objective is to reduce the burden of maintaining Electronic Media Records (EMR), instead they can focus on adoption of EMRs and other supportive EMR imperatives for clinical support system. Collaborative works among the physicians through remote video conferencing can be obtained through cloud. This support can be extended to rural areas and disaster hit areas with the help of wireless broadband and smart phones.

- **Health Information Exchange:** Health Information Exchange helps health-care organizations to share data contained in electronic media records.
- **Big Data and Analytics:** Healthcare is a great example of big data. As the digital data increases it is difficult to manage the big data storage. The storage devices hold a petabytes of data and these data hold the keys for clinical advancements. But, most of the time the data is not accessible to the researchers. The ability to access the data and analytical tools is a great source of drive for clinical and business intelligence. The analytical tools can provide better solutions for easy patient care and faster recovery by understanding the best practices. Cloud computing reduces the cost by storing the hardware devices locally and stores the EHRs, radio images, genomic data for clinical drug trials. Without using cloud storage, the remote access facility may not be succeeding easily.

Despite the huge growth many health care companies are still pushing back on cloud platform considering data security and privacy issues. But others are finding better security models and technology in the cloud. Moreover, most health care organizations moving to cloud computing only to reduce operational costs because many organizations do not have sufficient budgets. The new paradigm might overcome the problem of security and privacy excuses. Most IT organizations in the health care sector don't have the talent required to move their systems safely to cloud-based platforms and they may not understand the compliance and security issues as well as they should. However, its a peak time to get creative and innovative around the world to use the new technology. Especially, health care must get a much higher return on investment than other sectors from its cloud adoption. The amount of data that health care providers must deal with is daunting. That causes huge costs both for management and in inefficiencies, including some that lead to mistreatment due to ignorance among those treating patients as each has only some of the picture.

Challenges in Cloud Gaming in Health Care Services

There are many issues and challenges like QoS provisioning, architecture, services, and applications of cloud multimedia based application, dynamic resource allocation for health data processing in cloud, decision support system for cloud, data processing in a cost effective way are required to be addressed. Data maintained in the cloud may contain personal, private, and confidential information that requires being safe, must not be misused or compromised by unauthorized users. So, there is a biggest task in the cloud how to maintain data security, data privacy, data availability, data portability issues which is creating many worries for IT related health care. The various challenges involved in cloud based health care services are depicted in Figure 4.

- **Data Privacy and Data Security:** Data privacy is the major concern among the health care centre and is the reason for low adaption because putting the private personal information into a third party prevents the patient privacy laws. It might happen that data could be lost, misused, or fall into the wrong hands affects adoption. What the organization should do if the cloud provider

Figure 4. Challenges in health care through cloud service

loses data? A potential solution for this that the organization should maintain certain privacy at organization level and should comply with some standards such as NIST 800 146 cloud computing Synopsis and Recommendations. This method might be expensive, but security and privacy is more visible.

- **Data Portability:** Data portability is the main barrier to implement the cloud based health care organization. With traditional IT system, health care organization has direct control on physical control systems, services and data. But with cloud platform, if any vender refuses to provide service in between, health care organization suddenly won't be able to provide service to the patients or customers. The concern is that if the provider suspends any service or refuses for service that will lead towards interoperability issue across the cloud and makes a too much challenging to migrate for a new cloud. This risk highlights the need for provider agreements that includes termination rights, access rights, data retrieval at any time, termination assistance in moving to other provider etc before terminating or denying access the service.

- **Data Availability:** Data availability means that the computing resources must be available round the clock and must be usable. Denial of service attacks, natural disasters, and equipment outages are all threats for availability of data in the cloud.

REVOLUTIONARY CHANGES IN EDUCATION SYSTEM

The impact of cloud gaming on education brings a new revolution in the sense that it aims at the education to make it customized, individualized, and universally accessible. Seymour Papert predicted that "computers would play a vital role in Education" (Papert, 1984). The expectations of Thomas edition (Edition, 1920) that "Television will largely replace the textbooks". The predictions of Benjamin Darrow (Darrow, 1932) that "the role of teachers and textbooks can be replaced by radio". Now, Papert's prediction (1984) came into a reality. The paradigm of education has not been changed since a decade. The revolution of E-education affects student learning in various ways such as it affects the method of teaching; the teaching methodology followed by the teacher, structures of the school, the barriers between the home and school life and perhaps it affects the trajectory of entire future of human life. In the last century, the world is moving towards on-line but the education system is still restricted to the physical world. With the technological advancements a revolution of education is underway. The technological developments and emerging technology are bringing the innovations and offers a new a way of education that creates a platform for both Institutes and Industries. This technological advancement focuses on major three parts:

1. Internet and Open On-line Courses,
2. Mobile and Multi-faceted technologies,
3. 3-D Learning tools,
4. Virtual learning environments and learning analytics.

The main curiosity of these technologies is to merge the virtual world into physical world. Figure 5 shows a prediction model of education system how the cloud the educational institutes will be benefitted from the clod service.

Internet and Massive Open On-Line Courses

Internet and open source such as massive open on-line courses (MOOCs) is the first innovative technology and provides decentralized universally accessible information. The wide growth in Internet has produced the two open source technologies such as Web 2.0 and MOOCs. These two technologies allow the people to communicate,

Figure 5. Education systems through cloud service model

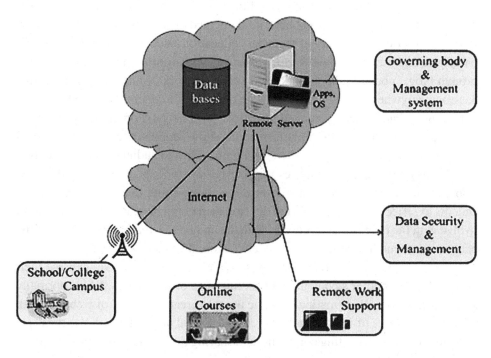

interact and present their views. MOOCs provide free open online courses and allow unlimited enrolments. MOOCs platforms are provided by leading universities, industry experts, and leading scholars. There are three first leading Universities such as Harvard, Stanford, Massachusetts Institute of Technology (MIT) to provide MOOCs. In 1911, Stanford University first lunched the 3 MOOCs platform where 100,000 students enrolled at a time. Later, MOOCs exploded across America. As of Dec 2014, many countries like Germany, Australia, Brazil, Turkey, India, and France are offering MOOCs. The major goal of MOOC providers is to offer MOOCs as an alternative to traditional education. MOOCs offer students traditional course materials such as readings, quizzes and problem sets. Students are taught via video lectures, can participate in online discussions and group studies. Communication between student and teaching staff is possible through MOOCs. It allows flexibility by allowing students to work at their own place and also impose the time restrictions. MOOCs predominantly offer tertiary level education and target students over the age of 18. However, students from the age of 13 are permitted with proper parental approval, to participate in different courses. For instance, some of the open source platforms that offer tertiary-standard MOOCs are Coursera.org, Edx.org, futurelearn.org, Udacity.com, OpenupEd.eu, openlearning.com, and Ulearniversity.com.

The new platforms such as wikis, blogs, podcasts, book marks and social media sites including face book and twitter runs on the top of original website platform. It is very common to see the students and teachers are using Web 2.0 for learning environment beyond the classroom coaching. The whole world is moving towards on-line. But in practical, it has not been implemented in our classroom coaching curriculum. In particular, primary or secondary education students who knows only how to navigate and use the on-line world. Making the classroom learning environments through blogs, podcasts, bookmarks and social networks, students can access the classroom anywhere at any time. Blogs are defined as frequently updated websites consisting of dated entries arranged in reverse chronological order (Walker, 2005). They are on-line, open source platforms that allow sequential entries like diaries or journals to be posted or published for a global on-line audience. Blogs are used as learning journals, gallery spaces for peer reviews and as display platforms for problem solving exercises. This allows the students think deeply, encourage the students to reflect, give feedback and develop something new. But main drawbacks involve with the blog is that it remains with the author's primarily control. So, if the teachers try to modify anything on student's blog, they cannot change it.

Wikis are designed so that numerous people can send, receive, express their ideas and modify other's content and post link with other sources. Wikis normally support team work. Bookmark allows the users to create a library of websites with different categories of images and other media. Social networking allows the users to log in for charting, posting comments and sharing the media. Users have to create a network in order to participate in the activities. Face book, twitter is the examples of social networking, where teachers can post the assignments, assist the students, reminding about other activities by providing flexible education system after the class hour. Teachers also can help the parents by posting the classroom activities in the social networking sites. Podcasting allows audio-based files to be created and distributed on a regular basis. This can be the support for the distance learner and can be watched as the guest lectures, case based lesions at anywhere at any point of time. Flipped classroom is the foundation of podcasting. But the drawback is they don't allow interaction or any type of collaboration.

Moreover, Web 2.0 allows the students to work within the class community, outside the classroom to share their views and get the inputs. It makes the students learning process independent, more interactive and helps the students to adopt their own learning procedure which is not possible in traditional classroom coaching. The Internet and open source tool has got global recognition and effective means of distributing high quality materials and accessible to the high quality materials for the students for developed or developing countries.

Mobile and Multi-Faced Technology

Second, the most revolutionary technology is mobile and multi-faceted technology emphasizes on education how the society is offering to the students. In view of some Industry experts and Educators that Cloud Computing, Mobile learning, multi-touch devices are the main building blocks for the new faces of the education system. This fact such as technologies benefits is not convinced by some educators. Out of many different opinions, some points are discussed here how technological developments with cloud impacts our education system. Cloud computing is the practice of using a network of remote servers hosted on the Internet to store, manage, and process data rather than using a local server. Cloud computing has become the storage platform of choice. In 2012, the CDW-G 2013 State of the Cloud Report highlights that cloud computing was increasingly adopted for the cost savings and efficiency. It could deliver, improved user mobility and increased opportunity for innovation (Ivica Boticki et.al, 2009). Once users are authenticated, they can use the programs anywhere and at any time. Schools are using cloud computing to provide students with easy, simple access to teachers' lesson plans, and the ability to submit their homework or access educational programs. Students can now also access and work on their files anywhere, increasing the efficiency and flexibility of homework. Adopting cloud computing in educational institutions creates lot of worries about data security. As the public cloud is based on the Internet, it is not always a secure educational network. To combat this, cloud computing providers are creating private and hybrid Clouds. Private Clouds are maintained on a private network and offer users the most security. However, users are still required to maintain and support all the technology infrastructure and software, which often eradicates the cost-saving benefits of cloud computing. Hybrid Clouds utilise the benefits of both public and private options through multiple cloud providers.

Mobile learning was redefined with the introduction of smart phones in 2001, mobile applications in 2008 and tablet computers in 2010. By 2013, these mobile learning devices, alongside laptops, have become incredibly capable, useful, and ubiquitous in the developed world. It's important to note that mobile learning devices are naturally encouraging exploration and learning in adults and children alike. The New Media Consortium 2013 Horizon Report says the distribution of these mobile learning devices "defy traditional patterns of adoption; schools and consumers alike have decided these devices are necessities, even economically disadvantaged families find ways to make use of mobile technology" (NMS, 2013). As the world is moving online, Web 2.0 platforms and 'flipped classroom' models are going to be the standard form. It is becoming imperative that students have constant access to mobile computing devices. Mobile learning devices, if implemented in educational institutions correctly, promise to make education individualised, customised and accessible for every student. Mobile learning devices are also increasingly necessary for students and educators alike, if they are to partake in the aforementioned revolution of education. Cloud computing is such example and defines the path for educational institutions how to store the information and where the students can access this information through mobile learning devices. Mobile learning devices makes the students learning capability more independent and provides a customised educational experience.

Game Based Learning and Gamification

Game based learning seems to be an effective way teaching that cannot be obtained through traditional classroom exam based systems. Game based learning is organized in such a way that students create interest automatically and enthusiastically without feeling bore without any teacher's guidance. Game based learning not only provides the effective way teaching but also provides distinct way of teaching. The path of progress within a game rewards the students for their achievement and directly makes the students learn new concept. Most of the games provide problem solving environments and by providing this it encourages the students to be creative with real world challenges. Game based learning helps the students to acquire knowledge and receives the feedback instantly from the virtual world by implementing the knowledge through experiments. It's quite interesting to analyze that the virtual world provides the students inadequate experience and helps the teachers safely by providing the information about the students' progress. The idea of video games to incorporate in education is not new and has originated in early 1990's (Epper, Derryberry, &Jackson, 2012). Games can be a very effective way of teaching "soft skills" for critical enquiry and rewarding method of instruction for students even infusing a sense of competition among the students.

Gamification helps designing the instructional concepts in game dynamics. It can be applied in non-gaming systems to improve user experience and user engagement. It can be used to monitor students' progress through any course, by rewarding points through badges or other credentials, providing instantaneous /regular feedback, monitoring the students' attendance through social media and all of this can be managed by the students through virtual Avatar (Lawton et.al, 2013). An article in the Scientific American claimed that gamification would be one of 10 life changing trends affecting almost every part of our lives, not just education (Pavlus, 2010). The difference between gamification and game based learning is that in actual games, the concepts are taught to transfer knowledge and skills instead of modifying the existing course contents or reframing the course contents. It has been argued that computer games can be considered to be complex learning environments requiring instructional support in cognitive activities, such as decision-making (Wouters & Oostendorp, 2013). Some serious games have been explored to teach practical skills, including medical procedures. (Knight et al, 2010) evaluated using game-based learning to teach triage and resuscitation skills in a Major Incident Medical Management and Support Course (MIMMS) and concluded that such games offered the potential to enhance learning and performance when compared to traditional educational methods. In this regard, (Pivec, 2007) convinces that games-based learning could support constructivist pedagogy allows the students to collaborate, interact in virtual environments, manage problems and learn through virtual experiences. Implementing games-based learning is not so easy task and may require actually producing the game for the concept in question. As most of the games are one-off products tailored to specific institutions that may not be easily adopted in other institutions. Designing games that are accessible to all the students and producing positive learner outcomes requires expertise to produce and leads to cost related issues (Epper et al., 2012). There is also a negative impact with every technology that it might happen some successful games may create distraction for students, or gamification leads to the opposite outcome related to attendance issues. Keeping this in mind to use gamification and game-based learning, Instructor need to define the course objective and must have a clear strategy of implementation. Institutional infrastructure and equipment should satisfy the requirements of the game or gamified content. Faculty and support staffs are required to produce, maintain games, and adapt course content accordingly (Epper et al., 2012).

3-D Learning Tool

Raspberry-Pi is the prime example of 3-D Learning tool which is giving students in schools hands on exposure to understand both the hardware and software aspects of computer science. Raspberry-Pi is a piece of technology which combines not only different types of technology described in the literature but also provides access open source software and programming tools. Raspberry-Pi is a credit/debit card sized computer mother board developed by Raspberry-Pi foundation supported by different Linux platform. Python is the main programming language and one common feature with Raspberry Pi is that all are open source and facilitates learning easier and brings creativity among the students. Further, to make the education more interactive and to actively engage the students, 3-D learning technology like 3-D printing is widely incorporated into curriculums. Cloud is also very emerging to broadcast event worldwide which is very useful for online streaming in education, remote lectures in college, broadcasting gaming event online on the internet.

Virtual Learning Environments and Learning Analytics

Students learning from Web 2.0, MOOCs, Cloud computing will be the extremely important for virtual learning. As more students are educated through the merging of their physical and virtual worlds through mobile technology and dynamic web sites, it is very much possible for the teachers to assess and monitor the student's progress. Virtual learning environment (VLE) provides access to classes, tests assignments, home works, reading materials as similar to the traditional classroom coaching. The students can interact with the teachers through threaded discussion, instant messages etc. Game based learning is an example of virtual learning system. Most of the young students learn though the fun and challenges. On the other hand, Learning Analytics is a new field of research attempts to focus on the data to analyse students' activities. It is defined as "the measurement, collection, analysis, and reporting of data about learners and their contexts for the purposes of understanding and optimizing learning and the environments in which it occurs (Siemens, 2013). Learning analytics tries to utilise the large amounts of data produced by the various systems used to monitor and improve the progress of students.

North America and Asia Pacific are introducing bring your own device (BYOD) in practice. The new learning of BYOD emphasizes M-learning through mobile learning devices. Qual IT is a cloud computing provider offers cloud computing solutions in self-service (IaaS and PaaS) and organizes regular on-line events and engages enthusiastic gamers. It provides on-line competitions of all kinds, tutorials, sharing news and discussions. Virtual learning environments and learning analytics has brought new paradigm to the Education. Today, people's physical lives have been merged with virtual lives due to fully inter-connected and digitalised society. In near future, students are going to practice it. As accessing of mobile devices such as smart phones, Laptops, i-pads etc. are increasing more among the young students, learning will occur more frequently via educational games and virtual learning platforms. Students can be evaluated and submitted their assignments by the Institutions entirely via virtual learning environments.

Flip class room is such example. It allows the students to access the information at any point of time at anywhere and allows the teacher to continually assess and accurately guide their students. This new technology is referred to as learning analytics. The integration of virtual learning environments and learning analytics will solidify the growth of education towards being a more sophisticated, individualised, customised, and adaptive system.

Benefits of Cloud Gaming in Education

- **Economics:** The primary advantages for many Institutions are economics. Cost reduction can be obtained from both hardware and software side. The hardware devices can be redeployed or removed. Internet can be provided free of cost from external providers so that some amount of software cost can be saved.
- **Flexible:** The flexible nature of cloud allows any Institution to use it more during the peak days of the year such as starting days of academic year or during examination period without any usage level planning before. This allows Institutions starts with small scale services and gradually builds them up without significant up-front investment.
- **Enhanced Availability:** Less Environmental Impact: Now, power consumption over worldwide is growing significantly. The usage of cloud reduces the institutions own electricity bill. In theory it seems the cloud optimizes the usage over a group of customers.
- **End-User Satisfaction:** Apart from the availability, end users require new applications. The new applications containing latest tools and features can be provided by innovative companies like Microsoft or Google. Students can use these office applications freely in their systems without purchasing it and keep up to date it. They do not have to worry about backing up or losing data anywhere as it is freely available in the cloud. They can access their data anywhere at any point of time through mobile phones.

A NEW ERA OF ENTERTAINMENT THROUGH CLOUD GAMING

With the tremendous growth of cloud, lots of services are getting extremely benefited with the unlimited source of resources from cloud. Entertainment is one of the services from this huge pool which has been improved continuously since past few years. The major area of entertainment in cloud gaming is Media, Broadcasting, and Gaming services which has been discussed here briefly.

Cloud Gaming in Media and Entertainment

With the growing demand of data, increasing number of customer and availability of data round the clock creates a demand for a robust solution and cloud possesses an important role here. Broadcasting media is a late converter of cloud computing but it seems to be an enthusiastic one. The benefit especially goes for an industry undergoing a transformation from the concept of 'TV Everywhere' to migration of IP networks to transmit the information. These two trends fit well together as broadcasting migrates from dedicated infrastructures to IT-based platforms for delivering videos to a vast array of devices rather than just conventional TV sets. This brings many challenges with different devices in all possible shapes and forms and increases the complexity of delivering the data with quality of service (QoS) guarantee without consuming the undesired portion of bandwidth.

For instance, BBC supports 18 different video formats having necessary resources and expertise but while doing so it overwhelms the other smaller providers. This has to be compromised by choosing just a few target platforms by restricting their audience. However, the cloud model now provides an emerging solution. Unfortunately, one of the biggest criteria that make the cloud model appealing is enormous bandwidth but the storage capacity consumed by the video is again holding it back. In particular, for larger operations, the general cloud conundrum consumes some considerable amount of bandwidth to upload the data and store the data within it. For example, if a broadcast mechanism delivers a video directly to the consumer that is one-way transmission. If the cloud is involved in the middle, the video has to be transmitted twice which has to compromise the cost for larger operations.

It is worth to consider that there are three major areas that can be benefited from the cloud model: Content providers such as big Hollywood studios, broadcasters such as BBC, and pay-TV operators like BSkyB. These categories might overlap with each other. For example, broadcasters may produce content and pay TV operators may own it. There are also many sub-divisions, some broadcasters are state-funded and other commercial broadcasters like ITV and 'Free to Air' are funded by advertising. All of these operators are interested in cloud as a vehicle to reach at the people as much as possible. Still, there are some conflicts of interest that can be avoided.

Content owners holding the rights to broadcast are anxious to avoid the existing agreements. Traditionally, rights to premium content such as movies and sports have been divided based on geographical regions often defined by country or even local regions. This can inhibit cloud distribution of video content but it is also an opportunity for the cloud where digital rights can be negotiated and applied. The cloud can provide economics of scale distribution for the content owner by serving multiple distributors (the distributers may be broadcasters or pay-TV operators) in order to avoid dealing with each one in turn. Netflix has more than 30 million subscribers and Q2 2013 revenue of $1.07 billion and it's not a small by any standards. It uses Amazon Web Services heavily and the numbers really tell the cloud journey (ZDNet article, 2014). Netflix's front-end services are running on 500 to 1000 web servers according to the customer's demand. These are empowered by hundreds of other Amazon Simple Storage Service (S3) and the NoSQL Cassandra database servers using the Memcached high-performance, distributed memories object caching system. This informs us that for a business of Netflix's scale, cloud-based solutions are definitely reliable, practical and feasible. It proofs that for an evolved complex and dynamic ecosystem like Netflix through cloud is not only possible but also it makes sense for other providers.

During Feb. 6-23rd 2014 (Olympics 2014), Microsoft Corporation was used for the cloud encoding and hosting platform provider for NBC Olympics, a division of the NBC Sports Group, during its production of the 2014 Olympic Winter Games in Sochi, Russia. As a result, people were able to watch Winter Olympics programmes through more than 50 live high-definition streams on demand. Through the power of cloud computing, NBC used Windows Azure Media Services, a highly scalable video service platform hosted in Microsoft's data centres, to publish and stream coverage of the 2014 Sochi Winter Games. People were able to access live and on-demand content through the Internet-connected TV, tablet, or smart phones via the NBC Sports Live Extra app available free on Windows 8, Windows RT devices, Windows Phones, Android, and iOS. In addition to this, viewers could go to NBC-Olympics to view live or on-demand Olympics events on a PC or Mac all being streamed with support from Windows Azure Media Services (As per Microsoft Press Release). In the Media & Entertainment space, various use cases have been emerged. Few of them are discussed below:

- **Flexing the Private Cloud:** According to a survey conducted by Meta cloud Inc. at the recent VM world 2013; 87% of IT professionals leveraged private cloud solutions citing reduced cost 38% and security 34% as the top most reasons for its deployment. Among all the cloud models, a private cloud seems to be a secure virtualized infrastructure on which the organization has complete control over it. It helps in identifying operational requirements and their hidden inefficiencies while providing flexibility to customized offerings and tools suitable for the enterpriser's need. It has also helped Disney (worth of $110 billion) to own its cloud outrights and have greater access control. While Disney opted for cloud stack's to deploy faster cloud model, what actually makes it interesting is that they had integrated additional tools (object storage) from open stack (one of the cloud Stack's leading competitors) into their private cloud. As a result, Disney now has a fully functional cloud built on Cloud Stack which is tightly integrated with the object storage tool from Swift. This shows that providers are now offering cloud technology that can be either used as standalone pieces or can be easily integrated with other technologies.

- **Reduced Data Centre Footprint:** Recently, Fox has announced their partnership with HP to make its supply chain cloud-enabled and migrate its traditional IT to the cloud platform. By using the cloud, Fox will be able to provide agile, cost-effective services on top of its Fox Enterprise Media Framework (EMF) that is currently used by various business units to manage, collaborate, and distribute its media assets globally. Fox expects this initiative is to reduce its data centre footprint by 70%, cut traditional computational and storage resources, provisioning cycle time from five weeks to 15 minutes and shift 50 percent of IT resources from commodity support to global service brokering. The common challenges that any in-house infrastructure face are frequent server crashes and limitations in bandwidth. Even the necessary precautions might prove to be cost-prohibitive. So when data centres are consolidated and virtualized, organizations are able to reduce rising costs and free-up resources that can be otherwise used to support innovation and growth.

- **On-Demand Digital Content:** In early June 1994, Disney announced a cloud-based initiative called 'Digital Copy Plus' which allows DVD buyers to download digital version of the file in a format that is compatible to iTunes, Amazon Instant Video etc. Content-intensive companies like Netflix, are not just leveraging the cloud's scalability to store terabytes and peta bytes of data but also make the content available anytime and anywhere. It has given rise to a new breed of services where almost all Media & Entertainment providers that includes Warner Bros to Walmart-owned Vudu, to offer consumers the chance to convert their physical DVD/Blu-Ray libraries into more portable digital files. The commercial CD market by itself is a huge potential area of revenue. As per the current estimates from Warner Bros, US consumers have bought 10 billion DVDs while 10 billion DVDs have been sold worldwide. Ultraviolet, which is a free cloud-based digital rights collection, allows users to stream a movie or a TV show by adding it to their online collection along with a 'proof of purchase'. For example, if a consumer bought a movie or a

TV show from a participating retailer on Blu-ray, Ultraviolet allows the consumer to download a digital copy on its smartphone or tablet. It has more than 70 companies participating including Sony Pictures, NBC Universal, Warner Bros, Paramount Pictures Group, Fox Entertainment Group, Drame Works Animation and Lions Gate.

- **Regaining Visibility:** Unlike traditional system, IT system is always challenging when it comes to real-time monitoring or historical analysis. Cloud-based solutions make the information available on the go and helps in facilitating better collaboration. By leveraging the cloud to streamline operations, content providers stand to gain significant cost savings, better quality and faster time to market for newer services. For instance, Warner Bros. has recently streamlined their digital supply chain with a cloud-based solution (Pega Cloud) to provide visibility into the critical path of new film releases across International digital and physical media supply chains.

CONCLUSION

Cloud computing is one of the emerging technologies that must be exercised on health care sector, education and entertainment services. One of the greatest advantages to use cloud based multimedia e-health care services which make patient care technologies cost effective as health care cost is going on increasing. The impact of cloud computing on education cannot be compared with the traditional class room coaching. It brings a new revolution in such a way that it allows the education to be customized, individualized, and universally accessible without any differentiating poor and rich. Moreover, the Cloud is very helpful in the entertainment services where the multi user applications like gaming where users from across the worlds are playing on a single game and storing the data on a central location. Cloud is also helping the users to retrieve the data at anyplace at any point of time. Overall, it is a multidisciplinary technology which can bring a paradigm shift on human life.

REFERENCES

Anderson, L. S. (1999). *Technology planning: It's more than computers*. Retrieved from the National centre Technology planning. Website: http://www. nctp.com/articles/tpmore.pdf

Boticki. (2009). *Context awareness and distributed events in Mobile Learning. Architecture for distributed and complex M-learning Systems: Applying intelligent technology.* Academic Press.

Darrow, B. (1932). Radio: The assistant teacher. Columbus, OH: R.G. Adams.

Epper, R., Sicart, M., Nacke, L., O' Hara, K., & Dixon, D. (2011). Gamification using game- design elements. In *Proceedings of the 2011 annual conference extended abstracts on Human factors in computing systems.*

Informatics, H. (2012). *Cloud based communication versatile communication platform helps foster collaborative care.* Retrieved from http://www.healthcare-informatics.com/article/

KLAS. (2013). *Cloud Computing perception 2013: The Hybrid Cloud in Healthcare.* Retrieved from http://www.klaresearch.com/ klasreports/#/krms/19/0

Knight, J. F., Cartey, S., Treganna, B., Jarvis, S. S., Smithies, R., & de Freits, S. K. (2010). Serious gaining Technology in major incident triage training: A pragamatic controlled trial. *Resuscitations, 81*(9), 1175–1179. doi:10.1016/j.resuscitation.2010.03.042 PMID:20732609

Lawton, W., Ahamad, M., Angole, T., Axel Berg, A., & Katsominnos, A. (2013). *Horizon Scanning: What will Higher Education look like in 2020?* Retrieved from http://www.international.ac.uk/media/2423997/horizons scanning report finalprint. pdf

NMC Horizon Project NMC. (2013). *The Higher Education Edition Olympic Games (2014).* Retrieved from http://news.microsoft.com/2014/02/06/nbc-olympics-production-of-the-2014-olympic-winter-games-to-utilize-microsoft-for-live-and-on-demand-streaming/

Papert, S. (1994). Why School reform is possible. *Journal of the Learning Sciences, 6*(4), 417–427. doi:10.1207/s15327809jls0604_5

Pavlus, J. (2010). *Sixty – Two Reasons why gemification is played out. Fast company design.* Retrieved from http://fast codesign.com/166.2656/sixtytworeasonswhygamificationisplayedout

Pivec, M. (2007). Editorial 'Play and Learn: Potentials of game based learning. *British Journal of Educational Technology, 38*(3), 387–393. doi:10.1111/j.1467-8535.2007.00722.x

Rhonda, M., Derryberry, & Jackson. (2012). *Game based Learning*. Research Bulletin. Center for Applied Research.

Siemens, G. (2010). What are Learning Analytics? Emergence of Discipline. *The American Behavioral Scientist, 57*(10), 1380–1400. doi:10.1177/0002764213498851

Walker, J. (2005). *Final version of Weblog definition*. Routledge Encyclopedia of Narrative Theory.

Wouters, P., & van Oostendorp, H. (2013). A meta-analytic review of the role of instructional support in game-based learning. *Computers & Education, 60*(1), 412–425. doi:10.1016/j.compedu.2012.07.018

Compilation of References

Abu-Libdeh, H., Princehouse, L., & Weatherspoon, H. (2010). RACS: a case for cloud storage diversity. *Proceedings of the 1st ACM symposium on Cloud computing*, (pp. 229-240).

Adithya, C., Kowsik, K., Namrata, D., Nageli, V. S., Shrivastava, S., & Rakshit, S. (2010). Augmented Reality Approach for Paper Map Visualization. *Proceedings of the International Conference on Communication and Computational Intelligence.*

Akl & Taylor. (1983). Cryptographic Solution to a Problem of Access Control in a Hierarchy. *ACM Transactions on Computer Systems, 1*(3), 239–248.

Akl, A. (2010). *A Novel Accelerometer-based Gesture Recognition System.* (Master of Applied Science thesis). University of Toronto.

Akl, S. G., & Taylor, P. D. (1983). Cryptographic solution to a problem of access control in a hierarchy. *ACM Transactions on Computer Systems, 1*(3), 239–248. doi:10.1145/357369.357372

Alexander, K. (2012, August). *Fat client game streaming or cloud gaming.* Akamai Blog. Retrieved from https://blogs.akamai.com/2012/08/part-2-fat-client-game-streaming-or-cloud-gaming.html

Amazon Web Services, Inc. (2015). *Amazon Web Services (AWS).* Retrieved from http://aws.amazon.com

Ameigeiras, P., Ramos-Munoz, J. J., Schumacher, L., Prados-Garzon, J., Navarro-Ortiz, J., & Lopez-Soler, J. M. (2015). Link-level access cloud architecture design based on SDN for 5G networks. *IEEE Network, 29*(2), 24–31. doi:10.1109/MNET.2015.7064899

Anderson, L. S. (1999). *Technology planning: It's more than computers.* Retrieved from the National centre Technology planning. Website: http://www. nctp.com/articles/tpmore.pdf

Arcella, A., Balzano, E., Cavaliere, S., & Iura, R. (2008). A Teaching kinematics: augmented reality and virtualization in the observation. *International Conference on Computer Science and Software Engineering.* doi:10.1109/CSSE.2008.1625

Armbrust, M., Fox, A., Griffith, R., Joseph, A. D., Katz, R., Konwinski, A., & Zaharia, M. et al. (2010). A view of cloud computing. *Communications of the ACM, 53*(4), 50–58. doi:10.1145/1721654.1721672

Compilation of References

Arsanjani, A., Ghosh, S., Allam, A., Abdollah, T., Gariapathy, S., & Holley, K. (2008). SOMA: A method for developing service-oriented solutions. *IBM Systems Journal, 47*(3), 377–396. doi:10.1147/sj.473.0377

Ateniese, G., Fu, K., Green, M., & Hohenberger, S. (2006). Improved proxy re-encryption schemes with applications to secure distributed storage. *ACM Transactions on Information and System Security, 9*(1), 1–30. doi:10.1145/1127345.1127346

Babu, L. D., & Krishna, P. V. (2013). Applying operations management models for facility location problem in cloud computing environments. *International Journal of Services and Operations Management*, 1-27.

Babu, L. D., & Krishna, P. V. (2013). Honey bee behavior inspired load balancing of tasks in cloud computing environments. *Applied Soft Computing*, 2292–2303.

Babu, L. D., & Krishna, P. V. (2013). Versatile time-cost algorithm (VTCA) for scheduling non-preemptive tasks of time critical workflows in cloud computing systems. *International Journal of Communication Networks and Distributed Systems, 11*(4), 390–411. doi:10.1504/IJCNDS.2013.057718

Babu, L. D., Krishna, P. V., Zayan, A. M., & Panda, V. (2011). *An analysis of security related issues in cloud computing. In Contemporary Computing* (pp. 180–190). Delhi, India: Springer.

Babu, L. D., Krishna, P. V., Zayan, A. M., & Panda, V. (2011). An Analysis of Security Related Issues in Cloud Computing. *Springer Communications in Computer and Information Science, 168*, 180–190. doi:10.1007/978-3-642-22606-9_21

Badre, A. (2001). *The Effects of Cross Cultural Interface Design Orientation on World Wide Web User Performance*. Georgia Institute of Technology.

Bajura, M., & Neumann, U. (1995). Dynamic Registration Correction in Augmented-Reality Systems. *Virtual Reality Annual International Symposium, Proceedings*. doi:10.1109/VRAIS.1995.512495

Bamanikar, Ursal, & Jadhav. (n.d.). Hand Gestures Recognition Based On Vision. *ASM's International E-Journal of Ongoing Research in Management and IT*.

Baresi, L., Guinea, S., & Pasquale, L. (2007). Self-healing BPEL processes with Dynamo and the JBoss rule engine. In *International Workshop on Engineering of Software Services for Pervasive Environments (ESSPE '07)*. New York, NY: ACM. doi:10.1145/1294904.1294906

Bengtsson, M., Wilson, T. L., & Zackariasson, P. (2010). Paradigm shifts in the video game industry. *Competitiveness Review: An International Business Journal*, 139-151.

Benington, H. D. (1983). Production of large computer programs. *Annals of the History of Computing, 5*(4), 350–361. doi:10.1109/MAHC.1983.10102

Bezerra, C. E., & Geyer, C. F. (2009). A load balancing scheme for massively multiplayer online games. *Multimedia Tools and Applications, 45*(1-3), 263–289. doi:10.1007/s11042-009-0302-z

Bhatt, N., Babu, M., & Bhatt, A. (2013). Automation Testing Software that Aid in Efficiency Increase of Regression Process. *Recent Patents on Computer Science, 6*(2), 107–114. doi:10.2 174/22132759113069990008

Bose, R., & Sarddar, D. (2015). A new approach in mobile gaming on cloud-based architecture using Citrix and VMware technologies. *Brazilian Journal of Science and Technology, 2*(1), 1–13. doi:10.1186/s40552-015-0012-1

Boticki. (2009). *Context awareness and distributed events in Mobile Learning. Architecture for distributed and complex M-learning Systems: Applying intelligent technology.* Academic Press.

Bucchiarone, A., Cappiello, C., Di Nitto, E., Gorlatch, S., Meiländer, D., & Metzger, A. (2011). Design for self-adaptation in service-oriented systems in the Cloud. In D. Petcu & J. L. Vzques-Poletti (Eds.), *European Research Activities in Cloud Computing* (pp. 214–240). Cambridge Scholars Publishing.

Bucchiarone, A., Cappiello, C., Di Nitto, E., Kazhamiakin, R., Mazza, V., & Pistore, M. (2009). Design for adaptation of service-based applications: main issues and requirements. In A. Dan, F. Gittler, & F. Toumani (Eds.), *Service-Oriented Computing. ICSOC/ServiceWave 2009 Workshops (LNCS)* (Vol. 6275, pp. 467–476). Berlin, Germany: Springer. doi:10.1007/978-3-642-16132-2_44

Buyya, R., Yeo, C. S., & Venugopal, S. (2008). Market-oriented Cloud Computing: vision, hype, and reality for delivering IT services as computing utilities. In *International Conference on High Performance Computing and Communications.* IEEE. doi:10.1109/HPCC.2008.172

Byong, K. (1998). Finger Mouse And Gesture Recognition System As A New Human Computer Interface. *Computer Graphics, 21*(5), 555–561.

Cai, & Chan. (2014). *Cognitive Resource Optimization for Decomposed Cloud Gaming Platform.* Academic Press.

Cai, W., & Leung. (2012). Multiplayer cloud gaming system with cooperative video sharing. In *Cloud Computing Technology and Science (CloudCom), 2012 IEEE 4th International Conference on,* (pp. 640-645). IEEE.

Cai, W., Leung, V., & Chen, M. (2013). Next generation mobile cloud gaming. In *Service Oriented System Engineering (SOSE), 2013 IEEE 7th International Symposium on,* (pp. 551-560). IEEE.

Cai, W., Zhou, C., Leung, V., & Chen, M. (2013). A cognitive platform for mobile cloud gaming. In *Cloud Computing Technology and Science (CloudCom), 2013 IEEE 5th International Conference on,* (vol. 1, pp. 72-79). IEEE. doi:10.1109/CloudCom.2013.17

Cai, W., Hong, Z., Wang, X., Chan, H. C., & Leung, V. (2015). Quality-of-Experience Optimization for a Cloud Gaming System With Ad Hoc Cloudlet Assistance. *IEEE Transactions on Circuits and Systems for Video Technology, 25*(12), 2092–2104. doi:10.1109/TCSVT.2015.2450153

Canetti, R., & Hohenberger, S. (2007, October). Chosen-ciphertext secure proxy re-encryption. In *Proceedings of the 14th ACM conference on Computer and communications security* (pp. 185-194). ACM.

Compilation of References

Canfora, G., Di Penta, M., Esposito, R., & Villani, M. L. (2005). An approach for QoS-aware service composition based on genetic algorithms. In *Proceedings of the 7th Annual Conference on Genetic and Evolutionary Computation (GECCO '05)*. New York, NY: ACM. doi:10.1145/1068009.1068189

Care, R., Hussein, A. H. H., Suarez, L., & Nuaymi, L. (2014). Energy-efficient scheduling for cloud mobile gaming. In Globecom Workshops (GC Wkshps), 2014, (pp. 1198-1204). IEEE. doi:10.1109/GLOCOMW.2014.7063596

Chakraborty, P., Sarawgi, P., Mehrotra, A., Agarwal, G., & Pradhan, R. (2008). Hand Gesture Recognition: A Comparative Study. *Proceedings of the International Multi Conference of Engineers and Computer Scientists 2008*.

Chang, W.-C., & Chang, W. C. (2014). Real-Time 3D Rendering Based on Multiple Cameras and Point Cloud. In *Ubi-Media Computing and Workshops (UMEDIA), 2014 7th International Conference on*, (pp. 121-126). IEEE. doi:10.1109/U-MEDIA.2014.52

Cheelu, D., Babu, M. R., & Venkatakrishna, P. (2013). A fuzzy-based intelligent vertical handoff decision strategy with maximised user satisfaction for next generation communication networks. *International Journal of Process Management and Benchmarking*, *3*(4), 420–440. doi:10.1504/IJPMB.2013.058268

Chen, Huang, & Hsu. (2014). Cloud gaming onward: research opportunities and outlook. In *Multimedia and Expo Workshops (ICMEW), 2014 IEEE International Conference on*, (pp. 1-4). IEEE. doi:10.1109/MMSP.2014.6958835

Chen, K.-T. (2014, July 10). *Gaminganywhere*. Retrieved November 10, 2015, from http://gaminganywhere.org: http://gaminganywhere.org/index.html

Chen, K.-T., Chang, Y.-C., Hsu, H.-J., Chen, D.-Y., Huang, C.-Y., & Hsu, C.-H. (2014). On the quality of service of cloud gaming systems. *Multimedia, IEEE Transactions on*, 480-495.

Chen, K.-T., Huang, C.-Y., & Hsu, C.-H. (2014). Cloud gaming onward: research opportunities and outlook. *Multimedia and Expo Workshops (ICMEW), 2014 IEEE International Conference on* (pp. 1-4). Chengdu, China: IEEE.

Chen, F.-S., Fu, C.-M., & Huang, C.-L. (2003, March20). Hand gesture recognition using a real-time tracking method and hidden Markov models. *Image and Vision Computing, 21*, 745–758.

Chen, K. T., Chang, Y. C., Hsu, H. J., Chen, D. Y., Huang, C. Y., & Hsu, C. H. (2014). On the quality of service of cloud gaming systems. *Multimedia. IEEE Transactions on, 16*(2), 480–495.

Chen, K. T., Chang, Y. C., Hsu, H. J., Chen, D. Y., Huang, C. Y., & Hsu, C. H. (2014). On the quality of service of cloud gaming systems. *IEEE Transactions on Multimedia, 16*(2), 480–495. doi:10.1109/TMM.2013.2291532

Chen, K.-T., Chang, Y.-C., Hsu, H.-J., Chen, D.-Y., Huang, C.-Y., & Hsu, C.-H. (2014). On the Quality of Service of Cloud Gaming Systems. *IEEE Transactions on Multimedia, 16*(2).

Chen, K.-T., Chang, Y.-C., Hsu, H.-J., Chen, D.-Y., Huang, C.-Y., & Hsu, C.-H. (2014). On the quality of service of cloud gaming systems. *Multimedia. IEEE Transactions, 16*(2), 480–495.

Chen, K.-T., Chang, Y.-C., Tseng, P.-H., Huang, C.-Y., & Lei, C.-L. (2011). Measuring the latency of cloud gaming systems.*Proceedings of the 19th ACM international conference on Multimedia* (pp. 1269-1272). ACM. doi:10.1145/2072298.2071991

Chick, G. C., & Tavares, S. E. (1990, January). Flexible access control with master keys. In Advances in Cryptology—CRYPTO'89 Proceedings (pp. 316-322). Springer New York. doi:doi:10.1007/0-387-34805-0_29 doi:10.1007/0-387-34805-0_29

Chow, S. S., Weng, J., Yang, Y., & Deng, R. H. (2010). Efficient unidirectional proxy re-encryption. In *Progress in Cryptology–AFRICACRYPT 2010* (pp. 316-332). Springer Berlin Heidelberg.

Choy, S., Wong, B., Simon, G., & Rosenberg, C. (2012). The brewing storm in cloud gaming: A measurement study on cloud to end-user latency.*Proceedings of the 11th annual workshop on network and systems support for games* (p. 2). Piscataway, NJ: IEEE Press. doi:10.1109/NetGames.2012.6404024

Chuah, S. P., Yuen, C., & Cheung, N. M. (2014). Cloud gaming: A green solution to massive multiplayer online games. *Wireless Communications, IEEE, 21*(4), 78–87. doi:10.1109/MWC.2014.6882299

Chuah, S.-P., & Cheung, N.-M. (2014). Layered coding for mobile cloud gaming.*Proceedings of International Workshop on Massively Multiuser Virtual Environments* (pp. 1-6). Singapore: ACM. doi:10.1145/2594448.2577395

Chu, C. K., Chow, S. S., Tzeng, W. G., Zhou, J., & Deng, R. H. (2014). Key-aggregate cryptosystem for scalable data sharing in cloud storage. *Parallel and Distributed Systems. IEEE Transactions on, 25*(2), 468–477.

Chu, C. K., & Tzeng, W. G. (2007). Identity-based proxy re-encryption without random oracles. In *Information Security* (pp. 189–202). Springer Berlin Heidelberg. doi:10.1007/978-3-540-75496-1_13

Chu, C. K., Weng, J., Chow, S. S., Zhou, J., & Deng, R. H. (2009, January). Conditional proxy broadcast re-encryption. In *Information security and privacy* (pp. 327–342). Springer Berlin Heidelberg. doi:10.1007/978-3-642-02620-1_23

Clay, A., Couture, N., Nigay, L., Rivière, J. B., Martin, J. C., Courgeon, M., & Domenger, G. et al. (2012). Interactions and systems for augmenting a live dance performance. *International Symposium on Mixes and Augmented Reality*, Atlanta, GA. doi:10.1109/ISMAR-AMH.2012.6483986

Claypool, M., & Claypool, K. (2006). Latency and Player Actions in Online Games. *Communications of the ACM, 49*(11), 40. doi:10.1145/1167838.1167860

Claypool, M., & Claypool, K. (2010). Latency can kill: precision and deadline in online games. In *Proceedings of the first annual ACM SIGMM conference on Multimedia systems*. ACM. doi:10.1145/1730836.1730863

Compilation of References

Clincy, V., & Wilgor, B. (2013). Subjective evaluation of latency and packet loss in a cloud-based game. Information Technology: New Generations (ITNG) (pp. 473-476). Las Vegas, NV: IEEE.

Cloud Gaming – Gaming as a Service (GaaS) | NVIDIA GRID. (n.d.). Retrieved April 10, 2015, from http://www.nvidia.com/object/cloud-gaming.html

Cloud Gaming. (n.d.). In *Encyclopedia*. Retrieved from 23rd January 2016. https://en.wikipedia.org/wiki/Cloud_gaming

Colombo, M., Di Nitto, E., & Mauri, M. (2006). SCENE: a service composition execution environment supporting dynamic changes disciplined through rules. In *Service-Oriented Computing – IC-SOC 2006 (LNCS)* (Vol. 4294, pp. 191–202). Berlin, Germany: Springer. doi:10.1007/11948148_16

Coogan, T. A. (2007). *Dynamic Gesture Recognition using Transformation Invariant Hand Shape Recognition*. M.Sc. Thesis.

Crump, G. (2014, March 26). *What Is Storage QoS?* Retrieved December 13, 2015, from www.networkcomputing.com: http://www.networkcomputing.com/storage/what-is-storage-qos/a/d-id/1127906

Darrow, B. (1932). Radio: The assistant teacher. Columbus, OH: R.G. Adams.

De Winter, D., Simoens, P., Deboosere, L., De Turck, F., Moreau, J., & Dhoedt, B. et al.. (2006). A hybrid thin-client protocol for multimedia streaming and interactive gaming applications. *Proceedings of the 2006 international workshop on Network and operating systems support for digital audio and video* (p. 15). Newport, RI: ACM. doi:10.1145/1378191.1378210

Deelman, E., Singh, G., Livny, M., Berriman, B., & Good, J. (2008). The cost of doing science on the Cloud: the Montage example. In *Proceedings of the 2008 ACM/IEEE Conference on Supercomputing*. Piscataway, NJ: IEEE Press. doi:10.1109/SC.2008.5217932

Deffeyes, S., & Katz, N. (2010). Augmented reality in the data center. IBM Academy of Technology.

Dejun, J., Pierre, G., & Chi, C.-H. (2011). Resource provisioning of web applications in heterogeneous Clouds. In *Proceedings of the 2nd USENIX Conference on Web Application Development*. Berkeley, CA: USENIX Association.

Dhinesh Babu, L., Gunasekaran, A., & Krishna, P. V. (2014). A decision-based pre-emptive fair scheduling strategy to process cloud computing work-flows for sustainable enterprise management. *International Journal of Business Information Systems*, 409-430.

Dhinesh, L. D. (2014). A decision-based pre-emptive fair scheduling strategy to process cloud computing work-flows for sustainable enterprise management. *Int. J. Business Information Systems*, *16*(4), 409–430. doi:10.1504/IJBIS.2014.063929

Dhinesh, L. D. B., & Krishna, P. V. (2013). Applying operations management models for facility location problem in cloud computing environments. *Int. J. Services and Operations Management*, *15*(1), 1–27. doi:10.1504/IJSOM.2013.053252

Di Nitto, E., Meiländer, D., Gorlatch, S., Metzger, A., Psaier, H., & Dustdar, S., ... Lago, P. (2012). Research challenges on engineering service-oriented applications. In *1st International Workshop on European Software Services and Systems Research (S-Cube)*. IEEE.

Diao, Z. (2013). *Consistency models for cloud-based online games: the storage system's perspective*. Liebe Teilnehmerinnen und Teilnehmer.

Dischinger, M., Haeberlen, A., Gummadi, K. P., & Saroiu, S. (2007). Characterizing residential broadband networks.*Internet Measurement Conference* (pp. 43-56). San Diego, CA: ACM.

Eisert, P., & Fechteler, P. (2008). Low delay streaming of computer graphics. *Image Processing, 2008. ICIP 2008. 15th IEEE International Conference on* (pp. 2704-2707). San Diego, CA: IEEE.

Eisert, P., & Fechteler, P. (2008). Low delay streaming of computer graphics. In *Proc. IEEE ICIP 2008*.

Epper, R., Sicart, M., Nacke, L., O' Hara, K., & Dixon, D. (2011). Gamification using game-design elements. In *Proceedings of the 2011 annual conference extended abstracts on Human factors in computing systems*.

Fahringer, T., Anthes, C., Arragon, A., Lipaj, A., Müller-Iden, J., Rawlings, C. J. ... Surridge, M. (2007). The edutain@grid project. In Grid Economics and Business Models GECON 2007 (LNCS) (Vol. 4685/2007, pp. 182–187). Berlin, Germany: Springer.

Fan, B., Andersen, D. G., Kaminsky, M., & Mitzenmacher, M. D. (2014, December). Cuckoo Filter: Practically Better Than Bloom. In *Proceedings of the 10th ACM International on Conference on emerging Networking Experiments and Technologies* (pp. 75-88). ACM.

Felemban, M., Basalamah, S., & Ghafoor, A. (2013). A distributed cloud architecture for mobile multimedia services. *IEEE Network*, *27*(5), 20–27. doi:10.1109/MNET.2013.6616111

Ferdousi, Z. (2008). *Design and Development of A Real-Time Gesture Recognition System*. (Master of Science in Computer and Information Systems Engineering Thesis). Graduate School of Tennessee State University.

Ferreira, P., Orvalho, J., & Boavida, F. (2007). A Middleware Architecture for Mobile and Pervasive Large-Scale Augmented Reality Games. *Fifth Annual Conference on Communication Networks and Services Research, CNSR '07*. doi:10.1109/CNSR.2007.2

Fiedler, S., Wallner, M., & Weber, M. (2002, April). A communication architecture for massive multiplayer games. In *Proceedings of the 1st workshop on Network and system support for games*. (pp. 14-22). ACM. doi:10.1145/566500.566503

Field, M., Gordon, S., Peterson, E., Robinson, R., Stahovich, T., & Alvarado, C. (2010). The effect of task on classification accuracy: Using gesture recognition techniques in free-sketch recognition. *Computers & Graphics*, *34*(5), 499–512. doi:10.1016/j.cag.2010.07.001

Fischer, J., Bartz, D., & Straber, W. (2005). Stylized Augmented Reality for Improved Immersion. *Proceedings of the IEEE Virtual Reality*.

Compilation of References

Freeman, T., & Keahey, K. (2008). Flying low: simple leases with Workspace Pilot. In *Euro-Par 2008 Parallel Processing (LNCS)* (Vol. 5168, pp. 499–509). Berlin, Germany: Springer. doi:10.1007/978-3-540-85451-7_54

Froehlich, A. (2015, November 05). *Cloud Computing: 8 Hidden Costs.* Retrieved December 01, 2015, from http://www.informationweek.com/cloud/platform-as-a-service/cloud-computing-8-hidden-costs/d/d-id/1321375?image_number=10

Gammeter, S., Gassmann, A., Bossard, L., Quack, T., & Gool, L. V. (2010). Server-side object recognition and client-side object tracking for mobile augmented reality. *IEEE Computer Society Conference on Computer Vision and Pattern Recognition Workshops (CVPRW).* doi:10.1109/CVPRW.2010.5543248

García-Valls, M., Cucinotta, T., & Lu, C. (2014). Challenges in real-time virtualization and predictable cloud computing. *Journal of Systems Architecture, 60*(9), 726–740. doi:10.1016/j.sysarc.2014.07.004

Gartner Says That Consumers Will Store More Than a Third of Their Digital Content in the Cloud by 2016 . (2012, June 25). Retrieved March 25, 2015, from http://www.gartner.com/newsroom/id/2060215

Geer, D. (2008). Reducing the storage burden via data deduplication. *Computer, 41*(12), 15–17. doi:10.1109/MC.2008.538

Geroimenko, V. (2012). Augmented Reality Technology and Art: The Analysis and Visualization of Evolving Conceptual Models. *16th International Conference on Information Visualisation.* doi:10.1109/IV.2012.77

Gibbon, D. (2010, April 05). *PS3 to allow PC games to run on it.* Retrieved from www.digital-spy.com

Google App Engine. (n.d.). Retrieved February 25, 2015, from https://appengine.google.com/

Gorlatch, S., Meiländer, D., Bartholomäus, S., Fujita, H., Theurl, T., Hoeren, T., … Boers, K. (2010). Cheating prevention in virtual worlds: software, economic, and law aspects. In *New Trends in Software Methodologies, Tools and Techniques – Proceedings of the 9th SoMeT_10.* IOS Press.

Gorlatch, S., Glinka, F., Ploss, A., & Meiländer, D. (2012). Designing multiplayer online games using the Real-Time Framework. In A. Kumar, J. Etheredge, & A. Boudreaux (Eds.), *Algorithmic and Architectural Gaming Design: Implementation and Development* (pp. 290–321). Hershey, PA: IGI Global. doi:10.4018/978-1-4666-1634-9.ch012

Gorlatch, S., Glinka, F., Ploss, A., Müller-Iden, J., Prodan, R., Nae, V., & Fahringer, T. (2008). Enhancing Grids for massively multiplayer online computer games. In *Euro-Par 2008 - Parallel Processing (LNCS)* (Vol. 5168, pp. 466–477). Berlin, Germany: Springer. doi:10.1007/978-3-540-85451-7_51

Guan, H., Yao, J., Qi, Z., & Wang, R. (2015). Energy-Efficient SLA Guarantees for Virtualized GPU in Cloud Gaming. *IEEE Transactions on Parallel and Distributed Systems, 26*(9), 2434–2443. doi:10.1109/TPDS.2014.2350499

Guo, F., Mu, Y., & Chen, Z. (2007). Identity-based encryption: how to decrypt multiple cipher-texts using a single decryption key. In *Pairing-Based Cryptography–Pairing 2007* (pp. 392–406). Springer Berlin Heidelberg. doi:10.1007/978-3-540-73489-5_22

Hampel, T., Bopp, T., & Hinn, R. (2006, October). A peer-to-peer architecture for massive mul-tiplayer online games. In *Proceedings of 5th ACM SIGCOMM workshop on Network and system support for games.* ACM. doi:10.1145/1230040.1230058

Hermet, G., & Combet, J. (2011). Mobile Internet Monetization: A Methodology to Monitor in Real Time the Cellular Subscriber Transactional Itinerary, from Mobile Advertising Exposure to Actual Purchase. *Mobile Business (ICMB), 2011 Tenth International Conference on* (pp. 307-312). Como, Italy: IEEE.

Herold, R., Vogel, U., Richter, B., Kreye, D., Reckziegel, S., Scholles, M., & Lakner, H. (2008). *OLED-on-CMOS Integration for Augmented-Reality Systems.* International Students and Young Scientists Workshop "Photonics and Microsystems". doi:doi:10.1109/STYSW.2008.5164134 doi:10.1109/STYSW.2008.5164134

Hey, A. J., & Trefethen, A. E. (2003). The data deluge: an e-sicence perspective. In *Gid Comput-ing: Making the Global Infrastructure a Reality.* Wiley. doi:10.1002/0470867167.ch36

Higginbotham, S. (2012). *Smart TVs cause a net neutrality debate in S. Korea.* San Francisco, CA: Giga OM, Feb.

Hincapié, M., Caponio, A., Rios, H., & Mendívil, E. G. (2011). An Introduction to Augmented Reality with Applications in Aeronautical Maintenance. *13th International Conference on Trans-parent Optical Networks (ICTON).* doi:10.1109/ICTON.2011.5970856

Hobfeld, T., Schatz, R., Varela, M., & Timmerer, C. (2012). Challenges of QoE management for cloud applications. *Communications Magazine, 50*(4).

Holthe, O.-I., Mogstad, O., & Ronningen, L. A. (2009). Geelix LiveGames: Remote playing of video games. *Proceedings of the 6th IEEE Conference on Consumer Communications and Network-ing Conference* (pp. 758-759). Las Vegas, NV: IEEE Press. doi:10.1109/CCNC.2009.4784713

Hong, H. J., Chen, D. Y., Huang, C. Y., Chen, K. T., & Hsu, C. H. (2013). QoE-aware virtual machine placement for cloud games. *2013 12th Annual Workshop on Network and Systems Sup-port for Games (NetGames),* (pp. 1-2). IEEE.

Hong, H. J., Chen, D. Y., Huang, C. Y., Chen, K. T., & Hsu, C. H. (2015). Placing virtual machines to optimize cloud gaming experience. *Cloud Computing. IEEE Transactions on, 3*(1), 42–53.

Hong, H. J., Chen, D. Y., Huang, C. Y., Chen, K. T., & Hsu, C. H. (2015). Placing virtual ma-chines to optimize cloud gaming experience. *IEEE Transactions on Cloud Computing, 3*(1), 42–53. doi:10.1109/TCC.2014.2338295

Compilation of References

Hong, H. J., Hsu, C. F., Tsai, T. H., Huang, C. Y., Chen, K. T., & Hsu, C. H. (2015). Enabling adaptive cloud gaming in an open-source cloud gaming platform. *IEEE Transactions on Circuits and Systems for Video Technology*, *25*(12), 2078–2091. doi:10.1109/TCSVT.2015.2450173

Huang, J., Wu, K., & Moh, M. (2014). Dynamic Virtual Machine migration algorithms using enhanced energy consumption model for green cloud data centers. In *High Performance Computing & Simulation (HPCS), 2014 International Conference on*, (pp. 902-910). IEEE. doi:10.1109/HPCSim.2014.6903785

Huang, C. Y., Chen, K. T., Chen, D. Y., Hsu, H. J., & Hsu, C. H. (2014). GamingAnywhere: The first open source cloud gaming system. *ACM Transactions on Multimedia Computing, Communications, and Applications*, *10*(1s), 10. doi:10.1145/2537855

Huang, C.-Y., Hsu, C.-H., Chang, Y.-C., & Chen, K.-T. (2013). GamingAnywhere: an open cloud gaming system. *Proceedings of the 4th ACM multimedia systems conference* (pp. 36-47). Oslo, Norway: ACM. doi:10.1145/2483977.2483981

Hu, G., Tay, W. P., & Wen, Y. (2012). Cloud robotics: Architecture, challenges and applications. *IEEE Network*, *26*(3), 21 28. doi:10.1109/MNET.2012.6201212

Hull, J. J., Erol, B., Graham, J., Ke, Q., Kishi, H., Moraleda, J., & Olst, D. G. V. (2007). Paper-Based Augmented Reality. *17th International Conference on Artificial Reality and Telexistence*. doi:10.1109/ICAT.2007.49

Ikko & Agarwal. (2012). *Gesture recognition: Enabling natural interactions with electronics*. Gesture Recognition and Depth-Sensing Texas Instruments, White Paper.

Infan, Muthurangasamy, & Yogananth. (2014). Resilient Identify Based Encryption for Cloud Storage by Using Aggregated Keys. *International Journal of Advanced Research in Computer Engineering & Technology*, *3*(3).

Infoholic, R. (2015, June 23). *Global Cloud Gaming Market: Trends & Forecast 2015-2020*. Retrieved November 28, 2015, from http://finance.yahoo.com: http://finance.yahoo.com/news/global-cloud-gaming-market-trends-104100437.html

Informatics, H. (2012). *Cloud based communication versatile communication platform helps foster collaborative care*. Retrieved from http://www.healthcare-informatics.com/article/

Inmobi. (2014, December 01). *Monetization Solution for Games*. Retrieved December 03, 2015, from http://www.inmobi.com: http://info.inmobi.com/rs/inmobi/images/InMobi-Monetization-Solution-for-Games.pdf

Jain, S. (2014). *An analysis of security and privacy issues, Challenges with possible solution in cloud computing*. National Conference on Computational and Mathematical Sciences (COMPUTATIA-IV), Jaipur, India.

Jane, M. (2013, April 13). *Publisher's cloud gaming platform hacked, providing access to unreleased games*. Retrieved December 3, 2015, from http://www.cloudpro.co.uk/saas/5470/ubisoft-shuts-down-cloud-gaming-platform-wake-hack

Jansen, W., & Grance, T. (2011). *Guidelines on security and privacy in public cloud computing.* NIST Special Publication, 144.

Jarschel, M., Schlosser, D., Scheuring, S., & Hoßfeld, T. (2011). An evaluation of QoE in cloud gaming based on subjective tests.*Fifth International Conference on In Innovative Mobile and Internet Services in Ubiquitous Computing (IMIS),* (pp. 330-335). IEEE. doi:10.1109/IMIS.2011.92

Jarschel, M., Schlosser, D., Scheuring, S., & Hoßfeld, T. (2013). Gaming in the clouds: QoE and the users' perspective. *Mathematical and Computer Modelling, 57*(11-12), 2883–2894. doi:10.1016/j.mcm.2011.12.014

Jebalia, M., Ben Letaifa, A., Hamdi, M., & Tabbane, S. (2014). A Coalitional Game-Theoretic Approach for QoS-Based and Secure Data Storage in Cloud Environment. In *High Performance Computing and Communications, 2014 IEEE 6th Intl Symp on Cyberspace Safety and Security, 2014 IEEE 11th Intl Conf on Embedded Software and Syst (HPCC, CSS, ICESS), 2014 IEEE Intl Conf on,* (pp. 1048-1054). IEEE. doi:10.1109/HPCC.2014.176

Jia, P., Hu, H. H., Lu, T., & Yuan, K. (2007). Head gesture recognition for hands-free control of an intelligent wheelchair. *The Industrial Robot, 34*(1), 60–68. doi:10.1108/01439910710718469

Juan, M. C., Botella, C., Alcañiz, M., Baños, R., Carrion, C., Melero, M., & Lozano, J. A. (2004). An Augmented Reality System for treating psychological disorders: Application to phobia to cockroaches. *Third IEEE and ACM International Symposium on.* doi:doi:10.1109/ISMAR.2004.14 doi:10.1109/ISMAR.2004.14

Jurgelionis, A., Fechteler, P., Eisert, P., Bellotti, F., David, H., & Laulajainen, J.-P. et al.. (2009). Platform for distributed 3D gaming. *International Journal of Computer Games Technology,* 1.

Kamarainen, T., Siekkinen, M., Xiao, Y., & Yla-Jaaski, A. (2014). Towards pervasive and mobile gaming with distributed cloud infrastructure.*13th Annual Workshop on Network and Systems Support for Games (NetGames)* (pp. 1-6). Nagoya: IEEE. doi:10.1109/NetGames.2014.7008957

Kanchana, D., & Dhandapani, D. S. (2013). A Novel Method for Storage Security in Cloud Computing. *International Journal of Engineering Science and Innovative Technology, 2*(2), 243–249.

Kate, M. K., & Potdukhe, S. D. (2014). *Data sharing in cloud storage with key-aggregate cryptosystem.* Academic Press.

Kaur & Prasanna. (2011). *Real Time Hand Gesture Recognition and Blink Detection.* Project report.

Kent, S. (2001). *The Ultimate History of Video Games: from Pong to Pokemon and beyond... the story behind the craze that touched our lives and changed the world.* New York: Three Rivers Press.

Kharpal, A. (2015, November 25). *Sony PS4 sales top 30 million in battle with Xbox.* Retrieved December 5, 2015, from http://www.cnbc.com: http://www.cnbc.com/2015/11/25/sony-playstation-4-sales-top-30-million-in-battle-with-xbox.html

Compilation of References

Kim, S. J. J. (2012). A User Study Trends in Augmented Reality and Virtual Reality Research: A qualitative study with the past three years of the ISMAR and IEEE VR conference papers. *International Symposium on Ubiquitous Virtual Reality*. doi:10.1109/ISUVR.2012.17

KLAS. (2013). *Cloud Computing perception 2013: The Hybrid Cloud in Healthcare*. Retrieved from http://www.klaresearch.com/ klasreports/#/krms/19/0

Knight, J. F., Cartey, S., Treganna, B., Jarvis, S. S., Smithies, R., & de Freits, S. K. (2010). Serious gaining Technology in major incident triage training: A pragamatic controlled trial. *Resuscitations, 81*(9), 1175–1179. doi:10.1016/j.resuscitation.2010.03.042 PMID:20732609

Kongdenfha, W., Saint-Paul, R., Benatallah, B., & Casati, F. (2006). An aspect-oriented framework for service adaptation. In *Service-Oriented Computing - ICSOC 2006 (LNCS)* (Vol. 4294, pp. 15–26). Berlin, Germany: Springer. doi:10.1007/11948148_2

Lai, A., & Nieh, J. (2006). On the performance of wide-area thin-client computing. *ACM Transactions on Computer Systems, 24*(2), 175–209. doi:10.1145/1132026.1132029

Lane, S., Bucchiarone, A., & Richardson, I. (2012). SOAdapt: A process reference model for developing adaptable service-based applications. *Information and Software Technology, 54*(3), 299–316. doi:10.1016/j.infsof.2011.10.003

Lane, S., & Richardson, I. (2010). Process models for service-based applications: A systematic literature review. *Information and Software Technology, 53*(5), 424–439. doi:10.1016/j.infsof.2010.12.005

Lawton, W., Ahamad, M., Angole, T., Axel Berg, A., & Katsominnos, A. (2013). *Horizon Scanning: What will Higher Education look like in 2020?* Retrieved from http://www.international.ac.uk/media/2423997/horizons scanning report finalprint.pdf

Lee, Y.-T., Chen, K.-T., Su, H.-I., & Lei, C.-L. (2012). Are all games equally cloud-gaming-friendly? an electromyographic approach. *Network and Systems Support for Games (NetGames), 2012 11th Annual Workshop on* (pp. 1-6). Venice, Italy: IEEE.

Lee, Y.-T., Chen, K.-T., Su, H.-I., & Lei, C.-L. (2012). *Are all games equally cloud-gaming-friendly? an electromyographic approach. In Network and Systems Support for Games (NetGames)* (pp. 1–6). Venice, Italy: IEEE.

Leung, V. (2014). Keynote talk II-Video game as a service: Cloud computing enabled video gaming anywhere on any device. In *Advanced Information Networking and Applications (AINA), 2014 IEEE 28th International Conference on*, (pp. xxxv-xxxv). IEEE.

Lien & Huan. (n.d.). Model-based articulated hand motion tracking for gesture recognition. Image and Vision Computing, 16, 121–134.

Li, H., Liu, J., & Tang, G. (2011). A Pricing Algorithm for Cloud Computing Resources. *Conference on Network Computing and Inform. Security*. doi:10.1109/NCIS.2011.22

Liu, F., Shu, P., Jin, H., Ding, L., Yu, J., Niu, D., & Li, B. (2013). Gearing resource-poor mobile devices with powerful clouds: Architectures, challenges, and applications. *Wireless Communications, IEEE, 20*(3), 14–22. doi:10.1109/MWC.2013.6549279

Li, Y., Tang, X., & Cai, W. (2015). Play Request Dispatching for Efficient Virtual Machine Usage in Cloud Gaming. *IEEE Transactions on Circuits and Systems for Video Technology, 25*(12), 2052–2063. doi:10.1109/TCSVT.2015.2450152

Lodge, N., & Wood, D. (1996). New tools for evaluating the quality of digital television-results of the MOSAIC project.*International Broadcasting Convention (IBC)* (pp. 323 – 330). Amsterdam, Netherlands: IET. doi:10.1049/cp:19960828

Lu, & Dey. (2015). Cloud Mobile 3D Display Gaming User Experience Modeling and Optimization by Asymmetric Graphics Rendering. *Selected Topics in Signal Processing, IEEE Journal of, 9*(3), 517-532.

Lü, T. (2004). *Design and Analysis of A Real-Time Video Human Gesture Recognition System.* (Ph.D. Thesis). Princeton University.

Lu, F., Parkin, S., & Morgan, G. (2006). Load balancing for massively multiplayer online games. In *Proceedings of 5th ACM SIGCOMM Workshop on Network and System Support for Games (NetGames '06).* New York, NY: ACM. doi:10.1145/1230040.1230064

Luo, M., & Claypool. (2013). *Uniquitous: Implementation and Evaluation of a Cloud-based Game System in Unity.* Academic Press.

Lyu, M. R., King, I., Wong, T. T., Yau, E., & Chan, P. W. (2005). ARCADE: Augmented Reality Computing Arena for Digital Entertainment. *Aerospace Conference.* doi:10.1109/AERO.2005.1559626

Madani, F. M., & Mokhtari, S. (2015). Virtual optical network embedding over elastic optical networks with set-up delay tolerance. In *Electrical Engineering (ICEE),201523rd Iranian Conference on*, (pp. 450-455). IEEE.

Manresa, C., Varona, J., Mas, R., & Perales, F. J. (2000). Real –Time Hand Tracking and Gesture Recognition for Human-Computer Interaction. *ELCVIA. Electronic Letters on Computer Vision and Image Analysis, 0*(0), 1–7.

Marchand, A., & Hennig-Thurau, T. (2013). Value creation in the video game industry: Industry economics, consumer benefits, and research opportunities. *Journal of Interactive Marketing, 27*(3), 141–157. doi:10.1016/j.intmar.2013.05.001

Mark Claypool and David Finkel. (2012). *The Effects of Latency on Player Performance in Cloud-based Games.* Burnaby, Canada: ACM Publications.

Mashayekhy, L., Nejad, M. M., & Grosu, D. (2015). Cloud federations in the sky: Formation game and mechanism. *IEEE Transactions on Cloud Computing, 3*(1), 14–27. doi:10.1109/TCC.2014.2338323

Compilation of References

Mathew, M., Sumathi, D., Ranjima, P., & Sivaprakash, P. (2014). *Secure Cloud Data Sharing Using Key-Aggr egate Cryptosystem*. Academic Press.

McCallion, J. (2012, November 12). *Gamers find themselves locked out of accounts as hijackers apparently change personal details without permission*. Retrieved November 11, 2015, from http://www.cloudpro.co.uk/cloud-essentials/5022/ea-owned-cloud-gaming-platform-origin-hacked

Meena, S. (2011). *A Study on Hand Gesture Recognition Technique*. Thesis of Master of Technology in Telematics and Signal Processing.

Meiländer, D., Bucchiarone, A., Cappiello, C., Di Nitto, E., & Gorlatch, S. (2011). Using a lifecycle model for developing and executing real-time online applications on Clouds. In *Service-Oriented Computing – ICSOC 2011 Workshops (LNCS)* (Vol. 7221, pp. 33–43). Berlin, Germany: Springer. doi:10.1007/978-3-642-31875-7_5

Meiländer, D., Köttinger, S., & Gorlatch, S. (2013). A scalability model for distributed resource management in real-time online applications. In *42nd International Conference on Parallel Processing (ICPP)*. IEEE. doi:10.1109/ICPP.2013.90

Meiländer, D., Ploss, A., Glinka, F., & Gorlatch, S. (2012). A dynamic resource management system for real-time online applications on Clouds. In *Euro-Par 2011: Parallel Processing Workshops (LNCS)* (Vol. 7155, pp. 149–158). Berlin, Germany: Springer. doi:10.1007/978-3-642-29737-3_18

Meister, D., & Brinkmann, A. (2009). Multi-level comparison of data deduplication in a backup scenario. *Proceedings of SYSTOR 2009: The Israeli Experimental Systems Conference*. doi:10.1145/1534530.1534541

Mell, P., & Grance, T. (2014). The nist definition of cloud computing, 2011. National Institute of Standards and Technology Special Publication, 800-145.

Mendoza, A. (n.d.). *Cold Storage in the Cloud: Trends, Challenges, and Solutions*. Retrieved February 15, 2015, from https://www.intel.it/content/www/it/it/storage/cold-storage-atom-xeon-paper.html

Michaud, L. (2012). Technical architecture and advantages of cloud gaming. *Communications & Stratégies*, 203.

Mishra, D., Zarki, M. E., Erbad, A., Hsu, C.-H., & Venkatasubramanian, N. (2014). Clouds+ games: A multifaceted approach. *Internet Computing*, (3), 20-27.

Mishra, D., El Zarki, M., Erbad, A., Hsu, C. H., & Venkatasubramanian, N. (2014). Clouds+ games: A multifaceted approach. *IEEE Internet Computing*, *18*(3), 20–27. doi:10.1109/MIC.2014.20

Morie, T., Miyamoto, H., & Hanazawa, A. (2007). Brain-inspired visual processing for robust gesture recognition. *International Congress Series*, *1301*, 31–34. doi:10.1016/j.ics.2006.12.010

Nae, V., Iosup, A., Prodan, R., & Fahringer, T. (2009). The impact of virtualization on the performance of massively multiplayer online games. In *8th Annual Workshop on Network and Systems Support for Games (NetGames)*. IEEE. doi:10.1109/NETGAMES.2009.5446227

Nakamura, T., Sorbier, F., Martedi, S., & Saito, H. (2012). *Calibration-Free Projector-Camera System for Spatial Augmented Reality on Planar Surfaces.* 21st International Conference on Pattern Recognition (ICPR 2012) Tsukuba, Japan.

Nandhini, K., & Santhi. (2012a). Retrospection of SVM Classifier. *Journal of Theoretical and Applied Information Technology, 38.*

Nandhini, K., & Santhi. (2012b). An in Depth Study of Emotion Analysis. *Research Journal of Applied Sciences, Engineering and Technology, 4*(24).

Nandhini, K. (2013). Touchte'l: Nanomaterial Based Touch Sensing. *International Journal of Applied Engineering Research, 8*(17).

Nandhini, K., & Raajan, N. R. (2013). Gesture Based Life Saving Approach. *International Journal of Applied Engineering Research, 8*(17).

Narkhede, A., Dashore, P., & Verma, D (2013). *Graphics Based Cloud Security.* Academic Press.

Nave, I., David, H., Shani, A., Tzruya, Y., Laikari, A., Eisert, P., ... (2008). Games@ Large graphics streaming architecture. *Consumer Electronics, 2008. ISCE 2008. IEEE International Symposium on* (pp. 1-4). Vilamoura, Portugal: IEEE.

Neilan, J. H., II. (2012). *Gesture Recognition Using Ensembles of Classifiers.* (Master of Science Thesis). Northern Kentucky University.

NMC Horizon Project NMC. (2013). *The Higher Education Edition Olympic Games (2014).* Retrieved from http://news.microsoft.com/2014/02/06/nbc-olympics-production-of-the-2014-olympic-winter-games-to-utilize-microsoft-for-live-and-on-demand-streaming/

Nojima, T., Sekiguchi, D., Inami, M., & Tachi, S (2002). The SmartTool: A system for augmented reality of haptics. *Virtual Reality, Proceedings.* IEEE.

Nurmi, D., Wolski, R., Grzegorczyk, C., Obertelli, G., Soman, S., Youseff, L., & Zagorodnov, D. (2009). The Eucalyptus open-source Cloud-Computing system. In *9th IEEE/ACM International Symposium on Cluster Computing and the Grid.* IEEE.

Nvidia. (2015, October 03). *Compare streaming platforms.* Retrieved December 10, 2015, from https://shield.nvidia.com/geforce-now-vs-playstation-now-vs-gamefly

Ojala, A., & Tyrvainen, P. (2011). Developing cloud business models: A case study on cloud gaming. *IEEE Software, 28*(4), 42–47. doi:10.1109/MS.2011.51

Oredope, A., Moessner, Peoples, & Parr. (2013). Deploying cloud services in mobile networks. In *Science and Information Conference (SAI).* IEEE.

Panke, Q., Xue, C., Lei, W., & Liqian, W. (2015). A novel stateful PCE-cloud based control architecture of optical networks for cloud services. *Communications, China, 12*(10), 117–127. doi:10.1109/CC.2015.7315063

Compilation of References

Pantel, L., & Wolf, L. C. (2002). On the Impact of Delay on Real-Time Multiplayer Games. ACM NOSSDAV, Miami, FL. doi:doi:10.1145/507670.507674 doi:10.1145/507670.507674

Papazoglou, M. P., & van den Heuvel, W.-J. (2006). Service-oriented design and development methodology. *International Journal of Web Engineering and Technology*, 2(4), 412–442. doi:10.1504/IJWET.2006.010423

Papert, S. (1994). Why School reform is possible. *Journal of the Learning Sciences*, 6(4), 417–427. doi:10.1207/s15327809jls0604_5

Park, Yu, Chung, & Lee. (2011). Markov chain based monitoring service for fault tolerance in mobile cloud computing. In *Advanced Information Networking and Applications (WAINA), 2011 IEEE Workshops of International Conference on*, (pp. 520-525). IEEE.

Pavlus, J. (2010). *Sixty – Two Reasons why gemification is played out. Fast company design.* Retrieved from http://fast codesign.com/166.2656/sixtytworeasonswhygamificationisplayedout

Persson & Samvik. (2009). *A System for Real Time Gesture Recognition.* (Master's thesis). Lund University.

Pivec, M. (2007). Editorial 'Play and Learn: Potentials of game based learning. *British Journal of Educational Technology*, 38(3), 387–393. doi:10.1111/j.1467-8535.2007.00722.x

Ploss, A., Meiländer, D., Glinka, F., & Gorlatch, S. (2011). Towards the scalability of real-time online interactive applications on multiple servers and Clouds. *Advances in Parallel Computing*, 20, 267–287.

Prakash, K. (2013, February). A Survey On Security And Privacy In Cloud Computing. International Journal of Engineering Research and Technology, 2(2).

Purkayastha. (2009). *Integrating Gesture Recognition and Speech Recognition In A Touch-Less Human Computer Interaction System.* (Master of Science thesis). University at Buffalo.

Raajan, N. R., Suganya, S., Hemanand, R., Janani, S. & Ramanan, S.V. (2012). Augmented Reality for 3D Construction. *Procedia Engineering, 38*, 66–72.

Raajan, N. R., Suganya, S., Priya, M.V., Ramanan, S.V., Janani, S., Nandini, N.S., Hemanand, R., & Gayathri, S (2012). Augmented Reality Based Virtual Reality. *Procedia Engineering, 38*, 1559–1565.

Raheja, J. L., & Chaudhary, A. (2014). *PreConsultation Help Necessity Detection Based on Gait Recognition. In Signal Image and Video Processing* (Vol. 8). Springer.

Raj, E. D., Dhinesh, B. L., Ezendu, A., Nirmala, M., & Krishna, P. V. (2014). Forecasting the Trends in Cloud Computing and its Impact on Future IT Business. In A. Ezendu (Ed.), Green Technology Applications for Enterprise and Academic Innovation (p. 14). Bedfordshire, UK: IGI Global. doi:doi:10.4018/978-1-4666-5166-1.ch002 doi:10.4018/978-1-4666-5166-1.ch002

Rajasekhara Babu, M., Venkata Krishna, P., & Khalid, M. (2013). A framework for power estimation and reduction in multi-core architectures using basic block approach. *International Journal of Communication Networks and Distributed Systems*, *10*(1), 40–51. doi:10.1504/IJCNDS.2013.050506

Raj, E. D., & Babu, L. D. (2014). Analysis on enhancing storm to efficiently process big data in real time. *5th International Conference on Computing, Communication and Networking Technologies (ICCCNT)* (pp. 1-5). Hefei, China: IEEE. doi:10.1109/ICCCT2.2014.7066747

Raj, E. D., & Babu, L. D. (2015). A firefly swarm approach for establishing new connections in social networks based on big data analytics. *International Journal of Communication Networks and Distributed Systems*, *15*(2/3), 130–148. doi:10.1504/IJCNDS.2015.070968

Raj, E. D., Babu, L. D., Ariwa, E., Nirmala, M., & Krishna, P. V. (2014). Forecasting the Trends in Cloud Computing and its Impact on Future IT Business. In *Green Technology Applications for Enterprise and Academic Innovation* (pp. 14–32). Hershey, PA: IGI Global. doi:10.4018/978-1-4666-5166-1.ch002

Ram, N. A., Reddy, N. C. S., & Poshal, G. (n.d.). *An Effective Scalable Data Sharing in Cloud Storage using Key-Aggregate Crypto-system*. Academic Press.

Rautaray & Agrawal. (2012). Real Time Hand Gesture Recognition System for Dynamic Applications. *International Journal of Ubi Comp, 3*(1).

Rautaray, S. S., & Agrawal, A. (2012). Real Time Multiple Hand Gesture Recognition System for Human Computer Interaction. *I.J. Intelligent Systems and Applications*, *5*(5), 56–64. doi:10.5815/ijisa.2012.05.08

Remote Play. (n.d.). In *Encyclopedia*. Retrieved from 2nd January 2016. https://en.wikipedia.org/wiki/Remote_Play

ResearchandMarkets. (2015, June 28). *Research and Markets: Global Cloud Gaming Market 2015-2019 - What are the market opportunities and threats faced by the key vendors?* Retrieved December 08, 2015, from http://www.reuters.com: http://www.reuters.com/article/research-and-markets-idUSnBw235751a+100+BSW20150623

Rhonda, M., Derryberry, & Jackson. (2012). *Game based Learning*. Research Bulletin. Center for Applied Research.

Ricker, T. (2009, March 20). *OnLive killed the game console star?*. Retrieved from Engadget.com

Robinson, J. (2012). *The Evolution of the Gaming Industry into the Pockets of the Consumer.* Univ. of Southampton.

Royce, W. W. (1987). Managing the development of large software systems: concepts and techniques. In *Proceedings of the 9th International Conference on Software Engineering (ICSE '87)*. IEEE.

Compilation of References

Ruiz-Alvarez, A., & Humphrey, M. (2011). An automated approach to cloud storage service selection.*Proceedings of the 2nd international workshop on Scientific cloud computing.* doi:10.1145/1996109.1996117

Rydning, J., Reinsel, D., & Iacono, D. (2013, May). *Cloud storage is hot again.* Retrieved February 11, 2015, from http://www.storiant.com/resources/Cold-Storage-Is-Hot-Again.pdf

Sam Machkovech. (2015*). GameFly launches cloud-streaming video game service on Amazon Fire TV Ars Technica.* Retrieved from 2nd June, 2015. http://arstechnica.com/gaming/2015/06/gamefly-launches-cloud-streaming-video-game-service-on-amazon-fire-tv/

Samba, A. (2012). Logical data models for cloud computing architectures. *IT Professional Magazine, 14*(1), 19–26. doi:10.1109/MITP.2011.113

Schreier, J. (2011, June 05). *Sony Hack Probe Uncovers 'Anonymous' Calling Card.* Retrieved November 06, 2015, from http://www.wired.com: http://www.wired.com/2011/05/sony-playstation-network-anonymous/

S-Cube European Network of Excellence. (2012). *Software Services and Systems Network.* Retrieved from http://www.s-cube-network.eu

Semsarzadeh, M., Hemmati, M., Javadtalab, A., Yassine, A., & Shirmohammadi, S. (2014). A video encoding speed-up architecture for cloud gaming.*IEEE International Conference on Multimedia and Expo Workshops (ICMEW),* (pp. 1-6). doi:10.1109/ICMEW.2014.6890685

Shea, R., Fu, D., & Liu, J. (2015). Cloud Gaming: Understanding the Support From Advanced Virtualization and Hardware. *IEEE Transactions on Circuits and Systems for Video Technology, 25*(12), 2026–2037. doi:10.1109/TCSVT.2015.2450172

Shea, R., Liu, J., Ngai, E. C.-H., & Cui, Y. (2011). *Cloud Computing: architecture and performance.* Computer Science and Interactive Media & Game Development Worcester Polytechnic Institute Worcester.

Shea, R., Liu, J., Ngai, E., & Cui, Y. (2013). Cloud gaming: Architecture and performance. *IEEE Network, 27*(4), 16–21. doi:10.1109/MNET.2013.6574660

Sheikhi, A., Rayati, M., Bahrami, S., Ranjbar, A. M., & Sattari, S. (2015). A cloud computing framework on demand side management game in smart energy hubs. *International Journal of Electrical Power & Energy Systems, 64*, 1007–1016. doi:10.1016/j.ijepes.2014.08.020

Shelke, M. P. K., Sontakke, M. S., & Gawande, A. (2012). Intrusion detection system for cloud computing. *International Journal of Scientific & Technology Research, 1*(4), 67–71.

Shina, M. C., Tsapb, L. V., & Goldgof, D. B. (2004). Gesture recognition using Bezier curves for visualization navigation from registered 3-D data. *Pattern Recognition, 37*.

Shi, S. (2011). Building low-latency remote rendering systems for interactive 3d graphics rendering on mobile devices. In *Proceedings of the 19th ACM international conference on Multimedia,* (pp. 859-860). ACM. doi:10.1145/2072298.2072493

Shi, S., Hsu, C.-H., Nahrstedt, K., & Campbell, R. (2011). Using graphics rendering contexts to enhance the real-time video coding for mobile cloud gaming.*Proceedings of the 19th ACM international conference on Multimedia* (pp. 103--112). Scottsdale, AZ: ACM. doi:10.1145/2072298.2072313

Shi, T., Yang, M., Li, X., Lei, Q., & Jiang, Y. (2015). An energy-efficient scheduling scheme for time-constrained tasks in local mobile clouds. *Pervasive and Mobile Computing*.

Shneiderman, B., & Ben, S. (2003). *Designing the user interface*. Pearson Education India.

Siemens, G. (2010). What are Learning Analytics? Emergence of Discipline. *The American Behavioral Scientist*, *57*(10), 1380–1400. doi:10.1177/0002764213498851

Slivar, I., Suznjevic, M., & Skorin-Kapov, L. (2015). The impact of video encoding parameters and game type on QoE for cloud gaming: A case study using the steam platform. *Quality of Multimedia Experience (QoMEX), 2015 Seventh International Workshop on* (pp. 1-6). Pilos, Greece: IEEE.

Sommers, J., & Barford, P. (2012). Cell vs. WiFi: on the performance of metro area mobile connections. In *Proceedings of the 2012 ACM conference on Internet measurement conference* (pp. 301-314). ACM. doi:doi:10.1145/2398776.2398808 doi:10.1145/2398776.2398808

Sony Computer Entertainment to Acquire Gaikai Inc., a Leading Interactive Cloud Gaming Company. (2008, November) Retrieved 2015-12-12.

Sony. (2008, November). *Started the company*. Retrieved from https://www.gaikai.com/

Sony. (2015, November 02). *Remote Play*. Retrieved November 04, 2015, from http://www.sonymobile.com/global-en/apps-services/remote-play/

Subashini, S., & Kavitha, V. (2011). A survey on security issues in service delivery models of cloud computing. *Journal of Network and Computer Applications*, *34*(1), 1–11. doi:10.1016/j.jnca.2010.07.006

Suganya, S., Raajan, N. R., Priya, MV, Philomina, A.J., Parthiban, D., & Monisha, B (2012). Real-Time Camera Tracking of Augmented Reality in Landmarks Environments. *Procedia Engineering, 38*, 456–461.

Sun. (2010, March 26). *NVIDIA GeForce GTX480 Video Card Review: Streaming Multiprocessor*. Retrieved from Motherboards.org

Sundaresan, S., De Donato, W., Feamster, N., Teixeira, R., Crawford, S., & Pescapee, A. (2011). *Broadband internet performance: a view from the gateway. In ACM SIGCOMM computer communication review* (pp. 134–145). Toronto, Canada: ACM. doi:10.1145/2018436.2018452

Sun, K., & Wu, D. (2015). Video rate control strategies for cloud gaming. *Journal of Visual Communication and Image Representation*, *30*, 234–241. doi:10.1016/j.jvcir.2015.03.012

Compilation of References

Süselbeck, R., Schiele, G., & Becker, C. (2009). Peer-to-peer support for low-latency Massively Multiplayer Online Games in the cloud. In *Network and Systems Support for Games (NetGames), 2009 8th Annual Workshop on*, (pp. 1-2). IEEE. doi:10.1109/NETGAMES.2009.5446229

Tiplea, F. L., & Dragan, C. C. (n.d.). *Key-policy Attribute-based Encryption for Boolean Circuits from Bilinear Maps*. Academic Press.

Tokunaga, E., Zee, A. V. D., Kurahashi, M., Nemoto, M., & Nakajima, T. (2003). Object-Oriented Middleware Infrastructure for Distributed Augmented Reality. *Sixth IEEE International Symposium on Object-Oriented Real-Time Distributed Computing*. doi:10.1109/ISORC.2003.1199250

Tzeng, W. G. (2002). A time-bound cryptographic key assignment scheme for access control in a hierarchy. *Knowledge and Data Engineering. IEEE Transactions on*, *14*(1), 182–188.

Ubitus Inc. (2015, November 02). *ubitus*. Retrieved November 10, 2015, from http://www.ubitus.net: http://www.ubitus.net/en/aboutubitus.html

Valente, L., Conci, A., & Feijó, B. (2005). Real time game loop models for single-player computer games. In *SBGames '05 – IV Brazilian Symposium on Computer Games and Digital Entertainment*.

Vale, S., & Hammoudi, S. (2008). Model driven development of context-aware service oriented architecture. In *11th IEEE International Conference on Computational Science and Engineering Workshops*. IEEE. doi:10.1109/CSEW.2008.31

Valve. (2014, december 15). *steampowered*. Retrieved December 5, 2015, from http://store.steampowered.com: http://store.steampowered.com/about/

Velasco, L., Contreras, L. M., Ferraris, G., Stavdas, A., Cugini, F., Wiegand, M., & Fernandez-Palacios, J. P. (2015). A service-oriented hybrid access network and clouds architecture. *Communications Magazine, IEEE*, *53*(4), 159–165. doi:10.1109/MCOM.2015.7081090

Verma, K., Gomadam, K., Sheth, A. P., Miller, J. A., & Wu, Z. (2005). *The METEOR-S approach for configuring and executing dynamic web processes. Technical report*. Wright State University.

Vogler, C., & Metaxas, D. (2001). A Framework for Recognizing the Simultaneous Aspects of American Sign Language. *Computer Vision and Image Understanding*, *81*(3), 358–384. doi:10.1006/cviu.2000.0895

Vouk, M. (2008). Cloud computing--issues, research and implementations. *Journal of Computing and Information Technology*, 235-246.

Walker, J. (2005). *Final version of Weblog definition*. Routledge Encyclopedia of Narrative Theory.

Wang, B., Chow, S. S., Li, M., & Li, H. (2013, July). Storing shared data on the cloud via security-mediator. In *Distributed Computing Systems (ICDCS), 2013 IEEE 33rd International Conference on* (pp. 124-133). IEEE. doi:doi:10.1109/ICDCS.2013.60 doi:10.1109/ICDCS.2013.60

Wang, C., Chow, S. S., Wang, Q., Ren, K., & Lou, W. (2013). Privacy-preserving public auditing for secure cloud storage. *Computers. IEEE Transactions on*, *62*(2), 362–375.

Wang, Z., Yang, X., Xiao, S., & Li, B. (2010). Relighting in Spatial Augmented Reality. *International Conference on Audio Language and Image Processing (ICALIP)*.

Waugh, R. (2011, December 13). *Modern Warfare 3 hits $1 billion in 16 days - beating Avatar's record by one day*. Retrieved December 2015, 10, from http://www.dailymail.co.uk: http://www.dailymail.co.uk/sciencetech/article-2073201/Modern-Warfare-3-hits-1-billion-16-days--beating-Avatars-record-day.html

Wautelet, Y., Achbany, Y., Lange, J., & Kolp, M. (2009). A process for developing adaptable and open service systems: application in supply chain management. In *Enterprise Information Systems (Lecture Notes in Business Information Processing)* (Vol. 24, pp. 564–576). Berlin, Germany: Springer. doi:10.1007/978-3-642-01347-8_47

Wei, Z., Pierre, G., & Chi, C.-H. (2012). CloudTPS: Scalable transactions for web applications in the Cloud. *IEEE Transactions on Services Computing*, *5*(4), 525–539. doi:10.1109/TSC.2011.18

Wen, Z.-Y., & Hsiao, H.-F. (2014). QoE-driven performance analysis of cloud gaming services. In *Multimedia Signal Processing (MMSP), 2014 IEEE 16th International Workshop on*, (pp. 1-6). IEEE.

Wikipedia. (2014, December 10). *Early history of video games*. Retrieved december 11, 2015, from https://en.wikipedia.org: https://en.wikipedia.org/wiki/Early_history_of_video_games

Wikipedia. (2014, March). *Origins of the computer game*. Retrieved December 01, 2015, from https://en.wikipedia.org/: https://en.wikipedia.org/wiki/History_of_video_games#Origins_of_the_computer_game

Wikipedia. (2015, January 27). *Traditional game*. Retrieved 12 11, 2015, from https://en.wikipedia.org: https://en.wikipedia.org/wiki/Traditional_game

Wilhelmsen, & Alexander. (2014). Using a Commodity Hardware Video Encoder for Interactive Video Streaming. *Multimedia (ISM), 2014 IEEE International Symposium on*. IEEE.

Windows Azure. (n.d.). Retrieved February 25, 2015, from http://www.windowsazure.com/en-us/

Wirsing, M., Hölzl, M., Acciai, L., Banti, F., Clark, A., Fantechi, A., ... Varró, D. (2008). SENSORIA patterns: augmenting service engineering with formal analysis, transformation and dynamicity. In Leveraging Applications of Formal Methods, Verification and Validation (Communications in Computer and Information Science), (Vol. 17, pp. 170–190). Berlin, Germany: Springer.

Wouters, P., & van Oostendorp, H. (2013). A meta-analytic review of the role of instructional support in game-based learning. *Computers & Education*, *60*(1), 412–425. doi:10.1016/j.compedu.2012.07.018

Wu, Xue, & He. (2014). iCloudAccess: Cost-effective streaming of video games from the cloud with low latency. *Circuits and Systems for Video Technology, IEEE Transactions on, 24*(8), 1405-1416.

Compilation of References

Wu, Yuen, Cheung, Chen, & Chen. (2015). *Enabling Adaptive High-Frame-Rate Video Streaming in Mobile Cloud Gaming Applications.* Academic Press.

Wu, Z. (2014). *Gaming in the cloud: one of the future entertainment.* Retrieved 12 12, 2015, from University of Southamtpon: http://mms.ecs.soton.ac.uk/2014/papers/17.pdf

Xu, L., Li, C., Li, L., Liu, Y., Yang, Z., & Liu, Y. (2014). A virtual data center deployment model based on the green cloud computing. In *Computer and Information Science (ICIS), 2014 IEEE/ACIS 13th International Conference on*, (pp. 235-240). IEEE. doi:10.1109/ICIS.2014.6912140

Xu, Y., Nawaz, S., & Mak, R. H. (2014, November 1). *A Comparison of Architectures in Massive Multiplayer Online Games.* Retrieved December 15, 2015, from www.researchgate.net

Yang, R. (2011). The Study and Improvement of Augmented Reality based on Feature Matching. *2nd International Conference on Software Engineering and Service Science (ICSESS).*

Yuan, Y. (2008). *Image-Based Gesture Recognition with Support Vector Machines.* (Ph.D. dissertation). University of Delaware.

Zaharias, P. A. (2009). The gamer experience: Investigating relationships between culture and usability in massively multiplayer online games. *Computers in Entertainment*, 26.

Zero Client Computing . (n.d.). Retrieved March 10, 2015, from http://www.digi.com/pdf/wp_zeroclientcomputing.pdf

Zhang, H., Reardon, C., Zhang, C., & Parker, L. E. (2015). Adaptive human-centered representation for activity recognition of multiple individuals from 3D point cloud sequences. In *Robotics and Automation (ICRA), 2015 IEEE International Conference on*, (pp. 1991-1998). IEEE. doi:10.1109/ICRA.2015.7139459

Zhang, Ranjan, Menzel, Nepal, Strazdins, Jie, & Wang. (2014). *An Infrastructure Service Recommendation System for Cloud Applications with Real-time QoS Requirement Constraints.* Academic Press.

Zhang, C., Yao, J., Qi, Z., Yu, M., & Guan, H. (2014). VGASA: Adaptive scheduling algorithm of virtualized GPU resource in cloud gaming. *IEEE Transactions on Parallel and Distributed Systems*, 25(11), 3036–3045. doi:10.1109/TPDS.2013.288

Zhu, W., Luo, C., Wang, J., & Li, S. (2011, March). Multimedia cloud computing. *Signal Processing Magazine*, 59-69.

Zhugeex. (2015, August 20). *Video Game Piracy On The Rise, Will Cost The Industry As Much As It Makes.* Retrieved November 20, 2015, from http://gearnuke.com/video-game-piracy-rise-will-cost-industry-much-makes/

Zoellner, M., Keil, J., Drevensek, T., & Wuest, H. (2009). Cultural Heritage Layers: Integrating Historic Media in Augmented Reality. *15th International Conference on Virtual Systems and Multimedia.* doi:10.1109/VSMM.2009.35

About the Contributors

P. Venkata Krishna received his B.Tech in Electronics and Communication from SV University, Tirupathi and M.Tech in Computer Science and Engineering from NIT, Calicut and PhD from VIT University. He is currently Professor in the Department of Computer Science at Sri Padmavathi Mahila Visvavidyalayam, University, Tirupati, AP, India. His research interests include High Performance Computing, Cloud Computing and Wireless and Mobile Computing.

* * *

G. S. Tamizh Arasi is a PG student studying M.S Software engineering in VIT University, Vellore, India. Her research interests are cloud computing and cloud computing security.

M. Rajasekhara Babu is a senior faculty member at School of Computing Science and Engineering, VIT University. He obtained his BTech in ECE from SV University, Tirupathi, A.P and MTech. in C.S.E. from NIT Calicut, Kerala. He took his Ph.D. in CSE from VIT University, Vellore, Tamil Nadu, India. He was instrumental in establishing Intel Multi-Core Architecture Research Laboratory in collaboration with Intel, India at VIT University. He produced more than 75 international/national publications and authored 3 books in the area of computer architecture, compiler design and grid computing. He edited 5 volumes of 3 international conferences proceedings and published by Allied, Macmillan and Springer Publishers. Dr. Raja Babu has served in various prestigious positions as Division Leader (TCS <), Program Manager, etc., in VIT University. Currently, Dr. M Rajababu is working in the area of energy aware applications for Internet of Things (IoT) and high performance applications for Multi-Core Architectures.

Balamurugan Balusamy is working as a faculty in School of Information Technology an d Engineering, VIT University,India.He completed his B.E (Computer Science) under Bharathidasan University and M.E (computer science) Under Anna

University. He research interests are Cloud computing,Cloud computing security and Cloud access control.

Dhanaraj Cheelu is working as Head of department in Computing Science and Engineering, Ravindra College of Engineering for women, Kurnool, Andhra Pradesh. He took his B.Tech. degree in Computer Science and Engineering from SRKREC Bhimavaram, Andhrapradesh and his M.Tech in Computer Science and Engineering from National Institute of Technology, Calicut, Kerala. He received his Ph.D. from VIT University, Vellore, India. He has more than 12 years of teaching and industry experience. His areas of interest include Heterogeneous Networks, Network Security, Image Processing and Theoretical Computer Science.

Dhinesh Babu L. D. received B.E in Electrical and Electronics Engineering and M.E in Computer Science and Engineering from the University of Madras and PhD from VIT University. He is currently a faculty in Software Engineering Division of the School of Information Technology and Engineering at VIT University, Vellore, India. He has served as Division Leader of Software Engineering Division. His research interests include Cloud Computing, Grid and Distributed Computing, Online Social Networks, Computer and Software Security, Software Engineering, ERP, Business Information Systems and Supply Chain Management.

Prajit Kumar Datta is a Vellore Institute of Technology Graduate and also a Special Achiever Awardee. He is currently working in data science team called as Enterprise Information Exchange in Bank of America. With an experience in both data science and software engineering in financial domain, he works with data on the research and analytics level, as well as leveraging that data to build impactful products. His interests are cloud computing, natural language processing, and data mining and is also eager to learn and apply his unique skillset to new, interesting, and challenging problems.

Sergei Gorlatch is a Full Professor at the department of Mathematics and Computer Science, University of Muenster since 2003. Earlier he was Associate Professor at the Technical University of Berlin, Assistant Professor at the University of Passau, and Humboldt Research Fellow at the Technical University of Munich. Prof. Gorlatch has 25 years of international research experience in Computer Science and has published about 200 reviewed papers and books. He often delivers invited talks at international conferences and serves at their programme committees. He was principal investigator in several international research and development projects in the field of parallel, distributed, Grid and Cloud computing, funded by the European Commission, as well as by German national bodies.

Sharon Moses J. received his BE in Computer Science from Anna University, India and his MTech in Software Technology from VIT University, Vellore, India. Currently, he is a researcher in School of Information Technology and Engineering at VIT University. His primary research interests include cloud storage, fuzzy systems, and recommender systems.

Marimuthu Karuppiah received his B.E. degree in Computer Science & Engineering from Madurai Kamaraj University, Madurai, India in 2003, M.E. degree in Computer Science & Engineering from Anna University, Chennai, India in 2005, PhD in Computer Science & Engineering from VIT University, Vellore, India in 2015. He is now an Associate Professor in School of Computing Science & Engineering, VIT University, Vellore, India. He has published more than 10 research papers in reputed international conferences and journals. He is a life member of Cryptology Research Society of India (CRSI) and Computer Society of India (CSI). His main research interests include cryptography and wireless network security, in particular, authentication and encryption schemes.

Nandhini Kesavan received B.Tech. degree in Computer Science and Engineering from Pondicherry University, Pondicherry, India, M.Tech. degree in Computer Science and Engineering from SASTRA University, Thanjavur, India and pursuing Ph.D. from SASTRA University, Thanjavur, India. Her research interests include Gesture Recognition, Augmented reality (AR), Image & Video Processing, Network Security and Cryptography. She has published 6 Research articles in National & International journals and 5 conference papers. She has also received Best Project Award in B.Tech.

Nirmala M. received her Bachelor's degree in Electronic Science from the University of Madras and Masters in Computer Applications from Madurai Kamaraj University. She received her M.Tech in Computer Science and Engineering from VIT University. She is currently an Assistant Professor (Senior) in the School of Information Technology and Engineering at VIT University, Vellore. Her research interests include Distributed and Cloud Computing, Computer and Network Security, Software Engineering, Databases, Data mining and Data Warehousing.

Dominik Meiländer is a Research Associate and Ph.D. Student in the group for parallel and distributed systems at the Department of Mathematics and Computer Science, University of Muenster, Germany. He received his diploma in Computer Science in 2009 from the University of Muenster. Mr Meiländer participated in two European projects and one European Network of Excellence. He published 16 papers in reviewed international conferences and journals in the areas of distributed computing. His main research interests are in the area of Cloud Computing and real-time applications.

Thusitha Murali is a PG student studying M.S Software engineering in VIT University, Vellore, India. Her research interests are cloud computing, machine learning, and big data.

Shivangshu Nag is a final year student at the Vellore Institute Of Technology, Vellore pursuing his B.Tech in the field of Computer Science and Technology. He is currently working as an intern at Inmobi Pvt Ltd as an SDET.

N. R. Raajan received B.E. degree in Electronics and Communication Engineering from Bharathidasan University, Trichy, India, M.E. degree in Communication Systems from Anna University, Chennai, India, Ph. D. from SASTRA University Thanjavur, India. He joined SASTRA University, Thanjavur, Tamil Nadu, India as a Lecturer in the Department of Electronics and Communicat ion Engineering since 2005 and is now Senior Assistant Professor, His research interests include Augmented reality (AR), Image & Video Processing, Hydrophone Communication, Signal processing and Wireless Network Security. He has authored a chapter on book titled speech enhancement, modeling and recognition algorithms and applications," Mathematical modeling of speech production and its application to noise cancellation". He has published 120+ Research articles in National & International journals and 30+ IEEE conference papers with 2 BEST paper awards. He also hold Certificate of Appreciation from TI in 2007 for Project presentation, Guiding "Automatic assistance for physically challenging people" and won the first prize. Recently He also served as TPC member & review member for 14 IEEE & ELSEIVER supported International Conferences apart from 3+ peer reviewed Journals.

Ebin Deni Raj received his B.Tech degree in computer science from Cochin university of science and technology, India and his M.Tech in Information Technology from VIT university, Vellore, India. Currently, he is a researcher in School of Information Technology and Engineering at VIT University. His primary research interests include Cloud computing, Big data analytics, Social computing, machine learning and social network analysis.

R. Deepthi Crestose Rebekah is working as Assistant Professor in Computer Science & Engineering Department, Ravindra College of Engineering, Kurnool, A.P. she took her B.Tech degree in Computer Science and Information Technology from R.G.M.CET, Nandyal, Kurnool & M.Tech degree in computer science from Kottam

College of Engineering, Kurnool, A.P. she has total 5 years of teaching experience. and her interested Research areas are cloud computing, wireless sensor networking.

Utkarsh Srivastava is a final year undergraduate from Computer Science background studying in VIT University. He is extremely passionate about learning and implementing technology. He also has deep interest in the field on Bigdata.

Vipul Kumar Srivastava is currently doing his Bachelor of Technology in Computer Science and Engineering from Vellore Institute of Technology, Vellore and is expected to complete his course in 2016. He is regularly involved in competitive coding. He has been recruited by SAP in the on campus placement process.

S. Sudha is currently working as Assistant Professor (Senior), School of Information Technology and Engineering, VIT University, Vellore, India. She is having several years of experience working in Industry, academia and research. She received his M.TECH in Information Technology from VIT University, Vellore, India. She is currently pursuing Ph.D. in VIT University. Her research interests include information Security, Wireless systems, Network Security and Cloud computing.

Aiswarya Thangavelu is a PG student studying M.S Software engineering in VIT University, Vellore, India. Her research interests are cloud computing, machine learning, and big data.

V. Madhu Viswanatham is currently Associate Professor, School of Computing Science and Engineering, VIT University, Vellore, India. He is having several years of experience working in academia, teaching, and research. He has guided one Ph.D Scholar and supervising Six Scholars. He received his Ph.D in Computer Science and Technology from SK University, Andhra Pradesh, India. He has supervised M.Tech and B.Tech students. He organized several workshops and faculty development programs. His research interests include information Security mobile, wireless systems, Image processing and cloud computing.

Index

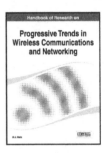
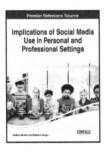

Printed in the United States
By Bookmasters